Blackwell Classic Histories of Europe

This series comprises new editions of seminal histories of Europe. Written by the leading scholars of their generation, the books represent both major works of historical analysis and interpretation and clear, authoritative overviews of the major periods of European history. All the volumes have been revised for inclusion in the series and include updated material to aid further study. *Blackwell Classic Histories of Europe* provides a forum in which these key works can continue to be enjoyed by scholars, students and general readers alike.

Published

Europe: Hierarchy and Revolt 1320–1480
Second Edition
George Holmes

Renaissance Europe 1480–1520
Second Edition
John Hale

Reformation Europe 1517–1559
Second Edition
G. R. Elton

Europe Divided 1559–1598
Second Edition
J. H. Elliott

Europe Unfolding 1648–1688
Second Edition
John Stoye

Europe: Privilege and Protest 1730–1789
Second Edition
Olwen Hufton

Revolutionary Europe 1783–1815
Second Edition
George Rudé

Europe Reshaped 1848–1878
Second Edition
J. A. S. Grenville

Europe Transformed 1878–1919
Second Edition
Norman Stone

Forthcoming

Europe in Crisis 1598–1648
Second Edition
Geoffrey Parker

EUROPE: PRIVILEGE AND PROTEST 1730–1789

Second Edition

Olwen Hufton

BLACKWELL
Publishers

First edition published by Fontana Press 1980

Second edition first published by Blackwell Publishers Ltd 2000

2 4 6 8 10 9 7 5 3 1

Blackwell Publishers Ltd
108 Cowley Road
Oxford OX4 1JF
UK

Blackwell Publishers Inc.
350 Main Street
Malden, Massachusetts 02148
USA

British Library Cataloguing in Publication Data

A CIP catalogue record for this book is available from the British Library.

Library of Congress Cataloging-in-Publication Data is available for this book.

ISBN 0-631-21513-1

0-631-21381-3 (pbk)

Typeset in 10.5 on 12pt Sabon
by Kolam Information Services Pvt. Ltd, Pondicherry, India
Printed in Great Britain by TJ International, Padstow, Cornwall

This book is printed on acid-free paper

Contents

Author's Note

A new edition of a twenty-year old book demands some re-thinking about the ways in which history has moved on. In the late seventies and for most of the eighties there was a concern to write general history with an eye to the interaction between classes, in particular to view the impact of high politics on the masses and their riposte to exploitation whether this came from higher tax, food costs in time of dearth or war demands. At the same time, those concerned to challenge the basis of monarchical power did not hesitate to appeal to 'the people' to lend force to their claims. Hence the title of this volume and the perceived need to interpret the eighteenth century – a century of much conflict which ultimately saw the unleashing of Revolution – in terms of contestation and social polarities, and one in which action was understandable in primarily social terms.

Over the past decade or so such an interpretation has not been displaced but the energies of historians have tended to demonstrate a growing concern with the cultural, with the effects of extending literacy, of changing consumption patterns, of gender and national identity. Moreover, and this particularly in the context of the bicentennial of the French Revolution, a new emphasis has been given to the alternative sites of political expression, debate, interchange and association which emerged in western Europe to challenge and effectively to undermine monarchical claims to absolute power and their transformation from a private to a public forum. The 'competing discourses', of critical voices promoting different alternatives to the ordering of state and society came from salons and Provincial Academies, or publications and the epistolary interchanges of a Republic of Letters whose internationalism defied state censorship. These associations served to reformulate how society and government were conceived in ways which presage the development of modern secular western society.

Some of the historiographical changes in emphasis have been integrated into this second revised edition in the relevant chapters and an updated bibliography has been added as a pointer to further study. In most respects, the original text has been allowed to stand since its main contentions have not been radically revised.

Introduction

If any single concept contributes towards an understanding of the eighteenth century, it must surely be that of privilege. Privilege was the foundation upon which society was constructed and all governments, however reluctantly, were forced to acknowledge this. Privilege existed in manifold forms, some purely honorific, others extremely lucrative. There were privileged individuals, like nobles and clerics who were often tax-exempt and who were tried in their own courts of law: there were privileged towns which had long since purchased exemption from royal taxation and which were, in some German and Spanish instances, virtually self-governing enclaves: there were privileged provinces endowed with their own law codes, in some instances with their own Diets which fought with monarchs over the power of the purse and effectively questioned, delayed or boycotted royal legislation, like those of Hungary or Bohemia. Other provinces, often these but lately joined to the central crown, demanded special consideration. Brittany refused to pay a salt tax: Basques refused any royal taxation at all. Sometimes privilege entailed the actual possession of men, the privilege of the Russian *dvorianstvo* or the Prussian Junkers: sometimes it merely endowed the owners of privilege with specific rights to labour services or rents in money or kind or the profits from basic community services – the oven, the mill and the wine-press. Lower down the social scale, privilege in England gave some the right to vote by residence in a particular cottage or on a particular estate or throughout Europe allowed some rural communities rights to glean at another's expense, or accorded some grazing rights on common land whilst denying them to others. Privilege gave some paupers the right to candle droppings in church and to the children of the poor the right to strip the hedgerows of blackberries and gather windfall fruit. In short, privilege of some kind touched everyone. Many forms were medieval in origin, but others were the particular product of the sixteenth and seventeenth centuries when monarchies, in order to purchase support of finance wars, had multiplied the numbers of nobles, offices, monopolies and concessions.

The late seventeenth century had been remarkable for the establishment of a number of strong 'absolutist' monarchies which seemed capable of persuading or at least of overriding power-sharing institutions so that they ceded the power of the purse. This was with a view to allowing monarchs maximum flexibility in raising taxes to support the new large standing armies which mushroomed in seventeenth-century Europe. But the strength of these monarchs has been much exaggerated. Everywhere in the seventeenth century absolutism was tempered by bad communications and local privilege. Still, the standing armies and the bureaucracies which raised the men and money to support them were real enough and they were the immediate inheritance of the eighteenth century. There was no chance that the century would be a peaceful one. The entry of Russia into European power politics from the reign of Peter the Great, with significant consequences for both Russia and the rest of Europe, the presence in north Germany of a strong state, Prussia, with decided territorial objectives, and the new dimension of conflict in America and India ensured war on a new scale. The European world had never experienced a war on so many fronts as the Seven Years' War which virtually shattered state finances and resolved next to nothing. Monarchs, then, could not slough off the financial burden of armies and bureaucracies and were condemned to a remorseless pursuit of the means to finance them, a pursuit which led them into a head-on conflict with privilege whether in individual, corporate or provincial form. This conflict dominated the century's political life.

But there were other concerns which gave the confrontation between power as vested in the ruler and privilege in its manifold forms a new acuity. The Enlightenment, which reached its full flowering in this period, projected the very concept of secular and religious authority out front. It questioned the divine basis of royal power, the absolute authority of Church doctrine and strove to make man's earthly happiness central to the ordering of society. It sought to formulate a new political culture. It lead an attack on privilege whether it came in the form of tax exemptions for the nobility and clergy or provincial customary rights. No intellectual movement turned its back so emphatically upon the past.

If privilege existed in a progressively hostile environment it did so as well in one of consequential social and economic change. The period is that of the 'vital revolution' – a reversal of the classical demographic see-saw of upward movement followed by cutback – in which the European population took off for the first time into sustained growth with considerable implications in the shape of new food and employment demands. The broadening of the base of the social pyramid more widely than ever before brought the dispossessed into the cities, threatening a world of privileged elites and monarchs cocooned in baroque splendour.

This volume is then about privilege, social and political, about monarchy, its struggle for survival and its relationship with society, about power politics on a new scale and about the social and economic changes which are the hallmarks of the eighteenth century. Above all it is concerned with the tensions which produced the demise of the old order and ensured that the days of *ancien régime* Europe were numbered.

PART I

Traditional Structures and the Forces of Change

I

Social and Economic Developments

On the eve of the meeting of the Estates General in 1789 a contemporary print showed a humble peasant whose bent back bore, lashed to him like the proverbial albatross, a fat ecclesiastic, representing the church, and a gaudily dressed noble representing the aristocracy. There was no reason why the artist should have stopped there. He could have piled on that same pair of shoulders kings and palaces, bureaucracies, armies, fleets and towns with their swarms of legal officials and varied industries. In so doing he would merely have been expressing the simple truth, axiomatic amongst the disciples of the Enlightenment, that agriculture was the basis of European economic life. Eighty-five per cent and upwards of the population of every European country lived by working the land and consuming or marketing the produce. Most of the rest lived by rents or dues raised from those who worked the land or, in the case of industrial workers, were dependent upon the purchasing power of those whose income derived from the land. Or else they looked to the tax-paying propensities of the agrarian masses.

There was of course no homogeneous European peasantry. In purely legal terms one might distinguish between a bonded eastern European and a largely free westerner – free, that is, insofar as, setting aside Denmark, parts of southern Germany and Holstein and Alsace, where serfdom persisted, the western European peasant was master of his own time, was free to move, and his life was less dependent upon the arbitrary will of a single individual than the serf of eastern Europe. In western Europe the relics of serfdom and vestigial seigneurialism which still claimed dues and payment for use of monopoly rights, the mill, the community oven and the wine-press, were a waning force, relics of a medieval past and a ready target for reforming criticism. East of the Elbe, however, serfdom was a relatively new and still growing phenomenon. In Russia, eighteenth-century rulers continued to put themselves behind the extension of serfdom because they deemed this the best way to fix, and hence tax and recruit from, an otherwise shifting population. In Poland and east Germany, lords had sought in the second half of the seventeenth century, in the wake of war, famine and pestilence, to bind the peasantry to the soil to ensure a supply of manpower. In Poland and east Germany, lords had sought in the second half of the seventeenth century, in the wake of war, famine and pestilence, to bind the peasantry to the soil to ensure a supply of manpower. In Poland where the political domination of the *szlachta* was highly developed, the process continued apace throughout our period and reflected the interests of landlords who could gain good prices for their grain in heavily populated western Europe in preserving their cheap labour. Eastern lands were in the main farmed extensively, not intensively. There was no shortage of land but the land had no value without men to work it, grain yields were low and fallowing the only method of replenishing the soil. Yet this primitive area by extensive farming could be made to yield considerable surpluses.

Serfdom is, of course, a legal, not an economic, designation. It tells us nothing about the quality or quantity of the serf's diet in comparison with that of the free western European peasant. Russian serfdom included serfs on *obrók* (making payments to a lord in money or kind) and those subject to *barshchina* (heavy labour services). Apparently bondage touched the *obrotchnik* far less than the peasant on *barshchina*. Yet *obrók* was the characteristic tenure of the porest northern regions where the lords judged the peasant knew best how to survive and left him to it. The word *obrotchnik* was synonymous with pauper. Western observers like William Coxe were insistent that in dietary terms even the Russian serf could, and usually did, live better than the western European smallholder and that the evils of the situation related entirely to the character of the serf owner and how he used his powers of punishment – particularly flogging and in the Russian case, exile to Siberia for attempted flight. Primitive local government and above all, abysmal communications, in some instances confined almost to rivers, ensured that the peasant of eastern Europe could fall victim to terrible famines which could go unrelieved. The Bohemian riots of the 1770s and the Pugachev revolts of 1774 were to demonstrate degrees of deprivation produced by famine, in the Bohemian instance by pestilence, and in both cases by the demands of war, perhaps without parallel in the century. But in normal times, east European society could produce enough for relatively adequate nourishment and, in the instances of Poland, Livonia and continuous territories, an impressive marketable surplus. Not until the nineteenth century did internal demographic pressure force upon Europe east of the Elbe the problems which the west had to face in the eighteenth century. Herein resides one of the most striking differences between the territories of the Hohenzollerns, the Romanovs and the Habsburgs and those of the west.

Any generalization about the west European peasantry must be hedged about with qualifications, so great were regional and local differences. The seigneur as an individual who could claim rents, dues and monopolies, had disappeared in Britain, and parts of the Netherlands, and a straight landlord/tenant relationship was the only one – other than outright ownership – that affected these societies. Which sector of society, nobility, clergy, bourgeoisie, peasantry, actually owned the land varied from region to region and country to country. Taken acre for acre most of it (50 per cent plus) was directly in the ownership of the peasantry. But the crucial questions related less to who owned the land than to the quality of that land, and whether or not the farmer had enough to support himself and his family. Did he have a surplus he could take to market? Was he forced at some juncture of the year to be a purchaser of grain? How dependent were he and his family upon ancillary employment? The typical continental peasant was a smallholder, an owner occupier. This was particularly marked in France, most especially in the poorer agricultural regions which constituted, by Turgot's reckoning, about 60 per cent of the country. But it was as true of the Belgian Campine or northern Italy.

In Spain, the droughts of the late seventeenth century had caused something of a flight to the littoral and an actual retraction of land under cultivation. Smallholding Spain was the west, the north and Galicia. The extreme south, La Mancha and Extremadura were characterized by directly exploited latifundia and Mesta privileges which, at least until 1786, required large areas of the interior to be kept open and untilled for sheep runs.

The feeble demographic record of the late seventeenth and early eighteenth century produced fairly sluggish agricultural prices which were little incentive for larger more affluent farmers to contemplate experimentation, or to increase production. There were exceptions to this. In Britain and the Netherlands when grain prices lagged, some transition occurred to livestock production. In East Anglia, for example, from c. 1660, the introduction of turnips, cultivated grasses, and heavy marling permitted the conversion of extensive tracts of thin, permanent sheep pasture into mixed farming country, primarily grain-producing but conducting an important beef and mutton fattening business as well. From the point of view of the surplus producer, British agriculture actually suffered from a minor crisis of over-production in the 1730s. Similarly Flemish agriculture, the response to the needs of a highly urbanized region, made significant advances in the production of stall-fed cattle and abundantly fertilized wheat. Yet, taken all in all, western Europe was singularly unprepared for what was, in historical terms, the major revolution of the century, the revolution in numbers of people.

The history of the population of Europe from the sixth until at least the eighteenth century might realistically be described as a continued and dramatic confrontation between a population with a natural tendency to growth and food supplies capable of only limited extension. The eighteenth-century economist, Malthus, backed by a wealth of irrefutable historical evidence, saw as the God-sent arbiters of the battle between population and supply, a twin force, famine, the product of harvest failure, and disease, which rising at intervals ruthlessly cut back population to a level more consonant with its feeding resources. It is in a sense ironical that Malthus should have been an eighteenth-century figure, the product of the century that witnessed the 'vital revolution' in which the population of Europe embarked upon a slow but irreversible upward movement. Yet Malthus was not myopic nor deliberately misreading the signs. There was nothing ineluctable about this upward movement to stop it being reversed and why it occurred at all has yet to be fully explained by the modern demographic historian. One factor which is apparent is that in Continental Europe the increase was not attributable to an upswing in the birth-rate nor to any miraculous breakthrough in medical knowledge (though inoculation may well have assisted already established growth). Rather did it arise from a lowering of mortality rates not so much in normal years as in abnormal ones by the disappearance of the great crises, the cumulative runs of bad harvests and plague outbreaks which were characteristic of an earlier era. In this way, 'the peaks not the plateau of morality were lowered'. In Britain, a slight reduction in age at marriage, reflecting availability of work, may be responsible for a slight increase in the birth rate.

After the second decade of the eighteenth century, western Europe may have known isolated years of diminished harvest returns and the poorer sectors of the community certainly remained a prey to typhus, smallpox, typhoid, enteric fevers of all kinds, tuberculosis, a disease clearly on the increase and known in fact if not by name – diseases which in any community at any time could cause an excess of deaths over births – but neither dearth nor disease could eliminate the overall tendency to growth. In part at least this significant change might be attributed to the disappearance of local or regional famines as a result of better communications which permitted a more effective system of national distribution of supplies in time of local hardship. Progressively, grain could be shifted more easily from a surplus producing region to alleviate one acutely in need.

One should not, of course, overestimate the rate of population growth nor endow overall population figures with an accuracy they cannot possibly possess. They were based on highly defective data such as irregularly held and often partially concocted government censuses. Between 1700 and 1800 the European population moved from some 68–84 million to some 104–115 million and one must honestly allow such a margin of speculation. Gregory King in 1696 (though his reck-onings have been described as fantastical by a French historian) arrived at a figure of 6 $\frac{1}{2}$ million British who had become 9 million by the census of 1801. Twenty million Frenchmen in 1714 had become 26–27 million by 1800. Six million Spaniards were counted in 1700: 10.3 millions by the census of 1796. Fourteen million Russians in the Empire of Peter the Great are, by some highly dubious government calculations, estimated to have doubled in number by the end of the reign of Catherine the Great. In Great Britain, the Austrian Netherlands and Scandinavia, the rate of growth between 1740 and the end of the century seems to have been of the order of I per cent per annum. In France, the most populous country in Europe throughout the eighteenth century, the rate of growth was about half as great. Yet in spite of this less buoyant rate of growth, the French population was at least three times greater than that of Britain throughout the period.

One must also beware of equating population growth with ubiquit-ous new-found prosperity. Everything depended upon how far eco-nomic growth in any particular country was capable of providing for more people. The first kind of economic growth that obviously mat-tered was that directed towards increasing the supply of food. Unless food supplies were significantly augmented by bringing more land under cultivation, by increasing crop yields or by the transition to crops capable of feeding more people on a reduced acreage or less fertile soil (millet, maize, buckwheat, rice, potatoes, etc.), then acute periodic famine would be replaced by less acute, but notwithstanding chronic, malnutrition. Moreover, the scramble for existing supplies would almost certainly push up the price of food. If employment potential was not increased either in the agrarian or the industrial sector then the population increase must lead to underemployment. It must place pressure on existing jobs (hence ensuring no rise in wages to counteract the rise in prices). Or, smallholding societies must be thrown back on a further division of holdings, progressively less capable of supporting the incumbent. In the last analysis, without an enlargement of job and food potential, the lower echelons of western European society were condemned to rapidly deteriorating living standards in which they ceased to starve but were never free from hunger and in which they knew underemployment, unemployment or the inadequacy of a wage in a bloated labour market to feed a family.

Historians once used the term 'agrarian revolution' to describe some of the agricultural changes which took place in the eighteenth century. But such an approach is very misleading. The century experi-enced a spate of agronomic literature – in France alone 1214 books and pamphlets were produced compared with 130 in the previous one. In every country, gentlemen farmers, leisured clerics and *literati* formed agricultural societies, French *sociétés d'agriculture*, Spanish *sociedades económicas de Amigos del País* which sprouted throughout Spain after 1770, Italian *accademie*, Dutch *Oeconomische-Patriotisch Beweging* (the Economic-Patriotic Movement) which indicate a widespread growing interest in agricultural topics and some appreciation of the need to raise the level of production. Certainly the appreciation of the potential for increasing production through scientific methods and the move away from small-scale subsistence farms to large, market-orientated ones, can count as indicators of a more modern approach. However, the practical effects of the agricultural societies was minimal. Indeed, the intendant of Burgundy referred to them, pejoratively, as places for gossip. True, the best of the literature, for example Jethro Tull's *Horse Houghing Husbandry* (1731), H. L. Duhamel du Monceau, *Traité de la culture des terres* (1750–61), Gottlieb von Eckhart, *Vollstandige Experimentalokonomie* (1754), Johann Georg Leopoldt, *Nutzliche und auf die Erfahrung Gegunrundete Einleitung zu der Handwirtschaft* (1759) was not totally without effect over ensuing decades. But its influence was confined to particular areas and to a landlord class which perhaps farmed itself, as did many English gentlemen, or in more serious fashion, the Junkers of the lands beyond the Elbe, who on their 'home farms' could incubate practices which might *eventually* be extended to the holdings of their tenantry.

Over western Europe as a whole, the swelling of agronomic literature did not mean an increase in yield per acre and that for good reason. Smallholding societies had neither the means nor the inclination to hazard experiment and above all were without the manure needful to revitalize the soil and lift production. In an effort to grow as much bread grain as possible these societies gradually sacrificed pasture with serious consequences in terms of dietary standards and soil replenishment. In some areas (Brittany, Lorraine), there may have even been a decline in productivity. Even in Britain where on the whole a better balance had been struck between grain-growing and fodder crops for the cattle whose dung renewed the fields, the upward trend in agricultural production faltered in the 1750s, failing for the next half century to keep pace with population growth.

Nor was western Europe relieved by the bringing under cultivation of marginal land, or land once used which had slipped from usage during the population cutbacks of the seventeenth century, a movement of overall significance. Some assault was made in Britain and eastern France upon commons' rights to force enclosure of the common land to the lord's advantage. Europe on the whole did not lack uncultivated land. But where such land existed in abundance was in Mediterranean Europe (territories south of the Cantabrian mountains, of the Pyrenees, the Massif Central and of the north Italian plain). To render such land fertile was a matter of water control. The irrigation of even an insignificant fraction of the vast extents of under-watered land in Mediterranean Europe was a task far beyond the organizational and capital resources of the times and where attempts were made – as they were in the environs of certain Spanish cities (Barcelona, Valencia) – to dig out watercourses and employ abundant night-soil as fertilizer, they were very small in extent. Further north, the bringing under cultivation of heathland, scrubland, marsh or fen certainly did not make a significant contribution to increased food production. Except in East Prussia, where small but impressive progress was made in reclaiming marshland, efforts in Ireland, Scotland, Norway, Sweden, Britanny and north-west Germany to incorporate heathland into rotations usually had disastrous long-term consequences resulting in the exhaustion of the heath, previously a valuable source of manure.

In limited areas, there was a switch to unpopular but high-yield foodstuffs, particularly maize and potatoes, which in the course of the nineteenth century were progressively to monopolize the diet of the poor. The eighteenth-century potato, a hard, irregular tuber which bore little physical relationship to modern strains, had by 1750 made a positive entry into the diet of the Irish peasant of Munster, into that of the Bavarian smallholder and with strenuous opposition, into that of the peasant of the Pyrenees, of parts of Aquitaine and of eastern France – particularly Alsace where its false association with typhoid occasioned protracted rioting in 1786.

Western Europe also continued to find some support in imports from the Baltic distributed through the ports of Danzig and Riga. Baltic lords were able to provide the Mediterranean lands and some north European cities – including London – with part of their needs in exchange for wine, salt, manufactured goods and bullion. The trade in wine to northern Europe and America was highly consequential in promoting the extension of viticulture from Gascony, along the coast of Portugal and Spain and across southern France into Italy. Those who argue an increase in French agrarian output for the eighteenth century do so most convincingly in terms of viticulture. But the extension of the vine was at the expense of bread grain because it reduced the amount of land available for grain production leaving any small proprietors in these regions very dependent upon buoyant wine prices and hence dangerously exposed in the wine slump of the 1780s or during the Baltic grain famine of the 1760s.

The natural corollary of the failure to lift grain production or to open up new land, or significantly to turn over to new crops was simple enough. Prices moved, slowly at first but then with considerable momentum, into an upward spiral. The demographic revolution, which in some instances had only begun in the 1740s, had by the 1750s and '60s produced a number of winners and losers. The winners are clear enough to define – anyone in command of a marketable surplus must profit from the enhanced prices his goods could command.

Good market prices saw the substantial farmer with a new-found wealth. This new-found wealth lies behind, and helps explain, the growth in sufficient consumer potential to transform the appurtenances of the substantial farm as well as the contents of the stately home. Satire mocked the wealthy farmer's wife who squeezed her bulk into fashionable clothing. Large landowners directly exploiting the soil were able to play the market to their own advantage, and could withhold grain if it suited them in the immediate post-harvest period to market it during the spring and summer, the time of the highest prices. Such people might have to negotiate with merchants for the marketing of their produce or deal directly for themselves. Or the profitmakers in such a situation might be those who took a cut of the peasant's crop in kind: the seigneur in the shape of dues: the church in the form of tithe and anyone from whom the peasant had been forced to borrow. The creditor might well be a grain merchant who advanced grain to the peasant to meet his needs if his own crop proved inadequate to carry his family through the year or if harvest failure had forced him to consume grain needed for the next sowing. Or he might be a seigneur or substantial peasant ready to make a loan, charging a great deal for his grain in the spring and early summer when prices were high. Loans were always repayable when the harvest was garnered and prices at their lowest. It was virtually impossible for the subsistence, or very modest farmer, ever to profit from rising prices because he was inevitably a purchaser when prices were high and a vendor when they were at their lowest. Moreover, for anyone unfortunate enough to have been reduced to the position of borrower, debt repayment at the next harvest clearly reduced his chances, even supposing his harvest returns were good, of making his way through the next year without borrowing again. Much peasant protest reflects the prolongation of crises in this way. Debt was the road the smallholder took in his descent to the labourers' ranks.

There was a second way to make money in this situation and this was by a closer, harsher and more business-like attitude towards the letting of land: the evolution of the shorter, and inevitably less favourable, lease which, when it fell in, could be adjusted to reflect market conditions in land. Generally speaking, there was not a western European nation which did not in some way experience this phenomenon in the second half of the eighteenth century. Hence one finds in England the gradual ousting of the copyholder by engrossing lords: in Ireland the rapid turnover in plots of under five acres: in France and Italy the increasingly unfavourable terms which sharecroppers (men who were without the capital to hire and stock a farm and to whom cattle and seed were advanced by the landlord against a rental payable at harvest time) were forced to accept. In Piedmont sharecropping leases which were the dominant tenure were gradually pushed up so that the lessee was paying his landlord an amount which advanced from two-fifths to a half of his harvest returns. Moreover, here, the hereditary tenure gradually disappeared to be replaced by three-, six- or nine-year leases, a phenomenon also noteworthy in the French Nivernais and the Limousin. (There was of course a ceiling beyond which the landowner would not go particularly on land capable of only feeble returns.) A variant on such practices was the subleasing found in parts of Spain. Here before the second half of the eighteenth century, the only way of making a significant profit from farming was to store the grain harvested against years of bad harvest and high prices. But from 1760–65 with rising demand for food and hence the increasing value of arable land, there rapidly evolved a keen interest in acquiring and re-assuming possession of lands.

There was also an ever-swelling number of middlemen employed by often absentee landowners to maximize their profits – agents, stewards, *fermiers* – some of whom made impressive profits from taking a direct cut in proceeds in kind: in negotiating new leases on behalf of their employers which might unbeknownst to them embody bribes for the agent and so on. The foundation of the fortunes of the House of Lamoignon, *fermiers généraux*, even in one instance *contrôleur général*, stemmed from a stewardship. Then there were the sub-contractors of tithe (sometimes grain merchants themselves) who negotiated a lump sum with the holder in exchange for garnering the proceeds – proceeds which were in kind and hence whose values rose yearly. Obviously the occupying farmer was not totally passive in his response to the demands of such a person as is emphasized by the mounting tide of tithe litigation or in one instance – that of southern Ireland – by the outbreak in the 1760s of some of the most violent rural revolts eighteenth-century Europe knew. Notwithstanding, the existence in the countryside of a host of intermediaries living parasite-like upon the farmer and who, in terms of wealth, occupied an impressive place in the rural economic hierarchy, was a general phenomenon.

If high prices for food improved the standard of living and disposable wealth of those who had access to food stocks the losers in such a situation are no less apparent: anyone who was forced to be a purchaser even for part of the year: any sub-subsistence farmer forced to subdivide property with each generation and eke out a living on less and less. Overall we are faced with the clear certainty that over much of continental Europe, demographic increase was accompanied by a gradual decline in average *per capita* calorie intake. In some areas this was not felt until the 1760s but in others, for example the chestnut-eating communities of parts of the Auvergne or of the Pyrenean slopes, or of the Alto Adige or the Trás-os-Montes of Portugal, or the rice-eating, malarial communities of Dauphiné and the Maremma Toscana, or amongst the cotters of Connaught, signs of strain were manifest from the 1740s. Entire mountain communities lived for months of the year principally on boiled chestnuts and a few vegetables in the summer, or on slops of maize or buckwheat. The only protein they ever saw was milk from a scrawny cow fed on weeds hand-picked by the roadside, or a little fat pork from a pig – the animal *par excellence* of the poor because it needed no pasture – that shared the family's hovel but whose better meat was sold at market.

It is tempting to posit the increasing polarization of western Europe into richer and poorer: to go so far even as to think in terms of rising *per capita* income and yet increasing misery on the part of the masses, a phenomenon familiar enough in parts of the world today. However, although this process of social polarization was a shared western European experience, its intensity varied significantly from country to country and even region to region. It is possible, for example, to turn to examples of French communities and find given as an answer to the question 'How many of your parishioners are indigent?' 'There are only two who are not': or communities in Tipperary wherein one great dairy farmer in command of 9000 acres along with his agent stood out in stark contrast to surrounding cotters on two-to five-acre plots: or the Tuscan Pistoiese where in occasional mountain communities like Treppio, out of 315 families, there were 60 pedlars or shepherds and the rest were smallholders spending six months of the year as seasonal migrants in the Maremma Toscana. Such extremes were obviously not the norm. Notwithstanding, the social polarization of western Europe as a whole over our period into the affluent few and the impoverished many is a factor with which to be reckoned for it had important consequences. The absence of a sufficiently large, affluent grouping with purchasing power in the countryside could have repercussions on industrial development. It would condition the type of urbanization a country experienced. Societies of paupers without possibility of relief in the shape of work or assistance money from wealthier elements in the community would probably be forced to move in search of work and could be responsible for what we might call an urbanization of poverty such as reached its apogee in Sicily.

Generally speaking, Great Britain (leaving aside Ireland) probably achieved the best overall social balance, contriving a cottager and pauper population of the level of some 30 per cent of the whole and being remarkable for the existence of a solid middling farmer grouping, substantial enough, and this was crucial to sustained industrial growth, to be a considerable purchaser of industrial goods. The Austrian Netherlands and Sweden probably fared second in such a league though here, as indeed in Britain, one is conscious of the increase in the lowest element. In 1751 in Sweden cottagers and paupers formed some 25 per cent of all peasants: in 1815 they had swollen to 50 per cent. In France an overall estimate of cottagers, paupers and 'exposed' elements amongst the urban population might realistically stand at 60 per cent but in some regions 90 per cent of the population of rural communities did not have enough either to see themselves through the year or to be spared deprivation at various stages of the life cycle, most particularly when children were young or in old age. Perhaps it was in France that the contrast between the affluent few and the impoverished many was most marked. Whilst it existed in part of western Germany, the under-populated regions of eastern Germany were prepared to reach out for the demographic excess of the west so that the latter was preserved from the worst evils of population pressure and extreme social polar-ization.

So much for the feeding of Europe. Demographic change engendering on the one hand more wealth and hence more consumer expenditure, a growing supply of people to be clothed and supplied with basic com-modities, and on the other, a mass of people anxious to accept industrial employment either to buttress a no longer self-sufficient holding, or as a substitute for work in agriculture, were factors which obviously played their part in promoting industrial development.

Taken overall, the eighteenth century was one of impressive though patchy industrial growth and by the end, Great Britain was fashioning new criteria of development. In 1730, however, the shape of things to come was far from apparent. Amongst industrial areas, England, Belgium, north-east France, Languedoc and Switzerland enjoyed a rough parity of development (agriculture/industry ratios roughly 2:1). Industrial development was largely dependent upon the internal market, but considerable quantities of goods went to eastern Europe, to the Levant and across the Atlantic and there was fierce commercial competition to seize and hold on to these 'foreign' markets. In eastern Europe and over much of Germany, woollen fabrics from England, Holland, France and Saxony fought a commercial battle. The Mediter-ranean was the scene of much wide-ranging commercial warfare. By the beginning of the eighteenth century the Languedoc woollen industry had captured the Levantine market and was to hold on to it until the 1760s whilst the English ousted the Dutch as principal pur-veyors to Spain and Portugal. But no one country enjoyed long-term advantages. Those producers first in the field with better selling vari-eties or prompter to discern market drifts could seize the initiative and reap the profits.

In 1730, the basis of textile production was woollen cloth or wool mixed with other fibres and manufactured in various sizes, qualities and quantities over much of Europe – though sometimes such industry did little more than supply the needs of the producing family. The two most noteworthy wool-manufacturing nations, Britain and France, had very similar records throughout our period in spite of the apparent dissimilarities in organization. French industry was guild regulated and physiocratic thought identified such practice with low industrial performance. But the physiocrats naïvely overstated the case. Guilds were the guarantors of quality and shoddy goods would not win markets. Indeed the freeing of industry from guild control in the 1760s is coexistent with the decline of the Languedoc woollen industry. In both France and Britain woollen production expanded in the course of the century, in the French case perhaps production was 70 per cent higher in 1780 than 1700. But, around 1760, growth momentum was lost. Exports declined markedly and total production may in the French case have been tending downwards. Similarly British production, marked by a rapid development in the West Riding which by the 1760s included fundamental technical innovation (the flying shuttle from the 1760s, the jenny from the 1770s and the carding machine from the '80s), entered a sharp phase-change around 1760. Exports fell and kept heading downwards and did not regain their 1760s level until well into the 1790s. The fall was most marked in East Anglia and the West Country and home production does not seem to have increased sufficiently to have prevented an overall contraction on the part of British industry.

The downward turn in woollen production might reflect any one or an amalgam of three factors. Firstly, there was increased competition from the development of importing nations of indigenous industries given state protection. England thus lost useful markets in Denmark, Norway, Sweden and even Prussia which built up a notable woollen industry after the acquisition of Silesia in 1740. In Portugal too, an official policy, inaugurated in 1758, of developing a rural cloth-making industry in parts of Beira and the Alentejo seems to have borne solid fruit. Moreover the growth of Venetian rural industry, a spontaneous rather than a state-promoted development, reduced French strength in the Levant.

Secondly, the low performance rate of the sixties might also be a reflection of a generalized sixties crisis. This crisis extended to Europe as a whole and affected several levels of the economic life of the continent. Government finances ran into difficulties: the international money market was severely dislocated, there were several bankruptcies amongst leading financiers and, perhaps the origin of all the difficulties, there are signs of stress in the agrarian sector which may reflect the changing demographic balance. The sixties were the occasion of grain riots throughout the villages and towns of England, of France, Holland and even of Spain because of the rising price of bread grain through bad harvests. Rising prices could curtail the purchasing power of consumers of basic textile goods and hence trigger off slump.

Thirdly, other textile products, particularly the use of cotton, perhaps contributed to the long-term demise of woollen goods. At the beginning of the eighteenth century, western Europe had not fully mastered the art of spinning the fine, strong cotton yarn needed to reproduce the calico-type materials of the Orient which so strongly appealed to the tastes of moneyed western society and with which, through the agency of the English East India Company, it was becoming increasingly familiar. A calico-craze in fact so characterized early eighteenth-century society that most of the governments of western European states chose to relieve distressed native textile interests by measures to exclude printed cotton fabrics from their territories. But the taste had been excited and was not to be denied. Enterprising men concentrated upon finding native substitutes for such eminently saleable materials and to founding textile printing establishments. Cotton manufactures sprang up in Britain and Prussia, in Switzerland which came to specialize in lawn and embroidered cottons, in Catalonia, in the Rouen-Amiens-Troyes nexus in France, and in Liège and the Belgian textile cities.

Eastern spinning skills were not in fact rivalled, however, until the waterframe and the mule provided mechanical solutions to the problems posed by fine spinning and that at the very end of our period. It was only in the 1780s – and in Lancashire alone – that waterframe and mule-spun yarn was being supplied in any quantity. Up to that point, the story is of a slow broadening of European competence to comprehend certain kinds of pure cotton cloth and cotton-linen mixtures of a finer type than those made hitherto.

These light fabric industries were an overwhelmingly rural activity except for the bleaching, printing, finishing and marketing aspects. Spinning, pre-mechanization, in particular, was a labour intensive craft practised by cottage-based women and children. They formed a readily exploitable labour force prepared to work for less than townswomen because for them industry was an ancillary income to that provided by a small agricultural unit. Even traditional industries, wool, lace and ribbon making, were still apt to creep into the countryside to find a cheap tractable force. This is not to suggest that rural poverty automatically engendered industrial enterprise. The need for employment was no determinant for the introduction of industry. But where industry did creep into the countryside it both proved a palliative to extreme rural poverty and stemmed the flood of peasant migration townwards. It also exposed the countryside to the vicissitudes of industrial performance.

Yet to a limited extent and in particular areas, industrial development (not Industrial Revolution) did make some small contribution to keeping the small farmer on the land. What it did not do was to remedy the marked imbalance between employment potential and the work force. Unemployment and underemployment remained and wages were depressed in all but a few favoured industries at very restricted times. To set against a rise of 65 per cent in food prices in France was a feeble 22 per cent growth in wages between 1760 and the Revolution. The day labourer was particularly disadvantaged and for the sick, feeble, old, and the victims of slump or crop failure there was no palliative of organized relief. In Catholic Europe, the frail support of voluntary almsgiving remained the most effective [sic] weapon against inflated numbers of those unable to make a living. In Protestant Europe, particularly in Britain and Scandinavia, governments sought to shift provision for poor relief on to the shoulders of parish or, as in Holland, on to the church community, with the result that parishes haggled over responsibility, erected legislation against outsiders, and in many instances made a condition of support entry into a workhouse. It was no accident that the eighteenth century became preoccupied, throughout the length and breadth of Europe, with the question of the poor. And whilst debates from armchair salons raged, millions of people eked out miserable existences and struggled with the uncomfortable option of a hungry unnoticed struggle in the country or a flight to the town where they could not be totally ignored.

Urban society was in many respects a mirror image of the conditions prevailing in the surrounding countryside and reflecting on the one hand the new wealth to be had from the marketing of agrarian products and the sale of consumer goods to those rich from agrarian revenues, and on the other hand, the growing poverty which forced the landless into the ranks of the dispossessed and kept wages in a bloated labour market depressed.

Towns were thickest on the ground in western Europe and grew smaller in number and size east of the Elbe. Generally, in no European country did urbanization exceed 20 per cent of the total population, the exception being the Low Countries, or more precisely Flanders, Brabant (24%) and the province of Holland (55%) and Sicily. Towns grew in the eighteenth century as bureaucrats multiplied, as maritime trade increased, as industrial development proceeded apace and as the dispossessed of the countryside sought out the towns.

Bureaucratization involved the increasing elaboration of the organs of central government (the trappings, for example, of enlightened despotism) throughout our period. In capital cities especially, courtiers, politicians, civil servants, lawyers, financiers with their demands for servants and service trades, multiplied in proportion to the increasing complexity of government, a trend begun in the sixteenth century and still continuing in the eighteenth.

The second reason for growth was the expansion of maritime trade, especially transatlantic trade. Glasgow, Liverpool, Bristol, Cork, Nantes, Bordeaux, Oporto, Lisbon, Barcelona, Marseilles, Leghorn and Hamburg testify to this. Already well established as major ports and experiencing only modest or no further expansion of their sea-going trade, were London, Amsterdam – these two continuing to tower above all other European commercial centres – and Rotterdam. But the ripples of maritime trade extended inland via the great rivers to Lyons, Rouen, Frankfurt-on-Main and the Rhine stations. Again, the growth of ports opened up opportunities to building workers, porters and dock labourers and to a servant and service populace. To read Arthur Young on his visit to Bordeaux as he experienced an architectural elegance and an affluence of existence he had never seen before, is to appreciate something of the extent of employment demand such a growth could engender.

The third force making, in some instances, for notable town expansion, was industrial growth. Yet one must be careful. All towns of any size were in some sense industrial towns. They housed garment and leather workers, building workers, furniture workers, candle-makers, soap-makers, brewers, distillers, bakers and so on. Capital cities, with their special congregations of wealthy, housed in addition numerous and varied producers of luxury goods: fine metalwares both base and precious, jewellery, clocks and watches, optical instruments, coaches and carriages, books, engravings etc. The biggest concentrations of industrial workers in Europe were those of London, Paris and Naples – the largest concentrations because these were the largest cities and not vice versa. Where there was urban growth, there was, as a consequence, industrial growth. The reverse process – industrial growth impelling urban growth – is a much rarer phenomenon. Indeed, Leiden, Lille, Rouen, Reims, Valenciennes, Cologne, Nuremberg and Augsburg were all textile cities which may actually have *lost* population in the eighteenth century as industry pushed out into the village and hamlet. Yet in Britain already by the end of our period, Birmingham and Manchester, Leicester, Nottingham, Sheffield, Leeds, Bradford and their satellite industrial villages demonstrated at least incipient growth attributable to industrial development. The emphasis, however, must be on incipient. In every European state the capital (national or in the case of a political agglomeration like the Habsburg lands, provincial) dwarfed all other towns and could absorb anything from 5–10 per cent of the total population.

The two most highly urbanized parts of Europe, Holland and Sicily, offer an interesting contrast. In the one, international trade, industry and commerce had from medieval times promoted intense, but in eighteenth-century terms, decelerating, urban development. In the other, exists an extreme version of a theme present in some degree in urban demography anywhere in Europe: towns as places of refuge for the extreme poor, sometimes the hopeless and the helpless: towns as monuments to rural poverty. The weight of urban population in Sicily is a testament to the growing collapse of its rural economy, unable, through a combination of human and physical factors to offer even the promise of support and subsistence to swelling numbers of its progeny. Sicily, the most town-strewn landscape in Europe, also boasted Europe's most conspicuous slum, Palermo, understandably last seat of western European plague.

The urbanization of poverty, a poverty born in the countryside but which manifested itself in town, created problems of public order, menaced public health and placed a strain on traditional patterns of provisioning. Mounting crime rates, particularly theft which in urban areas more than exceeded the rate of population growth, soaring statistics of children abandoned to foundling hospitals because their parents could not afford to keep them, plummeting standards of hygiene as municipal facilities failed to keep pace with the rate of influx, all bear witness to an urbanization of poverty. True the 8000 foundlings with which the Hôtel Dieu in Paris had to cope in the 1780s and which represented about a third of all city baptisms, were in many instances dispatched from villages. It was impossible to isolate the problems of poverty in rural society from those of the towns.

Linnaeus compared the stench of Hamburg to an open sewer. Most cities could be smelt several miles away so inadequate were facilities for drainage, sewage and refuse collection, though perhaps the most odoriferous were those commanding waterways, or built on river estuaries, such as Stockholm, Venice, Ghent and Bruges. In the back streets of even the most elegant towns, unless police could enforce prohibitive legislation, pigs foraged undisturbed. It is hardly surprising that town growth in the eighteenth century was nowhere self-generated but sustained and augmented by a rural influx. Moreover, in a sense the town murdered a good part of its rural refugees from typhus, typhoid, smallpox and tuberculosis which flourished in the cramped, insalubrious, polluted conditions in which immigrants were forced to live. Such immigrants were, of course, a volatile element in the urban community though historians of riot have demonstrated the greater likelihood of their being a cause of discontent rather than the instigators of popular movements. Be this as it may, the lower echelons of urban society were disquieting for authority to contemplate. Most of the courts, and in particular those of France, Spain, Portugal and of many German princes had decided in some instances a century before to maroon themselves in the artificially created, semi-rural gentility of palaces like Versailles, Mafra, Charlottenburg and Schonbrunn. Yet though the nobility and the affluent were drawn to the courts, they also sought the diversions of city life in spite of its dangers.

There was of course real wealth in the cities and larger towns of Europe though the degree of that wealth reflected the condition of the surrounding countryside for the money expended in the town was in overwhelming part that drawn from rents, dues and taxes paid by the rural community.

Affluent Europe had a whole series of wants and cravings in the form of clothing and artefacts to adorn the person, building and house decoration, furniture, metalware, porcelain, paintings, tastes for foreign foods like sugar and drinks such as tea, coffee, chocolate, fine wines and spirits, and for leisure pursuits, books and horses. The century experienced what has been called the 'discovery of childhood', that is of a childhood to be enjoyed by special toys, dolls' houses, carved animals, soldiers, musical boxes and instruments, and a childhood for which distinctive clothing must be purchased instead of having children garbed as little adults. The cravings of the rich engendered employment potential for craftsmen, and architects like Adam, furniture makers like Chippendale, porcelain manufacturers like Meissen, the continuing success of Sèvres, or of new men like Wedgwood, for publishers and printers – especially in Holland where censorship was at its lowest – of painters like Hogarth, Stubbs, Canaletto – who provided lasting mementoes of dearly purchased foreign travel – or Antoliñez whose paintings depicted the Spanish picture hawker who carried exhibitions into the homes of the wealthy. The laces and embroideries, elaborate stays and ribbons worn by Marie Antoinette and her ladies were of course produced by women's labour remunerated by derisory sums since the women either worked at home or on a living-in basis in an employer's house. A day's lacemaking, a labour which could eventually take the sight, in the Massif Central realized between 2–5 *sous* per day (a pound of bread cost about 2 *sous*).

The aristocratic and those of middling wealth who aped their betters put much of their wealth into circulation. Thirteen per cent and upwards of the population of every major European city were domestic servants and although in some instances the term implied girls performing some industrial functions on a living-in basis, and in others the maid-of-all-work in quite modest households, in the capitals an important sector of the servant class was concentrated in the employment of the affluent. The labour services demanded by the wealthy stretched far beyond resident domestics to wig-makers and powderers, corsetmakers and an incredible battery of service trades catering to the elaborate costume of upper-class eighteenth-century society. The cult of bodily filth practised even by kings in the seventeenth century gave way to washing and perfuming the body. Never before nor since has so much human effort been expended on dress and appearance nor to this point on the material appurtenances of life, building, furnishing and transport. The noble, ecclesiastic and wealthy bourgeois revelled in conspicuous consumption. Their servants and tradesmen noticed and 'aped' their betters. Maidservants cut into their wages so as to own two or three overdresses and clean shifts. Artisans too added to their possessions and a pocket watch (to be pawned in hard times) became a common possession.

Office-holding was perhaps less of an attraction to the newly rich than it had been in the past because the returns, other than in prestige, on such an investment were relatively slight but still this was another direction for the absorption of capital. Mercantile wealth was invariably concerned with acquiring the material accompaniments of an aristocratic existence, land with rents and dues, perhaps office, certainly lavish houses and clothing. The only outlet preventing the evaporation and loss of capital was lending to the government, in peacetime at fairly modest interest rates, though in time of crisis with the potential of greater gains. There existed a significant grouping of *rentiers*, people concerned with living on capital lent to governments or their agencies, sometimes against annuities, sometimes on a shorter-term basis. Banking and credit facilities were developing swiftly, if patchily, in Europe in the great ports and the capitals. Britain (1694), Austria (1705), Prussia (1765), Spain (1782) all had state banks. Geneva and Amsterdam were the centres of great banking houses. This development linked closer than ever before the worlds of trade, industry and public finance and in the sixties and eighties gave an international aspect to crises of credit.

Towns everywhere housed bureaucrats, great and small, who existed above all to tax, to police and to regulate society. Indeed, there were French, Italian and Spanish towns where one adult male in ten thus defined himself in the mid-eighteenth century, and German states which threw up bureaucratic dynasties offering their services, rather like mercenary soldiers, to Habsburg, Hohenzollern and Romanov. The top bureaucratic positions, like the French *intendant* or the Spanish *corregidor* were in the hands of the nobility, the more modest positions in those of men with an education, if few means, and the lowliest, like the offices of bailiffs in semi-redundant courts, scarcely afforded the incumbent a living. The bureaucratic structure of eighteenth-century Europe virtually defies analysis. The innovations of seventeenth-century monarchs had been slapped on top of a substructure of crumbling medieval courts and often redundant institutions. In France and Spain office was frequently venal. This meant it was the property of the owner and could be sold or bequeathed virtually at will. Then there were provincial and municipal bureaucrats or officials often concerned with the mechanism of taxation and not infrequently drawing an income from a cut of the proceeds. Customs, excise, the French General Farm which employed thousands to administer the unwieldy *gabelle* and catch smugglers and evaders, the *chinoviki* of Russia (literally men of rank), irregularly paid and ever-open to bribery, were consistently hated by a venerable popular tradition.

Then there were the swarms of lawyers, some with a prosperous business in distinguished courts like the *parlements*, courted by an affluent clientele and others dependent upon infrequent briefs from a rural society which believed justice ought to be free and was doubtless irregular in the payment of fees. Setting aside the poor and landless, eighteenth-century society was highly litigious to preserve rights in land and privileges, to promote an affronted individual's sense of honour which at almost every social level was far more sensitive than twentieth-century people can appreciate (even the fishwives of Marseilles and Montpellier regularly sued for compensation for insults) and lastly to obtain redress for very frequent violence. This made for plenty of business but insufficient to preserve many from a scramble for subsidiary work, regulating estate or hospital accounts or acting in France as parish *syndic*, a man who conducted parish business correspondence with the officials of the intendance, or seeking work in a seigneurial jurisdiction where fees were at their lowest. Amongst the lawyers and office holders were numbered many who were bitter, frustrated and critical. These were to be a dissident element in the eighteenth-century bourgeoisie.

Urban industrial production centred upon the small workshop where the craftsman drew upon the services of his family and those perhaps of a journeyman and an apprentice. Few wage earners earned more than sufficient to keep themselves and a small family in bread and lodging and the master craftsman in sickness, or when trade was for any reason dislocated, was precariously exposed and had few reserves to sustain him. This is not to deny the existence of wealthy iron masters or merchant clothiers whose influence extended over numerous out-workers, but they were not a numerous grouping. They were townsmen who organized the scattered labour of the villages, exploiting a rural labour force which could be used or abandoned at will according to market conditions and which was often paid less than the urban worker and caught up in a web of debt to the clothier.

Town and country were pitted against one another in every conceivable way. For the peasant the town was an oppressive, privileged, parasitical force bleeding the countryman to its own ends. The world of taxmen and officialdom, of seigneur and fat cleric, of rapacious clothier, of absentee landlord whether noble, cleric or bourgeois, presented an alien influence only too unpleasantly intrusive in rural life. Conversely, indigenous urban society dwelt in many cases in fear of an immigrant sector which was rowdy, violent and perhaps prepared to work for less than the town labourer.

The Irish immigrant in London, whether temporary or permanent, had his role to play in arousing popular discontent, manifest for example in the Gordon Riots. The influx of rural poor, Auvergnats, Beaucerons, Picards, Normans, into the French capital created new scales of policing priorities as an overworked force found it easy to assume the immigrant, dossing in wretched cellars or crammed in attics, frequently out-of-work and invariably hungry, was the most crime-prone sector of the populace.

The towns also suspected the producing farmer of having the upper hand in negotiations relative to the sale of grain. The modest urban consumer was endowed with an economic philosophy under onslaught in the changing demographic conditions of the eighteenth century. He believed markets should be regulated; that all grain sales should occur in the open market and not be conducted between farmer and merchant by sample or when the grain was standing in the field; that the small man should be permitted to buy first before the wholesale merchant and hence have his interests protected. He was also a protagonist of the just price, that is one which did not escalate with shortage or reflect fluctuations in supply. But grain was a commodity ever more precious and producers in western Europe were progressively evading established market practice. Insofar as many peasants were purchasers at certain times of the year they shared some interest in the town's concern with a moral economy. But neither trusted the other: both believed the other advantaged in the competition for supplies at fair prices: that the nearness of the countryman to the soil gave him an unfair advantage or conversely that the townsman was in a better position to influence town government to bring in coercive legislation. Grain riots were the commonest form of urban disturbance in times of shortage, especially where distribution practices were mistrusted, and even where grain was not the ostensible object of riot it usually lurked somewhere in the background.

The other question which was likely to bring on urban disturbance was the extension of commodity taxes. Escaping the brunt of direct taxation, indirect taxes on goods entering towns or articles of common consumption, above all on alcoholic drink and tobacco, fell more heavily on the urban dweller. Britain (fostered by the distillers) experienced a whole series of Excise Riots and disturbances as a consequence of fresh impositions on gin but sharpened by the popular belief that they were the precursors of extended indirect taxation. Indirect impositions were traditionally the recourse of governments in search of funds. Less frequent were industrial disputes. Yet, the legislation of 1762 extending all branches of textile production to the villages engendered some bitter rioting in Languedocian textile towns and demonstrations in Amiens and Lille.

Urban populaces, their nerves ever on edge, were also, in the capitals and provincial cities, open to manipulation by political dissidents, a theme to which frequent reference must be made. Rural disturbance on the other hand tended to focus on particular hate figures who were made to epitomize the problems of the countryside. A great deal of grievance centred upon the seigneur and his agents, the steward or the miller to whom rights of mill had been leased and who could be responsible for all kinds of delays and added costs. This was particularly manifest in France.

Further east it was seigneurial labour services which attracted dissension and which lay behind the massive agrarian disturbances in Bohemia and contributed to the Pugachev rising. These were riots on a scale which rocked government, but most rural disorder was highly fragmented and posed little real problem for the central government. Anti-tithe riots and movements to raze enclosure shook the Irish province of Munster intermittently over twenty years after 1760. Extensive as this movement was, it selected particular hate figures, tithe proctors or canters (men who leased the tithe against a sum and then proceeded to make a profit on the collection), or landlords responsible for par-ticular atrocities. Many victims however, some of whom were buried alive, were so because of vendettas. The French General Farm yearly lost a score or more of employees who were found murdered in hedge-rows. In one year alone fifty recruiting agents disappeared in the Auvergne. Violence was an attribute of both rural and urban European society. Town and country were defined more than anything else by their hatreds.

2

The World of Privilege

Eighteenth-century European society was still largely qualified by reference to estates or orders – the clergy, the nobility, the Third Estate, the last sometimes split into burghers and peasantry. The first two estates were almost invariably known as privileged orders, though they were far from enjoying a monopoly of privilege. The stratification reflected a medieval concept of division by function into a warrior elite, a priestly order concerned with the salvation of souls and lastly, those who depended on the other two orders for defence and spiritual succour. By 1730 such a stratification had lost much of its initial justification. If the clergy continued to pray and claimed tax exemption for doing so, several societies had lost sight of why such an activity should betoken special privileges: the nobility looked to pursuits far more complex than the art of war. A division into estates had never been intended to convey economic uniformity and the qualifications noble, cleric or Third Estate took progressively less account of social realities. An apparently vast social and economic chasm lay between say a Duke of Orleans and a Languedocian seigneur with a crumbling *château* and a handful of servants, unable to prevent the peasantry taking pot-shots at the doves to which his nobility entitled him, or between an Archbishop of Mainz in his palace and a humble parish priest in his hovel. Yet all were caught up in the tangle of privilege which characterized eighteenth-century Europe and which make it impossible entirely to disregard the concept of order as totally irrelevant. The two privileged orders had corporate interests which they struggled to maintain and corporately they were sufficiently powerful to sustain a struggle if not ultimately to win it. Moreover, in this struggle they were to be brought into a head-on collision with monarchy which traditionally had looked to an establishment of nobility and church to maintain its authority. The struggle was bitter because the corporate wealth of the two orders in land and manpower was, to say the least, impressive and because in many states institutions existed which not only guaranteed the continuation of privilege but gave the two orders a platform for countering opposition to their claims which could be, or seem to be, far broader than the mere defence of elitist privilege. Thirdly the struggle was sharpened by the fact that monarchy, on the one hand, and privileged bodies on the other, were endowed with a differing concept of the form and role of the state. In broad terms the one stood for a concept of centralized control wherein the state could directly reach each citizen and where that citizen had one simple allegiance: where the state could raise armies and tax according to its needs. The other stood for decentralization and fragmentation in which the state could not intrude upon traditional patterns of allegiance or override particularist influences. Such statements perforce must be developed further, but they are the three major explanations of why privilege was such a formidable force.

Squarely on top of the world of wealth sat the European nobility nowhere jostled in their economic pre-eminence except perhaps in England and the United Provinces where the collective wealth of gentry and commercial bourgeoisie demanded some recognition as an approaching rival.

The legal designation 'noble' usually extended to about 2–3 per cent of any European society with the exceptions of the United Provinces, where it was decidedly less because town patriciates had not taken titles or noble status: of England where as a legally definable grouping it was confined to a small peerage of 182 families: of Switzerland where for historic reasons a nobility did not exist: and of Spain where 15 per cent of the adult male population were nominally included (an inflated figure arrived at by the inclusion of the entire adult population of Guipuzcoa where nobility meant nothing more than the exemption of the province from royal taxation and justice). Even so the Spanish figure exceeded the European norm.

Nobility could everywhere be acquired in two ways: firstly by birth – the easiest and least disputed method – the second by creation by the monarchy. Monarchs might bestow noble status for a variety of reasons: to gain important political support (as in England): to enhance an administrative experiment by raising the status of certain royal officials (as in Prussia, Sweden, Russia, France, Spain and the Spanish administration in Lombardy): as a reward for loyal service in time of war (an important consideration for the hard-pressed Habsburgs): as a money making expedient (common in Spain and France in the sixteenth and seventeenth centuries): or even as a reward for merit, though this was relatively rare. In the eighteenth century the ennoblement of Rutherford in Bavaria for his schemes relating to poor relief, of Elie de Beaumont the philanthropist in Caen, or of occasional reclaimers of waste land fit into this small category. In France and Spain there existed a third method by which nobility might be achieved, that is by the purchase of certain offices which carried with them life nobility and thereafter, if the same family continued to hold the office, hereditary nobility after three generations. An estimate made in France at the end of the *ancien régime* calculated the number of these offices to be some 4000. This type of nobility was largely to be found in the *parlements* though *parlementaire* offices fell vacant with less regularity than did those of the *secrétaires du roi*. The *secrétaire du roi* had no obligations attached to his office once he had paid the large purchase price. For all these reasons, by the beginning of our period perhaps not even 5 per cent of the European nobility could boast an ancestry buried deep in the middle ages and well over 50 per cent had been ennobled since the beginning of the seventeenth century.

Nobles were usually privileged in two ways: firstly, they had the right to judgement by their peers, that is, outside the royal courts; secondly, the nobility (along with the clergy and the towns) continued to escape a significant part of royal taxation, though their exemptions in this respect have been much exaggerated. Moreover, there were also exceptions to this, for example, England. In eastern Europe, in Russia, Poland and Hungary, a noble was quite simply defined: he alone had the right to own men. Here generalization ends. Apart from these considerations the differences between the various elements in the European nobility are almost more apparent than the similarities and the historiography of nobility has tended to concentrate upon what a noble was not. A noble was not necessarily wealthy: he did not necessarily have a title: he did not necessarily own land: he certainly did not necessarily occupy a fief: he did not necessarily own seigneurial rights and mere possession of seigneurial rights was not a determinant of noble status: he was not necessarily a military figure as the medieval noble had been and he was not necessarily exempt from taxation. Yet, taking account of all these provisos, the noble who was not wealthy above the general run of men, did not boast some title – at best a province and at least a field – did not own land and seigneurial rights and have some connection (if not himself then his brother or son) with a military career and did not expect his status to proffer him something in the way of pecuniary advantages, belonged to a small minority about to sink through the planks of noble society into the undistinguished mass below. In continental European terms there was a psychological aspect to nobility. If it did not indicate a degree of affluence, education and expectation of military or office-holding status, then it would not be in the long run recognized and when this happened, the taxman would surely call. By the same token, a non-noble individual who encased himself in noble trappings, seigneuries and land, could slip – certainly in Spain and Italy – virtually uncontested into noble ranks. In France, purchase of an office would be needed to guarantee acceptance.

Too much attention has been given to the concept of the poor nobility, defined as families who employed less than six servants but never less than three, or who in the east owned less than twenty serfs, at the expense of the average and of the extremely affluent. What Lancashire cotton magnate even in the 1790s had a roll of employees which even approximated in number to the two or three thousand servants, farmers, gardeners, agents, lawyers on the payroll of the Duke of Orleans? Moreover such a concentration obscures an important truth. In the eighteenth century, and in many ways this was becoming increasingly true, aristocratic Europe was capitalistic Europe. Collectively the nobility owned, if they did not necessarily directly exploit, a considerable proportion of Europe's land (15–40%) and Europe's natural resources in the form of iron ore and coal and timber – the productive resources, with a few exceptions, of the century and of the future. True not all were thus involved. In the very special instance of Russia there were nobles, let us say in the frozen northern wastes of Simbirsk, who could not even profit from a local market since such a thing did not exist. Throughout most of Europe was found a petty provincial nobility which often directly managed its land, sent its sons into the army and lived in a very modest state. But on the other hand there was an urbane court nobility backed by impressive estates and natural resources. The Earl of Lonsdale's Cumbrian soil covered wealthy coal seams. Silesian and German and Baltic nobles provided Europe with timber. Laws of *dérogeance* which technically precluded the French and Spanish nobilities from participation in trade, did not withhold from them the profits to be culled from metallurgy, glassmaking and exploiting mines. The mines of Carmaux were directed by a co-operative of petty Toulousain nobles: those of Littry by the Marquis de Balleroy and the Spanish nobility were well to the fore in exploiting these lines of development. The Duke of Orleans himself owned two glass furnaces. The largest industrial enterprise in Europe, the mines of the Nord, was in the hands of the Compagnie d'Anzin, a largely noble enterprise. The world of maritime commerce was also wide open to noble entrepreneurial activity. They were heavily involved for example in the production of the great wines of Burgundy and Bordeaux and in the port and sherry trade of Portugal and Spain and such activity reached an impressive peak in the 1780s. Recently massive noble participation in the sugar trade of Nantes has been revealed, a significant and profitable outlet for the investor. Far from shunning mercantile endeavour the wealthy nobility sought it out. The ennobled sugar merchant felt no obligation to cast off the source of his wealth when he adopted a title. Then there was the armament industry or the intriguing company formed in 1781 to arm French naval vessels carrying letters and royal freight and of whom the shareholders were Prince de Rohan Rochefort, the Comte de Melfort, Comte du Hautoy, Chevaliers Lambert and Beige, a medical doctor, Guiraudet, and an arms' dealer named Fournier. They were joined in 1782 by Prince Frederick de Salm-Kribourg – a German. Noble capital lay behind the Compagnie de la Guyane Française founded in 1763 which had a monopoly of provisioning the French West Indies, encouraging emigration and supplying African slaving stations with provisions, and then conducting the slave trade itself. Shareholders in this enterprise included names like the Princesse de Lamballe, the Duc de Duras, the Marquis de Chaillon, in fact, the entire involvement was noble and utterly typical of noble interest in transatlantic trade. Marriage was the time-honoured way of transferring wealth between groups. The eldest daughter of an old family or even more of the newly rich could bring into her alliance upto a fifth of her family's wealth. The contracting families who arranged the marriage after a supervised, limited interchange between the couple expected something in return for their investment. Marriages established the standing of the two families, a more significant concern than romantic love. Heiresses from newly rich families exchanged their father's millions for titles and their families of origin shared the glory of the groom's house. Significantly the daughters of the old nobility remained within their own social group on marriage because their families feared loss of status. Marriage, however, certainly bolstered the wealth of those noble families who could find new money for their sons. The world of finance not only gave rise to new nobles but dragged old noble houses into involvement and alliances. The most recent historian of the French nobility writes, 'The *haute bourgeoisie* and *le parti des ducs* formed from now on a single society: a *société du bon ton*, of wealth and of power.'[1] When a Montmorency, a Broglie and a Biron married heiresses from newly ennobled financial houses one can see this integration in action.

More depended upon opportunity than on anything else. In Spain, whose overall economy was backward in comparison with her northern neighbour, it is possible to find nobles who seized opportunities afforded by significant state contracts to build up commercial careers. Juan Fernàndez de Isla, of distinguished lineage, embarked upon a splendid commercial career in 1746 as purveyor of naval supplies to the great arsenals of Ferrol, Cadiz and Cartagena, and by 1754 was master of an industrial empire including thirteen merchant vessels, trading offices in Cadiz, Murcia, Valencia, Madrid, Lisbon, Bilbao and Santander, a porcelain works, a paper mill, a tannery, two distilleries, four iron works and a hat-making business. Don Juan de Goyeneche whose fortunes were mainly made by supplying the royal navy with timber and manufacturing woollens which supplied the army with cloth, provides another instance. Everything shows that the Spanish noble could strike out on his own without social stigma, but those who did so hazarded their futures in an uncertain commercial world

---

1 G. Chaussinand-Nogaret, *The French Nobility in the Eighteenth Century*, trans. W. Doyle (Cambridge, 1985).

restricted by the very limited purchasing power of the Spanish populace and hence had to face the practical economic difficulties confronting any Spanish entrepreneur.

As a whole, the European nobility is remarkable in the eighteenth century for improved book-keeping (even a Spanish and Russian phenomenon), and for keener estate management – though this usually only meant collecting rents more efficiently and a tighter control over leaseholds. In part this may have been forced upon them. To take one example, there was, until the 1770s, little scope for investment of large noble income in Spain. There was next to no return on Spanish estates, even less on urban property, and no 'stock exchange'. Lending to the state was very risky and only possible in the form of annuities (to observe the continuing prohibition on usury). After 1770, however, rising land values and the formation of *sociedades anónimas* for industrial and financial investment opened up welcome opportunities for a group less likely to find enrichment in royal favour as scope for rewards in the Americas shrank. Admittedly, the considerable investor had the best opportunities and for most nobles new sources of investment did not surpass the older income from land and from landed privilege, seigneurial rights, tolls on roads, bridges and fords and, in the Spanish instance, tithe appropriation and municipal offices.

By the eighteenth century the relative importance of differing types of seigneurial levies had shifted very considerably. The 'profits' from seigneurial justice had been replaced by deficits so that many seigneurs only maintained courts as a status symbol or because they had some sense of obligation to the community. Other seigneurial levies, *cens* (quit rents) and *champart* (rents on reclaimed land), could assume between 2–10 per cent of the continental peasant's gross income. *Banalités* (oven, mill and press and sometimes slaughter-house rights) which were usually leased out could be very profitable. On the other hand, *cens* and *champart* were notoriously difficult to collect and deeply resented and, since usually a money payment, had not kept pace with inflation. Manuals concerned with how to exploit a seigneurie to full financial advantage recommended that lords re-convert into payment in kind, but there is no hard evidence to suggest these recommendations were generally put into effect. Where lords could take advantage of rising land values was in admission fines payable by the new incumbent when a farm was sold or leased. Thus *luismo*, or *lods et ventes*, or *laudemio* (usually 10 per cent of sale price) could be the most lucrative of dues – especially, it would appear, in Bavaria where it could rise to 20 per cent of the sale price. Seigneurial dues were in fact subject to a three-pronged attack: from below by the peasantry often prepared to pay high land rents but resentful of archaic dues payable to an individual who might not be owner of the land: from Enlightenment thinkers who saw them as an obstacle to the development of a free market economy and as part of a pile of medieval debris. Rulers, and this was particularly marked in the Habsburg lands, middle and south Germany and parts of Spain, saw them as severely curtailing the amount the state could ask in tax from the peasant when seigneurial levies consumed so high a proportion of his crop, and Joseph II at least was to take significant steps to regulate their incidence. No ruler, however, dared destroy them. When they fell in 1789, it was because they were attacked from below. Happy the noble who had diversified into commerce, finance and industry to support his landed wealth. He at least could contemplate his portfolio without hearing any rumble of criticism from without. His considerable landed wealth, and commercial and industrial involvement, guaranteed that in post-Revolutionary Europe noble wealth was still the most impressive.

Whilst its economic dynamic differentiated the eighteenth-century nobility from its predecessors so did its increasingly ambivalent relationship with the ruler and its consciousness of its changing role within the state. Until the mid to late seventeenth century monarchs had relied upon the nobility and its private 'feudally' raised armies to defend the state and had been obliged to countenance periodic opposition of nobles controlling armies with a view to pushing their own political ambitions. The French Religious Wars (1562–98) and the Frondes (1648–53) are prime examples of civil wars induced by politically dissident, armed nobilities bent on reducing, to their own advantage, royal authority. The rise of standing armies, however, first changed and then ended the nobility's power thus to dictate the pace of political life. At the same time, it stripped the nobility of its ancient warrior-based justification for its privileges. The concomitant growth in bureaucracies directly responsible to the king rather than to province and locality also – at least theoretically – threatened to curtail the strength of the nobility in the localities. The eighteenth-century nobility was one vitally concerned to hammer out for itself a new role to justify its social privileges. Since it was better educated, at least in its upper echelons, than ever before, whether in Jesuit school, salon or university, debate rather than the sword became the nobility's chief weapon and it participated to the full in the burning issues of Enlightenment thought. Indeed the society of the Parisian salons where issues and ideas of the day were discussed was at least in part aristocratic. Some members of the provincial nobility participated in provincial academies which were part of social life but also they were alert to discussions on the distribution of power. An important point of view held by many nobles was that the most desirable political form was aristocratic constitutionalism, a government in which power was shared between monarchy and aristocracy and which was seen in Europe as the British model. The relationship between monarchies and aristocracies was complex and tricky. Monarchs had ceased making massive creations of new nobles as a money-making expedient by the eighteenth century and on aggregate noble numbers were declining. Rulers were also concerned, particularly in the Habsburg lands, middle and south Germany and Spain, to prevent land slipping into noble hands and hence escaping the taxman. Middle German princes successfully introduced laws forbidding the acquisition by the nobility or burgesses of peasant land when a peasant purchaser presented himself and vigorous peasant protection policies were pursued in Thuringia, Electoral Saxony, Bavaria and Austria to curtail noble encroachment on independent peasant holdings. Nothing was perhaps quite as severe as Charles XI of Sweden's *Reduktion*, crown assumption of alienated royal land in the late seventeenth century, but the intent is fully clear. Nor were monarchs dispensing pensions and sinecures with the abandon characteristic of an epoch when they needed to purchase the support of dissident nobles. This was particularly marked in Spain. True the disposal of key posts in church, state and colonies (if they had them) remained the prerogative of monarchs and they continued to choose noble candidates. In this way the nobility had secured a virtual monopoly of the best positions in church and state. A French noble automatically became an officer upon entering the army and all European armies (except the British) were officered by the nobility. A noble who chose the church as career embarked as a canon not as parish priest. Moreover, kings did not choose ministers from any other sector of society.

But there was nothing automatic about a reward for support. In France, from 1695 and throughout the eighteenth century, successive inroads were made into the principle of noble immunity from taxation which the nobility could not resist. To a degree, and much more marked in some areas than others, the nobility lay in the way of monarchical aspirations to a centralized bureaucratic state. The patriciates of northern Italy and the Austrian Netherlands knew Vienna aimed at the elimination of their power. Everywhere the local magnates participating in the Diets and provincial institutions were conscious of monarchical efforts to render them relatively powerless by denuding them of financial control. Quite understandably, they moved into a defensive role. This was not of course everywhere the case. Monarchs did not seek to destroy their nobilities for they had no concept of life without them, but they did seek to neutralize them. In Prussia and Russia they were hitched to the service of the crown in army and bureaucracy – a situation east European monarchs used to their advantage and in the Russian instance subjected their nobility to considerable hardship. Moreover, the continental nobility continued to define itself by sending a son or more into military service.

Most remarkably of all, and without doubt marking a severance with the days when private armies maintained by noble houses had been able on occasion to threaten monarchies with civil war, the eighteenth-century nobility turned to intellectual argument in defence of their privileged status and took to political tracts and institutions such as provincial estates, *Reichstag*, or *parlements* as an arena for advancing or defending their interests.

They did not of course operate from a position of total strength. Only in Britain and Poland could it be claimed that they were able to force the pace of political life. Their privileged position was, as we shall see, under attack not only from monarchies but from Enlightenment thought which stressed the equality of men before the law and the blatant wrongs embodied in exemptions and 'gothic' privileges. It was as well to meet with criticism from an increasingly dissident sector in the Third Estate concerned with an extension of political participation to include them.

The world of privilege however had an intrinsic fluidity. Some privileges, not least seigneurial rights, were purchasable: others flowed from the actual process of ennoblement. In western Europe an affluent middle class with aristocratic aspirations, moved fairly easily into noble ranks and, even if it did not do so, endowed itself with the trappings of nobility such as seigneuries, above all land, purchase or lease of hunting rights etc. There was even in a few areas, like parts of the French Massif Central, a petty rural bourgeoisie with absolutely no aspirations to nobility which invested in seigneurial privileges which brought it a reasonable return on small investments and yet gave nothing back to the community in the shape of those services which the seigneur was supposed to provide. Sectors of the middle class courted privileged positions – British government patronage extended down through the bureaucracy and ministers were besieged for example for posts in the customs offices of the ports. In such a way a lesser world of privilege was hitched to the greater one and this in no small part contributed to its perpetuation.

Sharing the nobility's problems of finding a niche in the modern world was the Church, though here one should perhaps draw a rigid distinction between Catholic and Protestant Europe. In the main the Protestant Churches had slipped under state control. The Protestant Churches had passed into the web of state patronage, stripped of most of their landed wealth two centuries before by lay rulers, some of whom claimed headship of national churches. Frederick the Great of Prussia or Gustavus III of Sweden or the Duke of Newcastle when in ministerial office, used offices in the Church to reward loyal supporters. The English episcopate was small but had some political power in the House of Lords and it was one which could be marshalled in the government's interest. Frederick the Great used 300 canonries as rewards to military and bureaucratic families. In the United Provinces and Switzerland the Calvinist Churches were still actively concerned to maintain their hold over their flocks by strong parochial direction and the pastor's influence in the parish was a key factor in determining attitudes and allegiances. In Germany religion was allied to a concept of territorial identity and religious differences primed the pump of particularism.

If Protestantism continued to be a dynamic intellectual force in the eighteenth century it was so largely by reference to German pietism whose influence extended into the Dutch Republic and Scandinavia but which flourished best in the restrained but rigorous German Protestant universities. As a social and intellectual force Protestantism had perhaps reached its nadir in England. Here even the working classes had embarked upon a movement away from the established church – stemmed temporarily by Methodism whose spirit had a great deal in common with the Lazarist and Redemptorist missions of Catholic Europe. In no Protestant country did the Church provide a truly effective obstacle to state control. In the main its authority and privileges were not such as to incur the opposition of secular powers nor did it feel the uncomfortable blast of the impious Enlightenment, except perhaps in Scotland.

The Catholic Church, on the other hand, expressed, with varying degrees of national conviction, allegiance to a power outside its natural or central government, the papacy, an ultramontane influence, which was supposedly supreme, in the last instance, on spiritual issues. True this power had been trimmed down by historic concordats which limited the intrusive hand of the papacy over the appointment of officials but when dissension loomed over questions of orthodoxy, as it continued in the early eighteenth century to do over Jansenism, then the papacy and its Jesuit agents, the religious order which looked direct to Rome for leadership, had, at least theoretically, the last word. Annates and Peter's Pence still made their way to the Vatican especially from Iberia and the Habsburg lands. The papacy actually owned enclaves in French territory at Avignon and Valréas. But the papacy was by the eighteenth century a waning force patently unable to present an assertive profile, a phenomenon best demonstrated by its failure to save its protagonists, the Jesuits, from expulsion. Far more intrusive was the panoply of privilege which the Catholic Church had throughout the centuries arrogated to itself. The Church's corporate wealth in land, seigneurial rights, tithes, precious metals and art treasures marked it out as a fair rival to noble and kingly splendour. Up to 2 per cent of the population of the states of continental Europe described themselves as clerics and the property of the Church as an institution amounted to 7–20 per cent of the territory of Catholic states. Like the nobility, the clergy could, with certain exceptions (Italy) pretend to immunity from ancient direct taxation and where the hand of the Church stretched over a fifth of the territory of a province as it did in Lower Austria, then one can appreciate the seriousness of mortmain (literally dead hand) to a monarch intent upon increasing his tax revenues.

In fact clerical immunity to taxation in western Europe has been somewhat overstressed. The French clergy paid the *don gratuit*, a sum 'voluntarily' conceded by the *assemblée du clergé de France* but which had to be (and was) suitably considerable. The clergy of the Papal States paid a land tax constituting up to 40 per cent of the total levy and the Spanish Church ceded large sums to the monarchy in time of war, a process which reached its apogee during the nineties and left the church seriously depleted. The clergy were of course heavy taxers in their own right claiming anything up to a tenth of gross production in tithes, usually less in France, the Austrian Netherlands and Poland, sometimes more in the Iberian Peninsula. Tithes had often been appropriated by bishops, chapters and religious houses or alienated to lay figures (as in Spain) leaving the parish priest dependent upon small fees levied for services such as baptism and burial and masses for the dead. The lower clergy resented the misappropriation of parish tithes by the higher clergy and religious orders, a feeling shared by the congregation.

The Church of eighteenth-century Europe was in fact a rent garment and the divisions within were social, economic and psychological. Setting aside the important examples of Spain where it was still possible for merit alone to be the determinant of high office, and Italy where in some states the aristocracy held under 30 per cent of all bishoprics, the bishops and cathedral chapters were monopolized by the aristocracy who used family connections, outside and within the Church, to secure elevation to the most lucrative positions. In the German Empire the Imperial Knights dominated bishoprics, canonries and held the Electorates of Mainz, Trier and Cologne. The Archbishop of Lyons, keeper of the *feuille des bénéfices*, hardly left Versailles where he was open to suggestion as to whom the next incumbent to a vacant bishopric should be and since bishoprics varied in value from 10,000 to 200,000 *livres* competition within the ranks of the episcopate itself was intense. The average bishop was a member of the high aristocracy, who thus ensured they need not spend any family wealth on providing for this scion, owed his position to nomination by an influential member at court and was at an advantage if he already had a kinsman in the episcopate. He had never been a parish priest or a member of the regular orders (except in Spain and Italy where the regulars gave rise to some outstanding prelates). He usually leapt from university and ordination into the grand vicariate of a cathedral chapter and was often a bishop by his mid-twenties and certainly well before his mid-thirties. Nevertheless, when Philip V of Spain in 1735 assigned the temporal administration of the archdiocese of Toledo to his eight-year-old son, he flew in the face of current practice. The post-Tridentine Church fought shy of flagrant abuses. Once in office the eighteenth-century bishop stands out for his administrative qualities rather than as theologian or saintly recluse. He was an efficient bureaucrat conducting, often via his agents, more episcopal visitations than ever before to ascertain the quality of parish worship and the conduct of the parish priest, and the basic level of seminary instruction. Frequently he was a politician as well. The Austrian Netherlands and Germany had a number of prince bishops who were temporal rulers, the latter with a role in the *Reichstag* and capable of adopting firm political stances. Elsewhere they participated in the game of court politics. In Spain Cardinal Portocarrero of Toledo had been a paramount influence in intriguing for the accession of the Bourbon dynasty and Charles III was only too conscious of the episcopal strength on the Council of Castile. Cardinal Fleury and Loménie de Brienne, Archbishop, first of Toulouse and then of Sens, belong to a similar tradition. But this episcopate was not without its dispensers of charity such as the Archbishop of Braga, the Archbishop Rajey of Santiago de Compostela who provided food for 1300 people per day during the crisis of 1768–9. And there are innumerable French examples in response to the needs arising from famine and epidemic. Corrupt as its promotional practices may have been, the eighteenth-century episcopate was on the whole a distinguished one.

For every bishop there were at least ten times as many canons (2300 in Spain for sixty bishops) attached to cathedrals and fulfilling an undemanding and comfortable role in diocesan administration with more than their fair share of leisure and often with a network of patronage at their disposition. Again these chapters were mainly aristocratic and it was often within the bosom of the cathedral chapters that the intellectual dilemmas of the Catholic Church were most hotly debated: the debate between Jansenists and Jesuits, between traditionalists and partisans of a Catholic Enlightenment.

Bishops, chapters and, at the beginning of our period, religious houses were heavy spenders on building and precious artefacts. Servants and large numbers of agricultural workers looked to the church for steady employment. From 1720 to 1740, during the golden age of the Portuguese church, more than 5000 building workers regularly looked to the royal palace of Mafra for employment and the Church's prominence in the country's economic life is one traditional scapegoat used by Portuguese historians to explain the slow development of the national economy in the eighteenth century. In Austria, Portugal and through much of Italy, substantial churchmen and wealthy monasteries rather than the nobility dominated local economic and social life.

But the religious houses by the mid century had passed into troubled times. Everywhere, except in Poland, aggregate numbers were falling and decline was most marked in the ancient contemplative orders of the Benedictines and Cistercians. However, in Spain and Portugal the

Franciscans, numbering 15,000 in Spain, never had any difficulty in finding recruits largely because they recruited from the lower orders. Womens' vocations fell less dramatically largely because, for the middle and upper classes, there was no other viable alternative to marriage. The Iberian Peninsula had not produced the spate of active women's orders, like the Sisters of St Joseph or Daughters of Charity, who were responsible in the first instance for lifting female literacy in Catholic Europe, and in the second instance for providing France at least with a nursing service that Florence Nightingale a century later said she struggled to emulate. These uncloistered women's orders in fact represented a paradigm shift in the religious life. They constituted a precocious social service dedicated to caring and coping with the problems of the weak and they reached out to the localities where little other help existed. They proved capable of surviving the Revolution and indeed expanded throughout Europe, America and Asia in the nineteenth century.

Wealth was of course very unevenly distributed amongst the religious houses. Broadly speaking the ancient orders were the best endowed and men's houses more so than women's. The drying up of recruits left vast edifices like Vézelay with under a dozen monks in 1789. The rejection of the contemplative life clearly reflected amongst the educated upper classes the fashionable intellectual distaste for a life consecrated only to prayer and to personal salvation in a hereafter no longer unhesitatingly accepted. What is clear is that the emptiness of monasteries laid them wide open to assault from the state and crises of confidence occurred amongst the dwindling communities. The French *Commission des Réguliers* in 1766 endorsed the amalgamation of houses with under nine inmates: other houses asked collectively to be released from their vows. In Lombardy and Tuscany similar reductions sanctioned by Joseph II reduced houses in the first instance from 291 in 1767 to 200 in 1790, and in Tuscany the reduction was from 345 to 215 with a loss of 43% in personnel. In Spain a move to have separate Spanish congregations for Carthusians and mendicant orders brought them more clearly under royal control. In Portugal, an edict of 1788 required royal permission for youths to enter religion and amongst the nobility and the affluent urban classes there was a clear falling off. In 1789 in the great monastery of Sintra, for example, there were four frail, elderly monks. Clearly a death knell had sounded for the contemplative life.

This leaves only for our consideration the parish priest, the staple of parochial religious life. We know a great deal about this individual. He was recruited from the lower middle classes in the towns rather than from rural stock – a factor probably related to educational opportunities – and hence he was a man of limited economic resources. Even so, he was economically better placed than his poorer parishioners although he had to stretch his income to pay for a curate and for basic services like laundry. He was, as well, the first to be called upon by the parochial and even wandering poor. Setting aside rural Portugal and Spain and southern Italy, he was a far more 'trained' individual than his predecessors. This was due to the marked extension in seminary education nurtured first by the Counter-Reformation and then by the Catholic Enlightenment. He was also more aware of the bishop and higher clergy because his actions were subject to the scrutiny of a regular periodic visitation. For this reason, again setting aside Iberian and Italian backlands where irregularities could pass undetected, he was remarkable, to an unprecedented degree, for his impeccable private life. In eighteenth-century France, Germany, the Austrian Netherlands, Austria proper, Northern Italy, and Spain there was virtually no such thing as the lax parish priest. Nor was there any general crisis of vocations except in France where it was difficult to find incumbents for parishes in the poorest rural parishes in the Auvergne. Other countries, particularly Spain and Portugal, produced an uncomfortable and occasionally dissident surplus.

The eighteenth-century priest was frequently a critic of the ecclesiastical establishment. He knew himself to be overworked and to dispose of a pittance in comparison with the empty monastic establishments and the higher secular clergy, and he needed money to fulfil more adequately his parochial work. The spirit of opposition reached its highest peak in France where the standard of the parochial clergy was at its highest. This movement was known as Richerism and had as its basis the belief that the priest not the bishop was the significant element in the ecclesiastical hierarchy and that the former had, therefore, a right to adequate remuneration. Critical of religious houses, and indeed of the monastic ideal, indifferent in many cases to the authority of Rome, and overtly hostile to bishop and chapter, the parochial clergy was not to be counted upon to defend the old order in 1789.

The world of privilege was not confined to noble and cleric. With the few striking exceptions of Britain, Russia and Sweden, most European states retained, beneath a veneer of apparent centralization, a tangled reality of decentralizing institutions and authorities. Of these, the most important were the province and its organs of government, the provincial estates, and the towns of which the largest boasted virtual autonomy. The strength of provincial government *vis-à-vis* central authority determined the extent to which royal authority prevailed in a particular area. It could be argued that since most provincial estates were divided into nobility, clergy and Third Estate, who could, though this was not invariable, be tied to a separate voting procedure, the provincial estates merely enhanced aristocratic and clerical authority. But this is not the whole story. They contained an important commoner element and rested upon a significant popular consensus as guarantors of 'liberties' (in the eighteenth-century sense) and hence were appreciated by all levels of society.

It was, for example, the Estates of Brittarry which had preserved the immunity of that province from the salt tax and which yearly haggled about the amount payable by the province in direct taxation with the *contrôle générale* so effectively that the Breton peasant was one of the lowest taxed in France – and obversely that he received the lowest level of servicing in the form of policing, road construction and so on. The humblest peasant knew which he preferred. In Languedoc, which argu- ably had the most responsible and efficient provincial estates in France, and where voting was by head and not by order, not only did the estates keep down the level of taxes but guaranteed that such taxes as were collected were, as far as possible, used within the province. This explains why Languedoc had the best road system in France and as well the Canal du Midi, a costly enterprise which brought little in the way of returns to the central authority but something in the way of commercial activity to Languedoc. Small wonder that where provincial institutions were weak in France, the cry in 1789 was for a restoration and revivification of provincial estates. The policy of the Estates of Holland, and hence the interests of the maritime provinces, were those most effectively promoted at the Dutch Estates General and Holland claimed the right to provide the grand pensionary because maritime wealth formed the largest source of state revenue. The Cortes of Castille was in similar way the arbiter of Spanish political life and the interests of Castille preferred to those of any other province. Pro- vinces often were endowed with specific law codes incorporating pro- vincial custom which, because associated with provincial autonomy, bleakly asserted themselves against attempts from the centre to impose uniformity.

Then there were the privileges of the towns. In the Netherlands and northern Italy but also in Spain and Mediterranean France existed cities with highly developed powers of self-control. Most of these had in centuries past purchased immunity from royal taxation by paying a specific sum raised from indirect taxes levied by the municipal councils. Most of these councils were corrupt oligarchies and the brunt of taxa- tion fell on commodities of common consumption entering and leaving the towns. But it seems indisputable that the towns were highly favoured when it came to tax distribution – possible exceptions here were Britain and Prussia when the central governments imposed fairly stiff commodity taxes in the shape of excise duty. Every town dweller was privileged in comparison with his rural counterparts because no urban property tax equalled that on agricultural land. The towns also held guild monopolies which were designed to protect the towns from possible rural competition though they drew on rural labour when it suited them so to do.

We have observed that urban officialdom, particularly in France and Spain, was venal, that is to say the incumbent had purchased his office and could by definition dispose of it at will by sale or legacy. Hence office-holding was a form of property and, though monarchs might attempt abolition, in some French instances of entire courts of officials at a time, the concept of venal office as sacrosanct because it was a form of property continued to prevail.

There existed then a structure of officialdom embedded in courts and cities whose incompetence could escape unchecked central control. Monarchs were themselves responsible for the initial creation of venal offices – from which they had in the past drawn profit – and for concessions of tolls on rivers and bridges and of monopolies ceded to individuals or companies against money payable to the crown. Many of these concessions continued to be a source of revenue for the central authorities who, debarred from raising land taxes by provincial estates and *parlements*, could ill afford to sacrifice them. In this way monarchs were bound up in a privileged structure and torn between reform – and loss of revenues – or continuance which implied the failure to evolve a more efficient, streamlined system.

An appreciation of privilege in its manifold forms shows how far eighteenth-century Europe was from a universally acceptable concept of the state as we know it, that is, of a united autonomous political entiry at least theoretically recognizing no external sovereign control over its functioning, and permitting no other authority to stand between itself and its citizens. Taking such a definition, only England, Sweden and Russia might have qualified throughout the eighteenth century for such status. In the first two monarchy and aristocracy enjoyed full powers without the presence of provincial claims to separate recognition. In Russia provincial institutions had never truly evolved nor had the idea of power-sharing and government remained a primitive patrimonial concept.

The history of western European government from the middle ages onwards had been of a central authority seeking to eliminate, as far as possible, intermediary authorities and privileges which questioned central control. Success had been very partial. In 1730, for example, although the King of France pretended to absolute authority, his was a country rent with provincial anomalies endorsed by provincial *parlements* and estates, endowed with differing law codes, sometimes with distinctive languages, Breton, Occitan and Basque and having to recognize the particular privileges of nobility, clergy and some princes. The pope owned Avignon and Valréas, the Dutch House of Orange an enclave in southern France, and the king was hamstrung in the imposition of a central policy. His 'despotism' was hedged about with rules and regulations and where his authority began and those of provincial laws and institutions ended was almost impossible to define, a factor which monopolizes the political history of eighteenth-century France. Yet the King of France had perhaps greater freedom of manoeuvre than his Spanish counterpart who in 1730 had to juggle the respective interests not only of Aragon and Castille but of innumerable cities which claimed control over the surrounding countryside. In the Dutch Republic central authority was almost impossible to locate. True there was the Estates General, supposedly an amalgam of the corporate interests of the seven provinces, fraught with internal provincial dissensions, whose authority supposedly ran over the great cities. But in effect the Estates General never controlled them and could never truly resolve whether it did or did not wish in peacetime to have a stadtholder who might surreptitiously usurp power from particularist interests.

In central Europe a concept of the state was weakest of all and the ramifications of power within the 294 states of the German Empire almost impossible to define. A loose federation of states met in the *Reichstag* and professed allegiance to the Holy Roman Emperor. Yet within these very states were enclaves, cities, the estates of monasteries and Imperial Knights claiming *Reichsunmittelbar*, independence from all authority other than that of the Emperor. Habsburg territories were also a federation of which part belonged to the federation of the Empire. Between a Habsburg Emperor and his subjects lay a mesh of authorities, provincial, local and immediate – a serf on a noble estate expressed obedience to his lord who had claims on his time (and hence his earning capacity) and so upon his income. In addition, the lord was the filter of government decisions.

Fragmented entities, such as Italy and the Baltic states, were happy hunting grounds for rulers anxious to carve out an inheritance for their children and who grafted on to existing 'state' structures a small ruling elite. The southern Netherlands, taken from Spain in 1713, became part of the Austrian inheritance, though one which the Habsburgs would readily have exchanged for Bavaria. Yet how much authority, real power, remained in Brussels or Liège and how much did Vienna truly assume? Such a question had no immediate answer. One talks of the Prussian 'state' yet Prussia and Brandenburg were separated by a wide corridor of Polish territory and the 'state' also embodied Neuchâtel in Switzerland and Cleves and Mark on the Rhine, all with provincial traditions and institutions. What a ruler could do in Brandenburg he could not necessarily do in Cleves.

Before the Swedish example of 1772 no European state had a single document embodying a written constitution clearly laying down principles of where power resided. The pressure for such a document was to gain force after the American Revolution and the French Revolution with its succession of constitutions. In default of a constitution the question of who, within a particular territorial entity, had power to do what was a continuous, acrimonious debate. Central authority usually embodied in monarchy made demands in furtherance of a unity it deemed requisite to serve the general interest and particular institutions then replied with charges of despotism and violation of the essential 'liberties' of province and sectional interest. This long standing struggle assumed in the course of the eighteenth century a new vocabulary. The discourse of political criticism included a language of rights, the rights of man and of the citizen, a special endowment of the Enlightenment. Moreover, perhaps conspicuously in France, a new development was that of a political culture outside the formal institutionalized government structure, based on the salon and the media in the form of books and prints. The voice of criticism percolated further down the social scale and something identifiable as 'public opinion', such as moved the crowd in the great Revolutionary days of 1789, emerged.

3

The World of Ideas

Enlightenment: Shallow and pretentious intellectualism, unreasonable contempt for authority and tradition, etc; applied especially to the spirit and aims of the French philosophers of the eighteenth century. (The Shorter Oxford English Dictionary, *1865*)

The Enlightenment has never been a neutral subject for study. Its protagonists have pronounced it the critical departure permitting the development of modernity, of a secular society dedicated to the happiness of mankind and to the fulfillment of man's earthly potential. This meant the recognition of certain basic rights such as freedom of opinion, and hence to tolerance, or freedom from arbitrary arrest, in a political culture based on debate and consensus. Indeed, over the past three decades the study of the Enlightenment has been given many new dimensions. The eighteenth century has been interpreted as 'the century of the book', the period which saw an exponential growth in print and in the circulation of ideas relating to every conceivable subject. These ideas were hotly debated in the political salon but also filtered downwards as literacy increased. They crossed national frontiers as postal services became better. The result was, in this interpretation, that the period witnessed a variety of social transformations ranging from the emergence of a new political culture, to a new valorization and re-evaluation of childhood. The eighteenth century has been called 'the century of the child'. It has also been accredited with a change in the affective relationships of husband and wife and hence with the 'birth of the modern family' as affection between spouses allegedly replaced the gloomy formality of earlier violent times with a cult of sensibility. If we add to these attributes a revolution in economic thought in which emerged the modern notions of a free-market economy, laissez-faire, rather than protectionism; or the notions of a standardized judicial and penalogical structure applying punishments to fit the crime and abandoning savage corporal punishment for the notion of moral correction permitting a return to society, then we can urge the diversity of intrusions into the ordering of man and his world. However, an important departure must be that the intellectual reach of many eighteenth-century thinkers far outstripped their grasp of practical change. In the interface between ideas and their implementation, generalization frequently errs on the side of overstating the theoretical. For example, the concept of 'the century of the child' as argued from educational tracts devoted to developing the mind of the young child so as to help him realize his earthly potential or make him the ideal citizen, or through the toys and games and books dedicated to the young consumer, refers essentially to the child of the affluent since the century saw record levels of foundlings. Or if, little by little, standard codification of law was the aim of every enlightened ruler and generally spread throughout the Napoleonic Empire, improved penology needed financial resources in terms of policing and institutions which exceeded the means available to all European states. A plan was on the drawing board and there it often remained.

This said, ideas, above all, have given the eighteenth century its particular place in the evolving history of mankind and to neglect them is to sacrifice an important way stage in the evolution of a western identity. How we define ourselves as western Europeans – secular, tolerant, respectful of human rights (now much expanded as a concept) – owes much to Enlightenment discourse.

The German philosopher, Kant, described the Enlightenment as European man's coming of age: the point at which he stood firmly on his own feet, unsupported by the psychological scaffolding of the medieval and ancient world. This scaffolding, the unshaken belief that man was part of a divine plan and his earthly sojourn was a testing preliminary to hell or paradise, that he dwelt on an earth which was God-created and, according to Ptolemaic geography, the epicentre of the universe, that he must suffer the dual authority of the monarch (however apparently tyrannical) and the decisions of the Christian church as endowed with the only truth, collapsed in the view of Enlightenment thinkers because it was demonstrated by reason and scientific principle to be patently unsound.

The origins of this remarkable intellectual experience long predate the eighteenth century. Scientific empiricism in which exploration from first principles by experimentation and observation made possible the erection of new laws governing the nature of the universe – a long development from Copernicus, through Galileo and Francis Bacon to Isaac Newton – had been one point of departure and had cut across established doctrine in the most destructive way. Rationalism, of which Descartes was the most explicit exponent, had been another starting point. In man, it was argued, was an innate power of reasoning, capable, in the long run, of explaining phenomena, previous mysteries, by remorseless logic which permitted no assumptions. Essentially empiricism and rationalism led men in the same direction, that is to say, towards a concept of the world which was no longer God-centred but which existed for man and for man's enjoyment and which was man's only certainty.

Initially, this critical enquiry did not diminish a belief in a Christian God as formulated by the Church but rather lead to a destabilization of previous certainties. The science of chronology, when applied to Scripture revealed inconsistencies in the Bible itself, previously considered the unblemished repository of divine truth. Such discoveries were disturbing. Furthermore, to empiricism and rationalism must be added relativism, the product of a more abundant and ever increasing knowledge of a wider world. The opening up of the Americas and the penetration of Asia by Jesuit and Dominican missionaries had been going on for almost two centuries before 1730 but their reports (particularly the Jesuit *Relations* which were published from the mid seventeenth century) progressively led to a disquieting perception of the limitations of the European experience. Outside Christendom, it was quite clear, lay other peoples who had lived for thousands of years without any knowledge of Christ and Christian revelation, governed in some instances by authorities who did not justify their power by reference to the divine right of kings. A perception of alterity might indeed inspire both the urge for conquest and a missionary zeal to rescue the heathen but at the same time it contributed to intellectual uncertainty. If a Christian God had created the world and ordained its functioning, how did one explain the uninitiated masses? Some had recourse to the consideration of the odysseys of Noah's sons to help explain this paradox. Others were left with the uncomfortable question that perhaps Christendom did not enjoy a monopoly of truth? The Jesuits tried in China to reconcile the Christian and Confucian traditions and promoted the view that outside Christendom virtuous people could exist and that many of the values of these pagan people could be reconciled with Christian thought. Their approach was condemned as heretical but the contemplation of other cultures from an informed critical viewpoint became an established intellectual exercise. Indeed, it took a new turn in 1721 when Montesquieu produced his *Lettres persanes* in which an imaginary group of Persians arrived in Paris and applied their own critical understanding and innate sense to the spectacle and assumptions of Parisian government and society to reveal their illogicalities. The exercise set out to disturb and question conventional understanding and reveal its illogicality. It taxed the imagination rather than proposed any agenda for change.

Indeed, the process of enlightenment did not follow any single straight road. No single theoretical framework united critics. The questioning of divine truth left German Protestantism still firm. The divine nature of kingly power had long been discounted in Britain. Both these societies, however, from the late seventeenth century, developed a concern or preoccupation with the origins of government which fed into the development of theories of natural law and of government as a form of contract. If one adopted an anthropocentric approach and considered what impelled early men to accept government, an overarching authority, one could argue that the impulse behind their acceptance was the guarantee (a contract) of certain fundamental rights to include the preservation of self and property. Locke's *Essay concerning human understanding* (1690) and his *Two Treatises on Government* (1690) were critically important in defining these issues but his preoccupations were shared and no less intense in Germany where a distinguished tradition grew up in the universities of chairs of natural law held by scholars such as Wolff (1679–1754) and Pufendorf (1632–94). Natural law and the notion of contract, a legal terminology in which a language of the rights of men replaced divine right, became a fundamental point of reference for thinkers such as David Hume and Jean Jacques Rousseau. Furthermore, the notion of a contract guaranteeing certain basic rights opened up discussion on the very nature of rights themselves. Freedom from arbitrary government (tyranny), freedom to express opinions in print without censorship and tolerance of dissent, the right to occupy positions irrespective of privileged birth (*la carrière ouverte aux talents*) were the kinds of universal concepts at issue. The notion of rights was crucial in defining a criticism of existing society and has of course been ever since open to expansion as the rights of groups (women, children, ethnic minorities, gays) have in the twentieth century challenged the existing universal construct. In the context of the eighteenth century two women, Mary Wollstonecraft and Olympe de Gouges, picked up the concept of rights as embodied in the French Declaration of the Rights of Man of 1789 to demand women's rights. For Wollstonecraft this meant the right for women to have an education equal to that of men and an entry into the same professions: for de Gouges, amongst other concerns, it meant freedom from tyranny within marriage should such occur and fundamental mothers' rights such as the guardianship of children. In the context of the eighteenth century neither could claim success but, in the long run, the notion of rights has been the way forward in promoting an agenda of change.

The notion of rights had an economic dimension which was to be developed by a group of French thinkers, the physiocrats, of whom Quesnay was perhaps the most noteworthy and by Adam Smith and those who became known as the classical British economists. Essentially starting from the premise that men enter civil society under terms which guarantee the sanctity of their property, the promotion of conditions (the free market economy or laissez-faire) whereby they can maximize their wealth is for them an integral concern and leads to the general enrichment of society as a whole.

Any attempt to reduce Enlightenment thought to an instant synthesis must be doomed to failure. Setting aside a handful, most Enlightenment thinkers were not intellectual giants pursuing a forward path with rigorous certainty. Like the death-watch beetles of a gothic edifice, they gnawed their way through the intellectual underpinning of centuries but in many instances they were relatively unconcerned with reconstruction. The Enlightenment was circumscribed in time, place and extent. After a bold beginning in the late seventeenth century, as a movement it faltered, reached one crescendo in 1734 with the publication of Pope's *Essay on Man*, a distillation of deistical thinking, of Voltaire's *Lettres Philosophiques* which were observations on the relative freedom of British thought, the press, and establishment organs, and of Montesquieu's *Considérations sur les Causes de la Grandeur des Romains et de leur Décadence*, a new empirical approach to history which considered the political record of civilizations so as to bring out the strengths and weaknesses of differing types of government. Then it bubbled gently for the next decade or so to erupt in the late forties and then to experience some official condemnation in the fifties which engendered a spurt of optimism. But in the sixties it flourished again and by the seventies had contrived almost an establishment orthodoxy.

Generally speaking, the Enlightenment was a western and central European phenomenon, embracing above all France, Britain, the Netherlands, some of the Italian and German states and the Habsburg lands and in small degree Spain. It touched only the most literate and to convey in percentage terms who these might be is almost impossible. Literacy statistics usually relate only to the ability to sign one's name, so that, according to such criteria, two-thirds of Frenchmen and about a third of women could count as literate by the end of the eighteenth century. Levels in Britain, the Netherlands and parts of Germany were higher than this and those in Spain and Italy generally lower. Exposure to advanced reading matter, discursive newsprint and translations was most available in Britain. The United Provinces where censorship was weak also had a book trade organized to cater for an established reading public. Evading censorship by publication in the United Provinces and smuggling books into France was also a fine art and primed a sense of adventure among intellectuals of an intensity perhaps lacking elsewhere. The ideas of the Republic of Letters circulated at many levels: in the Parisian salons, in French Provincial Academies who set prize essay topics, in debating societies and like associations which formed in cities, and also in books, tracts, letters, prints.

It is always difficult to trace the filter-down effect of ideas or to establish the relationship between thought and political action. Not surprisingly, France, where revolution occurred in 1789, has been accredited with the most radical development in which the critical voices of intellectual elites in salon and academy reverberated in the capital. Popular journalists of the Grub Street variety, printmakers and street orators together moulded something which might be called public opinion. Critical of government, often supportive of the parlements, hostile to the royal family and of the foreign queen Marie Antoinette in particular, the media worked to undermine the standing of existing political authority amongst a broader spectrum.

It is also in France that, after the Revolution, one can most clearly point to policies which reflect Enlightenment ideas. The framing of the Constitutions, the Declaration of the Rights of Man, the stripping of the Catholic Church of its landed wealth, projects to relieve the poor and to destroy privilege or codify the law, reveal the Enlightenment in action. However, long before revolution was on the horizon, one can perceive that where ministers and individuals persuaded by Enlightenment logic were placed in positions where they could influence policy decisions, they did so. In this volume we shall encounter Sonnenfels and van Swieten, Turgot, Cocceji and Aranda who in differing contexts sought to change their national record.

Two factors cannot be overemphasized. First, many of the greatest minds were highly individualistic. Voltaire and Rousseau for example do not readily fit into what can be called mainline development. Second, Enlightenment had a different meaning and emphasis within different national contexts. The French Enlightenment was salon-based: one hostess succeeded or rivalled another. Madame de Lambert, Madame du Deffand, Madame Geoffrin, the last virtual patroness of the *Encyclopédie*, invited into their drawing rooms thinkers and writers who progressively formed coteries of like minds reinforcing each other in their stands against 'gothic' prejudice. The members of coteries themselves introduced into the salons friends, foreign visitors and disciples until by the seventies entrée into a salon was dependent upon the right connections. At that point some argue that the Enlightenment ossified. Others, however, whose work owes much to the German sociologist Jürgens Habermas, see the salon as an important, quasi-institutionalized forum for debate which was critical to the development of ideas in a society where power was not shared but concentrated in the hands of a ruler claiming divine legitimation. Though concentrated within the privacy of an affluent home and regulated by a hostess according to quite firm rules of procedure, the discipline imposed by this structure converted a private space into a useful public forum and the association of discursive men created an alternative voice (perhaps voices given the amount of dissent). Ultimately this nurtured the formation of a politically conscious civil society which moved towards political change.

The hostesses (*salonnières*) worked hard at their job and often conducted serious epistolary exchanges with foreign scholars and thinkers. However, we should not see these women as precocious feminists but as facilitators of conversation and communication, each providing a comfortable environment for the philosopher out of her purse and enriching his experience by welcoming intellectuals from abroad. Her work entailed a lot of planning, including an agenda of questions but she did not herself advance an opinion. The Abbe Morellet insisted that Madame Geoffrin, one of the most celebrated of the hostesses, had as her ambition 'to procure the means to serve men of letters and artists...to be useful in bringing them together with men of power and position'.

The French salons fostered a movement more profoundly hostile to established religion and more overtly concerned to limit the power of the monarchy than any found elsewhere. The equally intense German Enlightenment centred, more prosaically perhaps, upon the universities, the most vigorous in eighteenth-century Europe. Here strong princely authority was seen as the best means to safeguard the happiness of the individual whilst the persistent influence of Protestant pietism and of the Catholic Enlightenment restrained the German intellectual from the Franco-British drift towards deism, or, in isolated instances, towards atheism. Deism – belief in an unspecific divine presence, in a religion of benevolence without structured institutional form, but dedicated to the pursuit of human happiness – blossomed differently in a French climate than in a British one. Perhaps this was because, as Voltaire remarked in his *Lettres Philosophiques*, the Church of England had learnt to live with proliferating sects and hence could countenance deism without undue strain. In France, on the other hand, the Roman Catholic Church was bound to react vigorously and hence there was an almost giddy intellectual preoccupation in the salons with the particular cerebral odysseys of individual philosophers who gradually severed their ties with their religious heritage. It is no accident that Baron d'Holbach left his native Germany for Paris to wage his own personal war on God from the uncontrolled yet reassuring environment of a salon where the conservative traditionalist had no footing. One should compare Lessing's agonizing struggle to hold on to some shred of faith within a German university where traditionalist and innovator met on the same ground.

Yet whatever the national or individual differences, the Enlightenment waged war on common enemies: in religion against superstition, intolerance and dogmatism: in politics against tyranny: in society against prejudice, inequality and ignorance and against any obstacles to the realization of an individual's full intellectual and physical well-being upon earth. Hardest hit of all was the Roman Catholic Church as alleged arch-preserver of the illusions of the past. The Church had, during the Reformation, been obliged to cope with dissidents but it had never before had to cope with a movement clearly hostile to an institutionalized faith or one which had questioned the right of *anyone at all* to hold a monopoly of truth. The early Enlightenment had been in the hands of Jews like Spinoza or Protestants like Bayle but in the mid-thirties it was to settle itself in the capital of Louis XV whose title embodied that of Most Christian King and to entrench itself within a *société du bon ton*. Over the ensuing twenty years when Voltaire and Montesquieu occupied the limelight of the French Enlightenment, there was an active clandestine circulation of manuscript works or pamphlets smuggled in from the free Protestant presses of Amsterdam by the hundred in spite of government attempts at repression and official church condemnation. These works included such disconcerting material as an alleged recanting testimonial of a priest, Meslier, who claimed to have been an atheist throughout his life or, in the forties, one of an unbelieving abbé called Dumarais whose pamphlet *Le Philosophe* sought to define an individual – and no better definition applied to *les philosophes* – who had freed himself from the prejudices and misconceptions of a religious education and who recognized that religion was based not on reason, which alone should guide *le philosophe*, but on human ignorance, credulity and passion, on hope rather than actuality. *Le philosophe*, the abbé concludes, follows observation and the evidence of his senses: he is committed to society and to the improvement of man's condition through knowledge and above all to the pursuit of truth. Almost contemporaneous was the publication by Fontenelle of a treatise called *Nouvelles Libertés de Penser* (1743) which concentrated on the same concepts.

From the mid-forties onwards the *philosophes* were a distinct group ready to take on Church and state and some of their recruits were to be drawn from the bosom of the Church itself. The more advanced works of the early forties showed merely a movement towards deism. Worse was to follow. Whilst the Parlement of Paris was ordering the burning of quite conventional deistic tracts, like Toussaint's *Les Moeurs*, advanced thinkers like La Mettrie in *L'Homme Machine* (1748) were spilling over into atheism in works which denied the spirituality of man and the concept of 'soul'. Even the largely political milestone, Montesquieu's *De l'Esprit des Lois* (1748), arguably the most influential work of the century, levelled some weighty blows at the established Church in a careful argument for religious toleration and a critique of the Church's hold on society. Church education and a concept of holy charity which undermined the natural dignity of working men by allowing them to live like parasites on the largesse of those who thought they were purchasing a key to eternal salvation enslaved society to serve the Church's purpose.

The *Encyclopédie* (first volume published 1751) summarized in telling form how far the *philosophes* had advanced along the path of reason and its opening, d'Alembert's *Discours Préliminaire*, was a virtual historical enquiry into the impact of the modern scientific approach upon the thought processes of the ancient and medieval world. It was not until 1759 that the *Encyclopédie*, now in seven volumes, was placed on the Index. Helvétius's *De l'Esprit* (another monument to atheism) and Voltaire's *Poème sur la Loi Naturelle* (moderately deistic) were at the same time both condemned by the Parlement of Paris to the flames.

About five years later, came the first consequential French work on sensationalism, or knowledge from the senses, attributable to the Abbé de Condillac (and it should be noted that he too was a cleric). Sensationalism concentrated upon man's sensual discernment of pleasure, pain and satisfaction. Sensationalism in fact became the most noteworthy development of the fifties and sixties and the most influential works of those years were those of the Scottish philosopher David Hume, the most significant of all the *Treatise of Human Nature* (1740) and the *Natural History of Religion* (1757) which were echoed by Boulanger and President des Brosses. Hume argued for the unreliability of sensual evidence but embarked upon an explanation of the evolution of religion by reference to the primitive fears and aspirations of ancient man who was unable to explain natural phenomena and dwelt nearly with disease and famine. Religion was hence presented not as an imposture perpetrated from above but as a historical phenomenon developed from below out of men's senses and as such it was advanced as part of the history of humanity.

It is worth considering how far sensationalism reduced the centuries-old tomes of Christian theology to the level of a passing sentence in the developing story of mankind. At its most extreme, the concept of sensationalism could be the atheist's most primitive tool. In the hands of Helvétius and yet more strikingly, d'Holbach, it could be used to convert atheism into as dogmatic a creed as anything adumbrated by the Christian Church. *De l'Esprit* argued that if all our ideas come from our senses, then they emanate from a sensory equipment beyond our control and hence man's ideas are predetermined independently of any moral force – though education and the pursuit of virtue could act as conditioning factors. D'Holbach obliterated any such considerations. Man's sensory equipment made a machine of him: he had no free will: his only motor was necessity and education's only role was to explain necessity to the young. The *Système de la Nature* (1770) was the end of the line and with it d'Holbach splintered the *philosophes*, many of whom found the dogmatism of atheism more repellent than what it was designed to replace. Voltaire was amongst those who considered d'Holbach to have perpetrated an act of intellectual tyranny.

How far did the anti-clericalism and attack on conventional catholic practices and beliefs filter down society and constitute a discernible movement away from that church? Whilst recognizing the seeds of secularization among specific intellectuals there is abundant evidence to insist that popular beliefs were untouched and that whilst wealthy clerics may have provoked some anticlericalism this has nothing to do with popular faith. Those who have been concerned to estimate the numbers of those who did not attend a weekly mass have rarely come up with more than 2 or 3 per cent of men and hardly any women in the parishes of rural France. The impact of the Enlightenment on the practices of infant baptism, marriage and extreme unction was virtually nil. However, amongst elites, some of the more flamboyant aspects of baroque religion such as requests for hundreds of masses for the repose of the soul in Purgatory, elaborate funeral monuments and processions knew some modification. What is also striking is the decline in vocations to contemplative orders amongst both sexes. However, the female orders who operated outside the cloister continued to grow.

We have seen that individual clerics were converts to Enlightenment concepts. Indeed, the Roman Catholic Church, or at least segments of it, applied its own rational process to the criticisms levelled by moderate Enlightenment thought at the established Church and showed itself ready to re-mould itself along certain modified lines. This counter-movement, known as the Catholic Enlightenment, was almost as diffuse as the actual Enlightenment. In some instances, it was merely a continuation of Counter-Reformation principles. In others, it reflects something of the splintering perceivable in the French Church between Jansenist and Jesuit in the late seventeenth century and the term Jansenist is often stretched (somewhat deceptively as the initial movement was primarily theological, concerned with concepts of grace) to Catholic Enlightenment exponents not only in France but in the Austrian Netherlands, Austria and Italy. Certainly the Church produced laxists and rigorists, reformers and traditionalists which reflected a general intellectual crisis gathering momentum from the 1740s. Such conflicting views perhaps weakened the Church in its stand against government ministers and officials demanding change in accord with the philosophy of the Enlightenment. In the 1740s Muratori put forward to the papal curia a programme of reform on Enlightenment principles but this was rejected at the end of Benedict XIV's pontificate.

The Catholic Enlightenment sought to confound its critics by a movement designed to harden the spirituality of the faithful at parochial level and to apply a new moral austerity to the mores of the flock. This meant a new emphasis on the calibre of the parish priest's education aided by the considerable extension of seminaries in France, Germany and the Habsburg lands and greater supervision of the priest's conduct and his assiduity at catechetical instruction. It meant a very rigorous attitude towards superstition, miraculous claims, saints of suspicious origin and towards the more colourful yet implicitly pagan aspects of popular beliefs. Saints' days and holidays were reduced throughout the Catholic world and this without papal instruction. Bishops, particularly in France and the Habsburg lands, undertook a personal onslaught on processions in honour of local saints which were often the occasion for drinking and violence. They also regarded with dubiety an extension of the colourful missions to the people which had gained momentum during the Counter-Reformation but which achieved new levels in the eighteenth century with the activities of the Redemptorists.

In short, in the name of enlightened reform and to placate a small minority of intellectuals, the Catholic Church waged a war on the religious customs of the majority of its flock and in so doing perhaps made a fundamental error of judgement, for, in the long run, the intellectuals had severed their links whilst the religion of the masses, if weak in matters of doctrine, was based upon fervour and tradition. These, as the French Revolution was to demonstrate, gave it a force far stronger than any generated by the *philosophes*. It is instructive to see how Enlightenment thinkers and Jansenists could find common ground in condemning the activities of the *convulsionnaires* of Saint-Médard, allegedly miraculous cures effected at the tomb of the Jansenist, François de Pâris, of cripples and sick who went through convulsive tremors. To both this was an expression of error and superstition.

Another aspect of the Catholic Enlightenment was to acknowledge, though here there was a critical counter faction, the condemnation of the contemplative life: to denounce the activities of ultramontane 'laxist' orders (i.e. the Jesuits with their generous theories on divine forgiveness and their allegiance to Rome) and to concur in the dismantling of the clerical hold over high-level education. There was even preparedness, never truly absent in the Church, to decry wealth and pomp. In some instances, the Catholic Enlightenment was acknowledging the inevitable since state policy had singled out Jesuits and contemplatives and the wealth of underutilized monastic establishments for special condemnation. But in the Austrian instance, for example, the grouping known as 'the Great Ones' (Die Grossen) which was responsible for the demise of the Jesuits and the reformation of the universities included many priests and devout laymen under 'Jansenist' influence – like Ambrose Stock, director of theological studies in Austria and Ignaz Müller, appointed confessor to Maria Theresa in 1767 and Van Swieten, her minister, himself. In Spain the infiltration of the Enlightenment could be attributed to the regalist element in the Spanish Church which Charles III in 1759 began to use to accelerate change. The Church, in short, produced elements patently anticurialist who were prepared to welcome, and adapt to, change.

Yet the forces of reaction persisted. The Index grew yearly longer. The Inquisition, if tired and desultory, occasionally went about its work, and the Calas affair showed that even in France as late as 1762 it was possible for a Protestant to be tortured and broken on the wheel for the falsely attributed murder of his Catholic convert son.

The turmoil in religious thought was rivalled only by that in political thought. The common ground was the absorption of the main legacy of the seventeenth century, the doctrine of natural law: that in politics there are rationally discoverable principles, of universal application, to which states must adhere. This implied a search for the origins of political organization: the original contract whereby individual man had sought in political organization the guarantee of his well-being. What common interests held men together? Alongside the search for first principles the eighteenth century developed a contending concern, that of empirical observation of the motor of various states or political organizations. This oscillation between the two concerns, theoretical on the one hand, historical and actual on the other, could only produce some sharp divergences, most particularly in different national contexts. The most influential western European political thinker, Montesquieu, would have argued that this was, in effect, as it should be and that one could only argue about what ought to be on the basis of what is. Nevertheless, and here again some consensus was possible, in politics what was to be avoided was tyranny (variously defined) and what was to be achieved was freedom (variously conceived), freedom of conscience, freedom from oppression, exploitation and ignorance but not freedom to the extent of a licence for self-destruction. The function of politics was to guarantee the maximization of individual freedom without the curtailment of that of another. This ought to be the end of government. Arguing from the near observation of French practice (Montesquieu was a member of the Parlement of Bordeaux) and from the relatively close experience of British political structure, which he very imperfectly understood, and from what he had read about the ancient world and the Orient, he classified governments according to type. Each form he held to be characterized by a distinctive quality, a republic by virtue, a monarchy (tempered by aristocracy) by honour, but a despotism only marked by fear. Montesquieu left his readers in no doubt, though he did not explicitly say so, that he considered aristocratic constitutionalism to be the best means of guarding against the abuse of power by despotic authority. He discerned in the British model a balance of powers achieved by the separation of legislative, executive and judicial organs of government and by extrapolation left his readers assured that the traditional checks on French monarchy, *parlements* and provincial estates ought to be endowed with powers analogous to the British bicameral legislature to serve as an effective limitation on ministerial despotism.

Small wonder that the aristocracies of Europe from the Magyars to the Swedes found *De l'Esprit des Lois* to their taste whereas the Marquis d'Argenson's *Considérations sur le Gouvernement Ancien et*

Présent de la France (1764) enjoyed more limited attention. The d'Argensons were a family which had for generations enjoyed repeated ministerial office and the work posited a political situation in which the power of the *parlements* was minimized, venality abolished and popular magistrates elected in the localities as direct agents of an undiminished royal authority. Royal democracy was however a recommendation of small appeal in the context of the *ancien régime*. Similarly restricted was the highly complicated, little understood, *Du Contrat Social* (1762) of Jean Jacques Rousseau, perhaps the most taxing and controversial outpouring of the period, with its notions of popular sovereignty channelled by expediency (*raison d'état*) into particular political forms. Here was no rival to Montesquieu's clearly pragmatic and readily identifiable study pointing to the desirability of a royal authority hedged about with institutional checks.

Yet strong unfettered monarchical authority as the best means of guaranteeing individual freedom found its protagonists in western Europe amongst those who approached politics from a quite different angle from the proponents of natural law and an original social contract, that is from a group known as the physiocrats, not strictly speaking political thinkers, but a group often hailed as the founders of modern economic thought. Physiocratic doctrine gradually evolved in the 1760s largely as a result of the ideas of two men, Quesnay and the Comte de Mirabeau. As a movement, physiocracy transformed economics from the subservient role it played in political thought from Aristotle to Rousseau wherein it merely equalled a part of the management of the state and was determined by the socio-political order, to a new science, that of wealth. As a direct manifestation of the natural order and hence as determinant of the socio-political order, economics gained a new prominence.

Quesnay was an economic animal (perhaps the first ever) involved more than anything else in the mechanics of the production of wealth and in ways to increase the revenues of the state. Quesnay equated the product of the land – grain, wine, spirits, salt, flax, linen, wool and livestock – with wealth and held that the state's business was to create the environment for efficient production of that wealth which in turn would fill state coffers. The environment for efficient production was a free market economy (*laissez-faire*) which implied (though Quesnay was unspecific in his vocabulary) the emergence of capitalist farming. The job of government was to free the market from all restrictions upon the sale and distribution of grain. Here Quesnay turned to the concept of an authoritarian government alone capable of overriding particularist interests, a concept lent shape by Mirabeau whose point of departure was a profound belief in the sanctity of property and in the virtues of a hereditary nobility. Mirabeau absorbed a recognition of the sanctity of property into a novel development of natural law which became the basis of physiocratic political thought. Property precedes government and an intrinsic part of the original contract is the sanctity of property. Hence government derives from property and cannot tamper with the fundamental laws of property without social chaos. And building upon such premises, Quesnay insisted the most fundamental law of property to be the economic right of the landowner to demand the highest possible return on his investment. In this way was evolved the concept of legal despotism, an authoritarian government which existed to guarantee the interests of a market society based on capitalist relations of production.

Physiocracy of course had to confront the question of privilege and in general found it an obstacle to the right of the individual to exploit his property to the full. Tolls, customs whether internal or external, commodity taxes, the existence of tax-exempt individuals ought to be nullified and the state run solely on a uniform land tax scaled according to landed wealth. Only a strong authoritarian monarch could override privilege. There were other targets too in the physiocratic firing range, like the restrictive practices of guilds and state protection of specific industries.

The physiocrats indeed did two things: they sounded the death knell of mercantilism by pronouncing the virtues of free trade and they offered monarchy a new rationale as first servant of a state dedicated to the maximization of man's economic potential. In a western European context, the physiocrats were the exponents of the theory of enlightened absolutism. In this way, they pulled parts of Europe towards a set of intellectual concepts long held by German political thinkers who approached the question of authority not via economics but through different interpretations of natural law and empirical reference to a political structure far different from that of France.

In central Europe there was relatively little enthusiasm amongst theorists for Montesquieu's concept of aristocratically limited monarchy. Perhaps, as Leonard Krieger has argued, this was because the historical territorial fragmentation of Germany and its peculiar political structure wherein the prince was executive in his own state but representative within the *Reichstag*, caused German thinkers to associate their political freedom with strong princely authority and this eliminated the grounds for antagonism between subject and ruler. Dissension within a state was seen as reducing the strength of the state within the Empire. Whilst Leibnitz, for example, was prepared to acknowledge the existence of hereditary tyrannical absolute rulers, he urged that expediency, the need to avert chaos, and to present a strong face to the outside world, was a greater consideration and that a subject should have no right of resistance because the evils caused by rebellion were worse than the cause of complaint. The great trinity of exponents of natural law, Pufendorf (1632–94), Thomasius (1658–1728), Wolff

(1679–1754) all posited a contractual basis for the development of the state and believed reform necessary in existing government but none urged constitutional safeguards nor conceived of any alternative to unlimited princely power. But the prince was to be left in no doubt as to what was expected of him in the modern eighteenth-century world. His job had an enormity never before conceived. In Wolff's *Politics* the prince must supervise the economy, education, welfare services and where the latter were found wanting, set up needful orphanages, poor houses etc. Moreover, Wolff did not sacrifice grandiose principle to minute detail. Supervising the economy entailed controlling immigration and emigration, knowing the numbers involved in various trades, fixing wages and working hours and erecting heavy penalties against the work-shy.

The German Enlightenment was no less explicit than the French or Italian in insisting upon religious tolerance, opposition to social privilege and in urging man's right to the fullest possible life on earth but it conceived of princely authority as the securest means to that end. German cameralism, as such an approach was called, differed from the physiocratic view of government in one basic essential, in the emphasis it laid upon the right of the state to intervene at any level and hence in the positive role of government. In contrast physiocracy envisaged a state wherein the ruler removed the obstacles to every kind of freedom, economic, social, religious, and then merely saw that the situation was maintained. Cameralism had in the German states and central Europe a far greater influence upon government than that enjoyed by the physiocrats upon western European rulers and for obvious reasons. It grew naturally out of a long-standing appreciation of the role of German states within the Empire and until the late eighteenth century with the advent of romanticism and nationalism and a marked reaction against autocratic authoritarianism, had no serious rival. Physiocracy, on the other hand, was born abruptly in a context wherein limited monarchy was a serious contender as a concept of the ruler's place in society and where there existed institutions which already severely curtailed the monarchy's freedom of action. This simple distinction is the most crucial to bear in mind when one considers enlightened despotism, the relationship between an intellectual movement and the actual practice of government.

It has been fashionable for a century or more to line up the rulers of western Europe in the eighteenth century and to assess their degree of commitment to the Enlightenment and their degree of conformity to a model enlightened despotism. Such an exercise requires us to consider how attractive and indeed seductive were Enlightenment principles to monarchies grappling with the problems of how to finance armies and armaments in face of institutions hotly contesting the power of the purse and the tyranny of absolutism. Seen this way, Enlightenment philosophy rejustified monarchy stripped of the concept of the divine right of kings by endowing it with a new rationale, that of first Servant of the People. This approach permits as an extension the reflection that new despotism was but old despotism thinly revamped. What, after all, was new about an attempt to override noble privilege, to strip the Church of its wealth or to fill state coffers more efficiently? How different were the bureaucracies created by the eighteenth-century monarchs from those set up in the aftermath of the Thirty Years' War? Was enlightened despotism merely despotism in its last stage?

Whilst acknowledging the obvious sense in such an approach, it does, notwithstanding, not convey the entire story. Enlightenment influence was pervasive and it can be detected in the legislation of practically every ruler in the second half of the eighteenth century. The ambitions of rulers were nowhere furthered by law reform, by the extension of secular education or by religious tolerance but across every country some attempts were to be made in that direction. Yet Enlightenment influence is one thing, to translate the blueprint of the enlightened despot into a working model quite another. No ruler of a loosely knit state would make his state an experimental laboratory for a set of preconceived political principles. Moreover, local political traditions clearly limited attempts at change.

Within the context of the Empire, in individual states, Mainz, Trier, Saxony, there can be seen to be a close marriage between theory and practice. Elsewhere the strength of provincial and social institutions obviously made such a union impractical. Joseph II is of interest because as a convert to German cameralism he flew in the face of *raison d'état*, the premises upon which the Habsburg Empire had been constructed, with predictable consequences. For Frederick II on the other hand, dealing with territories which were part of the Empire and where the relationship between ruler and provincial estates was a harmonious though measured one, cameralism was an easier development. Yet an appreciation of local economic and demographic conditions ensured that Frederick II was not a slavish convert to *laissez-faire* nor to serf emancipation however much he might be attracted to western European philosophies. He does, in short, stand up to a cameralist concept of an enlightened ruler but not a physiocratic one. Elsewhere, the only parallel to the German state is perhaps Tuscany whose peculiar position within the Austrian Empire was analogous to that of a German state within the Empire and where in the late eighteenth century the Grand Duke Leopold contrived a situation conforming to cameralist principles and policies.

In religious terms the influence of the Enlightenment upon state policy was manifest in measures adopted towards contemplatives and above all towards the Jesuits. The expulsion of the Jesuits perhaps more than any other phenomenon reflects the temper of the times. The impetus for this came initially from the Portuguese and reflected at first colonial tensions. Troubles had been brewing along the Para River where the Jesuits had protected native Indian labour from harsh exploitation by colonists. In 1752 an interchange of territories between the Portuguese and the Spanish governments resulted in the Jesuits leading their Indian settlers on their farms and all the livestock away from these territories in resistance to the measure. In the Iberian peninsula their numbers were quite small (3000 in Spain) against the numbers of mendicant orders who frequently resented their influence over elite education. Even so, they only had seventeen colleges in Spain whereas in France they had over a hundred, and alumni who included Voltaire and Robespierre. In France, however, as we shall see, the Jesuits were associated with papal influence and with a political crisis in which the parlements stood out against the registration of the bull *Unigenitus* (see above pp. 218–19). Politics of a somewhat dubious honesty led to combined pressure from France, Spain and Portugal upon the papacy to expel the Society.

Neither Clement XIII nor Clement XIV was in a position to make a determined stand and the latter chose, as a means of buying peace with the Catholic princes, to sacrifice the Jesuits in the bull *Dominus ac Redemptor* (1773) ironically pushing the remnants of the order further into eastern Europe where neither Frederick II nor Catherine the Great felt moved to regard them as a threat to their authority. Predictably this papal act did not purchase better relations between the papacy and the European princes. In France the royal commission for the reform of religious orders was conducted without papal approval; and in the Habsburg lands and Portugal secular authorities proceeded to strip the church of much of its wealth and destroy its hold over education. Moreover the Italian cardinalate, incensed by Clement XIV's sacrifice of the Jesuits, thenceforth questioned his every move including his attempts to reform economic and social abuses within the Papal States. In the history of the papacy, the eighteenth century is one of vacillation and confusion.

There were no popular demonstrations in support of the Jesuits perhaps because they were an organization more concerned with elites than with the masses and the priorities of popular religion were not offended by the expulsion. It is important to emphasize that although the Enlightenment concerned itself with the realization of man's potential and his social and political rights, the attitudes of many thinkers to the illiterate masses was often overtly dismissive. The people were ignorant, credulous and lacking in rational skills. They were the slaves of base instincts, crime-prone, riot-prone and unreliable. But the *philosophes* were beset by the realization that they were the sector upon whose labour society as a whole depended and the *philosophes'* problem was how to reconcile the people's utility with their lack of reason.

Their utility meant they had a right to impartial justice, fair taxation and a measure of education. How much was the subject of prolonged intellectual debate and commanded little consensus. Most agreed that the educational fare of the masses should be directed to promoting their social utility and should focus on the vocational. A few, however, went further. Adam Smith, for example, believed that the ability to observe and the development of reason and conversation were life-enhancing attributes which should be available to all, even the poorest. The ability to reason would increase public tranquility. Condorcet too urged an extension of education to a broad spectrum. But many drew back and erected barriers between themselves as the enlightened few and the many. Education for the masses should be concerned not with know-ledge or literacy but teaching them the duties of their estate. The question of religion for the masses revealed the same double standard. While men of reason could question notions of Purgatory and eternal damnation as inventions of a Church intent upon maintaining its hold through fear, they were reluctant to let go of the concept of eternal damnation in the case of the masses.

This concept was one of the few weapons to hold the weak-minded and crime-prone in check and Voltaire thought the preservation of such a myth essential to the maintenance of standards in the lower orders. Diderot and Condorcet were prepared to accept this though Helvétius opted for a concocted religion of public utility based on the concepts of the sanctity of life and property.

The people had some ill-defined right to work. Where work did not exist then a good government would create it. They had no right to charity, no right to expect government to protect them by price fixation and protected markets and they were to be kept in order by an even-handed justice served by an extended police force.

This is of course a very basic summary. Religious tolerance and a relative relaxation of censorship may have gratified a number of intel-lectuals but it had no meaning for the masses. Catholic Europe remained attached to its saints' days and Sunday mass, to processions, images, superstitions like the ringing of the parish bell to avert hail-storms and the frequent requests to parish priests to excommunicate insects, and the masses clung to popular cults which both the secular and Catholic Enlightenment roundly denounced but which notwith-standing flourished – for example the expansion by means of Lazarist missions of the cult of the Sacred Heart in Mediterranean Europe. The Priests of the Mission carried on the work of the Counter-Reformation under the overt condemnation of Jansenist reformers and dealt in that immediate vivid religion of blood and threat of damnation so readily acceptable to the working classes. Furthermore, the state did not cater in any substantial way to educating the common people – though some attempts were made in individual German states and in the Habsburg lands. Such literacy as the French or Spanish peasant enjoyed was the result of religious schools and educational innovation throughout Europe concerned only the better-off.

Popular reaction to *laissez-faire* economics was one area where indifference was impossible. From the 1760s in France, Spain, Portugal, throughout the Habsburg lands and to a lesser degree in Britain and Scandinavia, governments were converts to the concept of freedom of the grain trade and the breaking down of traditional methods of protecting the masses by price fixation in time of dearth and by the obligatory use of regular markets. Eighteenth-century consumers thought in terms of a just price, a concept patently at odds with *laissez-faire* economics and reacted violently, particularly during the difficult sixties and seventies, to any government attempts to abandon controls. Indeed no issue caused more fundamental alienation between governing and governed. Of less consequence, but notwithstanding causing overt opposition in the towns, were attempts to break guild monopolies, the physiocratic illusory catch-all to explain the slow performance of certain industries, whose only consequence in France was to accelerate the shift of industry from town to country and thus engender a crisis of over-production in the traditional woollen industries.

Increasing bureaucratization, where it occurred in Germany, the Habsburg lands and the Iberian Peninsula, and more efficient tax-collection stood for greater intrusion. The government sponsored work-projects designed to provide employment for the needy by road building, razing medieval walls, constructing ditches etc, was no palliative to the problem of chronic rural underemployment because no government had at its disposition sufficient funds to make a properly structured assistance policy a reality. The Enlightenment's attack on voluntary almsgiving and its condemnation of the charitable institutions run by the Catholic Church can only have accelerated the decline in the efficacy of such relief. In short, the faith of the *philosophes* in the power of government profoundly to influence the life of the masses in a society without the means to provide its demographic surplus with work or sufficient food was entirely misplaced. This may well explain why essays in enlightenment policy look very different in a less populous central Europe than in an overpopulated west. One should not lose sight of this basic reality when approaching these men of vision. In 1816 the mayor of Toulouse was to engineer his way out of a food riot by shrieking at the populace *voulez-vous la charité des philosophes?* The hungry women of Bayeux in 1794 shattered Rousseau's bust to the cry of *à bas putain*. The people were not called upon to express their views of the *philosophes* and physiocrats very often but the Flour War and the fiasco of the assistance programme of the *Comité de Mendicité* in 1790 offer some pointers. In practical terms, the people could well do without them.

One can similarly minimize the immediate effects of what was probably the Enlightenment's most conspicuous achievement, the reform of law and the legal system. In every country law was an anomalous hotch potch embracing Roman, canon, provincial and customary law. Laws were piled on the statute book with scant regard for uniformity or scale of punishments. Law enforcement was perforce left to communities since, even where a police force existed, as in France, it was so slight as to be virtually ineffective. Community justice in first instance often lay in seigneurial courts and since there was no profit in such justice for the seigneur these courts rarely met. Otherwise it was a question of finding one's way through the system by bribery. The tangle of jurisdictions and differing penalties given by different courts ensured total confusion. There is a general consensus that crimes, particularly crimes against property, were on the increase in the eighteenth century which may simply reflect demographic growth or the particular stress of deteriorating economic conditions. Authorities in the first half of the century adopted the principle of justice by harsh example – the severe punishment of the isolated apprehended individual to deter the rest. One's treatment in prison depended upon ability to pay one's lodgings and European authorities used in preference branding, flogging and the galleys. Until the 1780s judicial torture was used on the condemned to make them reveal their accomplices. Hangings or breaking on the wheel were public occasions, justified by the belief that such spectacles would have a deterrent effect on the potential offender.

The inefficiency of justice and its patent inadequacy to cope with soaring crime figures were obvious even to observers of the first half of the century. The appreciation of the barbarity of torture and some circumspection about the taking of life when immortality was not assured were concerns of the Enlightenment. Perhaps the greatest and most influential work of the Enlightenment was Cesare Beccaria's *Delle delitti et delle pene* (1764) subsequently translated into every major European language before the end of the century. The work was a summary of Enlightenment concepts about crime, punishment and crime prevention and its influence was patent in innumerable law works, like Blackstone's *Commentaries on the Laws of England*, in the second half of the century. Briefly Beccaria posited the replacement of a justice (now referred to as pre-Beccarian justice) which was sporadic, varying from place to place, founded on the principle of deterrent by harsh example, by one which was uniform across the land and across social barriers, wherein the punishment fitted the crime and wherein the apprehension of all offenders was the goal. Beccaria ruled out torture and all barbarities. He was an opponent of the death penalty. At two levels, the abolition of torture and the general movement towards law codification throughout Europe, his work was of immense significance in the second half of the eighteenth century. But to put the work into practical effect was another thing. Beccaria's projects demanded a new or rapidly expanded police force, a costly item and one which no state in eighteenth-century Europe could afford, as well as reformed prisons or places of detention and a more informed magistracy. None of this was achieved in the eighteenth century but it was a vision for the future.

Enlightenment then, taken overall, enhanced the distinction between the converted few and the ignorant or unconvinced many. Physiocracy pitted producers against consumers: the attack on superstition, the credulous many against the austere and self-righteous few. Indeed, secularization or change in traditional religious worship delivered resounding popular victories against the Habsburgs in the Netherlands and Lombardy and to the all–intrusive Republican government of Revolutionary France. The limits of intellectual persuasion were abundantly demonstrated.

4

Armies, Interests and Conflict

Amongst the manifold issues hotly debated by Enlightenment thinkers one more than any other secured consensus: opposition to warfare as an unjustified waste of life and material resources in quarrels of no real concern to mankind in general. If only the Abbé Saint Pierre actually published a project for making peace eternal, others – Voltaire, Helvétius and the historians – were insistent upon the ultimate futility of armed strife. Yet history had left not a ruler in Europe in a position to heed their admonitions. Everything seemed to conspire towards making strife perpetual. The growth of large standing armies in the aftermath of the Thirty Years' War was a process no one tried to arrest and throughout the eighteenth century there was a massive growth in the size of professionally maintained troops whose numbers were increased yet further in time of war. A regular kernel of about 20,000 Prussian troops in 1675 had become 190,000 by 1786 though the country had not technically been at war since 1763 – the justification for such numbers reflecting apprehension at the 300,000 maintained by the Habsburgs and the Russian force of 458,000 (1796). The French maintained by the 1780s a peacetime force of 187,000 with plans to inflate to 224,000 in time of war. The British and Dutch, with much smaller populations and both avowedly associating large standing armies with 'foreign' tyranny, notwithstanding usually had a nucleus of not less than 25,000 regular troops to tide over the gap that must elapse in time of conflict whilst conscripts and mercenaries were raised.

All the major standing armies, even in times of peace, employed mercenaries and there were veritable mercenary peoples, the Irish, Scots, Swiss and above all those of the petty German states like Mecklenburg for whom military service in someone else's army was a major element in the national economy. The rank and file of the army were drawn from the lowest echelons of society since the rich and often the townsmen were able to escape from the motley methods used to raise a force. British magistrates directed the unemployed and able-bodied petty criminals into the force: in Russia each peasant household had to provide a conscript: elsewhere villagers drew lots. Such methods scarcely provided committed recruits and desertion was anticipated – in some years a tenth of the French army defected and the Prussian situation was no better. Nevertheless, troops on peacetime alert were trained to a degree never deemed possible in the days when entire forces had been disbanded in peacetime. Moreover, the command in continental Europe was largely in the hands of the nobility who believed a military career their birthright and who, on the whole, constituted an effective officer class. Inevitably venality crept in and, at least in Britain, France and Spain, the best positions were purchasable.

Powers with commercial or colonial interests were also tied to the maintenance of navies, though Britain and the Dutch Republic alone regarded the navy as more important than military strength. In wartime the British navy stood by the second half of the eighteenth century at around 80,000 men and the French at about 75,000. The ships they manned were warships, not the hastily converted merchantmen of the previous century. The British navy dwarfed all others with 174 ships (1783) but the combined French and Spanish fleets fell not far short (104 and 60 respectively) and many of their vessels were more up-to-date. Naval conditions were invariably appalling and the press-ganged, forcibly recruited navies were a prey to every conceivable undesirable disease from scurvy to yellow fever. One sick man could infect and kill an entire crew. Nor was there any better apprenticeship for a life later committed to smuggling or privateering.

Along with the growth of armies and navies came improved weaponry and such weaponry made possible a more sophisticated use of tactics. The bayonet had by 1721 replaced the pike even in the Russian army and this gave a new strength to the infantry. The battle of Mollwitz in 1741 showed, for the first time, that it was possible for the infantry to be the determinant of victory when it stood firm whilst the cavalry was routed. This was only a beginning. In terms of linear technique and advanced weaponry the Prussians were in a class of their own. Eighteenth-century battle formations were usually based on thin drawn-out lines of men, a deployment supposed to enhance fire-power. The aim was to pierce the enemy line and serve as cover for the artillery which performed the real work of execution. By reinforcing flanks of their line or by deploying extra men against the enemy's side, the Prussians adopted new tactical variants which the rest of Europe was quick to learn.

The new armies were not only drilled but properly uniformed and well-booted. An infantry was heavy on footwear. Hence the standing armies were significant consumers of textile and leather goods as well as of armaments and metalware. Naval construction was also a major employer: Chatham, Portsmouth, Brest and Toulon each employed in the region of 1000 men. In addition was the business and employment involved in the actual provisioning of these armies and navies in times of peace. Small wonder they needed massive bureaucracies to sustain them and that the work of government was directed above all to ensuring the revenues needful to keep them up and indeed extend them. Armies, navies, servicing debts (usually incurred by warfare) and the costs of raising taxes (to service debt and maintain armies and navies) were the major elements in state expenditure. The maintenance of courts, the rewarding of faithful servitors and expenditure on public services were in comparison mere bagatelle. Given the rudimentary nature of book-keeping by eighteenth-century governments, it would be dishonest to offer any spuriously precise breakdown of government expenditure. But when monarchs and members of royal families adopted military dress and martial poses and some actually took to the field, they gave visual expression to what was an obvious truth: that monarchs and the governments and bureaucracies they created were tied to their armies. The growth of the last meant an increase in the organs of government and in the demands monarchies must make in terms of money and men of their subjects in the name of state imperatives and interests. Such imperatives and interests varied from state to state but they all led in one direction, towards expensive defence or expensive aggression. Moreover, the journey led into the cul-de-sac of debate with those institutions who claimed some control over the power of the purse.

What purposes were eighteenth-century armies intended to serve? There were five active empire builders, Britain, France, Russia, Prussia and latterly Austria though the arena of their activities was sharply differentiated, the first two were overwhelmingly concerned with expansion outside Europe, the last three with internal expansion, at the expense of weak states, mainly anarchic Poland and collapsing Turkey.

Much of this expansion was based on economic ambitions. When Frederick the Great undertook the conquest of Silesia it was with a view to procuring a major industrial area offering impressive state revenues. His ambitions in Poland focused upon control of the lower reaches of the Vistula and hence the extensive grain and timber trade distributed through Danzig. Russia's peculiar economic situation condemned her to a remorseless outward push in search of wealthier grain-producing land. Britain, France, Spain, Portugal and the Dutch Republic already had colonies whose existence or extension was often justified by actual or potential trade with the mother country. Trade for the western European powers justified the existence of the flag and by trade was largely understood commodities which were not produced in, but which were valued by, the mother country: sugar, cotton, spices, dyes, tobacco and furs. Territorial extent had relatively little relevance in comparison with economic interests. By any rating, the smallest West Indian sugar island in the first half of the eighteenth century outweighed in value to the mother country, the entire snowy extent of Canada, productive only of beaver furs and salt cod. Given mercantilist beliefs in the virtually static nature of world trade, colonial trade had always involved inter-state rivalries and conflict. Yet the abandonment of mercantilism for *laissez-faire* provoked no reappraisal of the intrinsic aggressive competition involved in trade.

Sometimes the interests of states were strategic, the belief in defensible frontiers or the importance of sites like Gibraltar, so dear to British strategic planning. Sometimes they were based upon the old notion of the balance of power, fashionable since the threat of the uniting of the French and Spanish crowns in the Spanish Succession War. This threat receded after 1713 but the principle of the balance of power was invoked as a fresh justification for the Partitions of Poland, begun in 1772 and completed in 1793 and 1795, and to justify Austro-Russian involvement in the collapsing Turkish Empire.

Dynastic considerations were not of course entirely absent. Elizabeth Farnese's attempt to push Spanish claims in Italy in order to carve out principalities for her sons served no obvious Spanish interest whilst Charles VI's attempts to guarantee his daughter's accession to Habsburg lands visibly weakened Austria in the eyes of Europe. Religious differences no longer led to armed conflict. Yet hatred of the French and Spanish, linked with the insistent spectre of Irish papistry, was useful for arousing British public opinion in favour of war and Russian or Austrian advance against the Moslem could engender, at least initially, some popular enthusiasm.

Clearly, however, the great demarcation between west and east lay in the direction of its imperial thrust. Transatlantic competition drove a wedge between Britain and the three colonial powers of France, Spain and the Dutch Republic. Spanish-Portuguese rivalry in South America and a historic hostility between these two powers provided Britain with her oldest ally, Portugal. France and Spain expressed nominal support in successive family compacts but these bore witness to an apprehension of a common enemy, Britain.

Lastly the Dutch, world carriers of an earlier epoch, commanding the entrepôt trade between the Baltic and the Mediterranean, progressively failed to sustain their earlier commercial momentum and, bitterly resentful of British commercial strength, were precluded from any lasting tie with that country. In the east, Frederick the Great's essays to create a unified empire lying athwart the Empire by depredations on Habsburg and Polish territories and the hostilities of Austria and Prussia within the Empire made the two permanent enemies.

Looked at academically, the two spheres of influence appear so separate as to permit rivals in the one total indifference to the progress of rivals in the other. Yet it was not quite so clear cut. A British king was Elector of Hanover and hence far from indifferent to events in north Germany. The French were not only sensitive to any Habsburg extension in Rhenish Germany but to any factor which threatened to strengthen and hence disturb the balance of states within the Holy Roman Empire. From such an apprehension stemmed in good part French opposition in 1733 to a candidature to the elective throne of Poland which seemed to lay a precedent for confining the position to the electoral house of Saxony and making Poland a client state of Russia and Prussia. The French believed that the maintenance of Polish, Turkish and Swedish power was the best guarantee of containing the Habsburgs. Insofar as the Saxon dynasty did by massive concessions to the magnates hasten the demise of Poland, the French read the situation aright. But after 1733, and the short, unsuccessful War of the Polish Succession, the French stood aside from Polish affairs leaving the arena wide open for Russo-Prussian advance. Yet in so doing the French did not abandon their near interest in German affairs, and the War of the Austrian Succession demonstrated their over-anxiety to deal a body-blow at the Habsburgs.

The concern then of Britain and France in the German situation linked the two arenas of conflict, adding an immensely extended dimension to international affairs. Extra-European battles in the New World were frequently fought by very small numbers of men: battles in Asia by still fewer. Yet to arm and provision these forces and maintain their contact with the mother country demanded some command of the sea and hence what were by European standards mere skirmishes, were incredibly costly to sustain. France and Britain's role as extra-European colonial powers and important arbiters of European situations lent an intricacy to international involvement never before experienced and a duality to their policy which countries with purely European interests, Prussia and Austria in particular, found frustrating because such a bifurcation of interests rendered Britain and France unstable allies.

These were the constant factors regulating eighteenth-century international relations.

The western European states which looked to overseas empires were Spain, Portugal, Great Britain, France and Holland. In territorial extent, no empire in 1740 exceeded the Spanish which embraced most of South America, Mexico and the most significant Caribbean islands, Cuba, Puerto Rico and Hispaniola, and extended into the Pacific with the occupation of the Philippines. The Portuguese Empire was scattered and held together only by sea power. Confined to Brazil and Uruguay, to stretches of coast in West and East Africa, to Goa and Macau, the eastern trading posts in particular were of special interest. Portuguese trading stations in the east had fallen prey to encroaching Dutch interests in the seventeenth century. The Moluccas, Ceylon and the Spice Islands changed hands and the Dutch had laid down bases at Batavia and Malacca. In Africa they had a station at Cape Town and in the Americas Dutch traders occupied a strip of Guiana, the island of Curaçao and two of the Leeward Islands. British possessions included stretches of the seaboard of North America, the thirteen colonies stretching from Maine to the Carolinas, and these were complimented in the Caribbean by the 'outer islands' of St Kitts, Nevis, Antigua and Barbados. In India, Catherine of Braganza's dowry to Charles II had been Bombay, and this added to Surat and Madras and a post on the site of modern Calcutta gave Britain an important toe-hold on the peninsula. The French had entrenched themselves less successfully in North America and their influence was mainly confined to small settlements along the Saint Lawrence and the Mississippi base of Louisiana. But they held some of the main jewels of the West Indies, Martinique and Guadeloupe and San Domingo.

There were three types of colonial development clearly discernible by the beginning of the eighteenth century. The first, that of the exploitation colony, existed in torrid zones and was undertaken by Europeans with a get-rich-quick mentality. Such individuals did not look upon the colony as a home or the severance with their native land as finite but saw the colony as a place where they, in managerial or business capacity, could make a quick fortune. Such colonies were usually worked by enslaved labour. Where a native population could not be thus harnessed then one had to be imported. Typical of exploitation colonies were the Spanish settlements in South America which used Indian labour to exploit the mines or the sugar plantations of the West Indies worked by an unremitting stream of African slaves.

Settlement colonies were quite different. Here the colonist for one reason or another – religious, political, economic – had made a definite breach with his native land and saw the new land of his choice as his permanent home. The characteristic unit of production was the smallholding and the settler looked to his own efforts to support himself and his family. The English mainland colonies offer an excellent instance. Composed of differing groups of dissident religious minorities – not all of whom were British – or of political refugees, the colonies were characterized by their in-turning, independent, even hostile approach to the mother country. By European standards, the British were over-casual in the peopling of their overseas settlement colonies. The French, on the other hand, were remarkable for their careful scrutiny of potential colonists to secure religious and political orthodoxy. This perhaps explains why New France (Canada) had no more than 10,000 inhabitants when Colbert died in 1683 but it also explains the community of interests of the colonists with the mother country. The work of the Jesuits, both in Spanish America and New France, amongst both settlers and Indians, ensured that the religious uniformity of the mother country was perfectly matched in the infant colony.

The governmental structure of the colonies tended to reflect the type of government of the mother country. In the Spanish Empire viceroys and *audiencias* (legal councils) in close contact with the Ministry of the Indies in Madrid aped the governmental structure of Spain, whilst the government of New France closely resembled that of a French *généralité* with an intendant at its head, albeit with larger powers of initiative than the French model.

There was a third type of colony, that of the station, 'factory' or 'counter' which meant quite simply, trading post, and most of these were found on the coast of Africa, India and in the Pacific islands. Such stations were highly prized by a colonial philosophy which put commercial interest before territorial conquest. Indeed, the stations fitted more easily than any other form of colonial development into that element in mercantilist philosophy which could only justify settlement if it provided a market for the industrial efforts of the mother country. The trouble was that the value of the stations aroused intense competition and to guarantee their security, Europeans were led in the long run into both conquest and occupation. Much of this development, however, was only beginning in the eighteenth century. For the western world the eastern stations meant tea, spices, fine cottons which could not yet be produced by European techniques, silks, saltpetre and hard woods. The business of eastern trade was in the hands of great national trading companies. The British East India Company was formed by a syndicate of London merchants; the Dutch East India Company was a national institution directed by representatives of the maritime provinces, with shares open to all. Such organization reflected the fact that eastern trade was very much a heavy deficit trade, that is, the value of the goods leaving the area far exceeded what went in – the deficit being made good in bullion. Business was then most effectively transacted by a limited number of annual vessels dispatched by the big companies.

Having allies meant use of their stations. In this way the British alliance with Portugal was extremely valuable. The British East India Company and its French and Dutch counterparts could of course force the pace of events by involvement in local politics and actions which did not necessarily conform to policy in the mother country. Their servants, more than hastily imported troops, had to fend off attacks. There was a very real sense in which officialdom was the arbiter of colonial policy.

Eastern trade was limited and still in eighteenth-century terms concerned with luxuries. In the seventeenth century, the eastern trade had always been pejoratively contrasted with the vital trades of the Baltic in grain, timber, iron ore and naval supplies. In both the Dutch had enjoyed an ascendancy, though one progressively contested by Britain. Yet it was no longer Baltic but transatlantic trade which excited mercantile enthusiasm and which had become the focal point of international rivalry. Transatlantic trade was concerned with relatively few but extremely valuable commodities which appeared essential to the European economy. As well as the Spanish and Portuguese trade in precious metals and diamonds, sugar and tobacco had become an intrinsic feature of transatlantic trade, mass consumption articles that Europe believed it could not do without. These were followed by cotton, indigo, dyewoods and timber. The settlement colonies of the north produced something in the way of hides or furs but apart from Virginia, already a prime tobacco producer, and the Newfoundland fisheries, they were not significant suppliers to the mother countries. The transatlantic trade would have been a heavy deficit trade for Europe had it not been for the slave business which made possible a convenient triangular traffic of manufactured goods (cheap cloth and baubles) to the African coast where African slave traders marshalled hordes of suffering humanity to work the plantation colonies of the West Indies, the southern American states, and South America. On the third stage of the journey, the sugar of the Indies could be dispatched to a craving Europe. There was wealth to be culled in each branch of this trade. The sugar merchants of Bristol, Nantes, Orleans and Rotterdam were unsurpassed in their mercantile affluence. Individual fortunes were made in slaving but overall for British, French, Dutch and Portuguese slave trader alike, the profits could on occasion be more apparent than real and rarely exceeded 10 per cent of investment.

Every mother country sought strenuously to supervise the trade of its overseas empire by a rigid system of regulations controlling export conditions for the carriage and distribution of goods, and curtailing imports into the colonies from outsiders. The English Navigation Acts are typical of such an approach. In Spanish America, where the attempts by colonists, merchants and shippers to evade the regulations were the *casus belli* of 1739, the right to participate in colonial trade was the monopoly of a single trading agency, the *Casa de Contratación*. Two annual convoys from Spain, one to Vera Cruz and one to Portobello, officially supplied the colonies with essential European commodities produced in Spain and took out silver, indigo, cotton, dyewoods and cochineal. Only a limited number of ports could send goods out to Europe. Obviously the formalities and the expense of the convoy system pushed up the costs of the goods for the colonists and hence made them ready to connive with foreigners for a cheaper deal. The Caribbean swarmed with illegal traders even before the granting in 1713 to Britain of the Asiento – the right to supply the Spanish colonies with 4800 slaves per year – and the concession of sending an annual British ship (nominally of 650 tons) to Portobello. Given the all pervasive conviction amongst government, merchants, and shipping interests alike of the immense profit potential of colonial business and of South American trade in particular, the universal urge to cut in and evade regulations bred intense resentment. The British slaving interest deemed that, thanks to the activities of interlopers and the machinations of Spanish officialdom, they never realized their due from the Asiento. The Spanish were convinced that the British abused their privilege of sending an annual ship by using several vessels to reprovision the official one as it lay at anchor.

One uses the terms 'British' and 'Spanish' here in the most oblique sense. Often the men directly involved were crooks of the first magnitude, smugglers and men without scruples living on the pickings of illicit trade, but governments could not extricate themselves psychologically from involvement in business which promised, however nebulously, potential 'national' profit. The crash of Law's schemes and the South Sea Bubble in the twenties had shattered some myths about the profitability of Spanish American trade and at least prevented the British and the French from ever harnessing state finances to trading enterprises again. Nevertheless, there remained the conviction that wealth was there to be garnered and, even more insistently, as events of 1739–40 were to show, pressure groups, some with vested interests, emerged to push governments into assertive attitudes. The alleged disappearance of twelve 'British' vessels in the Caribbean in 1737, sunk by *guardacostas*, Spanish suspension of the Asiento in 1739 and the loss of Captain Jenkins's ear whilst engaged in dubious South American traffic – one of many such reported incidents – placed Walpole under pressure from a war lobby. Inflated claims for compensation from the Spanish, mounting war fever and an implicit faith in the superiority of the British navy pushed Britain heedlessly in the direction of war.

In the course of the War of Jenkins's Ear the British captured and demolished the fortresses of Portobello but attempts made to take parts of Florida and Santiago (Cuba) met with no success. Four years after the outbreak of war, British interests were no further advanced. More strikingly the British had played a very dangerous game for Spain had since 1733 been locked in a family compact with France designed, from Elizabeth Farnese's point of view, to forge an Italian inheritance for her son. Any major British success leading to a shift in power in the Caribbean would be a near concern of France and the outbreak of war placed that country on the alert. In 1741 Walpole felt himself obliged to recall Vernon from Cartagena to guard the Channel. Still worse, the sideshow of British involvement in South America threatened to link itself ominously with a conflict in Europe which promised to be of major significance. Why the War of the Austrian Succession, 'King George's War' as it was known in Britain because it reflected royal concern with Hanover and the monarch actually took to the field, should merge so naturally with Anglo-Spanish embroilment in the Caribbean perhaps needs some explanation. Britain had already ranged herself against Spain and potentially, if Spain could not stand as effective buffer, against France. Britain had already, by 1741, taken the conflict into European waters by using the fleet in the Mediterranean to prevent Spanish troops moving into Italy. The step had proved ineffectual. The overall lack of success resulted in February 1742 in the resignation of Walpole. There then emerged a cabinet with Carteret in the Northern Department committed to the lifting of England's slipped international prestige. Britain's intervention, first by diplomacy and then by military involvement in the war, a war primarily against the Bourbons, who, defeated in Europe would be unable to sustain imperial defence, was an almost logical development.

Since 1713 the problem of the order of succession for the Habsburg Empire, a problem which existed because Charles VI was at that time childless and continued because he only produced a daughter, whilst his late brother had also only begotten girls, had been nominally resolved by recourse to a Spanish precedent, the Pragmatic Sanction. This was a document stating the indivisibility of the Habsburg Empire and vesting the succession, in the absence of a male heir, in a female. In the first instance, this was to be Charles's own daughter, Maria Theresa (born 1717). Next in order of succession were placed his brother, Joseph I's, children and next those of his father by Margaret Theresa of Spain. The Pragmatic Sanction was accepted by the Estates of Austria and Bohemia and by the Hungarian Diet (1722) and over the next decade by Spain, France, England and Prussia. Notwithstanding these considerable efforts to gain universal recognition, the death of Charles VI in 1740 saw the succession hotly contested and the major European powers precipitated, some only too willingly, into a contest which threatened the dismemberment of the Habsburg Empire.

Charles Albert, Elector of Bavaria, presented himself as a male heir through his distant descent from a daughter of Ferdinand I of Habsburg (1556–64). Philip V, King of Spain, based a claim on a treaty between Charles V and his brother Ferdinand, on the occasion of the cession of the German lands, reinforced by a reservation made by Philip III of Spain when he too renounced the German lands. Urged on by his ambitious wife, Elizabeth Farnese, Philip V proceeded to think in terms of a conquest of Austrian Italy. Augustus III of Saxony, husband of the eldest daughter of Joseph I, also threw in his claims.

To compound confusion and make it total, Charles VI was not the only monarch whose demise in 1740 altered the fortunes of his country. The death of the cautious Frederick William I of Prussia saw his replacement by his much more active and ambitious son, Frederick II (the Great), who now advanced claims to a portion of Silesia (renounced by Frederick William the Great Elector in 1686). In exchange for the cession of the whole of Lower Silesia, Frederick II declared himself prepared to take the field on Austria's behalf to settle the Austrian Succession question within Germany. Moreover, whilst both Britain and France hesitated over a line to adopt, Frederick took events into his own hands and invaded Lower Silesia. He expected his action to force the French into a positive anti-Austrian alliance aimed at the dismemberment of the Habsburg Empire. In this, as might be expected, he was wholly successful.

However much Fleury might hope for nothing beyond a defensive alliance the war party at the French court won the ear of Louis XV. Belle-Isle was given the Frankfurt embassy and threw himself into the job of arming Europe against Austria. Agreements were reached whereby Frederick II was to be guaranteed in possession of Lower Silesia: the Elector of Saxony was to have the larger part of Moravia and Upper Silesia: Bohemia and Upper Austria would go to the new Emperor Charles Albert of Bavaria (Charles VII): the Italian inheritance would be shared between Spain and Sardinia. France would clearly seek the prize of the Austrian Netherlands. The French appreciated that three potential allies of Austria, Russia, the Dutch Republic and Britain, would have to be rendered ineffective. Russia could be prevented from intervention by a Swedish menace: the Dutch by the threat of invasion and Hanover would be immobilized by a stranglehold imposed by Prussia and the Elector Palatine (in French pay).

French involvement was almost immediate. The Prussians drove back to the Neisse an Austrian force at the battle of Mollwitz (5 April 1741): the Bavarians and a French force made their way down the Danube valley: in September 1741 Charles Albert entered Linz and was crowned Archduke of Austria. Within the month Upper Austria was in Bavarian hands and thence a Franco-Bavarian army advanced on Prague. At this point Maria Theresa threw herself upon the mercy of the Hungarian Diet and in return for inevitable concessions to the magnates, she secured men and some financing for two armies, one for the reconquest of Upper Austria, the other for Bohemia. Frederick the Great, convinced that the French were about to be defeated, assumed a low profile and the British began actively to negotiate peace terms at both Berlin and Vienna.

British diplomacy was responsible for the treaties of Breslau and Berlin wherein Frederick withdrew from the alliance against Maria Theresa in return for the cession to Prussia of Upper and Lower Silesia and the country of Glatz, a withdrawal which persuaded the Elector of Saxony to cease hostilities. It must have looked as if war was really coming to an end when the French surrendered Prague and a few days later Maria Theresa was proclaimed Queen of Bohemia. Bavaria also lay open to her.

At the root of Carteret's aspirations in 1743 was the formation of a kind of resurrected Grand Alliance (of Protestant and anti-Bourbon states) against France, an aspiration which, if realized, could serve England's colonial and commercial ambitions well. To this end, a remoulding of alignments amongst the German principalities was a prime necessity. The defeat of the French at Dettingen (June 1743) by the Pragmatic Army composed of English, Hanoverians and Hessians under Lord Stair and George II, frustrated French designs to prevent an Austrian occupation of Bavaria. It also allowed Carteret to pose as mediator in a tricky German situation wherein Austria was to be persuaded to evacuate the Palatinate and Bavaria, against the distant promises of Lorraine and the three German bishoprics when peace was made. Carteret's anti-Bourbon strategy had an Italian aspect epitomized in the Treaty of Worms (13 September 1743). This entailed an alliance with the slippery Charles Emmanuel of Sardinia, the price of which was an Austrian sacrifice of part of the Milanese in return for recognition of the Pragmatic Sanction. Secondly, it embodied an Austrian renunciation of claims against the rest of the Milanese and thirdly, made the promise that Britain would keep 45,000 men under arms in case of a further Bourbon offensive. In such a way Spanish and Italian claims to Maria Theresa's inheritance might be neutralized.

The strength of Carteret's alliances was apparent rather than real. Three factors contributed to a Prussian malaise about the permanence of the Silesian conquest. The first was the visible manifestation of a German alliance system emphatically outside the control of Prussia, the second, the apparent totality of Anglo-Austrian success in Germany, the third, a hastily constructed peace between Sweden and Russia after Sweden's disastrous failure to take Finland which promised the potential of a renewal of an Austro-Russian alliance (in fact made 26 July 1746). The Austrians were not enthusiastic about the results of English diplomacy. Silesia, Bavaria and the Palatinate in exchange for very long-term promises, all seemed immediate Austrian sacrifices whilst the British were merely held to subsidies for mercenary troops.

Relationships between Britain and Austria were strained long before the official rupture of 1756 but it was Frederick who pre-empted resumed international hostilities when he entered Saxony with 80,000 men and invaded Bohemia in late summer 1744. He did this having reaffirmed a treaty with Louis XV (now personally directing foreign affairs) and having agreed a protocol with Bavaria, the Palatinate and Hesse for the defence of the Emperor Charles VII and Germanic liberties. His action forced an immediate Austrian withdrawal from Bavaria, shattered Carteret's vision of a Germany mobilized against France and revealed the tenuousness of his schemes. Carteret now came under heavy barrage at home for the drain on the treasury of the promised subsidies. In December he was replaced by Harrington who, along with the majority of English ministers, was inclined towards a resumption of Walpole's policies. Given the advent of the Marquis d'Argenson as foreign minister in Paris, a known adversary of the Spanish connection, clearly change of some description was in the air.

In January 1745, Austria, Saxony, England and the Dutch Republic concluded an alliance. For the first two the enemy was Prussia, for the second, in large part, France. A cornerstone of Louis XV's war policy had been an offensive in the Low Countries and though, as yet, no real success could be reported on that front, the Dutch were edgy about French intentions in the Austrian Netherlands. In fact the second Silesian war was to see a shifting of French activity to that arena. The unexpected death of the Bavarian Charles VII in January 1745 saw his less ambitious son surrendering his pretensions to Austria and promising Francis Stephen, husband of Maria Theresa, his vote at the Imperial election which eliminated in unexpected fashion one nucleus of hostility. But May 1745 witnessed the battle of Fontenoy wherein the pragmatic Army was seriously defeated by Maréchal Saxe and a French occupation of the Austrian Netherlands began. A month later Frederick the Great defeated the Austrians and Saxons at the battle of Hohenfriedburg in Silesia.

By autumn of 1745 however the position of Maria Theresa looked once more very insecure. In one sense, the elimination of Bavaria and what seemed sure, the impending election of Francis Stephen as Emperor, rendered her German position about as healthy as she could have hoped. On the other hand, the defeat in Silesia (to be compounded by the battle of the Soor in Bohemia in September), the defeat of Charles Emmanuel before the French at Bassignano and his evident reluctance to continue an Austrian alliance (he was secretly intriguing with d'Argenson), and in addition English withdrawal from the Low Countries to cope with the '45 rebellion, clearly jeopardized other flanks of her empire. In December she was willing to conclude with Prussia a peace at Dresden ratifying the Treaty of Breslau on the point of the cession of Silesia and in return securing Prussian recognition of the election of Francis I.

For Prussia the war was effectively over but Austria had ends to tie as had Britain, the Dutch Republic, France and Sardinia. Of these, the British and French were now undoubtedly the two most widely involved and their record, as it stood in 1747, was roughly parallel. Neither could boast complete success but each had something to barter. The British, after the Jacobite defeat, had turned their efforts to the maritime war and the effective harrying of French traffic to and from the Antilles. French vessels were forced to adopt a convoy system with a minimum of four warships to a convoy, warships for which the merchantmen had to pay. Here the British enjoyed some success but probably of greater bargaining worth was the seizure of Fort Louisbourg on

Cape Breton Island regarded as the key to French existence in North America. The achievement was largely due to Commodore Warren and a squadron of three warships which cut off aid to the beleaguered fortress. The capture of Louisbourg meant possession of the most important French fort in North America, the potential destruction of French fisheries and the way lay open for an assault on Quebec, though an attempt to take that city failed hopelessly. To set against Louisbourg, however, was a mounting toll of disasters. Not least of these were the capitulation of Madras, besieged by the governor of Pondicherry, Dupleix, in September 1746, and several abortive attempts to effect landings on the Mediterranean and Atlantic coasts.

The French, on the other hand, assiduously pursued the conquest of the Austrian Netherlands until by the end of 1746 there only remained to Maria Theresa, Luxembourg and Limbourg with Maastricht. There followed, in April 1747, a declaration of war against the Dutch Republic and a French invasion of Zeeland. Successful though this manoeuvre proved to be, it also provoked an internal revolt within Zeeland which proclaimed William IV of Orange stadtholder, a move which rendered improbable an early peace between France and the Republic. English subsidies were provided to help the Republic. Cumberland, leading English troops, was however persuaded of the necessity of an early peace with the French and Maurice de Saxe, leader of victorious French forces, was no less convinced. Hence eventual weariness made possible the Treaty of Aix-la-Chapelle.

The price of French evacuation of the Netherlands and the cession of Madras to the British was the restoration of Louisbourg. The Caribbean question was nominally resolved by declaring neutral four disputed islands – Dominica, Saint Lucia, Saint Vincent and Tobago. Prussia was guaranteed in the possession of Silesia: the Pragmatic Sanction was to be maintained in Austria: the House of Hanover was to retain the succession in its German possessions and in Great Britain. Parma, Piacenza and Guastella were ceded to the Spanish infante Don Philip, against a barrage of reversion clauses. What is evident is that, with the possible exception of Frederick the Great, no one had any cause for satisfaction. The problems of the end were quintessentially those of the beginning. Peace had been achieved because Britain and France wanted a breathing space but the power struggle in the Caribbean, in North America, in India, had not been resolved. Similarly the contest with Spain over contraband and the Asiento had no resolution, though matters were patched up in 1748 by a four-year prolongation of the concession. Minorca and Gibraltar were not mentioned in the treaty. Sardinia gained some territory between Lake Maggiore and the Po but no outlet to the Ligurian coast. Most dissatisfied of all was Maria Theresa. Humiliated by Prussia over Silesia, she felt she had been pushed into peace by an unsatisfactory ally who had made no sacrifices and could not even be relied upon to keep promises (she was particularly resentful over the English failure to defend the Netherlands) and who, moreover, had encumbered her with totally unsatisfactory allies. High on Maria Theresa's list of grievances was the Treaty of Worms which had linked the fate of her Italian possessions with the slippery Charles Emmanuel. This was no lasting amnesty.

Whilst imperial powers indulged fancifully in the belief that colonies were passive executors of the policies of the mother country, in fact, the War of Jenkins's Ear had demonstrated that something like the reverse was true. Moreover, the War of the Austrian Succession had set the seal on future international conflict by underscoring Franco-British rivalry in India, by demonstrating the vulnerability of New France at the peace treaty and by the recalcitrance of the French in evacuating the 'neutral islands'. New conflict was in fact pre-empted by the activities of the settlers of the North American mainland and the focal points for hostility were the Ohio valley and the area to the south of Lake Ontario and Lake Erie. Both these areas were ones in which 'British' and 'French' colonists entertained territorial ambitions. The push towards Lake Ontario and Lake Erie was directed by Pennsylvanian settlers (largely Irish, German and Dutch) and their thrust into Illinois territory was marked by the construction of Fort Pickawillany. In the Ohio valley a number of rich Virginian planter families, amongst whom were counted both the Lees and the Washingtons, had formed a land company and this, the Ohio Company, founded in 1748, was given a crown grant of half a million acres.

Such activities came into head-on collision with the ambitions of New France, or more precisely with the policy formulated by La Galissonière, dynamic intendant of New France. His policy was intended to raise New France in the league of colonial values held in the mother country by presenting it as the point of departure for a new French empire. This empire was conceived as a sphere of interest extending from New France, south through Illinois and the Ohio valley and down towards Louisiana and the Gulf of Mexico and France's Caribbean possessions. Such a scheme, argued La Galissonière, would block the way to British domination of North America and the Caribbean.

The science of hindsight is a precise one: La Galissoniere's project was a non-starter. In time of war a power which held both the Saint Lawrence and the Gulf of Mexico and most of the coastal strip between could cut the lifelines of such an empire. In terms of manpower the French did not have enough immigrants to settle the Ohio valley. What gave it credibility was the determination with which the initial French thrust succeeded in ousting British settlers, and the good relationship between French traders and the Indian warrior tribes of the Ohio region who preferred traders to settlers and hence were less suspicious of

French than Virginian settlers. Fort Pickawillany was destroyed in 1752. French forts were rapidly constructed over the next two years and an attempt by a small force of colonial militia, led by George Washington, to arrest the construction of Fort Duquesne (on the present site of Pittsburgh) was repulsed. It was abundantly clear that the soldiers of French Canada, however sparse in number, could make real progress against 'British' colonists, some of whom were pacifist by conviction; most of whom were prepared to make no monetary or personal sacrifices for defence and whose inter-state jealousies and suspicions made nonsense of a common policy. Cognizant of this, the British government in 1754 dispatched two regiments of British regulars under General Braddock. Tragically for them they were promptly marched, after a long sea voyage, through settled Virginia into the unsettled and mountainous region to take Fort Duquesne which had been fortified by the French against their arrival. Over one thousand perished in the crossfire. British humiliation seemed complete. Yet worse was to come when Admiral Boscawen failed to prevent all but two ships of the French fleet carrying reinforcements entering the Saint Lawrence. Moreover in the Marquis de Montcalm the French had a commander of exceptional talent who in 1755 went so far as to capture Oswego, a British trading centre on Lake Ontario.

Taken altogether, this was war in all but name. What was abundantly clear, given the contrast between the coherent French and the disparate, quarrelling 'British' colonists, was that the British government would need to move in troops on an unprecedented scale if the French were to be overcome. This was no pleasant prospect for a nation lacking an extensive standing army. In full cognizance of this unpalatable truth, the British declared war on France in January 1756, a conflict which merged, a few, diplomatically-harrowing months later into the Seven Years' War.

For the diplomatic historian, who knew his heyday in the first half of this century when European history *was* diplomatic history, the diplomatic overtures to the Seven Years' War were paradise indeed. So complex, so unpredictable, so oscillating were the relationships between the powers which finally culminated in a series of alliances quite at variance with the alignments of the War of the Austrian Succession that the diplomatic events of 1750–6 have been called the 'Diplomatic Revolution', a rather grandiose designation obscuring an important truth. The powers with major irreconcilable interests in the mid-eighteenth century were Britain and France, on the one hand, Austria and Prussia on the other, and in no way did diplomatic events alter that fundamental principle. The so-called 'Diplomatic Revolution' meant a shift in the relationship between Austria and France, states with historic rivalries, and in the one between Britain and Prussia, which involved little fundamental change in reasoning because it involved no real sacrifice of principle. It was perhaps accidental that Britain and Prussia had not found common ground before during the War of the Austrian Succession. Certainly Fleury had been convinced that Austria and France might do so. Moreover, Austria in the course of the war had experienced real dissatisfaction with her British ally and the French, particularly after the Bohemian fiasco of 1743 when left high and dry by the Prussians, had cause to regard a Prussian ally with some circumspection. In eighteenth-century diplomacy fidelity did not stand for very much: antipathy and permanent interests were the only constant deciding factors. Europe had yet to acquire a diplomatic morality.

In Europe the re-acquisition of Silesia by Austria remained the overriding obsession of the Habsburg monarchy, which saw itself pushed towards internal financial reorganization and massive mobilization. The Austrian government also was ready to construct an alliance system which would menace Prussia and protect Austrian interests in the Netherlands and Italy. Since 1746 Austria had been in pursuit of an alliance with the Empress Elizabeth of Russia, Frederick the Great's personal enemy, promising an adjustment of the Polish-Russian frontier to give Russia control over Courland, compensating Poland with East Prussia. Such an alliance was the basis of Austrian diplomacy simply because it promised something no other alliance could – that is the needful retention of Prussian forces in an area other than Silesia which would ward off potential invasion into Habsburg territory. Convinced of England's lack of commitment to Austrian interests in the Netherlands and Italy, Kaunitz, Maria Theresa's minister between 1750–52, made a mission to Versailles to explore the possibilities of a French alliance against Prussia, the possible price of which would be some boundary concession along the frontier with the Austrian Netherlands. He was to return partially disillusioned to Vienna, thwarted, he had reason to believe, by *le secret du roi*. *Le secret du roi* is the expression used to describe a plan or scheme for the conduct of foreign policy which existed in the mind of Louis XV who, since the death of Fleury, had actively preoccupied himself with foreign affairs. Such a plan was secret as all diplomatic strategy was intended in essence to be. It was also highly academic. Louis XV's scheme consisted of a Franco-Polish alliance (Saxony and Poland being one) to stand as buffer to Russian pretensions along the Polish frontier, to which Prussia (to assume in the long run Hanover) would be forced to accede. A system of German alliances would enforce Austrian neutrality and hence would allow France to concentrate her entire efforts upon the most pressing issue of foreign policy, the defeat of Britain. Hence Louis XV and his advisers, Conti and the Comte de Broglie, envisaged no severance with Prussia but rather a diplomacy in which Prussia would be forced to act under French direction. Kaunitz did not understand the entire *secret* (perhaps no one did) but he picked up at least the idea that Austria was not in the forefront of French priorities.

The French monarchy was not of course unique in its personal, proprietary attitude towards its nation's diplomacy. The conviction that foreign policy must be secret, and hence the personal work of an individual, not a committee or even a lesser individual than the monarch himself, was a European commonplace. The implications of such an attitude were of course enormous. Where a king really was a logical and informed thinker about foreign policy, in the way Frederick the Great proved to be, then he indeed made his own decisions and was his own best diplomat. Where he was not, then a theoretically absolute monarch found himself in the hands of advisers who were invariably favourites: and where favourites existed so did factions ready to catch the ear of the king. If this was a dilemma of the French monarchy, it was yet more that of the Russian monarchy. The Empress Elizabeth allowed herself to be pushed now in the direction of a British alliance, now in the direction of a French connection, by the rival factions of the ageing Bestuzhev-Riumin (grand chancellor) and his enemy Vorontsev (vice-chancellor). Ironically enough, it was the Russians who shaped the course of diplomatic history in 1756 and the 'Diplomatic Revolution' can convincingly be represented as a Russian accident.

Britain's continuing obsession with the safety of Hanover in the event of conflict with France (potentially entailing a repeat of the experience of the War of the Austrian Succession) led in spring 1755 to a number of British diplomatic overtures at Vienna. The hardheadedness of Maria Theresa's line in some ways took the British aback. She put to the British a number of proposals as her terms for coming to British assistance in the event of a Prussian attack upon Hanover. Firstly, to guarantee the safety of Hanover and the Netherlands, Britain must employ German mercenaries and further finance 60,000 Russian troops who would be ready to attack Prussia in the event of a Prussian attack upon Habsburg territories. If such guarantees were offered, Austria promised to come to the assistance of Britain in Hanover.

Britain had some months previously abandoned an attempt at negotiation with Russia but clearly, in view of Austria's terms, the attempt must be made again and Hanbury-Williams was sent to St Petersburg with a view to concluding a subsidy agreement. To forestall such an agreement became the first concern of Frederick the Great and Hanbury-Williams's mission in fact saw the first Prussian tentatives towards an Anglo-Prussian agreement which would ensure Hanover's immunity from Prussian aggression. But Prussian overtures were cautiously received in London which waited upon the events of Hanbury-Williams' negotiations and sure enough, by August the latter thought he had an agreement with Russia. This provided for British maintenance of 55,000 Russian troops near the borders of East Prussia to be maintained at a cost of about £100,000 per annum which would rise to £400,000 if they should be called upon to cross the Russian frontier. But, the Russian Empress made certain conditions which in the long run Britain could not accept. The first demanded a decision in the peace-making: the second demanded three months' notice before Russian troops passed into foreign territory (so that they could be replaced from troops elsewhere in the Empire) and the third precluded the use of the Russian troops at all if the cause of European hostilities was a war confined only to America or Italy. Clearly the Russians were concerned only with a Prussian conflict but the accelerating pace of incidents in North America during the summer of 1755 rendered the English cognizant that for them this would be the arena of war and what, in the meantime, would be the fate of Hanover? Rumours filtered into Berlin that some Anglo-Russian alliance had been made, or was in process of completion and British nervousness plus Prussia's uncomfortable ignorance made possible the Convention of Westminster (January 1756), a treaty of neutrality between Britain and Prussia. For the Empress Elizabeth this was the end of the British alliance – though Vorontsev had yet to steer her towards a positive French connection.

In May 1756 Kaunitz succeeded in convincing Versailles that an Austrian, not a Prussian, alliance could best serve French interests in the defeat of Britain. The result looked good for Austria. In the event of an Anglo-French war she promised what in any case she intended, neutrality. In return she received a French promise not to invade the Netherlands. If the European possessions of either Louis XV or Maria Theresa were attacked, the offended party had the right to demand 40,000 troops of the other. A secret clause provided for conflict between France and Prussia which might arise if France attacked Hanover and Prussia under the Convention of Westminster came to Britain's assistance. In this event Austria would help the French and by this the Austrians understood they would attack Prussia in Silesia. This indeed was exactly what the Austrians wanted because they could then summon Russian aid to attack East Prussia. It looked neat enough but there were decided flaws. France did not want to see an extension of Russian influence in Poland and the Baltic area. Not withstanding, the imminence of conflict with Britain in America meant that she was at least prepared to countenance Vorontsev's overtures for diplomatic negotiation and ambassadors were exchanged.

With news of a Franco-Austro-Russian agreement reverberating in his ears, Frederick the Great was precipitated into aggressive activity convinced that if he allowed them time all might be lost but that as yet neither France, Russia nor Austria was prepared to take the offensive against him. When he took this decision, he could not have known that Austria, believing herself unready for imminent attack on Prussia (she estimated 40–50,000 more troops were needed than the 67,000 she had already since Prussia had 150,000 men under arms), had informed Russia that concerted action could not be taken until spring of 1757 and Elizabeth had reluctantly, and with considerable ire, called a halt to the massing of troops on the East Prussian frontier. In August 1756 Frederick took his enemies by surprise. He invaded Saxony (the Elector of Saxony was King of Poland) with 67,000 men and took Dresden (2 September). He was en route to Bohemia. At Lobositz, an Austrian force tried to repel his entry into Bohemia and tie him down in Saxony. It was defeated and the Saxons (some 18,000) capitulated at Pirna. Complex treaty arrangements were called into effect and in January 1757, the Austrians and the French signed an offensive treaty.

The moot question of 1756–7 was not the strength of the Franco-Austro-Russian alliance but the effectiveness of that of Prussia and Britain. In a sense the Convention of Westminster, designed to protect Hanover, had become astonishingly obsolete. At war with the three foremost military powers of Europe, Frederick was hardly well-placed to assist Hanover. British public opinion was split between the belief (of William Pitt and the City) that Hanover and Prussia should be abandoned to their fate and Newcastle's line that French energies were dissipated on a European offensive. The second approach gave some credence to a policy of 'conquering America in Germany' which could only be done by a subsidy policy to Hanover, Brunswick and Hesse. Time was shown to be of the essence and the British had delayed too long. France by mid-1757 had an army 100,000 strong marching on Hanover which defeated the British and Hanoverian forces at Hastenbeck and forced the Convention of Kloster-Zeven wherein Britain promised to pull the Hanoverian army out of the war. In any case Hanover was largely abandoned to French occupation and hence central Prussia exposed to a French invasion.

But this was not to happen. In June 1757 Frederick the Great had been badly defeated at the battle of Kolin whereupon he was obliged to evacuate Bohemia. His other forces under Marshal Lehwaldt sustained a defeat at Russian hands (at Gross Jaegersdorf) which seemed to promise the loss of East Prussia, and to crown all, Pomerania was invaded by Sweden. It also seemed as if the French advance of 55,000 men under Soubise would take Leipzig and that Saxony would be wrested from Frederick. This event was forestalled in perhaps the greatest of Frederick's victories over the French at Rossbach on 5 November 1757, and over Austria at Leuthen a month later, wherein something like 50,000 Austrian troops were lost or deserted. Confronted with such spectacular success, William Pitt radically revised his thinking and pressed for the formal abnegation of the Kloster-Zeven agreement. From then on, there was no separate British-Hanoverian policy. Not that an agreement between Britain and Prussia was speedily completed. Frederick wanted British help in the shape of a Baltic fleet to curtail

Swedish and Russian activities but Britain would not thus jeopardize the naval supplies needed for an American offensive. Britain thought in terms of a subsidy treaty and finally Frederick accepted the £670,000, the largest sum ever accorded by Britain to a continental state, which kept the mercenary armies of Ferdinand of Brunswick supplied until the death of George II. From then on for the British the spirit of the war was encapsulated in the phrase 'a war of usury in Europe and of territorial conquest overseas' – a bifurcated conflict in which Prussia confronted Austria and Russia and English-Hanoverian mercenaries neutralized the French in Europe so that the real war for Britain and France could take place overseas.

From Britain's viewpoint the war in Europe was but a sideshow and William Pitt as effective director of the war offensive incarnated the national viewpoint. It was Pitt who believed, and had done so as early as 1746, in the conquest of Canada as a means to securing the British North American colonies, gaining the fisheries and cutting off French naval supplies. He was a perfect convert to the implausibilities of La Galissonière's schemes. On the other hand, his basic interest was trade rather than territorial acquisition and his war plans embraced schemes for capturing the most lucrative branches of trade which, it could be argued, would justify war expenditure. Not until 1758 was he able to reverse Britain's fortunes on the American continent and when he did so, his success was in large part attributable to the unity of direction and clear grasp of strategy.

The plan was simply for a section of the British fleet to shut up the French navy in Brest and Toulon so that no relief forces could sail for America. This would make possible a three-fold thrust. The first part of the thrust was to be an attack on Louisbourg as a prelude to taking Quebec: the next an attack on Fort Duquesne in the contested Ohio lands and the third an attack on Montreal. The first part of the plan was a total success after a seven-week siege and heavy bombardments. The second resulted in the French themselves burning the fort and retreating. Military ineptitude on the part of General Abercromby cost the British the immediate seizure of Montreal by a disaster at Ticonderoga. Nevertheless, New France's days were numbered. In 1759 Amherst was instructed to seize Fort Niagara, and hence to sever another important strand in the Ohio scheme. Then, Brigadier-General Wolfe took an assault force to capture Quebec, heart of French Canada. The taking of Quebec (June 1759) is attributable to many factors: amongst them the high quality and experience of British forces, the excellence of Wolfe's command, the naval expertise of Charles Saunders in navigating the Saint Lawrence, the perspicacity of William Pitt in having ordered the charting of the river as an essential preliminary, the failure of the French to buttress a falling New France with fresh supplies of men, and the division of the French command between the personal rivalries of the Marquis de Vaudreuil, Governor General, and the Marquis de Montcalm, commander of the French regulars. The surrender of Quebec was certainly the most decisive episode in the collapse of New France. All that was really left was the surrender of Montreal which came in September 1760 and its collapse was complete.

Never very far from a central preoccupation for the British government were events in the Caribbean and probably only the successful blocking of the French fleet in Brest and Toulon purchased for the British the luxury of not having immediately to contest an American war on two fronts. The fall of Louisbourg however gave Pitt the opportunity to turn to the French sugar islands which were of immense value to French trade, with a view to capturing some important bargaining counters for the peace negotiations and to ensuring that if French vessels did run the blockade, they would concentrate their efforts upon relieving the Caribbean and not on coming to the assistance of Canada. Already in 1758 French slaving stations along the Senegal river in West Africa had been seized and this was tantamount, in the long run, to starving the French West Indies of manpower. British planters, hostile to the idea of having their trade undercut, were unenthusiastic about Caribbean conquest, but Martinique, as a nest of privateers, was a different proposition. It was against Martinique and Guadeloupe that 6000 British troops and a naval escort were instructed to direct their efforts in 1758. Guadeloupe proved easy to take, though the climate and disease soon took their toll of the invading force. The articles of capitulation drawn up by the victorious British allowed freedom of trade within the British Empire and precluded British planters from moving in until the signing of the peace. Certainly they did not undertake the destruction of the French plantations which British planters regarded as a total betrayal of their interests. Martinique did not fall until 1762. Dominica had by then already fallen, and Saint Lucia, Saint Vincent and Grenada were also taken. All this had been made possible by the naval victories of Lagos and Quiberon Bay in 1759 after which there was no effective French fleet.

British success was everywhere apparent. The tardy entry of Spain into the war in January 1762 which was largely attributable to the anxiety of the new monarch Charles III over British success in the Caribbean, and the reforming of a family compact with France, could only be described, in Glyndwr Williams's words, as 'not far from being suicidal' for Spain. The British took Havana, key to Spain's Caribbean empire and then, in 1763, Manila, centre of Spain's Pacific dominions. Even this, however, looked small beer in comparison with British advances in India under Robert Clive, 'Britain's heaven-born general' as Pitt described him. Clive, at the battle of Plassey (1757), virtually destroyed French claims in India, established British control in Bengal and achieved decided victories on the Carnatic including the seizure of Pondicherry (1759).

Yet the British were anxious to make peace. The war had stretched the financial resources of every participant to a degree none had deemed possible and Britain was no exception. Political machinations and the death of George II resulted in 1762 in Pitt's resignation and his replacement by Bute. The withdrawal of Russia from the war and the Duc de Choiseul's peace overtures were all pressures to cease hostilities. And what a curious peace the Peace of Paris (1763) was to be. Explicable only by some perverse persuasion that to inflict too great a defeat on France was to store up wars eternal, French losses were in no way commensurate with the extent of French defeat. To Pitt, the Peace was a waste of all Britain had achieved. He too believed in the possibility of a Bourbon war of revenge but he believed it would come regardless of the terms of a settlement and he was to be proved right.

The debating point of the Peace was whether the British should cede the Caribbean islands of Guadeloupe and Martinique or Canada to the French. The ministers had few doubts that if Canada were returned it would have made total nonsense of the war. Choiseul offered to Britain the cession of all French possessions on the mainland and to Bute this meant that mainland America was now secure. On the other hand the French were given back their fishing rights on the Grand Banks of Newfoundland and the sugar islands of Guadeloupe and Martinique. This was certainly to the satisfaction of the British sugar interest though they would have preferred the destruction of the plantations. The West Indian islands of Grenada, Dominica and Tobago were retained by Britain as were Senegal and most important Indian conquests. Louisiana, ceded by France to Britain, was exchanged with Spain for Florida and Havana was restored to the Spanish. Anglo-Spanish commercial treaties were renewed. To Pitt, Canada without the fisheries was nothing. Perhaps he exaggerated their worth but of the unsatisfactory nature of the Peace, there can be little doubt.

Some of the flaws of the Treaty were unanticipated. Certainly the balance of greatness as a colonial power had been tipped in favour of Britain and perhaps the most significant question to ask about the Seven Years' War is why France was so unsuccessful? To this question there is no quick or simple answer. To Alfred Cobban the 'Peace of Paris was the price paid for government by weak and wavering ministerial groups and court factions'.[1] This is fair criticism given the court intrigues which had replaced d'Estrées, the victorious French general who had forced Cumberland into the Convention of Kloster-Zeven, by the Duc de Richelieu, who had squandered French triumphs in Hanover, dissipated the French army's strength and made possible Prussian victory

---

1 A. Cobban, *A History of Modern France* (London, 1962), p. 77.

at Rossback which Napoleon reckoned to be the single most important event in the collapse of the French monarchy. Equally apparent was the unpreparedness of French sea-power which resulted in the severance of the mother country from her empire. Perhaps too the Austrian alliance was a mistake when French aims were so patently predominantly anti-British, though that alliance was not to be formally abandoned until 1789. Lastly, how did one really come to grips with the British? In the course of the Seven Years' War, the French had come progressively to believe in the use of an invasion force. The lack of an effective standing army in Britain must render such a strategy wholly successful, if once a landing could be effected. It is significant that within two months of concluding peace, Choiseul was at work upon the construction of a naval force and speculating upon a suitable landing place. Very clearly the Peace of Paris was not to be of lasting duration.

The Peace of Paris and the Treaty of Hubertusburg mark the most significant dichotomy in eighteenth-century diplomatic history because they mark the point at which the two issues, the colonial and overseas preoccupations of England, France and Spain, and the ambitions and rivalries of the three eastern European powers, were suddenly and logically severed as *casus belli*. Both France and Britain turned their backs on Germany. The decision so to do was largely a financial one. The British would have liked the existence of some alliance which would somehow have protected Hanover but politicians clearly recoiled before the harsh economic practicalities of a subsidy treaty – and no east European power would defend Hanover for nothing. The French had sustained a very costly defeat and had emerged with the conviction that France's best interests, her economic future and her prestige, would best be served by a low profile in German affairs so as to muster all her energies to reconstruct a trading empire. This entailed above all the building of a new navy to reverse the experience of the Seven Years' War. The abandoning of German preoccupations gave the French a new single-mindedness. Since the Spanish were also intent upon a war of revenge to gain restitution of Gibraltar and Minorca, the family compact held firm. Such firmness however was made to operate in French favour. The French adamantly refused to be pre-empted into aggression by the Spanish before they were ready and hence the decision not to back Spain in 1770 on the issue of Spanish claims to sovereignty over the Falkland Islands.

Attitudes in eastern Europe also contributed to a quieter period in diplomatic relations. The immediate reason for this was financial exhaustion – though this did not mean any real reduction in armed forces. Indeed, for Joseph II, a lesson of the Seven Years' War was the inadequacy of the numbers under arms and the need to bring yet more into the military. But it did mean some recognition that a war to reconquer Silesia was not within Habsburg means. Frederick the Great had come close to disaster: perhaps only good fortune had prevented him from having to face a joint Austro-Russian attack. Rapprochement with the Habsburgs was not a reality and in 1784 the Prussian army was to ensure that the Habsburgs did not extend their influence within the Empire by exchanging Bavaria for the Netherlands. Nevertheless, the War of the Bavarian Succession was not for Prussia a war of conquest. Moreover, through Russian intermediacy, a degree of concerted action between Habsburg and Hohenzollern on the Polish issue became possible.

Russia in fact was the pace-maker of eastern European diplomacy after 1763. In part this was due to her ambitions in two areas, Poland and the Ottoman Empire, both contiguous to Russian territory, where putative gains could be made without necessarily incurring protracted military commitment. These now became the focal points of east European activity. Perhaps most significantly of all, in the twenty years after the Seven Years' War only Russia, in spite of the myth of an ever-bellicose Frederick the Great, was prepared to put an army into the field. Hence for the first time in our period, the much invoked principle of the balance of power had some reality to be perfectly demonstrated in the amoral dismembering of Poland in which the three eastern European giants acted in unison, none of the three ceding an inch in rapaciousness to the other two. These partitions demonstrated that the old concept of the balance of power based upon the idea of equitability of power for action had been redefined to emerge as a right to an equality of shares in any spoils. As Vergennes, the French foreign minister, remarked: 'for two centuries the great powers have concentrated their entire attention, often to the point of exhausting all their resources, on preventing any one of them from becoming preponderant. Now a new combination has replaced the system of general balance; three powers have set up one of their own. It is based on the equality of their usurpation and thus the balance of power is made to tip heavily in their favour.'

In short, whilst one part of Europe moved into the bitterest struggle to date for the forging or retention of a transatlantic empire in which the key factor was to be, yet again, the colonists themselves, the other side moved still further in the direction of empire building in the fluid frontier regions of eastern Europe.

That conflict between Britain and France was slow in materializing after 1763 in the west reflected more than anything else fiscal pressures. Even Britain experienced strain. The national debt had almost doubled from £70m to £130m: the land tax had risen to four shillings in the pound. Country gentlemen were hence paying out more than 15 per cent of their incomes in land tax and the government was involved in the introduction of new and highly unpopular taxes and in tightening up on any conceivable anomaly in the English customs system. Nothing in fact in the domestic or international sphere can be understood without constant reference to government penny-pinching in the aftermath of the Seven Years' War. Though Choiseul was convinced of the inevitability of imminent conflict and was striving to reconstruct the French navy (from 35 battered ships of the line in 1763 to 64 ships and 50 frigates in 1771) some of this had to be done by public subscription in view of the financial straits of the government. Choiseul initially projected a war for the reconstitution of some kind of Caribbean-based French empire with a possible reconquest of Senegal and Indian possessions which would take place within five years of the Peace of Paris. Hard financial thinking however determined France's powers of action and in 1770 Choiseul's Grand Design received a significant check from the *contrôleur général*, Terray. Choiseul, anxious to demonstrate to the British the strength of the Family Compact, was ready to support the Spanish in their claims against Britain to the Falkland Islands. To this, Terray opposed the near bankruptcy of French finances. Choiseul tried a policy of attributing this to the financial ineptitude of the *contrôleur général* but was abandoned by the king and stripped of his office.

In short, French foreign policy between 1763–76 was essentially low key and this subdued tone was due to the force of financial circumstances. Yet it could not be argued that any considerable change had taken place in royal finances by 1776 when the American colonies revolted against Great Britain. French anglophobia clearly dictated a strongly sympathetic line towards the rebels. A handful of French volunteers (including the young Lafayette) almost immediately crossed the Atlantic, to help the colonists' cause. By 1778 when it was apparent that the colonists were more than holding their own (after the capture of the British army led by Burgoyne at Saratoga) the French foreign minister, Vergennes, and the American envoy to Paris, Benjamin Franklin, had negotiated treaties of alliance and commerce between France and the American colonies. France agreed to enter the war and not make peace until American independence was achieved: to give up all claims to North America east of the Mississippi and in return was given a free hand in the Caribbean. Much of French help on the American continent proper was to be in the form of subsidies and these were gradually to be reimbursed by American tobacco and by favoured trading agreements between the two countries. Certainly the French expected a grateful North America to look to her for the manufactured goods currently furnished by Britain. Hence there was far more in the French entry into the war than mere revenge or philosophical notions about liberty and the answer to the question why did France get involved and hence clinch American success must take account of Caribbean and trade ambitions. The marriage between the American colonists and France was largely one of convenience. Indeed, in the course of the war, French preoccupations in the Caribbean were to infuriate the colonists.

Britain's quarrel with the American mainland colonies had an ineluctable quality about it. Attempts after 1763 to cut down the costs of maintaining them by a package of measures raised thorny constitutional problems within colonial assemblies which enjoyed a good deal of autonomy and were persuaded that arbitrary taxation was destructive of the power of representative institutions. These measures included defusing relations with the Indians by a proclamation guaranteeing that unofficial white settlement west of the Appalachians would be controlled and hence Indian land protected – a decision hardly coincident with the expansionist ambitions of the colonists – and efforts to raise revenues by taxes on foreign imported sugar and then by a stamp duty (1765). The absence of a French enemy making Britain indispensable was clearly important. At the same time, Britain's efforts to keep relations with French Canadians fairly harmonious by the Quebec Act which extended the boundaries of Canada to the Ohio river – hence severing the claims of Massachusetts, New York and Connecticut – were interpreted as a misplacement of favours. Incidents over efforts to regulate the importation of tea by according the East India Company a monopoly of supply resulted in the incident known as the Boston Tea Party which destroyed one such consignment. The formulation of radical politics was given practical form in September 1774 when the first continental Congress assembled at Philadelphia and the radicals, led by Samuel Adams, triumphed over the conservative elements, drawing up a declaration of rights which demanded the repeal of thirteen existing acts (including the Quebec Act) and denouncing revenue-raising acts. At the same time commercial relations with Britain were severed. Five months later the first shots were fired at Lexington.

Could war have really been averted? Probably not. The American colonies had reached a degree of political maturity and were possessed of economic ambitions which must bring them inevitably into conflict with the intrusive authority of a mother country to whom they were only tenuously committed. Emphatically the American colonies could not be squeezed within the confines of the Old Colonial System and the scale of relationships with the mother country dictated by the colonial philosophy we have described. But for Britain, an old philosophy clearly could not be discarded without another to take its place. Colonial refusals to co-operate on defence gradually sucked England into armed repression and a war she was doomed to lose.

Why did Britain lose the war? The American population was only about 2 million strong: that of Britain stood at about 8 million. British soldiers, or whatever mercenaries they dispatched, were trained regulars in stark contrast to the American forces. Moreover, Britain possessed much more developed armaments industries. That said, however, the odds were heavily against Britain. At the beginning of the war Britain maintained only a small military force in America. By the time a larger force had been assembled and transported across the Atlantic, a regular army had had time to train and to work out a strategy. British offensives were to reveal how great were the problems of supplying and co-ordinating troop movements across the Atlantic and over a large land area with very primitive communications. Britain was confronted with the enormous and unfamiliar basic problem of winning a war when it was needful not merely to defeat an enemy army and occupy the main centres, but to subjugate a civilian population as well. Moreover this civilian population believed in British defeat and hence for the British it was not so much a matter of putting down a rebellion as of effecting a reconquest. All this applied before the entry of the French and Spanish into the war in 1776. But their entry obviously multiplied British troubles. Now it was Britain who was menaced with a war on several fronts: in European waters, in the Caribbean and in India. Initially Vergennes chose to concentrate French efforts upon the Caribbean.

In June 1779 Spain entered the war intent upon the reacquisition of Gibraltar and Minorca and hence a combined naval force superior to that of Great Britain had to be reckoned with. Although a Franco-Spanish invasion of Britain in 1779 proved abortive, this diversion into home waters meant the retention of forces on this side of the Atlantic and, to add to Britain's confusion, war broke out with the Dutch Republic after disputes over the Dutch supply of naval stores to France and Spain. In the same year the Armed Neutrality of the North – an alliance between Russia, Sweden, Prussia, Denmark and Portugal – contested Britain's authority to stop them, as neutral powers, supplying the colonies. Against such odds there was little hope for Britain.

To what extent was American victory attributable to French inter-vention? The colonists' performance was aided by the fact that England had to face a war on several fronts, and that the French navy was able to keep America supplied with arms (probably Dutch in origin). Most crucial of all, perhaps, was the role of the French in the battle of Yorktown, singly the most important episode in the war. Even without French intervention, however, it is a fine point if any long-term victory in North America could ever have accrued to the British.

British loss of naval superiority was accompanied by depressing news from India where a strong combination of Indian rulers with French encouragement were rapidly destroying British power, and from the West Indies where Admiral de Grasse one by one took St Kitts, Mon-tserrat, Nevis and was preparing to attack Jamaica. Only a brilliant victory by Admiral Rodney, the battle of the Saints, in April 1782 saved Jamaica, and the same admiral was responsible for the defence of Gibraltar. Rodney's successes gave Britain something approaching bargaining power at the peace negotiations towards which public opinion and political desperation impelled her.

The negotiations were conducted on Britain's behalf by Lord Shelburne, a curiously unsuccessful politician whom posterity has judged an adroit negotiator, and one who looked to the future, not the past. Influenced by the new school of economists led by Adam Smith, he believed that what mattered was good commercial relations between Britain and the new American state and to that end he opposed French and Spanish moves to restrict the United States to the Atlantic littoral and defined it as the land south of the Great Lakes, north of Florida and westward of the Mississippi. A growing nation must be free to open up the west. Canada and Nova Scotia remained British, Louisiana, French, and Florida, Spanish. Vergennes, faced with French financial problems, found Shelburne more sympathetic than his Spanish allies who pressed preposterous claims. Britain, the American issue solved, could hold her own in the Caribbean and indeed most French conquests (except Tobago and Saint Lucia) were restored. France regained Senegal, though her main disappointment was in India where Vergennes had hoped to open up new spheres of influence and found himself reduced to a restoration of the trading stations and a strip around Pondicherry. Spain regained Minorca but did not edge the British out of the Gulf of Honduras.

For France the purchase price of British defeat was a constitutional and fiscal crisis which was to topple government, a long-term effect which no one could have foreseen but which demonstrates the degree to which the increasingly demanding commitment to trade, empire and allied interests dictated the pace of western European political life.

On the other side of the world whilst Britain and France were preparing to fight this totally debilitating duel, the fate of Poland hung in the balance. The idea of a partition of Poland did not suddenly emerge in the aftermath of the Seven Years' War for it had throughout that war been the *leitmotif* of Russian involvement in the hope of making an adjustment of the Russo-Polish frontier and, initially, of stripping Prussia of Polish Prussia. Grainlands, significant rivers, important Baltic ports were obviously prizes to be coveted even before one considers that Prussia was severed by Polish territory or that Zips, a Polish enclave, was contiguous to Hungary. Poland was to be picked off, leaf by leaf, as Frederick the Great put it, for several reasons, to be summarized under the headings internal weakness and external cupidity. In Poland aristocratic constitutionalism had run amok. An elective monarchy and an administration run by a senate and the *Seym*, the one composed of the greatest magnates, the other of their henchmen or nominees amongst the *szlachta* or gentry, ensured anarchy. In the *Seym* each individual had the right to nullify proceedings by his personal vote, the *liberum veto*. The king's control could only be purchased by rewarding the members of the Senate with pensions and sinecures and hence constructing a patronage network. Such control was purely fictional: the great magnates were virtually sovereign in their own palatinate and the *szlachta* would not budge an inch without them. This system was not productive of an effective national army – 18,500 officers and men could hardly confront the hundreds of thousands of men Russia, Prussia and Austria could jointly put into the field – nor, and this was a closely related question, of a substantial national revenue. Three-quarters of the population were serfs labouring under crippling *corvées* with detrimental effects for the national revenue which had to be raised by levies on merchants and trade and by extraordinary taxes on Jews and minorities. In any case, money was in extremely short supply.

Since 1733 the King of Poland had been a placeman of the Empress of Russia, first Augustus III (Elector of Saxony) and secondly, after 1764, Stanislas Poniatowski, former lover of Catherine the Great. The latter's election to the Polish throne was secured by a Russo-Prussian agreement as part of a deal in which Prussia guaranteed Russia assistance in the event of aggression by any power other than Turkey and Russia promised support for Prussia in the event of an attack upon her western dominions. It was a kind of rejoinder to the continuance of a Franco-Austrian alliance and perhaps as meaningful. Russian policy at this juncture was to preserve Poland as a weak client state, although a faction at the Russian court (headed by the Chernyshev brothers) advocated a revision of the existing frontier. What was to push Catherine along the path of dismemberment was a certain amount of passive encouragement from Prussia (an encouragement perhaps over-emphasized by Russian historiography), ready, if it could be achieved effortlessly, to join Pomerania and East Prussia together, and, more significantly, by events in Poland itself. For Poland, at such a critical time in its history, was to become ensnared in civil war. This arose over the rights of religious dissenters (the 200,000 Protestants and 600,000 Orthodox, the latter dwelling in present-day White Russia and the Ukraine). Both advanced claims for full equality and the Orthodox pressed for the termination of pressure to adopt the Uniate rite. Catherine encouraged their claims for a mixture of reasons, the promotion of anarchy, Enlightenment toleration and, as far as the Orthodox were concerned, for eminently 'Russian' reasons. Prussia, on the other hand, gave some slight encouragement to the claims of the Protestants.

The result was the formation of confederacies amongst the dissenters with evident foreign support and the existence of these prompted similar confederacies for the defence of the faith and of liberty and of the right of Poles to manage their own affairs without foreign intervention. The Confederacy of Bar came to embrace most of the latter. All the confederacies were guerrilla organizations given to looting, raiding and general brigandage. If the Confederacy of Bar had a political programme it was the diminution of royal power and the abolition of the *liberum veto*.

In the midst of such conflict, in which Russian troops unofficially engaged, the Ukrainian populace of southeastern Poland revolted against their Polish landlords and those whom they claimed were 'Jewish' middlemen and against the methods of conversion used by the Uniate church. A massive revolt, as much anti-seigneurial as anything else in its attacks on manor houses and seigneurial agents, swept the area, in the belief that Russian support would back the rebels. But in pursuit of fleeing Polish Confederates, the Ukrainians burned the Ottoman town of Balta and the Turks (with French encouragement) seized the pretext to declare war upon Russia so as to get in a blow whilst Russia was embroiled in Poland. Hence Russia in 1768 found herself in a curious position. On the one hand the Polish question clearly demanded a 'Russian' solution if Russia's grip on the country was to be maintained. The Confederacy of Bar had to be broken lest it led to a political settlement destructive of the 'happy anarchy' which so suited Russian interests. More likely than this, however, was that if Russia did not heavily involve herself, Prussia might take advantage of the civil war to lop off the Polish enclave between Pomerania and East Prussia. In another direction were Russian dreams of expansion towards the Black Sea. Catherine knew exactly what she wanted out of a Turkish conflict and her aims were ambitious: a Black Sea port: free passage of the Straits: the 'independence' of the Khanate of the Crimea. A vigorous direction hence had to be given to this untimely conflict.

By 1770 Russian armies were in Azov and Bucharest and a Turkish fleet had been destroyed at Chesme and Russian war aims were enlarged to embrace the actual annexation of the Crimea and of the fortresses of Kerch and Yenikate in order to control the Straits of Kerch which joined the Sea of Azov with the Black Sea, and the annexation of Moldavia and Wallachia to pay for the war. But to exploit Russia's tactical advantages was impossible with troops tied down in Poland. There was, moreover, every sign that European powers were not going to sit back and allow Catherine to annex the Ottoman Empire undisturbed. There were rumours of an Austro-Turkish alliance (in fact preliminaries of an Austro-Turkish agreement were signed in 1771 although Austria was very hesitant about it) and clearly Austria was not prepared to countenance unchecked Russian advance towards the Balkans. Frederick the Great, fearing to be dragged into a conflict, and in light of his treaty obligations which he now viewed as of no conceivable advantage to himself, was pressing Catherine to make peace and it was he who from early 1771 suggested to the Empress of Russia that international conflict might best be avoided by a tripartite division of certain Polish territories. This would, along with a dropping of Russian insistence upon the occupation of Moldavia and Wallachia, placate Austria and would settle the Polish issue so that Catherine could, undiverted, negotiate with the Porte. One by one the Confederate armies had surrendered to Prussian or Russian armies and hence the first partition, affecting something like a quarter of Polish territory, could be easily accomplished.

In his forecasts Frederick had been absolutely right though even without the Turkish issue the partition of Poland was an imminent likelihood and all the Turkish question did was to accelerate it. In August 1772 Prussia assumed West Prussia and the bishopric of Warmia (Ermeland), Austria a triangle based on the Carpathians and Russia the regions east of the Dvina, the Drúc and the Dnieper. Two million Poles passed under Austrian rule, some million and a half under Russian sovereignty and about half a million under Prussian – though the value of Prussian territory in strategic terms was far in excess of the annexations of the other two.

Fortunately for the Turks, no sooner had one obstacle to Russian advance been eliminated than another took its place. The dragging on of hostilities took a heavy toll of men not only in warfare but from disease. Moreover, this was a war the Russians had to finance themselves and hence had to have recourse to the increased taxation which was at the root of some of the disturbances connected with the Pugachev Revolt. The sheer extent of this revolt made the government, anxious to divert the army, conscious of the need for peace.

Negotiations with the Porte were strenuous but eventually the Russians emerged at the Treaty of Kutchuk-Kainardji with Azov, the mouths of the Dnieper and the Bug, the fortresses of Kerch and Yenikate, the free passage of the Straits and secured the independence of the Crimea. Both Britain and France viewed events in Poland and Turkey with great apprehension but neither was in a position to intercede. Neither the First Partition of Poland nor Kutchuk-Kainardji marked the end of a particular issue. By the early 1780s Russian designs on Turkey had blossomed into a 'Greek project' in which Russian influence was to extend to the Dniester and an independent Dacia was to be created (roughly Roumania), a Byzantine empire was to be revived and governed by Catherine's grandson, Constantine, whilst Ottoman Balkan possessions were to be offered to Austria and France was to be silenced by territory in North Africa. All this was conjectural and it was not until 1787 that such a project was to bring eastern Europe to the brink of war.

As for Poland, the shock of the First Partition did bring the tardy recognition amongst members of the *Seym* that some reform was needful and that individualism and anarchy could only bring destruction. Provincial diets in the 1770s surrendered some of their fiscal powers to the *Seym*: the landless *szlachta* were proscribed from the *Seym* and attempts were hence made to curtail the patronage powers of the magnates. Most striking of all were the efforts made to streamline revenue collection. These included attempts to establish a national budget, the rationalization of taxes on Jews and the clergy, and the introduction of new taxes on salt and tobacco as well as a new stamp duty. All this lifted revenue but what it could not do was to preserve the country from the rapacity of its neighbours nor two further partitions in the nineties.

The international scene on the eve of the French Revolution was more apparently quiescent than it had been for many decades. The old hatreds remained, some half patched up, if none obliterated. Two empires had been lost in the west whilst in the east two were rapidly growing. Hitched to the process was the fate of monarchies and the developing state.

PART II

Central and Eastern Europe

5

The Holy Roman Empire

'The German State stems from the territorial principality. It is not by nature a monarchic state as are the states of West Europe.' (Schlesinger, 1954)

Amongst European political forms, the position of the German states and indeed of the entire Holy Roman Empire, was in the eighteenth century quite unique. To contemporary observers – like Voltaire, always prone when confronted with phenomena he imperfectly understood to sacrifice accuracy to the pithy phrase – the Empire had ceased to be either holy, Roman or an empire. Its holiness and Romanness had been lost in the struggles following the Reformation and the imperial style assumed a central authority which the Emperor simply did not possess. To such observers, the Empire appeared in institutional form both decadent and moribund and none paused to enquire what function the Empire was designed to serve and how adequately it fulfilled its allotted purpose. This was because they, like ensuing nineteenth-century commentators, started from the concept of the unified monarchic state efficiently embracing one people whose particularist interests were secondary to their perception of unity.

Yet, looked at closely, such a concept had little relevance to the 294 states or 2303 territories and jurisdictions of the Empire comprehending those areas we know today as Germany but extending deep into central Europe into the traditional Habsburg lands. The history of early modern Germany was that of a federation of territorial principalities and in some of these individual principalities the notion of the state or of sovereignty was quite different from a western European one. This applied less to the super-states of the Habsburgs or the Hohenzollerns or even to middling states like Bavaria, Hanover and Saxony where authority was clearly vested in princes and estates, the one drawn from a single dynasty, than to the myriad Imperial Cities and free towns or the ecclesiastical states of the Rhineland where municipal authorities or elected prince-bishops claimed themselves as much *Landesvater* as any other secular dynastic ruler. Or, one needs to consider the particular position of institutions such as the great and ancient monastery of Fulda, or individuals such as the ancient German nobility, the Franconian, Swabian or Rhenish Knights arrogating to themselves a quasi-totality of political, economic and social rights: *guttsherrschaft* (land-lordship), *gerichtsherrschaft* (rights of justice) and *landherrschaft* (rule subject to no one *within* the Empire). *Reichsunmittelbar* (allegiance only to the Emperor and his authority limited to his presidency of the *Reichstag*) was the resounding claim made by Imperial City, Imperial Knight, monastic enclave or canonical benefice alike (though none but the first could claim representation in the *Reichstag*). Such small territorial entities, the smallest covering no more than a few square miles, were in effect self-governing but to survive and protect their integrity, they had to form associations, historically the ten German circles or spheres of influence. Hence, for example, though the towns of Regensburg, Freising and Bamberg, set in Bavarian territory, refused to acknowledge the rights of the Elector of Bavaria and were governed by elected ecclesiastics, they fell within the Bavarian sphere of influence through simple geographical reality. Just because some of the principalities were small does not mean to imply that they were lacking a sense of loyalty or identity. On the contrary, particularism implied a highly developed sense of identity and it was as possible to feel allegiance towards, for example, the Bishop of Speyer, as it was towards an Elector of Saxony.

The Empire had behind it a chequered and indeed bitter history of conflict. Historically, much of this had focused on religious dissent and religious distinctions still continued to play an important part in German particularism. The result of seventeenth-century conflict had been to guarantee the principle of religious uniformity within states whilst admitting the religious pluralism of the Empire itself, but several incidents in the eighteenth century, such as the expulsion of Protestants from the Archbishopric of Salzburg, served to maintain an awareness of undercurrents of religious difference. Moreover, though religion made natural allies of some principalities it was not invariably a binding factor. It did not for example ineluctably push those states with Catholic dignitaries as rulers towards alliance with Austria, particularly when the latter was a convert to Enlightenment principles which struck at the very foundations of church wealth and authority and seriously questioned the Church's role as landowner. Pushed to their logical conclusions, such principles denied the right to existence of the ecclesiastical principalities and hence were to be unconditionally rejected. This is merely one instance of fragmentation of interest. German land was rich, her rivers important trading arteries, her ports consequential in the Baltic trade and the Empire did not exist in isolation. Surrounded by covetous neighbours, German history had always been marked by jockeying of Habsburg, Bourbon and Vasa for territorial aggrandizement.

The Treaty of Westphalia (1648) was expressly designed to resolve the German problem by achieving a balance of interests. In particular no sovereignty was left so powerful that it could infringe the territorial integrity of another. To this end, Habsburg extension outside hereditary Habsburg territories was limited by a strong French presence on the left bank of the Rhine: intrusive Vasa influence in the north was offset by a Brandenburg reinforced with western Pomerania, and within the Empire electorates, princedoms, free cities and so on were restored to their primitive position. An institutional framework was resurrected to guarantee the continued existence of the component elements. The mechanism of Empire needs close examination because more than anything else it is the key to its survival. Imperial institutions on the whole performed a remarkable work of conciliation and arbitration in face of two powerful members, Austria and Prussia, who did not invariably abide by the rules.

The constituted authority of each German state had the right to control its own domestic affairs and to a large extent its relations with foreign powers and to send delegates in the person of its elector or immediate ruler or, in the case of the Imperial Cities, representatives to the *Reichstag*, a federative body concerned with matters of general interest to the Empire as a whole and which met under the presidency of the Emperor. The imperial office was nominally elective but in fact had become hereditary in the Austrian branch of the Habsburg family and this principle survived even the succession crisis of 1740. Theoretically the imperial office gave the incumbent certain 'reserved rights' allowing him to veto specific measures submitted by the *Reichstag*, to make promotions in rank and confer fiefs, titles of nobility and university degrees. He also represented the Empire in its corporate dealings (virtually non-existent) with foreign powers. The *Reichstag* was an imperial congress organized into three chambers. The first was the College of Electors, the eight who actually carried out the imperial election and who included the three ecclesiastics, Archbishops of Mainz, Cologne and Trier, and only two dignitaries, the Elector of Hanover and Margrave of Brandenburg in the Protestant interest. Second came the College of Princes, Counts and Barons, and third the College of the Imperial Free Cities. Very clearly the Catholic aristocratic bloc was numerically preponderant to a degree far transcending actual territorial weight. With voting powers at the *Reichstag* were 65 archbishops, bishops, abbots and priors, 45 dynastic princes, 60 dynastic lords and representatives of 50–60 Imperial Cities. Yet the 65 ecclesiastics had only about 14 per cent of the total land area and something under 12 per cent of the total federal population (c. $3\frac{1}{2}$ million) to set against the 45 dynastic princes who controlled c. 80 per cent of the land and c. $22\frac{1}{2}$ million people, leaving lords and Imperial Cities with about a million each and the Imperial Knights with about half a million.

Notwithstanding its weight in the *Reichstag*, the Catholic interest was wary of matters which set Catholic against Protestant in imperial politics for historical experience had demonstrated only too well that religious dissent was the prelude to foreign intervention. The component members of the Empire had a common interest in resolving internal conflict within their own rambling confines. To that end existed not only the *Reichstag* but the *Reichskammergericht*, a great law court concerned with administrative matters and particularly infringements of established authority, and the *Reichshofrat*, an imperial tax chamber. The former was a significant element in the processes of arbitration and conciliation and promoted the awareness of a collective German interest. The existence of such a mechanism for arbitration protected for instance the principality of Anhalt against absorption by Prussia or stopped the ruler of Hesse-Darmstadt from annexing the counties of Isenburg or Solms. Certainly it restrained the ambitious Dukes of Mecklenburg and Wurtemberg from attempting to pursue territorial claims and as late as 1803 it was able to prevent Bavaria from compelling the Franconian Knights to become her subjects.

Though the corporate institutions of the Empire were unwieldy, slow and cumbersome and seem on scrutiny frail preservers of the peace, on the whole they worked and there was less of a German problem in the eighteenth century than there had been in the sixteenth and seventeenth centuries, or would be in the nineteenth or twentieth. This was remarkable in the light of the fact that the *Reichsarmee* was painfully small and the imperial taxation designed to finance it slow to materialize. Most significant of all, Joseph II as Emperor in effect turned his back on the Empire, deeming that its fragmentation and federal form embodied the undesirable characteristics he wanted to eliminate in his reform of the Habsburg lands.

To a degree Joseph II's attitude is understandable. During the succession crisis in 1740 Frederick II of Prussia had seized Silesia and a Bavarian had been temporarily set up as Emperor. The institutional mechanism of the Empire had in no way prevented this from happening. Yet Joseph's own attempts in 1784 to lay hold of Bavaria during a disputed succession, resulted in the formation of a League of Princes which included the Catholic states in alliance with Prussia whose military strength was used to cut short Habsburg pretensions. The Emperor's ecclesiastical policy and his overt ridiculing of the Congress of Ems at which the Archbishops of Mainz, Cologne, Trier and Salzburg sought to put their church in order according to the principles of the Catholic Enlightenment further distanced the Emperor from his 'natural' supports. This is not to presume Frederick II unconditional in his support of the Empire. He is said to have considered pulling out of it entirely. But since Austria was progressively disinterested in the Empire he knew where his true interests lay, and on the whole, setting aside the seizure of Silesia, he abided by the rules.

The tendency, as the eighteenth century advanced, was for no one to have a good word to say for the Empire. By 1795 even middling states like Saxony and Hanover believed its days numbered and that they would in an ill-defined way profit from its demise. The strongly author-itarian character of the early German Enlightenment found its fullest expression in advancing the duties and powers of the territorial prince and the later development of romanticism and the concept of a *volk* with a unified past had scant sympathy for the federal principles on which the Empire was based. Notwithstanding, in the last century of its existence, imperial institutions lent some security to, and furthered the internal political development of, the component parts.

The eighteenth-century Empire, then, existed in spite of a crisis of confidence, of an Emperor who no longer believed in it, of a short but uncomfortable civil war (1756–63) and in spite of the rise of a northern power, Prussia, intent upon territorial aggrandizement. Its history obviously has to be written with reference to the separate and special evolution of Prussia and the Habsburg lands whose dominions trans-cended imperial frontiers and whose quarrels resounded throughout the Empire. But it should also be written with reference to the fragmented parts, and here we live in relative ignorance for historians tied to a nationalist past have fought shy of the Empire in the eighteenth century and only in the divided conditions of the late twentieth century is it gaining a more sensitive and sympathetic press and with it detailed analysis of the workings of middling and small principalities.

Amongst these the Electorate of Mainz demands special attention as an example of an ecclesiastical principality ruled by an archbishop elector whose ecclesiastical authority extended over several dioceses but whose territorial power was confined to some scattered territories flung across the Rhineland, Franconia and Thuringia, and which centred on the city of Mainz (30,000 inhabitants). Archchancellor of the Empire, the Archbishop of Mainz was in prestige terms 'second only to the Emperor'. In practical terms, though he was a significant former of policy within the *Reichskirche* (the Catholic church within Germany) and within the *Reichskammergericht*, his authority was confined to his electorate. Even within that small entity he was forced to recognize the independence of the cathedral canons, endowed with *Reichsunmittelbar* within their benefices and who could then stalwartly set themselves against any extension of his authority. Ironically the Archbishop/Elector of Mainz was specifically elected by the canons and like them was drawn from the elite families of Imperial Knights who slipped so easily into all the best imperial positions and for whom electorates like Mainz afforded continuing enrichment. Yet, once in office, archbishop and canons, should the former prove in any way active, were set upon a course of collision.

This anachronistic framework smacked of almost every abuse condemned by Enlightenment thought yet it proved possible during the electorates of Johann Friedrich and Emmerich Joseph (1743–74) and then more strikingly during that of Friedrich Karl von Erthal (1774–1802) to use it as a basis for enlightened reform. Indeed, it has been urged that enlightened despotism had greatest reality in such small German states where it was equated with a strengthening of the individual internal mechanism of principalities within the confines of the Empire. In the Electorate of Mainz what it meant above all was the electors' attempts (or those of ministers such as Stadion) to impose a broad programme of educational reform for almost every level of society, determined efforts to stimulate the economic development of the principality and religious reform designed to lend full expression to the principles of the Catholic Enlightenment.

One is of course dealing with a very small territorial entity and the effects of the economic measures are difficult to gauge since clearly Mainz, whose economic life had historically pivoted on the Rhine traffic, did not live in isolation but was part of western Germany. Germany's political fragmentation, innumerable customs barriers and river tolls clearly did not contribute to the realization of full economic potential – a major criticism levied at the old Empire. Yet more significant for Mainz had been the declining importance of Rhine traffic in the seventeenth century. This could be attributed in part to the new importance of the Atlantic ports but mostly to Germany's unfavourable demographic record which depressed industries and curtailed mercantile activity. At the same time, the agrarian population, decimated by famine and plague, slid still further into seigneurial bondage.

In the second decade of the eighteenth century, German economic life as a whole entered a healthier phase. Labour services and rents remained high but there was no indication of the slippage into pauperdom evident in France and the United Provinces and the balance between arable and pasture, and hence the maintenance of the productivity of the arable land by efficient manuring, remained relatively constant. In short, reforming measures were enacted within a fairly favourable context, in spite of French invasion during the forties and the dislocation caused by the Seven Years' War.

That said, the record of Mainz and its share of Rhine traffic in wine and agricultural produce is more impressive than that of other Rhine stations such as Cologne or Frankfurt. This could well be attributable to Stadion's efforts in the late 1740s to encourage mercantile activity by favourable credit facilities, by developing a consultative and advisory committee of merchants and government officials, by re-establishing annual fairs, by offering inducements to foreign merchants such as exhibition rooms, stressing the religious tolerance accorded to the mercantile sector and reducing the dues on some imported goods. Mainz retailers were compelled to purchase at the fair, a pragmatic protectionism demonstrating Stadion to be no slave to current economic philosophy. Contemporaries were certainly impressed and Frankfurt in particular was convinced that electoral policy had stimulated the revival of Mainz.

Attempts by Stadion in the forties to make primary education compulsory clearly had no avail but under the next elector, Emmerich Joseph (1763–74), essays were made in educational reform intended to project the electorate into the van of eighteenth-century progressive policy. Teacher education was improved by a new College of Education and teaching manuals revised to bring them up to date on Felbiger, Muratori and Lessing. Reason and development of the memory were to be sharpened by broader curricula involving science and natural history and this was accompanied by a real extension in primary and secondary schools. To go further and reform the grammar schools involved a confrontation with the Jesuits who had a monopoly of higher education. Emmerich Joseph was a convert to the Catholic Enlightenment and hostile to the theological stranglehold of the ultramontane orders but he did not follow Portugal, Spain and France into expelling the order until Clement XIV ordered its dissolution in 1773. The demise of the Jesuits permitted the introduction of a number of new and illustrious professors into the universities of Mainz and Erfurt which then enjoyed some of the renewal experienced by German Protestant universities within the Empire.

Emmerich Joseph's most radical departure however stemmed from his leadership of an episcopalian party within the *Reichskirche* which aimed at a marked reduction of papal power within Germany. This was coincident with a number of personal grievances stemming from papal intervention in the Rhenish bishoprics – Emmerich Joseph was piqued at the high entry fees demanded when elected to the Bishopric of Worms – but the party's views embodied all the distinctly anti-papalist attitudes of the Catholic Enlightenment. A conference held with his fellow bishops produced the Koblenz Gravamina demanding the abolition of dues to Rome, of papal control over German benefices, limiting the activities of papal nuncios and proclaiming the end of monastic immunity from episcopal jurisdiction. The *Gravamina* (1769) were to be the exact precursor of the Conference of Ems in 1786 in which the dignitaries of the *Reichskirche* attempted to put their house in order according to the principles of the Enlightenment. On both occasions the Archbishops looked to Joseph II for support and were gravely disappointed. An anti-papalist himself, Joseph II was also an anti-episcopalian with no intention of involving himself in a reduction of the power of the pope if it implied an augmentation of the powers of the bishops and those states which were Catholic, but not administered by prince-bishops, hung back.

On other issues victory was simpler. Emmerich Joseph and Friedrich Karl von Erthal achieved stricter regulation of the monastic life, an end to future mortmain, the sale of Jesuit property, and an undercutting of clerical privilege – for example, the chapter's right to exemption from customs dues. There were also the inevitable attempts to tidy up popular mores by curtailing leisure activities, pilgrimages, dancing and drinking on fête days which smacked of the profane. Not surprisingly, on his death in 1774, the chapter was able with popular support to engineer a minor aristocratic reaction, nullifying during the vacancy what Emmerich Joseph had done. Clearly the populace had little taste for change which cut across the immediate religion of the flamboyant baroque or imposed learning on their children or threatened in any way the ritual associated with traditional faith. Yet Friedrich Karl von Erthal was undismayed and not only carried on the work of his predecessor but immersed himself yet further in measures to allow the peasant redemption from the more onerous seigneurial dues (at levels, let it be said, that only the wealthiest peasants could conceivably have afforded, demanding redemption payment of twenty times the value of the due) and by formulating a programme of institutionalized poor relief.

The record of Mainz is significant because it demonstrates how in the most conservative and anachronistic of the lesser German states it was possible for a wind of change to blow, albeit in gentle fashion. It is not a unique instance. Clemens Wenceslaus of Trier, Franz Ludwig of Wurzburg and Bamberg, Max Franz of Cologne were able to push their respective territories along the path of reform demonstrating that Germany was far from asleep. In spite of the devastations caused during the Prussian occupation, Electoral Saxony contrived a recovery without a loss of peasant status or change in its political framework. The middling German states like Saxony and Bavaria still preserved the mechanism of the estates which acted as a check upon the dynastic ruler's policy. The concept of enlightened absolutism here has less reality and political debate, though slight by British or Dutch standards, has a clearer existence. The rulers vigorously pursued policies designed to curtail mortmain, the extension of clerical privilege and to prevent peasant land slipping into the hands of the nobility. In the most fragmented areas of Germany where power was at its most diffuse, inhabitants looked to the structure and institutions of the Empire to guarantee their rights and privileges. Lippe for example, in Westphalia, self-governing but conscious of its powerful neighbour Brandenburg, preserved its independence and the privileges of its cities against any encroachments by the ruling dynasty or outsiders by frequent successful appeals to the *Reichskammergericht.*

The Empire then existed by a delicate balance of privileged interests and anachronisms, severing western Europe, whose political development had been in the direction of the unified state, from an east whose political experience had been quite other. Though it was to be the Napoleonic invasions which caused a fundamental rupturing of the traditional position, nothing threatened the physical existence and destroyed the intellectual underpinning of the Empire more than the reverbatory struggle of Habsburg and Hohenzollern and the anomaly of an emperor who had reasons for believing the preservation of the Empire contrary to the best interests of the Habsburg dominions. Some of the most fundamental questions one can ask about government in Vienna, are what made its rulers in the second half of the eighteenth century turn their backs on their traditional position and how convincingly could they thus reject the experience of centuries?

6

The Habsburg Lands

The Habsburg dominions, some within the Empire, others without, were a striking hotchpotch of random and disparate interests. The uniqueness of the Habsburg monarchy was that it was only a political entity in the most tenuous sense and that the forces tugging it apart were far more apparent than the forces which held it together. Notwithstanding, it continued to exist and though in the eighteenth century important losses were sustained, as an eastern European power it still had some vitality as the immoral dismemberment of Poland was to demonstrate. The historical truism that Austria was a declining power from the fifteenth to the twentieth centuries needs examining closely in light of the Austrian Empire's persistent, to some eyes, perverse, refusal conveniently to disintegrate. Somewhere there must have been a hidden dynamic, one which depended upon an anachronistic, perhaps indeed obsolete, motor, but one which, with occasional breakdowns necessitating a few overhaulings, sustained it largely intact for the five-hundred-year span between the middle ages and the First World War. Embedded in the concept of the perpetual decline of the Austrian Empire is the inherent contradiction of its survival and such a concept only exists because of a western European conviction that one ought to be able to apply to the Empire norms and criteria which apply elsewhere. In fact, perhaps the main reason for its survival was that like the Empire itself, the Habsburg lands were a political entity of a radically different kind from most other European states and that this entity performed, and very successfully, quite different functions.

Historically, the loose agglomeration of Habsburg territories in eastern Europe, had found some unity of expression in defending their immediate interests, and those of Christendom, against the Turk. Without association they would assuredly have fallen. With association, in the seventeenth and early eighteenth centuries, an expansion at the Turk's expense occurred. This lent security to the existence of the component elements of Habsburg territories, above all Hungary, a new-found security which goes some way to explaining Hungary's intransigent attitude towards Habsburg demands. Crises occurred within this empire when the idea of community of interests was in some way obscured or when the union, far from guaranteeing the individuality of the component elements seemed to threaten their particularism.

The Austrian Empire was in 1730 a loose agglomeration of territories: Austria proper (divided into Upper and Lower Austria and the Tyrol), Bohemia, Silesia, Moravia. All of these were part of the Holy Roman Empire. The other Habsburg territories were Hungary, Milan, Naples and Sicily (exchanged in 1738 for Parma and Piacenza) and the southern Netherlands acquired at Utrecht, and in fact never psychologically committed, to any degree whatsoever, to the concept of belonging to an Austrian Habsburg. Each of these component elements had its own privileges, distinctive character and individual political tradition. Each had its own concept of the Emperor's role and the limitations upon his power within their particular territory. When, in the late seventeenth century, other European powers, such as France, Sweden, Prussia, Russia were moving in the direction of strong centralized government no parallel movement occurred in the Habsburg lands. Nevertheless, it is from this period that in Vienna, in government circles, there emerged a debate between the concept of empire (*Reichsidee*) and the concept of the unified state (*Staatsidee*) with a gradual swing to the latter as a philosophy for government action. One must stress the theoretical nature of this persuasion. Habsburg rulers were confronted with the spectacle of central governments in other lands able to secure, to a greater or lesser degree, the power of the purse: able to override the traditional institutional checks upon monarchical authority and having done so to finance armies and military campaigns and wage war on an unprecedented scale with an unprecedented efficiency. To a Habsburg, hamstrung at every level by particularist interests, such governments were in an enviable position. But there was nothing that could be done at this juncture to give the *Staatsidee* real shape. Habsburg control over Hungary was for example severely limited. Only in 1687 did kingship become hereditary in the Habsburg family and the Magyar nobility lose the right of armed resistance to their ruler, whilst a serious nationalist revolt occurred in 1703 terminated by a treaty in 1711 re-confirming Hungarian privileges. *Staatsidee* was a dream. It was, perhaps, given the particular conditions of the Habsburg territories, an insidious illusion. Yet it was the *Staatsidee* which was to make Joseph II in particular review the workings of his own territories and to alter his entire attitudes towards his own dominions and towards the Holy Roman Empire.

It is worth looking at the mechanism whereby Habsburg territories were governed in 1730. The two most significant bodies in the administration of the Habsburg lands from Vienna were the *Gehei-merat*, the conference or secret council headed by the *Obersthofmeister* (the nearest the Habsburg lands came to a Prime Minister), and the *Hofkammer* or council of finance. The first existed to debate domestic and foreign policy, a futile exercise given its lack of control over financial matters which were specifically the concern of the *Hofkam-mer*. This administered the revenues contributed by the different states to the sovereign but one must be careful to define the strict limitations of its powers which were confined to the purely routine administration of the sums allocated by the separate Diets for very specific purposes. The *Hofkammer* had no independent initiative in determining budget-ary matters. In each separate state the sovereign had domain and regalian rights (customs, tolls, income from mines, etc.) but from the sums thus raised, as well as from direct taxation voted by the Diets, were deducted the costs of provincial and local administration, salaries, roads and public buildings. What reached the *Hofkammer* was invari-ably insufficient for the running of the army which was, of course, its principal concern, and it was the *Hofkammer* which had to have recourse to borrowing from the bankers of Genoa and Holland, pled-ging as security the anticipated revenues from customs and mines, a state of affairs which the creation of the Bank of Vienna (1705) by Joseph I had in no way improved.

Working on the reports of the *Hofkammer*, the *Geheimerat* could make policy recommendations to the Emperor but their implementation depended not merely upon the Emperor's assent (this was no French *conseil du Roi*) but upon that of the Diets and local administrations. In a sense, since the king's will was not the law, as in France, the secret council had no real constitutional power. It was merely an advisory body which had weight only because of the stature of the participants. Generally, for example, the two Chancellors of Austria and the Chan-cellor of Bohemia were participants.

There was a further council, the *Hofkriegsrat* or war council which was concerned with military matters, equipment, wages and troop movements. It waited upon money from the *Hofkammer* and foreign policy statements from the *Geheimerat*.

Several of the individuals who sat in the Emperor's councils held high office and possessed great territorial wealth in their own localities. At one and the same time they owed allegiance to their own country and to the Emperor. Hence local interests could exert more direct pressure upon the Emperor than the latter could upon the localities where he was often very inadequately represented. Nominally at least, each state had a lieutenant resident in its capital who was responsible for admin-istering in the Emperor's name and who was the Emperor's man. But his work had to be done in conjunction with the Diet and its executive agents. Even more tellingly, all judicial and financial officials, though possibly nominated by the Emperor, were dependent upon the local Diet and hence served that before their prince.

There is perhaps no question more difficult to answer than where did power reside in the Habsburg lands but it is one which must be attempted – though we must deal in constant qualifications – because it is intrinsic to the problems of government. At the local level, real power lay with the Diets or provincial estates, aristocratic meetings of the great landed nobility which decided what financial contributions and troop levies should be made to assist the running of the Habsburg dominions and which were schooled to head-on collisions, should the occasion demand it, with the central authority. Whatever these meetings decided upon must in the last analysis prevail, for they were government in the localities. Their officials, those who made contact with the people, were the filter for government policy. Clearly the Diets were bastions of aristocratic privilege, but they were also guarantors of local privilege, meaning those provincial rights and immunities which often served as a block to the untrammelled demands of a prince whose interests might stretch beyond, or even run counter to, purely local concerns. For this reason, the aristocratic Diets could claim to rest on a bedrock of popular sanction. To take a hypothetical example from these random territories, no Hungarian was prepared to pay *ad infinitum* towards a war in Germany or Italy. That he was prepared to consider any payment at all for such a purpose, reflected a perception, of fluctuating clarity, that as a frontier territory with Turk and Slav, Hungary's best interests were served by a link with Vienna. But that linkage must be between equals, reflected by a separate coronation in Pressburg guaranteeing that the Emperor was aware of the separateness, individuality and dignity of the Hungarian people.

This said, we must also emphasize that the social structure of the Habsburg lands imposed grave limitations upon a central government whose essential preoccupations were the maintenance of the integrity of its territories and the honour of the House of Habsburg and which must concern itself with armies and the taxes to support them. The agrarian economy was still in Bohemia, Galicia, Moravia and Hungary and sporadically in Austria, Carinthia, Carniola and Styria, seigneurial in form. Dues and domain farming were the norm and the tax burden that the state could impose upon the serf must be limited by the amount he must pay to his seigneur and his restricted earning capacity due to the demands of labour services. The nobles, some of whom sat in the Diets, were, in first instance, seigneurs, and the very source of their wealth lay in land, dues and labour services. They might also be army officers, members of Habsburg councils, diplomats or bureaucrats and as such, employees of the prince, but they were his rivals for the revenues of the peasant whom they held to be subject of his seigneur before he was subject of his sovereign. This implicit assumption encapsulated the Habsburg dilemma. For what government in the conditions of the eighteenth century could effectively function if it could not claim primacy in the direction of its subjects?

Looked at in one light, the Habsburg solution might be to sell the *Staatsidee* to the dominions and embark upon a centralization programme beginning with the reform of the mechanism of taxation so that taxes could be levied without the intrusion of the Diets and extending state control over a peasant populace, thereby increasing peasant contributions to the central treasury at the expense of seigneurial revenues. Other measures were in comparison mere tinkering with the system to make it yield a little here and there. Such measures might include new trade monopolies for government profit, improved banking and credit facilities, an onslaught on ecclesiastical revenues or a further bleeding of those territories (the Low Countries, northern Italy) where funds could be more readily mulcted from a 'free' populace. Charles VI had recourse to all these means of revenue raising. Temporizing though such measures undoubtedly were, they did not threaten the entire premises upon which the Habsburg Empire was constructed. The fiscal problem in the Habsburg lands to a far greater degree than even in France, was a constitutional and social issue. The *Staatsidee* was a threatening concept. Perhaps the best approach to Habsburg government in the eighteenth century is to recognize that all the rulers appreciated the essential difference between *ad hoc* expedients and radical change but they would have been fools not to opt for the first as long as possible lest the second should precipitate the disintegration of the Empire, that is, provoke the very condition centralization was intended to avoid. What marked the government of Maria Theresa (1740–80) and Joseph II (1780–90) off from that of Charles VI (1711–40) was that the option of the palliative as opposed to radical surgery appeared to have been removed. Even under Charles VI, losses in the Polish Succession War had revealed the inadequacy of the Austrian army. Now in the course of two short years, 1740–41, the Habsburg monarchy underwent a crisis which convinced the Emperor and officials alike that without an extension of central control, making possible increased taxation to finance defence, the days of Habsburg rule were numbered. At best, the age of Habsburg glory was past and the vultures were gathering to pick over the entrails. From that point on *Staatsidee* was adopted by Vienna as a philosophy for survival.

The crisis of the Habsburg monarchy was of an inadequately trained, equipped and provisioned army and a contested succession. In her memoirs, written in 1750, Maria Theresa described the confusion of the first few months following her succession in 1740. If one sets aside her claims of political innocence, ignorance and lack of political education as obligatory female rhetoric (to be compared with Elizabeth I's body-of-a-weak-woman speeches) one is left with the hard facts of her lack of experience in diplomacy, her advanced pregnancy (Joseph II was born in March 1741) and the death of her one-year-old daughter in January 1741. Obviously these were psychological, physical and emotional obstacles which had to be surmounted. Let us add that when Frederick II seized Silesia in December 1740, the leading ministers left Maria Theresa without counsel because they feared to compromise themselves with what seemed a doomed succession and, understandably enough, local magnates in territories occupied by Prussians and Bavarians paid homage to their new overlords. Her armies defeated at Mollwitz (April 1741), the Queen threw herself on the mercy of the Hungarians, and some six weeks after the birth of her son made the journey to Pressburg. In return for a guarantee of Hungarian rights, privileges and liberties, she was crowned ruler of Hungary. Secure at least in that role, she then embarked upon a series of abortive diplomatic negotiations to buy off the Electors of Bavaria and Saxony. When these failed, convinced that the hereditary lands of the Habsburgs were to be dismembered, she went, bedecked in widow's weeds, to the Hungarian Diet and by an impressive performance, secured the raising of 40,000 men and the guarantee of six cavalry regiments.

In this instance, Hungary saved the Habsburg Empire. Although unbeaten, Frederick II was prepared to make peace if Silesia were ceded. Maria Theresa had no option but to acquiesce in this condition, albeit temporarily, at Breslau in 1742. The English alliance held and the combined forces of the Habsburg Empire succeeded in cutting off the French army in Bohemia where the local nobility had already accepted the Elector of Bavaria as overlord though he had not been crowned. The French contrived a brave retreat and without their support Bavarian pretensions were nullified.

In April 1743, Maria Theresa was crowned in Prague at a cost of 100,000 *gulden* and the Diet accepted an annual tax obligation of 500,000 *gulden* and a further 700,000 *gulden* in extraordinary levy to help meet war costs. The succession contest within the Empire had been hard won. Maria Theresa had on the whole done well. What irked her was the cession of Silesia though it was Frederick the Great who actually resumed hostilities in 1744, perhaps unwilling to countenance any Austrian success which might jeopardize his possession of Silesia. The Second Silesian War (ended by Treaty of Aix-la-Chapelle in 1748) did not rejoin Silesia to the Austrian crown.

If she took stock of events since 1733, Maria Theresa could only be aware of the substantial losses incurred in Italy so that only Lombardy and Tuscany remained: that all lands south of the Danube and the valuable fortress of Belgrade had been ceded to the Turks: and that Silesia, economically the most advanced of the Habsburg hereditary lands, had been lost to Frederick. The Empire clearly was not surviving in the cut-throat world of eighteenth-century war and diplomacy. Maria Theresa saw no alternative but to try to equip herself with the same powers other European monarchs seemed to enjoy. The first wave of reforms with this end in view extended from 1748–c. 1755 and are sometimes called the first *rétablissement*.

The architect of the first *rétablissement* was a Silesian *émigré* called Friedrich-Wilhelm Haugwitz. Haugwitz belonged to the new men Maria Theresa called in to balance the ageing noble paladins bequeathed as ministers by her father and of whom one, the Supreme Chancellor Count Friedrich Harrach, actually led a noble opposition to Haugwitz's proposals. Indeed, Harrach's proposals were more than just demolitionist. He enunciated a counter scheme to centralization which ceded more political authority to the estates in return for increased subsidies and a more efficient way of levying and collecting them. His was perhaps the policy of the future but at the time seemed the product of an arch-reactionary, and one must question whether the eighteenth-century estates were capable of reforming themselves. Haugwitz and Koch believed an efficient means of streamlining financial administration must come from the centre. Historically the estates fought over the actual sum to be levied as royal taxation, divided it, collected it and made deductions from it, before dispatching the rest to the *Hofkammer*. Haugwitz could see no way of divesting the estates of their power to decide *how much* the monarchy should be paid but hoped to concentrate on their powers of collection and dispatch so that the maximum amount possible of the initial levy actually reached Vienna. Haugwitz's proposals also extended to bringing seigneurial land under the taxman's hand. The aim of his proposals was to provide for a standing army of 108,000 men. Moreover, he was particularly averse to a situation wherein there had to be a yearly reckoning between central government and estates and pressed for the guarantee of subsidies several years in advance.

Maria Theresa, in spite of Harrach's opposition, accepted the rationality of Haugwitz's demands and left it to the minister to convince the estates of the need for more money without an extension of their political powers. Before the Diet of Moravia he was surprisingly successful and got a ten-year guarantee. That of Bohemia proved more recalcitrant but finally agreed to a reduced figure and that any tax on seigneurial land could only be on an 'extraordinary' basis. The Estates of Upper and Lower Austria accepted the proposals in full. Styria, Carniola, Gorz and Gradiszka agreed to grant money for three years. Carinthia refused point blank. Here an extraordinary tax on seigneurial land could only be collected by unconstitutional means. Nevertheless, overall, Haugwitz had demonstrated that to secure the territory of the Habsburg Empire the Diets were prepared to make some sacrifice. Even more he had increased by upwards of 25 per cent revenues from

Bohemia and Moravia. At the same time, new agencies of central government were created, called circle authorities (*Kreisbehorden*), in many provinces to supervise billeting of troops and to ensure that peasants were not so oppressed by seigneurial taxation that they could not pay state contributions. Finally, *Directorium in Publicis et Cameralibus* united the *Hofkammer* and the chancelleries of Bohemia and Austria to lend firm central control to financial matters.

These efforts at centralization achieved something but Hungary, northern Italy and the Netherlands were in no way more closely linked with central control. Maria Theresa's hand tightened over the traditional Habsburg lands to form a tougher bastion of resistance to Prussia. That this alone was inadequate to secure her ends was to be demonstrated by the experience of the Seven Years' War.

Haugwitz's reforms had produced the wherewithal to finance a standing army and cover ordinary peacetime expenditure. That army had been conspicuously improved and an officer class nurtured by Daun, most prominent of military reformers, had been schooled in strategy and the art of manoeuvre. The foundation of the school at Wiener Neustadt in 1752 was part of a plan to ensure that the nobility's training as army officers would cede nothing to Prussia and Russia. This army was not intended merely to deter a putative aggressor. It was designed to re-take Silesia and to re-establish the Habsburgs, at least as the foremost of German princes. Yet it was not adequate and it did not have sufficient financial backing to achieve those ends. It could in the main *hold* an aggressor and prevent significant advances but after four years of war, there was no prospect of regaining Silesia and Austria was only able to continue through substantial loans on which the interest payments added enormously to the annual burden on the treasury.

No one could have foreseen the financial upheaval which the Seven Years' War would inflict upon every European power. As the Prussians devalued their currency and reminted coins and the Tsarina's emissaries pursued Dutch capital, Maria Theresa in 1760, whilst still at war, embarked upon a further round of reforms and chose to carry them out Prince Wenzel Anton Kaunitz. Kaunitz as negotiator of the French alliance, and Chancellor of State, felt his diplomatic achievements had been betrayed on the domestic front and was responsible for the second *rétablissement*. Like all statesmen he had in part to demonstrate his political acumen by token demolitionary work upon the achievements of his predecessor. In Kaunitz's case this consisted of scrapping the *Directorium in Publicis et Cameralibus* as a cumbersome bottle-neck, and resetting up the *Hofkammer* and the Chancellery. But he made clear that fundamentally he aimed to develop a new creation, the central Council of State (*Staatsrat*), composed of eight senior officials with himself as president. This advisory body existed to investigate all other official bodies and to draw up plans for reform. Its strength lay in the fact that its members were one in their approach to reform and hence were a solid ministerial backing for Maria Theresa's reforming efforts.

The money to finance the Seven Years' War had to be found and the means chosen were three-fold: firstly, to extend to Hungary the same principles applied by Haugwitz to Bohemia and Moravia and Austria, that is to say, a 'God pleasing equality' which brought seigneurial land under the taxman's hand and furthermore secured a long-term guarantee on a voted subsidy: secondly, to bring directly into the tax bracket a hitherto privileged group, the clergy, and at the same time to ensure that no further land passed into mortmain (i.e. was owned by the clergy as a result of bequests and hence escaped taxation): thirdly, to increase the amount payable by the serf to the state by reducing or limiting the amount owed by him to the seigneur.

In every way these measures were a logical extension of Haugwitz's approach. In the case of Hungary, they enjoyed but limited success. It was one matter to convince Bohemia and Moravia and those provinces which had direct experience of the Prussian menace to make concessions involving a sacrifice of constitutional and economic privilege, another to convince the Hungarian noble. Even by employing a remarkable ruse, the publication (obscuring the fact that it was on government initiative) of a book by a Hungarian scholar, Adam Franz Kollár, which put forward the superiority of royal over noble claims, the Hungarian Diet ceded no real ground. The amount of Hungary's tax liability was increased minimally in 1764 but not at the expense of the nobility and only then when Maria Theresa agreed to condemn Kollár's book. From then on Maria Theresa laboured to neutralize the Hungarian noble by a gradual policy of 'Austrianization'. This implied bringing the noble to Vienna, using him in imperial service, honouring him at court and neglecting to use the Diet during the last years of her reign. Yet this did not stifle Hungarian separatism. It was a sentiment which knew how to slumber but not die.

The attack on clerical and seigneurial privilege was a policy well in tune with Enlightenment sentiment, though one must be careful how one uses this fact. There was indeed an impressive Austrian Enlightenment but much of the impetus for reform came directly from fiscal pressure rather than from any deep-rooted conviction of the need for social equality. True the intellectual underpinning of Enlightenment philosophy lent a respectability to policies running counter to powerful vested interests and may have caused ministers to persist in courses they might previously have abandoned as too uphill. A good instance of the alliance between fiscal exigency and a conviction of the quintessential rectitude of an attack on church wealth came with the measures to tax the clergy and Kaunitz's resolute onslaught upon clerical privilege. No church in Europe disposed of a greater proportion of national wealth than did the Roman Catholic Church in the Habsburg lands. Moreover, given the continued inflow of landed bequests to monastic foundations, this income could only grow at the state's expense. Church land was lightly taxed land, virtually 'dead' land as far as the state coffers were concerned. The church had a monopoly of education: it insisted upon an uncompromising policy towards Jews and heretics: it expressed basic allegiance in first instance to Rome.

We are familiar with Enlightenment attitudes towards the established church which concentrated upon several facets of ecclesiastical power. Extremists attacked the very basis of religion, the existence of a Christian or any other god. Between them and the devotees of established religion there lay many intermediate attitudes which even the doctrinally orthodox might accept. Maria Theresa was a woman of conspicuously orthodox piety: anti-semitic: anti-Protestant: faithful to the minutest detail of Church teaching on faith and morals. At the same time she was a willing convert to proclaiming a moratorium on the further growth of church land or to the belief that the monasteries produced too many idlers and had too much apparent disposable wealth – like the Abbey of Melk in Upper Austria which had a surplus of 27,000 florins per annum. Hence she willingly enough accepted Kaunitz's policy designed to deflect some of this wealth to state coffers.

The Habsburg Duchy of Milan was chosen as a testing ground to see what exactly might be done. In 1765 the *Giunta Nationale*, a lay body, was set up to deal with all ecclesiastical matters. A year later all land acquired by the church less than fifty years previously was declared subject to full tax liability and, in default of payment, was to be sold. In 1767 church land was frozen by a law forbidding its acquisition by religious bodies, and religious houses were required to submit estimates of income and expenditure and of their numbers. The intention was to see how many houses could be suppressed by the amalgamation of the smallest.

In spite of papal protest, the measures were extended in 1769 to the hereditary lands and a specialized ecclesiastical department in the Court Chancery under the direction of Franz Joseph Ritter von Heinke, a former pupil of Christian Wolff at Halle University, embarked upon a further series of measures. Of these, the most noteworthy limited the number of entrants to religious houses and prevented the acquisition of further wealth by the monasteries. The first was achieved by prohibiting the taking of religious vows before the age of twenty-four and restricting the numbers to those specified in the house's foundation charter. The novice's dowry was also limited to cash or moveable goods not exceeding 1500 florins.

These reforms were the basis of the policy confusingly attributed to Joseph but in fact formulated during his mother's reign, and during the co-regency of Joseph and Maria Theresa which began when Francis died in 1765. Paul Joseph Riegger, Professor of Canon Law at the University of Vienna, was responsible for providing the intellectual justification for the changes which were fully consonant with Maria Theresa's brand of piety. The single greatest influence upon her was without doubt that of Gerhard van Swieten, her Dutch physician. Van Swieten was a Jansenist, whose brand of devotion set him up in immediate opposition to the laxist and flamboyant elements in baroque Catholicism and who stood for a reinvigorated faith based upon better instruction, scrupulous morality and an austerity denying the immediacy and attraction of popular cults. Not surprisingly, Van Swieten was a conspicuous influence in the programme of educational reforms which sought to remould the universities by removing a Jesuit control productive of magnificent scholasticism but of little use in producing a priesthood for parochial work. Van Swieten was made personally responsible for reform of the medical faculty which rapidly secured a remarkable European reputation.

The net result of university reform was a real secularization of the universities and a new emphasis on mathematics and political science. Adherents of the Enlightenment secured key posts. A reform of the grammar schools along similarly secular lines was less successful because qualified lay teachers were lacking and the same consideration, plus lack of financial backing, impeded the implementation of a far-reaching programme for primary education devised by Johann Ignaz Felbiger who also laid the plans for a new teachers' training college. Felbiger was from Silesia. Indeed the whole reform programme showed at the intellectual and bureaucratic level how truly coherent this multinational empire could be with its reforming bureaucracy drawn from every corner. Equally striking was the demise of Jesuit influence which had sought to subordinate the state to the considerations of the Universal Church. Without doubt the reform programme transcended fiscal exigency even if fiscal exigency gave it its urgency.

The same might be said for such reforms as were directed towards a reduction of seigneurial privilege. The burden of taxation was borne by the peasantry and if the state was to raise its levies it could only, perforce, do so at the expense of taxes paid in labour, money and kind to a seigneurial lord. Enlightenment philosophy, in stressing man's right to be arbiter of his own destiny, was clearly condemnatory of serfdom, but the implications of a confrontation with the privileged classes in the estates was something before which any Habsburg must recoil. The first significant attacks upon seigneurial privilege were in fact made from below in the revolt-ridden conditions prevailing in Bohemia in the 1770s.

The Bohemian revolts of 1775, chronologically, though probably accidentally, coincident with the Pugachev revolts, were the product of multiple factors. These were cumulative harvest failure, between 1765 and 1770, in areas which had borne heavy recruiting demands and had been the actual arena of war, and virulent epidemics engendering a considerable, if statistically imprecise, population cutback (though it is speculated that it was fifteen years before Bohemia caught up on the population loss of 1771). Sporadic peasant risings in Bohemia occurred from 1768. The majority of Czech peasants were serfs subjected to a heavier *robot* (labour services) payment than in the other Habsburg hereditary lands. Attempts to prevent the export of grain and to restrict labour services to three days per week were feeble palliatives. Two factors, however, continued to convey to the Czech peasant that the state was his ally against the oppressive seigneur. Firstly, in 1771, Joseph II travelled throughout Moravia to get a first-hand impression of the situation and was appalled by what he saw. Alms were rushed in, but too late and too sparsely to do much good. More significantly, the state showed itself anxious to punish seigneurial scandals. This started as early as 1768. A good instance was the Mansfeld affair. The Prince von Mansfeld had an important domain near Prague where the prince's employees embarked upon reprisals against tenants who refused certain *corvées* and used beatings and torture. Reported by his tenantry to Vienna, Mansfeld's estate was investigated and the prince condemned to pay 2000 florins to the foundling hospital at Prague and to compensate the peasantry for damages. There were other enquiries into the conduct of Count Lazansky and into the running of the Margrave of Baden's properties at Lovosice and into the implementation of the prohibition on seigneurs to inflict corporal punishment enacted in 1768.

Such enquiries drew a great deal of attention both in university circles and at grass roots where it was believed major reform was on the way. Indeed, the nearest parallel to the Bohemian rising was perhaps the Great Fear in France in 1789 where rumours of reform held back by a self-interested seigneurial group precipitated revolt. The first incidence of revolt occurred in January 1775, within the circle of Koniggratz where *châteaux* and churches were pillaged. This pre-empted the activities of a secret society planning revolt under the direction of a free-peasant, Antonin Nývlt, and committed to fund-raising for arms to undertake a march on Prague on 16 May, the date of the pilgrimage to the shrine of Saint John Nepomuk when substantial crowds would have gathered in the city.

The army quelled the insurrection in Koniggratz but the winter and spring were marked by the formation of peasant terrorist bands – some 1000 strong – menacing stewards and domain administrators and refusing to do *robot*. Nývlt himself in March entered into negotiations with the authorities of the *château* of Nachod to secure the abolition of *robot*, a movement which might have been the precursor of a general trend, had Nývlt not been lured into an ambush. Another band, several thousands strong, under Mathieu Chvoyka, was defeated by the army at Nový Bydzov. Stripped of their leaders, the peasant movement still planned a march on Prague but, chronically under-armed, they were routed by regiments of soldiers – though with little bloodshed.

Rumours that an imperial instruction written in gold, liberating the peasantry, was in existence underscored the quasi-millennial character of the movement and thousands of minor outbursts occurred in the summer, the hungriest months. Pacification came in late August when the real instruction from the Empress, statutorily limiting the *robot* to three days per week at the heaviest time of the agricultural year, was read by soldiers independently of the seigneurs, and a general amnesty was proclaimed to rioters.

The peasants had scored a partial victory at the expense of the seigneur but the real victor was the state which was able to use the incident to intimidate seigneurs, if only to a limited degree. Maria Theresa favoured a scheme devised by Franz Anton von Raab to trans-form *robot* into a cash payment and to divide up domain land into leaseholds for a liberated peasantry. Introduced on to a number of royal estates in Bohemia, the scheme remained limited to them. The most significant advance made in the history of the Habsburg peasantry in Maria Theresa's reign was the increasing preparedness of the state to intervene in the relationship between peasant and lord, but, given the strength of the latter, the material condition of the serf knew no overall improvement.

How does one summarize the achievements of Maria Theresa's reign? How thoroughly had she sold the *Staatsidee* to her dominions? At least in the Habsburg hereditary lands the notion of the legal sovereignty of a central authority which alone could command obedience had made inroads into a concept of law which only guaranteed particular and personal privilege. But the emphasis must be upon 'inroads'. Faced with the exigencies of war, sacrifices had been made and the power of local estates conspicuously diminished. The Habsburg hereditary lands looked tighter knit than ever before. The assertion of the right of the state to bridle the untrammelled expansion of church wealth and to resist an ecclesiastical monopoly upon the educational formation of the elite were positive steps. Yet there still lay a world of virtually untouched seigneurial, ecclesiastical and particularist privilege. The Austrian Netherlands, and more significantly, Hungary, were in no way converts to an extension of the administrative powers of Vienna. Moreover, the reforms had, with difficulty, provided for a force of 108,000 men. This force had not been enough to re-take Silesia or impose significant reverses upon Prussia and the debts incurred during the Seven Years' War were not offset by enhanced revenue from Maria

Theresa's historically significant, but, in terms of what they yielded in hard cash, puny, attacks upon privilege.

When she died in 1780 her son, Joseph II, frustrated in his powers of decision during a fifteen-year regency, might well be excused a degree of impatience in his belief that a more radical approach to privilege could, working on past experience, and should if the Empire were to survive and prosper, be adopted without hesitation. Childless and lonely, incapable, it would appear, of arousing love in his family and dogged by ill-health, Joseph was endowed with singlemindedness and a conviction of the rectitude of his actions on the one hand, and a kind of frenetic energy which demanded immediate results on the other. It was an unfortunate mixture. Perhaps alone amongst eighteenth-century rulers, Joseph II had a plan. He saw his dominions as ensnared in the undesirable social and political accretions of centuries and that his role was primarily to create a *tabula rasa*. The removal of social and political inequalities, he believed, would lift the economy as a whole because the man labouring in his own interest must be especially productive. The emancipation of the masses from the distorting influence of powerful vested groups who maintained their hold through a monopoly of the organs of communication would make possible, once established, a 'God pleasing equality'. The embodiment in law of social equality, of religious tolerance and a severe but uniform penal code, would lead, ineluctably, towards the perfectly functioning state and the harmonious society. To achieve the common good the ruler, who alone could be disinterested, must enjoy a monopoly of public authority, both executive and legislative, and his agents of execution, the bureaucracy, would ensure the implementation of his demands.

Such a streamlined philosophy delineates Joseph as the perfect disciple of the Enlightenment as do his measures attacking privilege in the name of social equality and the unitary state. But Joseph's policy at one significant level took a direction which showed that government demands upon the new unitary state were to be used in a way not necessarily consonant with everyone's interpretation of public welfare. Joseph II was greedy for territorial acquisition and committed to a dynamic foreign policy designed to secure prestige and a share of any spoils. To that end he wanted to maintain an army 300,000 strong – almost 300 per cent greater than the army of the Seven Years' War – which could only stretch the taxable resources of the Empire. Joseph II's unitary state was geared to the glorification of the Habsburgs and to satisfying Joseph's inner vanity to cut a figure in the style of Frederick the Great upon the battlefield. It may be that Joseph, like the French Revolutionary Assemblies, believed that military success cemented a nation together and hence his military policy was a logical extension of his social and political measures. Whereas Prussian rulers had been content to make military exploits wait upon the firm consolidation of domestic policies, a healthy treasury and a relatively united country, Joseph sought to do everything simultaneously.

Joseph's administrative reforms were directed towards reducing the power of the estates, creating a uniform administrative system throughout the Habsburg Empire served by a bureaucracy closely controlled from Vienna using German as its language and drawing upon a single code of law. The new plan was to divide the Habsburg monarchy into thirteen administrative units: Bohemia, Moravia and Austrian Silesia, Galicia and Bukovina, Lower Austria, Inner Austria (Styria, Carinthia and Carniola), Tyrol, Further Austria (the Habsburg possessions in south-west Germany), Transylvania, Hungary and the Banat, Croatia, Lombardy, Görz, Gradiszk, Istria and Trieste. A noteworthy omission from these plans is the Austrian Netherlands. At this juncture, Joseph II clearly realized the problems of incorporating them into his unitary state. His intention in 1779 was to surrender them for the throne of Bavaria. Only the failure of the Bavarian Succession War caused him to change his plans for the Netherlands. The thirteen units were largely contiguous and each had a *gubernia* or provincial government staffed by Vienna. Though they did not have the power of the purse which remained with the estates, they absorbed all other powers.

Most conspicuous was the attempt to extend to Hungary the mechanism by which the hereditary lands were governed. The Hungarian Parliament, a bicameral institution with an upper house of about 300 magnate families and a lower one of some 25,000 gentry, had in fact not been convened by the monarchy since 1765 and it was not this body which offered any threat to any extension of central control so much as the county assemblies (congregations) in which the gentry reigned supreme, controlling all local appointments in administration, justice and the church. When Joseph refused to be crowned at Pressburg in 1780 and four years later actually removed the ancient Crown of St Stephen to Vienna, he was indicating in no uncertain terms the shape of things to come. In 1785, Hungary was divided into ten units, a division based not on ancient provincial divisions but upon demographic considerations. The country assemblies were preserved in name but lost any powers of appointment. New imperial commissioners (*intendants*) and their subordinates (*vizegespane*) took their orders from Vienna. Perhaps the greatest affront of all to a people convinced of their ancient equality with Vienna, was the decree of 1784, in which, making exception only for Lombardy and the Netherlands, German was introduced as the official language. For the central government it was, without doubt, a matter of practical convenience. The Habsburg lands were largely serviced by a bureaucracy composed of German noble families who found in the Empire attractive career prospects. But even if Hungarian or Polish or Czech officials were used, if they dealt in a common language, then they could be moved around at central will.

In 1786, the administrative framework of the Duchy of Milan was worked out in detail. The Duchy had previously been ruled by the Milanese patriciate who controlled the Senate and the *Magistrato Camerale* (the supreme judicial body), and a hotchpotch of individual provincial authorities, also largely monopolized by the local nobility. Maria Theresa had already made inroads into Milanese autonomy by circumscribing the actual power of the Senate and the *Magistrato Camerale*. Now the Duchy was divided into eight administrative units with characteristic Habsburg-style officialdom. Senate, *Magistrato Camerale*, and any provincial institutions with pretensions to government were swept away. The old judicial structure was replaced by a three-tiered set of courts and a code of law in line with that operating in the Habsburg lands.

Only the Austrian Netherlands remained to be brought into line. Least loved of Habsburg possessions, least understood in Vienna, they were recognized to be the richest, the thorniest and most recalcitrant in accepting central change. Comprised of ten separate provinces, each with a set of provincial estates, three-tiered in the French model, and serving as guarantors of provincial privilege and with cities whose virtual autonomy was medieval in origin, the Austrian Netherlands has been termed 'a rationalist's nightmare'. In 1787 the reformer's hand sought to abolish all existing administrative authorities and to replace them with nine provinces (again based on utilitarian considerations) each with the equivalent of intendants and officials who were the creation of Vienna. This brought the Austrian Netherlands fully into line with the administrative framework of the rest of the Habsburg lands. Most conspicuous was the loss in power of the great urban patriciates. Privilege in the Netherlands was indeed an intricate growth, carefully nurtured through succeeding regimes by the provincial estates. Tax exemptions extended far beyond the clergy and nobility to privileged cities and enclaves and royal revenues from the Netherlands fell far short of meeting administrative expenditure. Apart from an annual grant from the estates, much of which was creamed off to support the governor general's court, the monarchy had only been able to touch the income from the royal domain, external customs duties, postal revenues, fees payable upon appointment to high office, for titles and concessions, annual recognition of city charters, some of the profits of justice from royal courts and confiscations of goods left unsold or uncollected after a specified time in the ports. To collect such revenues was immensely cumbersome and disproportionately expensive. The abolition of the power of the estates removed the intermediate body between the Emperor and his privileged or unprivileged subjects though without a thorough reform of the basic premises upon which taxation was based.

The question of tax reform was obviously allied to a larger issue, that of the socio-economic structure of the Empire as a whole. A serf-based society had, to Joseph's thinking, nothing to recommend it. Not only did it deny personal freedom but as long as a lord could take first cut of the proceeds of peasant labour, the serf was precluded from paying his fair share towards the running of the state. Then there was the consideration, very real to Joseph, that serf labour was not truly efficient labour and that hence the economic performance of the country as a whole was impaired by the perpetuation of the practice. Even where seigneurialism was relatively vestigial, as it was in parts of the Netherlands, it served no useful purpose.

Joseph's earliest measures removed the more personally degrading aspects of serfdom and granted freedom to move from one estate to another, provided all prior obligations had been met, freedom to marry without the consent of the lord and to pursue any trade or profession. More significant to the peasant were the ordinances of 1780 which guaranteed, without conceding proprietorship, the hereditary tenure of his property and the curtailment of *banalités* (milling, baking, fishing and hunting rights). Untouched was the issue of emancipation and who would own the land if emancipation was granted. Moreover, the failure to curtail the lord's rights over the peasant's labour meant that the state was still restricted in the demands it could make of the serf. With this in mind, and with a view at the same time to obliterating the unnecessary complications of the state tax-system and towards achieving full social equality came the plan, enunciated in 1784, of a uniform tax on land which permitted no exemptions on the grounds of privilege.

The implications of this plan were enormous. Firstly it entailed a *Kadaster* (a land-survey) of everyone's landed assets to ascertain on a uniform basis property values throughout the Habsburg lands, which could not be carried out overnight. It took from 1784–9 to complete. Secondly, the state needed to know exactly what proportion of peasant income was due to the lord. Joseph's plan insisted that 50 per cent plus of a peasant's income must remain his own so that he could restock his land and live comfortably; something under 20 per cent would be consumed by village contributions; would constitute the state levy and 17.7 per cent that due to the lord. Furthermore, the cash payment was all the lord could expect. Labour services must be remunerated. In short the plan implied an end to domain farming and given the relative shortage of manpower in some territories, would have made agricultural labour prohibitively expensive. The opposition to the measure ensured that it was never put into effect.

The rest of the package offered during the decade of his personal reign included an attack on restrictive guild practices as imposing fetters upon industrial growth. These were at their most extensive in the Netherlands and Czech lands of Bohemia and the morsel of Silesia which remained, that is the more industrialized sectors of the Empire. That the Enlightenment's view of the guilds was overstated – their abolition in France for example merely shifted production from the towns to the country where people would work for less because they had a few acres of land behind them and served to depress certain urban economies – is abundantly clear. Joseph judged them too powerful to attack at one blow, merely abolishing their monopoly of trade (their strongest asset), their property, and allowing the importation of foreign craftsmen, measures which in the long run weakened the urban hold on manufacture and, as in France, moved it into the countryside where the workers were unprotected. Nonetheless the guild-regulated artisan nature of Habsburg industry continued largely to prevail.

Probably more significant in lifting economic performance was the one aspect of Joseph's policy which ran directly counter to Enlightenment principles – protectionism which savoured more of mercantilism than any other economic philosophy. In 1784 a tariff barrier was erected around Hungary and the hereditary lands to exclude foreign goods by the imposition of heavy external customs dues. These even applied to raw materials used in Austrian manufacture. Simultaneously tax relief and bounties were instituted to help native manufactures. Certainly Bohemia and Moravia had reason to look back on Joseph's reign as one of marked expansion for which the state might claim some credit. The growth of the state's income from 65,777,780 *gulden* in 1781 to 87,484,740 *gulden* in 1788 reflects that the Austrian Empire as a whole more than held its own in the expansion of the European economy in the period.

Always, however, one must make special provisos to understand the Netherlands' record. Isolated territorially from the rest of the Empire, its economic performance was more linked with exogenous factors than with Joseph's policy. In particular, the neutral policy pursued by the Austrian Netherlands during the League of Armed Neutrality, and the need for British merchants during the American War of Independence to find netural ports, accelerated an inflow of trade into their coastal cities giving the area a mercantile prosperity which collapsed dramatically after 1786. Two years later, grain regulations designed by the Emperor to keep grain within the Empire to satisfy local demands at a time of generally poor European harvests and a disruption of the grain market by the outbreak of hostilities between Sweden and Russia in the late spring of 1788, cut across the aspirations of Flemish merchants, drawing upon the most productive agriculture in Europe, to take full advantage of the increased price of grain upon the international market. Apart from this measure, the highly developed smuggling rackets which were a quintessential part of the Netherlands' economy, meant that Josephine legislation usually remained a dead letter.

To boost economic performance might well be in the long run the most meaningful way to increase revenues, but it is of little immediate help to a monarch in search of funds and it would be lunacy in any case to suggest that even over the decade of Joseph's reign, the Austrian Empire made significant steps towards industrialization and a capitalist economy. To cope with imminent expenditure state revenues could be best enhanced by extending state control over privileged exemptions. In particular, since the nobility/serf issues were to be dealt with by the reforms issuing from the *Kadaster*, this involved a confrontation with the church. No less devoted than his mother to the precepts of Christian teaching and to the basic premises of the Roman Catholic Church, Joseph was much more a child of the Enlightenment and a more fervent pupil of Van Swieten and Muratori than she. Their particular brand of devotion was of a purged faith stripped of the accretions of baroque piety, of Virgins, relics, votive tablets, statues, pilgrimages, festivals (semi-pagan in origin) and permeated instead by better instruction and personal consciousness of the importance of high moral conduct. Joseph II certainly lent himself wholeheartedly to this particular brand of Catholicism. But he took their work further into the realms of religious tolerance to Protestants and Jews and towards a concept of a Christianity characterized by good works (though Saint Vincent de Paul a century before would have heartily endorsed this). In Joseph's attacks upon the church, one can discern at least a dual intent: the one practical, the other moral, fully expressing an Enlightenment rectitude. On the one hand came the measures extending state control over the church, absorbing church land and above all dismantling the monasteries: on the other came the patent of toleration, significant measures of public welfare, and measures destroying censorship. In Joseph's policy pragmatist and idealist met.

In extending state control over the church, the primary issue concerned the power of the pope within the Habsburg lands. Joseph's point of departure was that the pope was the head of the Church merely because a figure head was needful to express the Church's unity. Johann Valentin von Eybel's pamphlet *What is the Pope?* summarized the Josephist view in asserting that the medieval papacy had usurped that power which belonged to every bishop (the authority to bind and loose had been given by Christ to *all* the apostles, not merely St Peter), hence papal jurisdiction should not extend outside the papal see. Even the pope's claims to decide on faith and morals were challenged by a spate of Josephist writers as false, since such authority lay truly with the councils of the Church. The practical measures which ensued from such reasoning included those prohibiting publication of papal communications without imperial permission, or episcopal appeals to Rome without the Emperor's prior consent. The Bull *Unigenitus* which had condemned Jansenism, was officially denounced. Monasteries in the Habsburg lands were declared released from control by the heads of their order resident in Rome. Perhaps most important of all was the stipulation that bishops must take an oath of allegiance to the state. All this by 1782 virtually amounted to the creation of a national Habsburg church. Pius VI chose, perhaps unwisely, to confront the Emperor face to face, by a visit to Vienna in March – April 1782, a visit which demonstrated that the populace was hostile to Joseph's changes but that the pope had no power to persuade the Emperor, however graciously he might receive him, to change his mind.

There followed a two-fold attack upon church wealth. The first was directed against the monasteries: the second was aimed at the secular church and involved a radical restructuring of clerical income. There can be little doubt of Joseph's (and the Enlightenment's) general contempt for the monastic ideal, and in particular, the contemplative life. In all, starting with the contemplative orders, 700 monasteries were suppressed and 38,000 religious out of 65,000 – over 50 per cent – pensioned and moved out into the world. The proceeds from the sale of the property belonging to these houses were in part paid into a fund set up for charitable purposes and to finance more parish clergy. Church estates were indeed immense: in terms of area they owned half of Carniola and three-eights of Austrian Silesia. Certainly after Joseph's reforms the pattern of landownership was drastically changed, though who the new purchasers were is more obscure.

The assumption by the state of secular ecclesiastical property was with a view to reducing the vast incomes of the episcopate (drawn as to 100 percent from great noble families) and converting them into salaried (quasi civil servant) officials. These were paid respectively 20,000 *gulden* annually for an archbishop (in some instances a salary reduction of 80 per cent) and for bishops 12,000. The proceeds from the sale of land were to be used to pay the parish clergy a living wage and to increase the number of parishes so as to arrive at a better priest/congregation ratio. The parish clergy, it was realized, could be important in disseminating not only greater religious knowledge to their flock but also government ordinances and could explain developments in agricultural techniques. The pulpit was after all the main vehicle whereby the state could reach the masses. An enlightened and reformed clergy was hence a first priority in the creation of the unitary state.

The proceeds from the sale of church land were also partially used as the basis of a social welfare programme. This may not have been Joseph's initial intention for he went so far as to announce to his minister in Brussels that church wealth should be used for religious purposes only. As a Catholic power, the Habsburg lands still looked to voluntary charity and private institutions to succour the sick, the aged, infirm and unemployed. Without radically departing from the principles of Tridentine 'holy charity', a commission headed by Count Johann Buquoy recommended, and saw realized, the foundation of foundling homes, maternity hospitals (which, given the ignorance of antisepsis, multiplied the numbers of women dying from puerperal fever) and general hospitals very much on the model of the French *hôpital général* founded by Saint Vincent de Paul in the 1650s. In part the capital used was raised from church property. The hospital in Vienna had 2000 beds to cater for the old who were past work and the physically disabled. Joseph's creations should not be viewed as a comprehensive scheme of public welfare. As in all such schemes, city dwellers were favoured to the exclusion of country people since the numbers of beds were limited and waiting lists existed. But it was something far more substantial than what had gone before.

Whilst political and economic considerations lurked near the surface in measures attacking clerical wealth and extending state control, the same could not be said for the Patent of Toleration, the first of its kind, which was enacted in 1781. It summarized the revulsion felt by Joseph for religious persecution and misunderstanding and gave total freedom of worship and civil equality to mainline dissenters – Lutheran, Calvinist or Orthodox – but not to the fringe sects which had always proliferated in Bohemia and Silesia. Extended also to the Jews in late 1781 and 1782, these for the first time were allowed to worship freely, to build schools, to attend universities and take degrees. Afraid however that popular anti-semitism might react violently to any ostensible and evident expansion of Jewry, those living in Vienna where a crowd ripe for incitement existed, were more carefully circumscribed and in particular forbidden to build a synagogue or form any communal organization. Another aspect of the policy of tolerance was the relaxation of censorship (excluding pornography and overt atheism) and the unrestricted importation of foreign and Protestant writings.

Much of the spirit of religious tolerance was also embodied in the civil law in process of codification and can be seen in legislation relative to marriage. The power to grant separation was no longer the prerogative of Rome but of the local bishop (as in France). Interdenominational marriages were proclaimed legal and divorce recognized if adultery, abandonment, or criminal conviction before the courts could be proved. Mortal sin was no longer a major crime before the courts. Magic and sorcery were demoted from the rank of capital crime and capital punishment was replaced by the living death of penal servitude – the pulling of barges up and down the Danube was the nearest Austria could come to the spell in the galleys so favoured in French law. Perhaps most significantly of all, a great deal of emphasis was placed upon the uniformity of punishment. This had been the mainspring of Cesare Beccaria's *Delle delitti et delle pene* and contrasted starkly with the random sentencing current in other European countries in the same period.

All this then, together with an extension in primary education and a plethora of rather picturesque measures designed, for example, to encourage breast feeding and to limit the wearing of corsets – which

Enlightenment thought deemed likely to produce foetal abnormality – constituted the Josephist package. At first encounter one is impressed with its total consistency: its remorseless dealing with privilege and the debris of centuries: its wholehearted commitment to the creation of the unitary state and social equality. It is easy to see that certain powerful groups, the clergy, the nobility, the urban patriciates and magistrates, the guild masters, would be immediately alienated but to offset this, surely the measures would purchase the support of the peasantry, of the Protestants, of the Jews, of new officialdom? If the magnates of Hungary and patriciates of the Netherlands were hostile to the package, surely the new coherence of the hereditary lands would carry them along on the tidal wave of change? This, presumably, was Joseph's reasoning and convinced of its quintessential rectitude, hesitating only here and there, by for example not extending many measures to the Austrian Netherlands until 1786–7, and leaving from serf/seigneur questions the thorny issue of the ownership of land, he went ahead, only to die in 1790 a bitter man. 'Here lies Joseph II, who was unfortunate in all his enterprises' was his self-composed epitaph.

What went wrong? The answer is 'everything'. Traditionally and properly, the failure of the Josephist package is given in terms of the victory of provincialism over the concept of the unitary state and of privilege over social equality. Before we consider these reasons, however, let us state something which should be obvious but which is often forgotten. Joseph's programme radically shook society to a degree which can, as yet, only be guessed at. The massive assumptions for example of ecclesiastical wealth in the shape of land, seigneurial income, and monastic buildings, did far more than strip a set of parasitic religious of their wealth to the advantage of parish clergy and welfare institutions for the poor, but robbed craftsmen, employees, purveyors of consumer goods in the monastery's employ of an income. When the Abbey of Melk, for example, spent 27,000 florins annually on its new buildings, most of it went to craftsmen. Indeed the baroque building mania of monasteries within the Habsburg lands in the eighteenth century dispensed wealth over a vast social spectrum. Now one had to be a recipient in a welfare programme to enjoy a cut. Then there was the complex question of land transfers. No monastic dissolution accompanied by land sale, whether in England in the sixteenth century or France in 1790, has been effected without some strain. A change of landlord, in the French and Habsburg instance, meant exchanging a fairly lax traditionalist landlord for someone anxious to capitalize his investment. Whole villages could be affected. Every time law courts were streamlined, someone lost his job. In particular, the radical reformation of the tangle of urban and provincial jurisdiction which characterized the Netherlands and to a lesser extent north Italy, cut at the employment of thousands. The property of the guilds had buttressed many a small workman in distress and had offered very limited protection to the widows and orphans of guild members, sometimes allowing the widow to continue production in her husband's name. Where was such protection now? How could one persuade an urban master, a relatively humble man on a bread and vegetable diet employing perhaps a couple of journeymen, the profits of whose labour were probably not much smaller than those of the master himself, of the virtue of throwing industry open to the countryside? To understand the vehemence of response, one must stand in such a man's shoes and share the anxiety of the farmer who was apprehensive about his new landlord.

The *ancien régime* was a set of vital economic relations. However corrupt, however reprehensible to the reformer privilege in one shape or another might be, one could not destroy it without disturbing the livelihood even of the most humble. There were psychological implications too. Loyalty to province came next to loyalty to kin and village: one mistrusted the outsider. What confidence could anyone, humble or substantial, feel in a German-speaking bureaucracy or in a reformed law which emanated from an alien source? To take another direction, everything we know about popular religion in the eighteenth century, anywhere in Europe, underscores its total revulsion for anything savouring of the Jansenist ethic. Vivid, immediate, semi-pagan, the religion of the masses wallowed in the accretions of baroque images, fête days, processions and cared nothing for better instruction, more exigent morality and a religion pared down to its purest essentials.

Hence Joseph, however much he might be seen as the serf's ally against the evils of his grasping lord, could not look to a broad basis of popular support for his measures. An archbishop in the Netherlands, resentful of power loss, of income loss, or outraged over the civil legislation regulating divorce, could rally popular support in defence of the old order and of his particular interests amongst the urban masses. Indeed some of the most violent revolts in the Netherlands were led by women against Joseph as antichrist. What provoked them specifically can only be surmised, but since 1786 they had been the victims of slump, of an economic hardship it was over-easy to identify with the regime and, like the women of France in 1795, they chose religious demonstrations as an effective vehicle of protest.

Joseph II's policies were in fact defeated both at the national level and by specific social groups. The most vociferous protests occurred in Hungary and the Netherlands, but even in the hereditary lands attempts to impose a uniform judicial system and to undercut the provincial estates were bitterly resented as cutting across traditional privileges recognizing the separate character of the component elements in the hereditary lands. By the end of his reign even here Joseph had to make concessions. The Hungarian nobility, however, rather than accept the tax decrees, took to the sword and as the *Kadaster* approached completion in 1788 actually made overtures to the King of Prussia for help against the Habsburgs. Beset with problems resulting from his own foreign policy and with a disastrous war against the Turks, Joseph could look to no body of support to counter the opposition of the Magyar nobility and peace could only be purchased by scrapping the entire reform programme.

In the Netherlands, the opposition was more diffuse, but no less effective, with aristocratic patriciates, the high clergy, and the urban populace involved in sporadic insurrections. Rumours of a mass conscription where in the people of the Netherlands would be drafted into the imperial army to wage war on Turkey, inspired the citizenry to organize themselves into armed corps. Almost daily from 1787 the provincial estates, led by Brabant, expressed vociferous opposition and demanded immediate revocation of all administrative and judicial decrees, the re-establishment of all religious houses to which the religious wished to return, the surrender to the estates of all annexed religious property and the full restoration of the powers of the estates.

The lives of ministers were threatened: blood-soaked flags recalling the struggle against Philip II of Spain were ostentatiously waved; patriotic songs recalling in some instances the revolt of the Netherlands were chanted by an urban mob ready for an outlet for its grievances. Making common cause with the 'Patriot' party, loyal to the ideals of a Netherlands whose ancient powers were restored, were the University of Louvain, the Primate of the Netherlands, Archbishop Frankenberg, ironically Silesian by birth, and the Bishops of Namur, Antwerp, Bruges and Ruremonde who entered the arena in late 1787. A disastrous harvest and trade recession only intensified a situation in which the local Habsburg administration understandably panicked and could not be called upon to hold a firm line. For a year Joseph tried to appease the bishops with theological arguments. In the meanwhile, the political situation deteriorated further with several provincial estates withholding taxes and the whole Netherlands question was complicated by the abrupt political changes occurring in France in 1788–9.

Liège was to become the most dangerous heartland of revolt and groups formed, such as *Pro aris et focis* (For Hearth and Altar), inspired by the lawyer Jean François Vonck, committed to the overthrow of monarchical absolutism and the delegation of political power to a broader social group. Indeed, it was the Vonckists who forged an army, sought to enlist foreign support and were to be the most organized nucleus of revolt.

Yet the immediate situation was to eventuate in a victory for the Patriot programme of a return to the old order of provincial autonomy and of aristocratic, clerical and municipal privilege. And the Vonckists, whether or not they should, as they frequently have been, be labelled 'democrats', cast their glances towards France and threw in their lot with the politicians of Revolutionary France. The end of this saga transcends the limits of this volume but it should be remembered that the implementation of Joseph's reform programme in the Netherlands unleashed both conservative and radical forces of opposition. Nothing and no one was on his side.

Even in the Habsburg hereditary lands which did not erupt into open revolt, beyond the formation of armed peasant bands to defend statues and banners against the imperial officials who sought to destroy them, significant concessions had to be made. Joseph could not even impress his subjects with a successful foreign policy to compensate for heavy taxes and recruiting demands. His foreign ventures opened disastrously with the failure of the War of the Bavarian Succession. Joseph put forward specious genealogical pretensions to the Bavarian electorate on the death of the Elector Maximilian Joseph in 1777 and backed his claims with an invasion. This incurred an immediate Prussian reaction leading to massive troop movements into Bohemia and immense territorial devastation resulting in the Peace of Teschen (May 1779), wherein a few square miles of territory passed to the Habsburg crown.

There followed abortive attempts to open the Scheldt which cost him the French alliance. Joseph's main achievement was the alienation of almost every European power. Several German princes, Hanover, Saxony, Mainz, Prussia and fourteen others formed a League of Princes to forestall any further German ambitions Joseph might nurture. His last involvement was his most disastrous. Spurred on by Balkan ambitions, he followed Catherine the Great into war with the Turks in 1787 and at the head of an army 200,000 strong, he personally led a catastrophic advance into Ottoman territory. His army, decimated by typhus and typhoid epidemics, was forced to retreat and Turkish forces devastated southern Hungary. Whilst the Turks were thus occupied, Catherine annexed the Crimea and reached the Dniester. Colossal war debts left the Austrian treasury with a debt of 400 million *gulden.*

Small wonder that freedom of the press opened up criticism of the monarchy, criticism which Joseph magnified and chose to repress by a secret police force organized by the Minister of the Interior, Count Pergen. This police force, to justify its existence, in turn invented plots and counterplots. Yet there was no revolutionary situation in Vienna in 1789, in spite of bread riots. An aristocratic city whose central role had been strengthened rather than weakened by Maria Theresa and her son, it rode out the revolutionary tide and survived by rejecting the *Staatsidee.* Joseph II however died a defeated and broken man, the most conspicuous victim of eighteenth-century privilege.

7

Prussia

The history of Prussia, the other mammoth of the Empire, in the eighteenth century, traditionally takes the form of a panegyric to two rulers, Frederick William I (1713–40) and Frederick II (1740–86) who, acting in auspicious circumstances, made possible what has been called 'the miracle of the house of Brandenburg'.[1] This 'miracle', expressed in concrete terms, was the acquisition of 76,000 square miles of territory, over a third of the Prussian state as it was in 1780. The population of this expanding state rose in the course of the century, in spite of slow natural growth, from 2.2 million to 5 million. The new territory was acquired by conquest in the case of Silesia, or by inheritance in the case of East Friesland, or by diplomatic negotiations, reinforced by Prussia's evident military strength, in the case of West Prussia – Prussia's gain from the unsavoury first Partition of Poland.

In the power politics of the eighteenth century, Prussia obviously did very well. Behind the acquisitions lay the reality of the army with the most impressive reputation of its day. This army in its later stages was 150,000 strong, and though numerically inferior to the forces of the Habsburgs and the Romanovs was superbly drilled and led in the field by a king with a military expertise no other ruler of his day possessed. Behind the army lay the bastion upon which its success rested, a healthy treasury, which ensured that the military was both fed and paid. This achievement has been attributed to the sacrifices of a hard-working peasantry, to the work of a bureaucracy which left Europe gaping at its efficiency and to the parsimony of the rulers. The Prussian 'miracle' has been written up in terms reminiscent of those Tacitus used when he contrasted the virtuous German with the effete Roman.

What made the difference between Prussia and other continental states was the moral force that emanated from the greatest of the Hohenzol-

---

1 W. Hubatsch, *Frederick the Great. Absolutism and Administration* (London, 1976).

lerns and the superb quality of the Prussian bureaucracy, one of the first
great modern civil service systems of Europe.[2]

In the same spirit is the assertion that Prussia ran a first-rate army on
the resources of a third-rate state. The implications of such a historiographical approach lay a great deal at the feet of personality and moral
fibre and whilst accepting that both have their role to play in historical
interpretation neither should be offered as total explanation. From the
1670s there had emerged in the German principalities a tradition of
maintaining strong standing forces whose aid could be purchased by
other foreign powers to pursue particular dynastic policies. These
standing armies, whose size was disproportionate to the state revenues
behind them, and which could not have existed without foreign support, progressively came to be built into the structure of German
politics and without them it is impossible to understand the German
politico-social structure. The growth of one army precipitated the
growth of another in order to secure immediate survival within
Germany. The use of these armies by foreign powers whether directly
as mercenaries or in alliances embodying subsidy payments or territorial
concessions, dictated the shape of German, and indeed European,
politics.

When in the late seventeenth century the nascent Prussian state began
to create an army, it did no more than Hanover, Brunswick, Mecklenburg, Saxony or Bavaria and a third of that army helped the Habsburgs
save Vienna from the Turks. Yet events, and in particular two if not
three power vacuums, permitted Prussia in the eighteenth century to
pursue a path in European politics which made it unique amongst
German states. The first, and most important, was the collapse of
Swedish power in north Germany in the early eighteenth century: the
second the increasingly anarchical Polish political situation which in
first instance made the elections to the Polish crown the occasion of
constant take-over bids by interested parties and ultimately exposed
that country to dismemberment. The third was the visible weakening
of Habsburg power within Germany in the first half of the eighteenth
century and the tenuous hold, due in part to a disputed succession, of
the Habsburgs over their most distant territories.

This is, of course, a crude, quick analysis. Even in the power politics
of the late seventeenth century the Great Elector had bartered his armies
and his alliances, with conspicuous shrewdness, though he was far from
being total master of the situation. At the turn of the seventeenth
century, Prussia had been caught between two wars, the Great Northern
War and the War of the Spanish Succession. True interest demanded
Prussian involvement in the first by helping Peter the Great demolish

2 W. L. Dorn, *Competition for Empire, 1740–1763* (New York, 1940), p. 53.

Swedish power with a view to acquiring West (or Polish) Prussia, Swedish Pomerania and a Baltic outlet. But Peter the Great could not afford to pay the subsidies on which the Prussian army depended whereas the Grand Alliance directed against Louis XIV could. For his participation, Frederick William I in 1713 at Utrecht picked up some territorial crumbs in western Europe (Mors and Lingen, Tecklenburg near Cleves; Neuchâtel on the western borders of Switzerland and Upper Gelders in the Spanish Netherlands). He then prepared to put his army in order but was precipitated by Charles XII into more active participation in the last episodes of the Great Northern War. By the Treaty of Stockholm (1720), Prussia acquired the eastern half of Swedish Pomerania stretching from the Oder to the Peene and the important Baltic port of Stettin. This acquisition probably more than any other determined that Prussia, whatever the intellectual predilections of her rulers, was emphatically an east European power – albeit one with significant toeholds (Cleves, Mark, Gelderland, etc.) in the west.

Both Frederick William and Frederick the Great recognized in their scale of priorities that the western territories, whatever they might yield in income, were less integrally a part of the Prussian state than territories contiguous to the Prussian heartland. Such a scale of priorities was no secret. West German states in particular lived with dynastic impermanence. They were familiar appendages in European treaties. Their provincial estates and homage ceremonies were geared to surviving transitions of allegiance whilst preserving the privileges and customs of their territories and in this process they were helped by the institutions of the Empire. Before Frederick the Great, no Prussian king had dared fly in the face of the ancient mechanism governing relationships within the Empire, and even Frederick accepted certain rules. As ruler of German territorial states the Prussian king was utterly circumscribed by possessions held as Elector of Brandenburg (he was no king in the Empire). Every legal reform needed permission from the Emperor in his capacity as chairman of the *Reichstag*. Every measure affecting law, taxation, recruitment and troop quartering had to respect provincial privilege in accordance with the imperial constitution. To talk of a policy of centralization and the all-embracing power of a despotic king is to demonstrate total ignorance of the whole character and rationale of the Empire. In order to achieve manoeuvrability the Prussian king had to look outside the Empire. His trump card became the dual character he assumed as ruler of non-German territories. This meant that he could secure a role in European politics which he could not enjoy within the Empire where his influence was circumscribed. A conspicuous tendency of Prussian rulers in the eighteenth century was to place their efforts into building up and stimulating the economies of their non-German and marginally German territories (East Prussia, Silesia, the Oderbruch venture and West or Polish Prussia) using in large part the domain revenues drawn from their west German holdings. When Frederick the Great referred to his possessions it was as 'mes états' and any concept we have of the unitary state as applied to Prussia must take account, as in the case of the Habsburg lands, of a highly developed provincial particularism. But it was a particularism which, on the whole, the Hohenzollerns did not have to antagonize to stay alive in European power politics.

The Prussian government by 1730 had a startling simplicity attributable to the efforts of Frederick William I. He gradually shifted business from the Privy Council in Berlin, which had previously served as an advisory body on all matters of foreign and domestic policy, to the king's private chamber (*Kabinet*) at Potsdam. The physical distancing of king from Privy Council symbolized the isolation of an institution able to offer written advice but with no direct control over the king's decisions. From Sans Souci in Potsdam issued a string of edicts and written instructions to ministers and civil servants. Such edicts rarely flew in the face of ministerial advice but ministers could not feel that they had necessarily influenced legislation. This distancing of king and Privy Council did not mean that the latter ceased to sit but that it did so less frequently and its meetings crystallized into small committees. One discussed foreign affairs, a second, the *Justizrat*, judicial policy, and a third, the *Geheimer Staatsrat* (Privy State Council), was concerned with domestic policy. These committees then drafted memoranda for the king's consideration.

In 1723, Frederick William I had amalgamated the military and fiscal agencies of his states into a single organization, the General Directory (*General-Ober-Finanz-Kriegs-und Domanen Directorium*) composed of about twenty people of whom the four most important were ministers, each responsible for two kinds of duty. Firstly, each must supervise the administration of a quarter of Prussian territories and secondly, each must present specialized knowledge of one of four categories of subject, frontiers and agriculture, general budget, army, postal system and coinage. Each was committed to making regular reports to the king and it was upon the views of these ministers that the king was most heavily dependent, though theoretically, he was not obliged to heed their advice.

Each principality had a Board of War and Domains (*Kriegs und Domanenrate*) comprised of councillors or commissars whose job was comparable with that of a French intendant and whose relationship with the minister of the General Directory responsible for the area was much the same as that of a French intendant with the *contrôleur général*. Below the boards in the towns were tax commissioners (*Steuerat*) and in the rural districts noble commissioners (*Landrat*) made up of local Junker seigneurs. The last also made up rural district councils and retained control of the most significant unit of traditional justice, the *Regierungen*. In other words, although the upper echelons of the bureaucracy were national appointees, at the bottom, the functioning of the Prussian state was dependent upon locals and in that respect was no different from any other European state.

It differed from them, however, in two crucial respects. In Prussia in the eighteenth century there had been, and continued to be, a steady growth in public law and a concomitant shrinkage in the powers of traditional law. This meant that there was a marked development in the demands and intrusions the state could make upon an individual or community in its own name. Whilst the traditional rights of provincial estates and nobilities were respected in regard to ancient land taxes, other state matters, such as taxes other than land tax, military affairs, local government, the administration of regalian rights (specific royal privileges), prices, wages, roads, monopolies, were the direct concern of the state and the citizen had no appeal against royal decisions.

The growth in public law did not lead to any proliferation of new courts or special legal officials. On the contrary, the king's executives in the provinces were just endowed, should the occasion arrive, with powers comprehensive enough to allow them to function as on-the-spot judges of those who refused their demands.

The second distinctive feature of the Prussian state was the nature of its revenues, the type of taxation it levied. Whereas other European powers looked mainly either to direct or indirect taxation and in the case of most of Germany to the *Bede* (a land tax similar to the *taille*) the Prussian monarchy to a considerable extent lived off its own. Domanial and regalian rights constituted in 1740 about 51 per cent of state revenue: second in importance were the excise taxes which formed a further 20 per cent and then came the *Landkasten* or land tax and finally miscellaneous taxes on industry and commerce.

The significance of such a revenue structure is worth spelling out for it gave the ruler of Prussia a freedom of manoeuvre unparalleled elsewhere. He was direct owner of a large proportion of Prussian soil (in East Prussia more than 50 per cent). His properties were leased out to a steward who had to keep registers of receipts and accounts and submit them to a provincial college which corresponded directly with the king and had to provide the General Directory with precise information. Hence the Directory was perfectly informed of the productivity of every farm. It could augment the value of the lease if there was a demand for stewardship or diminish it if recruitment was difficult. It could force changes of crop rotation and demand experimentation if it thought revenues might thus be raised. Hence maximum flexibility could be achieved and newly asserted or colonized land, initially held on favourable terms, could little by little be made to contribute more.

Excise taxes could also be fairly easily levied and readily augmented. As a non-traditional tax, they need not be contested by provincial estates. As taxes on consumption, particularly drink (though by the end of the eighteenth century there were 2775 excisable articles subject to 67 rates and demanding 8000 tax officials), the bulk of excise taxes levied were in the cities. Probably they were no greater burden on the townsdweller than the combined *aides* and *octrois* levied in France but whereas in France most of the revenue went towards municipal finances, in Prussia these were kept to a minimum and the state itself was arbiter over the disposal of the excise. Generally the cost of levying the excise was about 12 per cent of the yield.

Land taxes, on the other hand, were the least flexible form of state income and relative emancipation from heavy dependence upon them certainly gave the King of Prussia an edge over other European monarchs. Land taxes were ancient and hence fraught with exemptions and, worst of all, had to be agreed with provincial estates. True the power of these institutions had been somewhat curtailed by 1730 in Prussia but a monarch who did not need to make demands need fear no opposition anyway. Is it needful to contrast the fate of the Habsburg monarch or other German prince forced to bargain with his provincial estates and to see expenses deducted by them from the revenues of the land taxes?

Alone of European monarchs, Frederick the Great inherited a surplus from his predecessor, 10 million *thalers* which, in spite of the demands of war, would be converted into 54 million *thalers* by the end of his reign.

It is almost standard practice to accentuate the parsimony and business acumen of the Prussian monarchy in order to explain how a 'backward' economy could be geared to war. Whilst not denying the talents of both Frederick William I and Frederick the Great (and what could happen to the state under a weak monarch would be demonstrated in the ensuing reign) one should be careful to stress not so much the backwardness of the Prussian economy as its peculiarities and to recognize the advantageous position from which the eighteenth-century Hohenzollerns started.

Prussia was 'backward' by western European standards in the first instance simply because the king was to such a great extent direct landowner and seigneur of his kingdom. This meant he received the revenues of immediate landlord and seigneur as well as state revenues. The bulk of the domain revenues of other sovereigns had long been alienated and most were limited now to forest rights alone. Moreover, if economic growth in eighteenth-century Prussia did not equal that of some western European nations, such growth as existed, in bringing new land under cultivation and improving food supplies, was in the direction that mattered for the bulk of the populace. It may well be that the retention of serfdom and the incidence of the excise retarded the growth of capitalism in Prussia by a century or more but at least scantily populated Prussia was not bedevilled by a surplus population of landless or unemployed. There was no land hunger and no extensive problem of poverty or vagrancy to rival conditions in parts of France by the sixties. Furthermore, to present the Prussian serf as particularly oppressed or highly taxed is thoughtless. If he parted with 30 per cent of his income to the state, he did no more, and possibly less, than the French peasant who on average probably parted with 30 per cent to king, lord and church and 30 per cent to his landlord. Scarcity of manpower ensured he had at least enough to eat. Indeed, his position as a serf guaranteed him a degree of economic protection and, like the serf of the Habsburg lands, he was not necessarily the protagonist of serf-emancipation. True the range of wealth visible amongst the serf community was not as great as that amongst rural society in France or the Low Countries but this is to enter other realms. Never did the Prussian army like that of Catherine the Great have to be deflected to quell risings at home.

It is also possible to exaggerate the efficiency of the Prussian bureaucratic machine in comparison with that of other European powers. Outside domanial management there was nothing streamlined about the levying or collection of tax: taxes were slapped on taxes: the excise was characterized by 67 tariffs and the introduction of a general farm on the French model to manage indirect taxes was regarded as a reforming measure. Perhaps the most that can be said about the Prussian bureaucracy is that less revenue stuck to its hands than in other countries, a characteristic perhaps attributable to the direct responsibility of tax officials and bureaucrats to the General Directory. The worst that can be said of it was that at the top it was an indisputable bottle-neck. Cabinet government overstretched the capacity of the monarch, not least when he was at war and unable to give his attention to the day to day running of the country.

The question, where does power reside in the Prussian state in 1730, is fairly simple of resolution. Clearly the king held in his own hands a great deal of power: his bureaucrats were no venal officials undisturbable in office but royal nominees who could be dismissed if inefficient or corrupt. There existed few institutional checks upon the royal will in the shape of powerful provincial estates. Notwithstanding, sheer bulk of business involved some delegation. Ministers who existed to present information could be far from objective and, most importantly, as Miss Behrens has pointed out, even Frederick William I conceded that he must be 'soutenieren' or give support to his bureaucracy, if he wished to be 'souteniert' (supported). What this meant, as Frederick the Great was also to recognize, was a monopoly of the best positions by the local nobility and a staunch support by the monarchy of noble interests in the localities. Perhaps the uniqueness of the Prussian case lies in the community of interests which was to be found between ruler and nobility which made possible a collusion not found elsewhere. Such institutions as existed where confrontation between monarchy and nobility could be nurtured were neutralized. One institution existed, the army, in which the noble officer class and the monarchy were in perfect harmony. The intertwining of the interests of the autocracy, aristocracy, army and bureaucracy and their points of difference distinguish Prussian history in this period.

Apart from the creation of the General Directory, Frederick William I's achievements lie in the direction of developing a class of able, dependable and hardworking officials, for reforming the Prussian army, and for the resettlement (*rétablissement*) of East Prussia by encouraging immigration from neighbouring territories and according subsidies. The population in this area increased from 160,000 to 600,000 in twenty years. Perhaps his administrative achievement was the most noteworthy. Frederick William's officialdom, the bureaucrats prepared *travailler pour le roi de Prusse* (that is, to work hard for indifferent pay), were in their highest *echelons* drawn in part from the indigenous nobility and had previously been judges, army officers, or had managed large estates. These were supplemented by immigrants from other German states drawn from families who traditionally sent some of their scions into Habsburg, Vasa or Bourbon service and who were now attracted by the extension of Prussian state service. But the most significant element was of common stock. Expansion opened the way for these new men to get ahead as Frederick William set himself to break court-cliques and the concept of placemen. Hence half the ministers and five-sixths of the councillors of important chambers were non-nobles in 1740. Promotion above a certain grade brought with it, inevitably, ennoblement which meant that a type of *noblesse de robe* was in the process of evolving, though these bureaucrats, if inefficient, could be speedily and humiliatingly dismissed. The employment of retired soldiers or those nobles no longer fit for service and the transference, in time of peace, of noble army officers, expected to set a model for blind obedience to royal commands and for quick, unflagging and disciplined activity, into the civil service, also became a marked feature of Frederick William I's civil bureaucracy. At two levels, however, that of the *Landrat* and in the officer class of the army, the noble stranglehold on high position remained undisturbed. In short, the bureaucracy as it emerged under Frederick William I was a fusion of old and new. Patronage was obviously not fully eliminated – someone had to recommend one's activities to the king – and education and a degree of financial backing were obviously essential prerequisites to office-holding which meant that the inflow was from a limited social spectrum. Venality was not totally destroyed but the king did emancipate himself from a bureaucracy emanating from court nobles whose power in the localities rested on the distribution of offices.

Though scarcely recognized in principle, in practice a strong element of heredity crept into the civil service which was probably inevitable in a state composed of scattered territories and scanty population. Hence sons and nephews stepped into positions vacated by fathers and uncles, unresisted, unless they showed themselves incompetent, by the central control. In short the 'open' nature of Prussian bureaucracy under Frederick William I had already built into it aspects which ensured such openness steadily receded and indeed, since some posts earned ennoblement, that it became progressively noble as well as closed. High ranking posts in the central administration even under Frederick William I were the preserve of a few select noble families.

The army with which Frederick the Great was to embark upon the conquest of Silesia in 1740 was, of course, the legacy of his father. He had in significant part 'Prussianized' the army and secondly had made it an integral part of Prussian society. In 1713, two-thirds of the army were foreigners mostly recruited, often forcibly, by armed raids, from those German states which did not themselves run standing armies. By 1739 the proportions had been reversed. Of the 81,000 troops who composed Prussia's fighting force, two-thirds were Prussian and the officer class, almost in its totality, was native born and drawn from the Prussian nobility, members of which were forbidden by the king to seek employment in armies abroad.

For recruitment purposes, Prussian territories were divided into cantons, each supplying men for a particular regiment. The regiments thus raised were kept at full strength only between April and June and for the rest of the year a proportion were on furlough, working the land, which cut support costs. (There is a close analogy here with Swedish practice in the late seventeenth century.) Those maintained full time were housed in garrison towns, largely with burgher families. This home-basing of regiments achieved a linkage between the civilian and military populace not readily achieved elsewhere and does not appear to have created friction in the country as it did elsewhere in Europe, perhaps because manpower was scarce in Prussia and a son recruited into the ranks was not lost to the land. This did not eliminate desertion in the Prussian ranks. Indeed, the desertion rate was, during Frederick William's reign, of the order of 35 per cent per annum and was particularly high amongst the forced recruits from Mecklenburg. These figures rose considerably in the course of the Seven Years' War. Neither Frederick William nor Frederick the Great had any confidence in the loyalty of the common soldier. Neither expected, after battle, to be able to pursue the enemy because a considerable proportion of the Prussian force would simply have disappeared, a problem they shared with every other European monarch. They coped with it, however, in a somewhat different way. They relied on the loyalty of an officer class which did not hesitate to enforce a brutal discipline upon the common soldier and on a drilling routine which rendered the soldier under battle conditions an automaton. The common soldier advanced because programmed to do so and because, locked as he was between officers who would have shot him had he lagged, he had no alternative.

Perhaps little distinguished the Austrian from the Prussian soldier, but much differentiated the Austrian and Prussian officer. The latter, bound by kinship, mutual interest and an *esprit de corps*, scions of a Junker grouping whose economic well-being and social standing depended upon civil or military appointment, experienced directly a feeling of oneness with the king. This was because Frederick William and his son after him made it clear that the king was one of them, the chief officer, the soldier-king. He shared the privations of the field and a way of life that shrugged off luxuries. It was at the military level that the vaunted collusion of ruler and Junker became most apparent. Whatever the course of Prussian expansion, the Junkers as a group could feel confident that it was in a direction which furthered their immediate economic interests by providing scope for their advancement either as officers, civil servants or landholders. When a Magyar officer in the Habsburg army took to the field in defence of Czech territories he could not immediately perceive how this would benefit him. He was at odds with his service whereas, from the seventeenth century onwards, in Prussia close co-operation existed. Service in the army was a source of income of first-rate importance for the Prussian Junker, endowing Junkers as a whole with the protection of the state and a confirmation of their control over their serfs.

Frederick William I is often contrasted with his son as a man of little refinement for whom the intellectual climate of western Europe held no attractions, and the stormy relationship which existed between himself and his son during the latter's adolescence is used to explain some fundamental differences between the two. In fact the similarities between them are more apparent. True Frederick the Great throughout his life paid formal allegiance to ideas stressing the obligations of the ruler to use his powers in the interests of his people. His *Anti Machiavel* (1741) and *Essai sur les formes de gouvernement* (1781) embody a concept of monarchy dedicated to the good of the state. Certainly he was more preoccupied than his father with issues such as religious tolerance and education. Yet for both, military strength and administrative efficiency, the power-state which suppressed the interests of individuals to an austere and demanding concept of the common good, the duties of both ruler and ruled rather than their happiness or liberty, were the true essentials. To many Europeans, even German writers like Wieland, Lessing, and Winckelmann, Prussia seemed the most abhorrent of despotisms in the degree of control exercised by the ruler over the ruled, the constant intervention of the state in the freedom of the individual, the blatant inequalities within the social structure and the gearing of an entire society to militaristic ends. All these facets of Prussian life served fundamentally to alienate western European partisans of the Enlightenment.

Their yardstick, however, was a western European one and German intellectuals in particular failed to appreciate that Prussia was increasingly an eastern not a western European power forced to make out in the shifting world of east European politics. Her centre of gravity was situated east of the Elbe and affinities lay with eastern not western Europe. This shift was given real form under Frederick the Great and Prussia's role within the Empire became increasingly difficult to define. Under Frederick William I, Prussia remained solidly committed to the idea of the Empire even when this entailed humiliation at Habsburg hands. The best instance of this was on the issue of Prussian claims to the Rhenish provinces of Julich and Berg, to which Charles VI had acceded in 1728 in return for Prussian acceptance of the Pragmatic Sanction. In 1738 when the Habsburg Emperor signed a treaty with France and the maritime powers, he judged Prussian acquiescence something he could sacrifice and he repudiated the claims. Frederick William accepted this slight, smarting. The House of Habsburg was to pay for this action for Frederick the Great radically parted company with his father in the deference he was prepared to give to the concept of the Holy Roman Empire.

In 1740 a concept of the Empire in which princes were equals under Habsburg presidency was largely nullified. The invasion of Silesia showed that Frederick ignored the constitutional authority of the Habsburg Emperor. His substitution of King *of* Prussia for King *in* Prussia indicated that his kingship was unqualified by imperial custom. In 1750 the prayer for the Emperor was dropped in Prussian churches. In the aftermath of the Seven Years' War Frederick considered pulling out of the Empire altogether. But he did not do so, in spite of the niggling rules to which this exposed him, probably on the grounds that it gave him a leverage within Germany which a formal severance would have destroyed, a truth demonstrated in the Bavarian Succession War wherein Prussian military strength prevented an extension of Habsburg power within Germany.

Nevertheless, the state Frederick the Great controlled was no mere German electorate, but a power astride east Germany looking yet further eastward. His invasion of Silesia, the first significant action of his reign, was a calculated risk which bore no relation to the specious hereditary claims later advanced to support his action, but to his eastward ambitions. Not only did he reject the Pragmatic Sanction and invade Silesia but his success earned him the French alliance and a valuable territorial acquisition, hard evidence of his drive to forge a state for which the Empire had little or no relevance. The next two decades were devoted to ensuring that he did not lose his acquisition.

In economic terms, the acquisition of Silesia was Prussia's most significant asset. By 1750 the province produced 45 per cent (10 million
thalers) of Prussia's total exports and bought 44 per cent of her imports.
It represented, in industrial terms, the most advanced sector of the
Prussian state. Frederick can be credited with a grasp, unusual amongst
monarchs, of the significance of economic matters. He added to the
General Directory a fifth department radically different from the other
departments conceived on a regional basis. The purpose of this department was to view the Prussian economy as a whole and to formulate
and implement policies relating to trade, agriculture and industry which
had universal application.

In his approach to economic matters, Frederick was no pupil of the
Enlightenment, his ideas savoured less of Quesnay than of Colbert. The
economy must be tightly controlled by state directive: existing manufactures must be helped by protective measures: foreign artisans must be
encouraged to set up manufactures of products which Prussia presently
purchased abroad. The Fifth Department under von Marschall who was
an eloquent mercantilist, also set itself to advise existing industries on
production problems and to collect statistics from which local production and consumption could be estimated. One can exaggerate the
efficiency of von Marschall's work. For the first fifteen years or so of
its existence (by which time the state was plunged into the Seven Years'
War) precise information was difficult to amass and much had to be
surmised. Clearly an economic policy could not be given firm direction
in wartime and the dislocation engendered by the Seven Years' War
carried on well into the seventies. There is evidence to suggest that the
woollen cloth industry – employing by the end of Frederick's reign
about 60,000 workers – experienced solid expansion. The most obvious
reason for this was the continuing, steady demand to serve the needs of
an army standing by the end of the reign at some 150,000 strong.
Otherwise, the domestic market remained sluggish. Although there
were more people to clothe than before, peasant spending power was
limited and virtually static. Rough domestic industry often made the
family self-sufficient and kept it out of the cloth market. Noteworthy
advances were made in promoting the production of quality linens, fine
woollen cloth and, in Silesia, cotton production in state factories often
with imported artisan labour. Perhaps most significant of all, as an
export, was the production of silk. Here it was a question of the state
protecting and encouraging private initiative and a curious but effective
system of localized protection. The Krefeld silk industry, the most
consequential of state exports, was permitted only a limited domestic
radius for its sales to help the nascent industries of Kurmark, Stettin and
Königsberg. There was also, again at the luxury level, important state
direction given to the manufacture of porcelain. The impact of such
industrial growth on the overall economy was slight but the Prussian

state – as it existed in 1740 – did become self-sufficient in supplying its industrial needs in the course of Frederick's reign. That a trade surplus existed, was, however, due to the acquisition of Silesia. Here the development of already considerable metallurgical industries and coal mining, the foundation of new glassworks, state subsidies accorded to put depressed industries like the production of fine linen back into production, in spite of the vicissitudes of war, enjoyed distinct success. Frederick the Great would have been the first to recognize that as a result of his efforts Prussia was far from being a highly industrialized state but his aim for self-sufficiency was more than achieved.

An element of pragmatism ran through Frederick's approach to economic questions. Never, for example, in respect of the grain trade did he allow himself to be led astray by the will-o'-the-wisp of *laissez-faire* which exposed other western European nations to dislocation. Some of the Prussian states were situated in the midst of other states (Poland, Mecklenburg, Saxony) who were heavy grain producers whilst local farmland was of indifferent quality. Clearly local producers in normal times needed a protection from cheap foreign competition which was stringently enforced. Every effort was made to keep the price of grain relatively constant. In Silesia which was never self-sufficient in grain, subsidies were placed on grain imports from the rest of the Hohenzollern lands to keep the price within bounds. The existence of a great standing army entailed the running of state magazines and indeed, particularly after the bad harvests of 1739 and 1746, the state leant particularly heavily upon official grain stores to protect the country in time of dearth. In 1771–2 when the failure of the eastern European rye crop brought Saxony and Bohemia to the point of starvation and rye rose to five *thalers* a bushel in these areas, in Prussia, thanks to the opening of grain reserves, it stood at half that amount.

The state backed the consumer against the speculator by fixing market prices and curtailing the use of grain for distillation. Such a policy did not fly in the face of Junker interests. Prussia was an agrarian society based on serf labour. Shortage of manpower meant that without the legal fixation of labour, large-scale farming would have been impossible. The state by confirming the landlord's hold over his men, by protecting him against foreign imports, by being a consistent purchaser on the army's behalf and to fill the *Landmagazine*, gave security to his existence. Amongst reforming farmers of the eighteenth century, an element amongst the Junkers was able to elbow a place next to the yeoman farmer of East Anglia or his Flemish counterpart because this element was secure enough to make experiments to lift production. The subjection of serf to lord was intensified by the union in the Junker class of landownership (*Grundherrschaft*) with jurisdictional rights (*Gerichtsherrschaft*) which made the lord judicial, administrative and often military official as well. Yet, setting aside the abnormal conditions produced by the Seven Years' War, and the difficult years of harvest failure and pestilence in the early 1770s, one cannot on available evidence point to a deterioration in the standard of living amongst the serf-population. Junker and king alike had an interest in keeping men alive.

The government's schemes for new settlements in the thinly populated areas of Pomerania, East Prussia, Kurmark and Silesia drew in immigrants from Rhenish Germany. The landless, if they were in good physical shape, had no difficulty in finding work. About 250,000 persons were attracted into Prussia as rural settlers and in the pioneer frontier territories, serfdom did not exist. Not all the resettlement schemes brought immediate profit to the crown. The Oderbruch venture (draining the Oder swampland) cost a million *thalers* which were not recovered in Frederick's lifetime in the shape of taxes or trading surpluses. Such ventures, however, emphasized the vitality of Prussian expansion. Dank, stark and apparently cheerless as the flatlands of Polish Prussia and East Prussia undoubtedly were, they did not, like the fertile French Beauce, house a population of paupers and as long as land could be brought under cultivation, taxes could be levied and relatively healthy soldiers produced.

A great deal of effort was put by Frederick the Great, acting through the War and Domains chamber and rural commissioners, into raising agricultural productivity. In particular, on reclaimed land, on royal domain and the lands of private landlords backed by government funds, stimulus was given to projects designed to promote more cattle rearing and hence to realize adequate supplies of manure which German agronomists in particular regarded as the first prerequisite for increasing grain production. Stall feeding of cattle during the winter, on the English and Flemish model, demanded fodder crops like lupins, sainfoin and clover and subsidies from the government made experimentation possible. Personally opposed to the idea of serfdom, Frederick insisted that on royal domain lands steps were taken to commute labour services into payment in kind. In the interests of crown revenue he offered short-term leases which could be made to reflect market value. Domain revenue was considerably higher in 1786 than in 1740 and given that in Silesia the Habsburgs had parted with much of their domain land, this reflected a more business-like approach to the management of domain land in existing territories. There is no evidence to suggest that leaseholders found difficulty in meeting the higher rents. The debate which centres upon whether Frederick was prevented from abolishing serfdom by a self-interested Junker group is a non-starter. Sound sense showed that a shortage of manpower and a similar lack of ready money in the agrarian world, made the commuting of domanial labour services to a money payment throughout agrarian society totally unrealizable. Frederick was insistent that some check should be placed on the abuse of the lord's power. In no circumstances could services demanded exceed 3–4 days per week. Physical punishment was forbidden. But, the individual who had to supervise the lord was the *Landrat* and he was very much a man of the provincial estates which were overtly hostile to attempts to interfere in the relationship between lord and serf. Even so, setting aside the instance of Silesia where landlord/serf relationships were tense (and even here the main uprisings were after 1787) there would appear to have been a relatively harmonious relationship between lord and man. Given the troubles which rent relationships in the agrarian world of the Habsburgs and the Romanovs in the sixties and seventies, one is impressed by the relative tranquillity of the Prussian lands.

This tranquillity was the more remarkable given the strains borne by Prussian territories in time of war. Actual war costs during the Seven Years' War were formidable, far outstripping the reserves of the state treasury, as well as contributions levied in Saxony and British subsidies. Extra loans amounting to 4 million *thalers*, symbolic, though scarcely productive, sacrifices such as the melting down of royal table silver, the debasement of the coinage through re-mintings, the falling behind in salaries paid to civil servants and amounts owed for forage and provision for the armies, point to strain within the economy. Even worse, entire provinces were subjected to foreign occupation which cut off their ability to render men and money. East Prussia was occupied by the Russians in 1758. East Friesland, Cleves and Silesia also suffered temporary occupation in which invaders seized what there was to be had in terms of grain, fodder and pillageable wealth. (Saxony in turn suffered similar treatment during the Prussian occupation.) The internal dislocation and immense suffering engendered by the war in which, in the final battles, the king was using old men and virtual children for soldiers are only too apparent. As a result of the war Prussia lost about 400,000 inhabitants, some 10 per cent of its population, an enormous loss for a country with such a low population density. In East Prussia alone 90,410 dead were reported and land lay idle. Peace necessitated a reconstruction programme at almost every level – further resettlement schemes, attempts to reorganize the financial resources of the crown on a more profitable footing, attempts to make a fragmented bureaucracy more efficient, to re-create an army and efforts to give greater meaning to the idea of Prussia as a unitary state. These efforts embodied legal reforms and steps in the direction of a more tolerant and humane state. In these enterprises the post-war situation was advantageous in only one way: the total exhaustion of every single belligerent in the war. In European terms, the Seven Years' War was a Pyrrhic victory and the prospect of further European conflict on any significant level receded. After 1763, Frederick the Great sought rapidly to refill the depleted ranks of the army. That army now became a deterrent force which was largely unused. The battle for Silesia had been won.

The basis of the new reorganization was a land survey to ascertain the productivity of farms, the exact location of frontiers, the exact worth of royal domain, and the potentiality for land improvement schemes. All this took time to compile and in the meanwhile the financial chaos prevailing had in some way to be resolved. Frederick chose to deal with his problems by adopting the method of Colbert, that is, the introduction of the *Régie*, a general farm, in which a syndicate of individuals (mostly Prussian but with an element of professional French taxmen involved) became responsible for the collection and administration of indirect taxes – particularly the excise – and in return guaranteed the monarchy a fixed return. The *Régie* (as in France) had no control over the rates it levied. The advantage of this system to the monarchy was that the mechanism for an unpopular tax ceased to be royal and it could be left to private enterprise to adopt efficient if tyrannical methods of collecting tax. The abuses of officialdom within the *Régie* severely antagonized both the populace in general and the regular bureaucracy. For the monarchy it was clearly an expedient to meet the exigencies of the post-war situation. After 1766, when the *Régie* was founded, the monarchy gradually trimmed its powers. It lost, for example, in 1769 the prerogative of collecting and administering postal revenues. Westphalian peasants avoided the *Régie* by taking their produce to non-Prussian markets and here Frederick admitted defeat. Nonetheless at the end of the reign, the *Régie* produced a surplus for the state treasury of 23 million *thalers*.

In many ways the Prussian bureaucracy had stood the test of war. Though Frederick expressed himself unresentful of its relationship with invading powers he harboured some grievances and was not sorry to lose through sheer old age many of the high officials of the General Directory. This institution more and more reflected the increasing complexity of the Prussian state as new departments and bureaux were added to cope with topical business. These were the diplomatic service, ecclesiastical administration, departments for mining and metallurgy (1768) and forestry (1770), for building and for the administration of justice. Frederick preferred specialized departments whose work applied to the country as a whole rather than regional offices responsible for all branches of administration. Obviously this preference could not have universal application. There had to be room in the General Directory for both the regional and the general. It is seriously to be questioned whether Frederick's changes did much more than start the General Directory functioning again in the aftermath of war and increase the demarcation disputes between departments anxious to hold on to such power as they had. Equally obviously, such changes as were introduced by Frederick into the General Directory and its sub-chambers were far from achieving unity of command over Prussian territories as a whole. Silesia never came under the jurisdiction of the General Directory but

preserved virtually intact the powers of the provincial estates to negotiate directly with the crown and throughout other provinces, Gelderland, Pomerania, West Prussia, the General Directory only tardily
gained power. Everywhere the ancient provincial estates were allowed
to remain and were used.

For good reason; Frederick's attitude towards a bureaucracy he never
ceased to abuse in quartermaster's language, was indeed ambivalent.
What became apparent to the Prussian monarch was that the bureaucracy was assuming a life of its own. Though an autocrat could not
exist without a bureaucracy, and the Prussian one in particular had
shown itself to be committed over and beyond the call of duty to the
interests of the state, Frederick clearly had misgivings. Looked at
closely, the Prussian bureaucracy in the aftermath of the Seven Years'
War seemed to be consistently increasing in power within the state.
Although there was no structured examination procedure until after
1770 – and that for new entrants to the bureaucracy – the tendency was
for high officials to be those with experience behind them. The sons of
officials with a good education were accorded preference. The higher
echelons of the civil service hence became the preserve of an increasingly professional elite, some of whom were drawn from ennobled
houses, some not. In 1770 a Higher Examination Commission under
Hagan's inspiration marked the introduction of a state examination
system which ensured that a minimum standard applied and hence
that elimination for incompetence was reduced.

A moot concern amongst historians is the degree to which Frederick
appreciated that the bureaucracy upon which he, as autocrat, was
forced to lean and which had been a significant factor in reducing the
power of local institutions within Prussia, was becoming over-powerful.
Increasingly a narrowing elite was endowed with administrative know-
how, responsible only to the crown which, try as it might, obviously
could not totally supervise everyone. The long-term view of the Prussian
bureaucracy as it continued into the nineteenth century was that it
showed itself capable, without the leadership of the monarchy, of taking
the initiative in reforming both itself and the army. Certainly, from the
reign of Frederick William I the strength of the bureaucracy was growing and every step in the direction of increasing its proficiency and
educational worth enhanced its stature and self-esteem. Its conflicts
with the local ancient aristocracy were legion, and anything or anyone
to whom it was opposed stood limited chance of success. Rosenberg has
argued that the introduction of the *Régie* was intended as a significant
blow at the established bureaucracy on the part of the monarchy to
prevent a further growth in its power by stripping it of its control over
indirect taxation. What lends the most weight to Frederick's apprehension as to the overweening power of the bureaucratic apparatus
within his dominions was the new emphasis he gave in a programme

of large-scale administrative reform which began in 1766 to the local Junker aristocracy. This in effect was to mean the adoption of policies which seemed directly to cut back upon the work of his father because the reforms sanctioned the reemergence of agencies of corporate self-government, many of which pre-dated the formation of the Prussian state. Hence Frederick gave more power and political influence to the Junkers than they had had for more a century. 'By supporting the natural foes of bureaucratic centralization and by promoting the re-introduction of elements of representative government, representative of the landed Junker interest, he sponsored, in effect, a partial restoration, though in altered form, of the old territorial *Ständestaat*.'[3]

Indicative of this trend was the extension and standardization of the office of *Landrat* throughout the Prussian provinces. This individual, although in a sense a significant state servant, was very much the representative of the provincial estates. He was a rural commissioner within a *Kreis* (or circle) responsible for supplying information on the economic standing of the villages within his *Kreis* and seeing that regulations were observed. Though salaried by the crown, the *Landrat* was nominated by the estates and the Instruction of 1766 made clear that one of his main functions was to see that no minor bureaucrat played the role of petty tyrant over the hardworking peasants. Hence the provincial estates whose existence the bureaucracy wished vehemently to terminate gained, via the *Landrat*, an extension of influence.

This attempt to balance bureaucratic power by aristocratic particularist power was obviously crucial to Frederick's very eclectic concept of the Prussian state. However, one should not take his urge to decentralize too far. In one direction, though success was not total, an important step was taken towards a more authentically unified state by the legal reform programme of Heinrich von Cocceji. The basis of this reform was the attempt to standardize courts throughout the Prussian state so that a unified procedure could be followed. Secondly, it was hoped, to fix legal costs and so remove (at least theoretically) the ability to buy one's way through the courts. Thirdly, the purpose was to streamline and standardize rates of payment to lawyers and judges and hence reduce the costs of judges: fourthly to insist upon minimum qualifications for judicial office to ensure a competent and honest bench and lastly to have a uniform law code. These measures cut across the power of the estates to appoint judges from the local nobility and theoretically the measures, if fully adopted, constituted a significant blow to particularism and local privilege. But what Cocceji's reforms left largely untouched, beyond insisting that seigneurs employ qualified personnel, was the issue of seigneurial justice which continued in East Prussia to be

3 H. Rosenberg, *Bureaucracy, Aristocracy and Autocracy: the Prussian Experience, 1660–1815* (1958), pp. 168–9.

regulated according to the traditions of particular domains. Standardization was only possible on royal property. Then, there was the tricky issue of reconciling a standardized, centralized justice with the regional peculiarities of provincial institutions which had to be respected. In the end provincial anomalies were in part preserved and a standardized system only had judicial authority over disputes of town against town, disputes concerning royal domains and of domain leaseholders in respect of their leaseholds or questions of taxation, disputes over brewing rights and effences against government agents such as tax-collectors, police and the military. Any offending official had also to be tried in the royal judicial structure.

Cocceji's law code was still only in project form when he died in 1754. Matters perforce slumbered during the Seven Years' War and indeed were not taken significantly further until the Chancellorship of von Carmer who in 1780 was ordered to proceed with codification of the laws in German. Working on Cocceji's projects, and tailoring them to cope with the complexities of divergent common law practices in the component provinces proved an enormous task. Draft followed draft. The entire corpus was not made law until 1791 and not enforced until June 1794. The *Allgemeine Landrecht für die Preussischen Staaten* (General Common Law for the Prussian State) has been seen by jurists and historians alike as the most significant and durable monument of the Prussian Enlightenment, embodying the fundamental principles of Beccarian justice, uniformity of punishment and humanity insofar as torture and barbaric punishments were absent and punishment was clearly related to the scale of the crime. How effectively the uniform code could be applied depended less upon the courts than upon a universal police force to bring offenders to justice and the Prussian state in the late eighteenth century was not prepared to spend enough in this direction. Nevertheless, the codification of Prussian law placed Prussia in the front rank – along with Revolutionary France and the Habsburg Empire – of states seeking to standardize and apply Enlightenment principles to law reform.

In another respect too, Frederick the Great's Prussia continued the tradition dear to Enlightenment ideals of religious tolerance. Frederick was a non-believer who held, like Voltaire, that religion was good for the masses. At the outset of the reign 90 per cent of the population was Lutheran Protestant, 3 per cent Calvinist and 7 per cent Roman Catholic but the annexation of Silesia brought into the Prussian system a predominantly Catholic population and over the Silesian Catholic Church were several bishops subordinated to Austrian archbishops. Frederick was anxious not to alienate the Catholic population, but it was not always easy to tread a neutral path. He, with some justification, mistrusted the Silesian higher clergy. His efforts to secure control over nominations to higher benefices naturally provoked reaction from both the papacy and Silesian church officials who resented the intrusion of a Protestant king. He was more successful in taxing ecclesiastical wealth and in freezing the amount of property under ecclesiastical control. The Catholic Church had also to learn to live with a Protestant minority given for the first time equal civil rights. Any religious sect was tolerated as long as it claimed no special position within the state, or, in the case of Roman Catholicism, did not insist upon a supra-national role. Friction between the state and the Roman Catholic Church was never fully eliminated and tension between Lutheran and Calvinist persisted.

As far as the state was concerned, the Jews were also tolerated but their full integration in society was something that official policy could not achieve. What they did have, by the General Privilege of 1750, was the right to be undisturbed in all matters relating to the administration of their schools, synagogues and cemeteries.

Amongst European peoples, the component groups of the Prussian state ranked low in standards of literacy and the amount of formal education available. Estate owners were by law forced to make some provision, but it was not possible to establish common educational standards and most estate owners refused to relinquish children for schooling except during the dead season. Moreover, a significant project begun in the 1750s for the training of teachers was interrupted by the outbreak of war. In August 1763 the *General-Landschut Règlement* tried to make a basic primary education obligatory, though the opposition of estate owners and the lack of qualified teachers meant that between theory and practice opened a vast chasm. Nevertheless the 1770s, particularly when the minister Zedlitz-Leipe espoused the reform of higher education, saw a significant extension in the quality and loyalty of new teachers who were increasingly emancipated from a pattern of education organized by the clergy. In the Frederician state, education was very much a social frill dependent upon what the state could spare and never an overriding priority. Even so literacy rates conspicuously grew.

The 'formidable despotism' which supposedly characterized the reign of Frederick the Great was much more apparent than real. Insofar as Prussia was a unitary state, it was one which lived with social privilege, provincial particularism, social prejudices which could defeat government pronouncements on toleration and education reform, and which all curtailed the manoeuvrability of monarchy. The autocrat even feared that his own bureaucrats might become a force who would one day further limit his own authority – and history was to prove him right. In his reforming zeal, Frederick may well have been the child of the Enlightenment and he may have laid claims to despotic authority, but his control was far from total and only existed at all because he never flew in the face of his true supports, the Prussian nobility. He accomplished as much as was possible but he wrought no miracles.

8

Russia

'The history of Russia is the history of a country which colonizes itself.' (Kliuchevskii)

By 1730 Russia had emphatically entered the mainstream of European development. As a military presence with which European governments would have to reckon she was 'westward' looking insofar as technologically, and to a degree psychologically and culturally, she patterned herself on a European, rather than an Asiatic or indigenous, model. That said, one cannot apply to Russia standards and concepts of society or even a vocabulary of political and social history which we use elsewhere in Europe. Russia had had no Renaissance and no Reformation: nor was it to have a native inspired Enlightenment. True under Catherine the Great Russia is held to have experienced in common with other European powers the phenomenon of enlightened despotism. But Catherine's role is a contentious one, as is indeed the entire concept of enlightened despotism in Russia. For whereas in the west the term implies a confrontation or an overriding of traditional constitutional checks on monarchical power, Russia had never evolved such clearly defined constitutional checks. In a western sense Russia was without a legal tradition, so that it was impossible to appeal to a body of law against the state. Hence the entire premise upon which monarchical government was based radically differed from that of the rest of Europe, even though some concept of the rule of law was entering Russian political life after 1760. Moreover, alone amongst European states, Russia was a country of fluid frontiers, and was committed by economic and political motives to a remorseless outward expansion. In the eighteenth century, this was directed above all towards an extension of control over a mass of semi-nomadic peoples only part Russian in origin and posing particular problems to government. There are other major points of contrast as well. Russia, apart from a handful of princely families, did not have a hereditary aristocracy entrenched in particular localities and able, because of vast landed wealth and an ancient lineage, either to oppose or actively promote the interests of the central power in the localities. Lack of primogeniture, a soil which rapidly reached exhaustion, and a tradition of state service in army and bureaucracy lifted the Russian noble out of his birthplace and combined to create a rootless group over dependent on patronage and land grants from the tsar.

To pick out yet another difference: whereas the whole tendency of European development in the eighteenth century was towards a weakening of the ties of serfdom, in Russia the reverse was true. Demographically of course, Russia was an underpopulated country by western European standards and the land worthless without the men to work it and hence the fixing of manpower continued to be a necessity for the landowing class. But more than this, the extension of serfdom could be allied to the whole process of colonization. Nomads are reluctant taxpayers of dubious allegiance to the central power and prepared to work the land only in their own interests. Serfdom was hence a means of hitching them to the Russian state and at the same time a means of rewarding a service nobility for its efforts in the service of the state. In short, an appreciation of the interplay between crown and society is crucial to an understanding of the course of Russian history in this period, and so is the recognition that any 'westernization' that occurred did so within a set of traditions and relationships which were anything but western. We must seek to define 'westernization' because it meant something quite different in 1785 from what it meant in 1730. Originally conceived by Peter the Great as a means to military success, westernization shifted from meaning the adoption of western technology and bureaucratic developments which were essentially tsar-imposed, into a movement ultimately – i.e. by the mid-nineteenth century – critical of the entire premise of autocracy. Something of that transition took place within the period 1730–1785 and involved a fundamental reorganizing of the relationship between the tsar and the *dvorianstvo* (service nobility). If Russia had a political history in the eighteenth century and it is indeed difficult to talk about politics in an autocracy where the only social group with sufficient wealth and education to develop a political mentality was the *dvoriantsvo* which almost perversely to western eyes refused to do so, it must focus in large part upon the radically changing relationship between the tsar and this significant social element.

The major constitutional difference between Russia and the west in the eighteenth century was that the tsar, unlike a western king, was both sovereign and proprietor of his kingdom. This difference stemmed from a medieval situation wherein the tsar, owner and absolute master in Muscovy of a servile Muscovite population, gradually extended his control outward, simultaneously reducing a formerly free population to bondage, and extending the practices previously used in running what was in effect a huge private estate to an ever increased area. Outside Muscovy the tsar's effective power was in fact curtailed by poor communications and the inefficacy of a very rudimentary government machine. The Russian Empire had three great expansive phases. The first in the fifteenth century absorbed Novgorod and adjacent princedoms. The second in the eighteenth century took in Estonia, Latvia and the territories of the Gulf of Finland and moved on, under Catherine the Great, to achieve the integration of Poland and the Ukraine and further south New Russia and Crimean territories which opened up the route to south-east Kazan. The third, a nineteenth-century one, carried Russia into the Caucasus, to Georgia and Bessarabia, and the mouth of the Danube, and also temporarily gave her Finland and the Duchy of Warsaw. Nevertheless throughout this vast expansion, the principle that the tsar was both sovereign and direct owner of absorbed territories was never relinquished. The concept of a patrimonial regime and the tsar as patriarchal figure, *dominus* as well as *rex*, permeated every level of society. The heterogeneous mass of semi-nomads and serfs who opted for a false Peter III in the shape of Pugachev never for an instant departed from this concept of the tsar as father, owner and absolute controller of their lives.

Russian aggrandizement was not of course dedicated to the sole gratification of the tsar and although all power nominally resided in his hands, in practice he depended upon a body of support as all rulers must. A restricted agricultural year, thin soils which became rapidly exhausted, the lowest agricultural yields in Europe, engendered a perpetual land hunger for the better soils of the west and south. Expansion meant need of an army and an army entailed officers, rank and file and the resources to support them. Hence the ruler looked to his servitors for support in conquest and rewarded them by massive handouts of land and men which, in the process, shored up the internal position of the monarchy by creating a situation of mutual advantage. These are general principles applicable to the entire course of Russian history from the fifteenth century onwards, but at no time were they more apparent than in the eighteenth century.

Peter the Great's military successes in the Great Northern War (1700–21) were attributable to the modernization of the Russian army on western lines, with up-to-date equipment and tactical know-how, drilled, uniformed and efficiently provisioned. This was achieved by a limited social revolution in which an officer class and a bureaucracy for recruitment and fiscal purposes were created out of an ancient nobility and, for want of a better word, a gentry and in small part from able commoners. Given official definition in the Table of Ranks (1722) the *dvorianstvo* or service nobility was unique. According to Petrine legislation, all males claiming noble birth were required to enter one of the fourteen branches of state service, and every state servant was automatically considered noble when, by merit, he had attained to a sufficiently high rank. In short, nobility was the product of service and could neither be acquired nor maintained without it. Rank gave social status and not, as elsewhere, the reverse. Theoretically, at least, the *dvorianstvo* was an open aristocracy particularly at the lower end of the Table of Ranks into which able commoners were able to thrust their way. Noble privileges did not extend beyond the right to own serfs and the life of the noble, particularly in the army, was indeed hard. Frequently transferred from place to place, from military to civil duties, irregularly and ill paid and often arbitrarily set aside in the path to promotion, the Petrine service noble was totally at the mercy of the state. If his services should be rewarded in the form of land it would be in lots scattered throughout the Empire affording him no toehold in any one particular region. His sacrifices were evidently extensive as was the swelling volume of noble petitions of complaint which reached Moscow.

In two ways Peter I's reforms were an overwhelming success. At the military level Russia was able to embark upon a new period of expansion and furthermore the tsar had succeeded in creating a group of people totally committed to the idea of service to the state as their *raison d'être*. They were undoubtedly more devoted to military than civil employment where the average nobleman, ill-equipped to cope with paper work, was conscious of his inferiority to the common clerk. But to set against success are three major considerations. Did Petrine reforms create a homogeneous Russian nobility? How content was the service nobility with its lot? What were the long-term prospects for Petrine changes as a means of running a military and bureaucratic machine? The answer to the first two questions was provided in 1730 when a constitutional crisis revealed a divided nobility with radically different aspirations.

Peter II's death in 1730 created a succession problem. Peter I had decreed that a ruler might nominate his successor from the ruling dynasty but Peter II died without an obvious legitimate heir and the choice of monarch fell to the men responsible for the direction of state affairs, high state officials, military men and church leaders. The situation made possible the beginning of an era of palace revolutions immediately affording the opportunity for the ancient Russian princely aristocracy, a handful of families who had opposed the Table of Ranks and the entire existence of the *dvorianstvo*, but who enjoyed the advantage of membership of the Privy Council (a purely advisory body), to put forward a plan to transfer some political power from the crown to themselves. They presented Anne of Courland (1730–41) with a number of conditions prerequisite for their support and indeed chose her because they assumed a woman of limited political strength. The movement was led by the Golitsyns and the Dolgorukys and aimed at changes to make the council analogous to the German *Reichstag* in which a princely senate had political initiative. Faced with the alternative between an autocratic tsar and an aristocratic body which experience had shown to be hostile to their existence, the *dvorianstvo*, though politically inexperienced, intellectually poor and inarticulate, nonetheless threw their entire weight behind the maintenance of tsardom in its ancient form. Such an action must have demonstrated to the new tsarina who her faithful servants were but did it persuade her gradually to sell out to the *dvorianstvo* by reducing their obligations to the state and hence gradually transforming them from dependent state servants into an independent elite? Certainly her reign is remarkable for the law of 1731 which permitted the *dvorianstvo* complete discretion in the bequest of land. Then, five years later, came the laws which permitted one member of every family exemption from state service so that he could remain at home and manage the estate, hence assuring a steadier revenue from land and which also reduced obligatory state service to twenty-five years. The *dvorianstvo* may, though it is a very academic point, have profited from a closer legal definition of obligation but looked at in practical terms how extensive were such concessions? Twenty-five years is a long spell and may have exceeded average tenure of office based on life service. Moreover, the state reserved the right to rescind such provision should the need arise. In time of peace especially, general obligatory state service for a large military personnel was costly and significant economies might be made by a reduction of the paid officer class. In addition upward mobility for the younger and more efficient might be secured by the elimination of the oldest elements. All these are points to be debated before one pronounces Anne's measures as significant steps in the liberation of the *dvorianstvo*.

Yet it is possible to discern from the 1730s a certain growth in *esprit de corps* among the *dvorianstvo* and an unqualified acceptance that service was a nobleman's lot and, in order that he should rise quickly through the ranks, that he must have an education to set him on the path to speedy promotion. Peter the Great had established a number of special schools but in 1731 Anne was persuaded to found a number of corps of cadets open only to the nobility and whose graduates were automatically promoted to full officer rank. This was only the beginning of an important process allying a concept of nobility with an advanced foreign-modelled education open only to the children of noblemen.

Perhaps as well, Anne's style of government – a niece of Peter I she had long lived in Courland and her mistrust of the Russian court nobility caused her to import Germans into all key positions –

promoted a further consciousness of corporateness and effectively obliterated something of the dichotomy between the old Russian princely families and the *dvorianstvo*. Ostermann was in control of the cabinet, Munnich the army, and worst of all Anne's favourite Biren was made High Chamberlain, a position he used to amass a huge private fortune. He was not representative however of 'German' rule which was remarkable for its ruthless efficiency in tax accountancy and the prosecution of lax or corrupt Russian officialdom. The Secret Chancery gained new strength in its persecution of any critics. The Golitsyns and the Dolgorukys were obviously eliminated but so was anyone who sought to question German rule. Peter I's esteemed servant, Volynsky, fell to the torture of the Secret Chancery after a vehement denunciation of Biren. It is not surprising that Anne's death was followed by a reaction against the Germans and a further sordid round of plots and counterplots in which Anne's two-month-old nephew Ivan VI and successive regents were overthrown by a *coup* in 1741 in favour of Elizabeth, daughter of Peter I.

The engineers of this plot were the Russian Guards. Elizabeth had behind her as well the entire nobility and anyone opposed to German influence at court including the French and Swedish ambassadors anxious to sever the German connection. Both France and Sweden had been humiliated by Russian success in the War of the Polish Succession (1733) wherein Stanislas Leszczynski, son-in-law of Louis XV, was ousted and a Russian candidate installed on the Polish throne and both hoped to profit from the constitutional chaos which resulted from Anne's death. Sweden in 1741 went so far as to invade Russia. But whatever the faults of government in the 1730s, there had been no abatement in military commitment and by the Peace of Abô (1743) Sweden was stripped of the province of Kymmenegard.

Indeed, one can over-emphasize the discontinuity of the era of palace revolutions. The period of 'German' rule was a difficult period for the old court nobility who aspired to high office, but apart from that no abrupt ruptures were made with Petrine policies. Elizabeth was Russian in every way, colourful, independent like her father, and with a flair for picking the right ministers out of a court rent by factions. Bestuzhev and Peter Shuvalov (however financially corrupt the latter might be) were men of talent. By comparison with Catherine the Great, Elizabeth was no European intellectual anxious to publicize her cerebral talents, yet her reign has amazing continuity with Catherine's and some of the reforms carried out or projected in Elizabeth's reign have been attributed to Catherine. In particular, the criminal law was updated, insofar as crimes, particularly against property, were rendered more specific and plans were laid for an overall discussion of legislative reform by a representative assembly. Moreover, if one seeks any one figure to whom one might attribute the most considerable importation of Enlightenment influence into Russia it should be not Catherine but Elizabeth's favourite and cousin to the influential minister, Ivan Shuvalov. Indeed in many ways the Shuvalov family epitomized Elizabeth's reign. Alexander Shuvalov headed the Chancery: Peter Shuvalov himself, although he amassed an immense fortune at the state's expense, was teeming with reform projects, some of which were put into effect. These included internal customs reform: fiscal changes – an attempt to diversify state revenues by introducing an excise tax on spirits and salt in order to curtail the ceaseless upward move of the poll tax – changes in local government administration, army recruitment and provisioning. He sought to lift the national economy by stimulating economic activity in the private sector, granting monopolies in industry and trade.

The era of palace revolutions was also that which saw an unprecedented development in the metallurgical industry with an increase of 250 per cent in output between 1725 and 1762, and the development of an important export trade in iron ore. Such evidence militates against an interpretation of the period as one of stagnation and indeed against an approach to Russian history which makes everything attributable to the personal characteristics of the ruler. The overriding consideration of Elizabeth's reign was in fact commitment to the Seven Years' War. Many of the changes, some of which could be described as reforms, and developments reflected not a reforming spirit *per se* but the chronic need to deal with the problems arising out of the strain placed upon the Russian economy by military demands. War was the catalyst of change in eighteenth-century Russia and the Seven Years' War in particular had far-reaching consequences. Not only did it engender economic crisis, but a reordering of the relationship between state and noble and state and peasant. The noble was of course the officer class and the one responsible for troop recruitment and tax levies. The peasantry was that group from which men and money had to be raised.

The Russian peasantry was composed of so many divergent types that generalization is indeed difficult. Broadly speaking, they were in the eighteenth century divided about equally between state peasants and proprietary serfs of which the latter, living on privately owned land, were personally bonded to a noble. In the territory forming ancient Muscovy proprietary serfs formed the bulk of the rural populace: elsewhere they were a significant minority. In the borderlands, those regions of the south and east, proprietary serfdom was extending in the course of the eighteenth century as the Russians took in Tartars, Kalmyks and Bashkirs. The church also held a number of peasants in bondage but under relatively light conditions.

State control was obviously greatest over state peasants but though these paid a fairly high poll tax they were otherwise free. Proprietary serfs paid poll tax through their owner. The demands the state made of them were obviously limited. Some kind of balance had to be struck between landlord and state demands bearing in mind that the landlord was a service noble whose income could not be arbitrarily curtailed in order to enhance state revenues without arousing immense noble discontent. The majority of serf owners owned under 100 men whose labour did not result in a significant surplus to be expended either on lord or state. Hence the state could not impose a limitless poll tax. As it was, attempts to increase the levy to meet the demands of war resulted in peasant flights to uncolonized land. The state therefore had recourse to indirect taxation on salt and spirits (the latter a 'luxury' and hence likely to be borne by the more affluent) and to bringing church peasants under state control so that these peasants (effectively reduced to crown serfs) could bear heavier state taxes. Such expedients were allegedly only for the duration of the Seven Years' War. The state also embarked on a less specific long-term policy of bringing the nomadic peoples of the south-east under central control and, by land grants to faithful servitors, reducing erstwhile free peoples to bondage. In short, there was a clear levelling-down process in the interests of the central treasury. The state had a stake in this levelling-down process. In extending a proprietor's rights over previously free peoples, the latter became accessible to the taxman's hand. From 1730 onwards a series of laws bound the serf more closely to the noble's will, stepping up penalties for flight and facilitating transferences from one part of the country to another. One cannot say with any degree of precision to what extent the economic situation of the Russian peasant deteriorated in the eighteenth century (or even in certain instances if it deteriorated at all) but clearly there was a down-grading in the legal standing of significant elements, a slippage made more pronounced by the continuing demands of war. The degree to which discontent was rife was to be demonstrated by Pugachev's revolt.

Shuvalov's financial expedients and attempts to bring previously free groups within the tax orbit did not preserve Russia from recourse to currency devaluations nor from an immense deficit. When peace came in 1762, the Russian treasury had never presented a gloomier aspect. It was perhaps as a measure of economy that the autocrat took a step which is regarded as one of the most controversial acts in eighteenth-century history. Peter III decided to dispense with obligatory state service on the part of the *dvorianstvo*.

It could be claimed that with this stroke alone, the monarchy created a privileged westernized leisure class such as Russia had never previously experienced and that since privilege without obligation was every nobleman's ambition, the autocrat was giving in to his nobility. In support of such a contention the Manifesto on the Freedom of the Nobility was the work of Peter III who, weak and incompetent, was no match for *dvorianstvo* pressure. Yet, looked at more closely, the Manifesto, however it might tally with deep-rooted ambitions amongst the *dvorianstvo*, was in fact the work of an influential group *within* the government, in particular the Vorontsov brothers. Since the 1750s they had vociferously urged that Russia's interests would best be served by deflecting the Russian nobility into closer estate management and keener involvement in local administration and economic enterprise, thus creating a gentry on the English model. There was ample evidence, they argued, to suggest that the *dvorianstvo* would remain emotionally committed to the idea of military service and hence that nothing would be sacrificed on the military front. None of these points were specifically embodied in the Manifesto however which concentrated wholly upon the relation of the nobility to service. The document in liberating the *dvorianstvo* from obligatory service levelled a few blows at them. It stipulated, for example, that those who left military service could only enlist in the civil service if there was a vacancy and could not be guaranteed reabsorption into the military at a later date. The state, in short, was shaking off any commitment to the *dvorianstvo* and reinforced this principle by providing for the education of a number of merit-worthy commoners to fill the lower bureaucracy. However one views the Manifesto of February 1762 it marks a fundamental breach in the relationship between autocrat and noble and the most rational explanation of the tsar's action, is the urgency to make economies. By ridding itself of unwilling servitors, the state might effect a fair and smooth transition from a war to a peacetime situation.

For the more affluent members of the nobility, the option on state service was joyously received. It aligned them more closely with western traditions and though they remained committed to the idea of service, they very clearly had everything to gain from the situation. For the poorer nobility the reverse was the case. The profits from state service and automatic entry into a service with a salary, however meagre, and with rewards, however distant these might be, were crucial to them. The removal of the direct bond between themselves and the autocrat threatened to strip them of a frail lifeline and to expose them to competition from below. The short-term effect of the Manifesto however, was an immediate exodus from the service of the poorest, most ill-educated and inefficient nobles who had long staffed the lowest and least rewarding offices, and who saw in emancipation a chance to reconstruct a livelihood from the land. This probably accorded well with Peter III's hopes. Obsessed as he undoubtedly was with the comparative efficiency of the Prussian bureaucratic and military machine, he clearly viewed the Manifesto as a means of streamlining the Russian service. To the same end, efficiency, came the measures which rendered permanent state control of ecclesiastical lands and provided jobs in administering the collection of dues from previous church serfs for superannuated government servants.

Peter III's reign lasted no more than six months. Victim of yet another palace revolution, his murder was probably due to his efforts to reduce the authority of the Senate. Though this body could claim few constitutional powers backed by the force of law, in practice under Elizabeth the thirteen senators had constituted the highest governing body of the state. The measures of June 1762 made clear that Peter III intended to reverse the policy of his predecessor. 'We...command that from now on the Senate issue to the public no decree with force of law, or [which] even serves to interpret previous laws, without submitting it to Us and obtaining Our approval for it.' Given that Peter III showed also a clear penchant for Germans and was proposing a radical realignment of Russian foreign policy by an alliance with Frederick the Great, which found little support except amongst the tsar's favourites, the alienation of the autocrat and what had become by 1762 a quasi-institutionalized court nobility was very apparent. The importation of German ministers and bureaucrats who stemmed neither from the court elite nor from the service nobility had already caused one reign of terror under the Empress Anne. The elimination of Peter III by the time-honoured Russian method of palace assassination prevented a recurrence of such a phenomenon. However much Peter may have served the interests of the upper nobility by emancipating them from obligatory service, such an act was insufficient to preserve him. The *dvorianstvo* did not rally in his support. The *sine qua non* of Russian autocracy was that it rested upon the understanding that favourites should not absorb political power and royal whim should not determine rewards and promotions, and Peter III clearly contravened that important principle. It is significant that Catherine the Great's first act was to restore the Senate to the position it had held in Elizabeth's reign.

Until recently, historians insisted that we view Catherine the Great's reign (1762–96) as marking in some ill-defined way a breach with the past: a significant stage in the Europeanization of Russia. Such historiography pivoted on the question of whether or not Catherine the Great deserved to be numbered with other enlightened despots and was concerned to weigh her personal predilections and intellectual agility against the legislation for which she was responsible. Or put another way, it undertook to balance the realities of serfdom and privilege against theories of the equality of man and natural justice. The conclusions were overwhelmingly insistent upon the divorce between sentiments evinced and principles put into effect: a severance explained by the realities of politics – Catherine was only too aware of the need to stay on the right side of those who put her on the throne.

In a meaningful sense, this approach is counterproductive and artificial because it detracts from an appreciation of the significant developments in Russian political and social life in the period by stressing discontinuity and because it demands we attempt to apply to Russian society and politics criteria which simply have no relevance to the Russian scene. Indeed, it is worth momentarily depersonalizing the course of Russian history with a view to accentuating the hard core of continuity. The influence of the Enlightenment had already been felt under Elizabeth. The Shuvalovs had projected several legislative and administrative reforms which merely waited upon peace. Most important, the overriding commitment of the central power was to the colonial push. This in the seventies gained considerable momentum as the central authority extended its control over the nomadic peoples of the south-east, and by a mixture of diplomacy and a threatening presence extended outwards into Poland. Such an extensive and ambitious programme necessitated a continuing close relationship between autocrat and noble, and in a different way, a particular relationship between the latter and the peasantry. Military service for any but the most impoverished nobles had become part of a noble's life scheme and such services continued to be rewarded by grants of land and serfs. Military demands fell inexorably upon the peasants. They paid for the expansion as soldiers with their lives and as civilians with their taxes. In newly colonized territories erstwhile free peoples were pressed into bondage by state interference whilst the opening-up of previously underpopulated lands involved enforced transferences of bonded labour from one part of the Empire to another.

This expansionist policy had little to do with the whims of any one particular ruler. In part it might have been dictated by economic considerations. By 1800 the heartland of Russia, ancient Muscovy, was unable to provide its population with bread and was forced to look south for imports from richer, less exhausted soils. But much more, this remorseless, outward move was by the 1760s automatic and continued to be so. It would stop only when it encountered stubborn opposition such as the British in Afghanistan in the nineteenth century, or the Chinese in Manchuria in our time. Western Europeans have long lived with concepts of historic or natural frontiers: both are concepts alien to the Russian experience. So when Catherine the Great continued the policy of colonization and expansion it need not be depicted as a way of courting the allegiance of the *dvorianstvo*. What it did mean of course was that neither forgot that their interests were interknit. Crucial determinants in the ebb and flow of an expansionist policy were the resources of the central treasury and, secondly, as the Turkish War was to demonstrate, the degree of preparedness of the population to submit to untrammelled fiscal demands. In 1762 a considerable deficit in the treasury stemmed from expenditure in the Seven Years' War and like other European governments in the sixties, history has to be written by reference to the dire straits of the central treasury. The reality of that deficit did not cease with Peter's murder. Just as Peter III had adopted economy measures *vis-à-vis* church serfs and the *dvorianstvo*, so his successor was forced, whatever her intellectual leanings, in the same direction. Having initially revoked Peter's decree transferring church serfs to crown control within a few years it was reinforced so that the dues they paid could go directly to the privy purse. Rewards for service had to be in men not money because the state's disposable revenues from poll tax, customs and excise, spirits, its own lands, loans raised in Holland and Italy and *ad hoc* expedients such as paper banknotes with dubious backing, permitted the ruler no scope for manoeuvre. Moreover, to achieve military ends, demands in money and men continued to be made. Whoever the ruler, these were the continuing realities of the situation.

One can advance further along a 'depersonalized' interpretation of the period. Whoever had assumed the role of tsar in 1762 would have been obliged to offer the *dvorianstvo* some further definition of its status. The Manifesto of Peter III left too much unresolved. It stripped a group of people both used and abused in state service of its obligations, leaving them defensive of their privileges and apprehensive as to their role in the state. Catherine's predisposition was towards the concept of no privilege without obligation but aware of the degree to which the higher nobility had welcomed emancipation and the actual state of the treasury, an abrogation of the Manifesto was hardly feasible. It is then hardly surprising that the period was one of legal definition and clarification and, since noble privilege extended to the ownership of men, definition which related to serf as well as to noble.

Obviously one can take depersonalization too far. The political history of an autocracy to a degree pivots upon the individual autocrat and the ministers he or she chooses from court factions. Factional politics had already produced the very palace revolution that brought Catherine to power but that achieved, Catherine demonstrated a cynicism and perceptive qualities peculiarly her own in picking her way amongst politicians and favourites. Her ministerial choice demonstrated a masterly refusal to allow any one individual or group an ascendancy. Panin stands out amongst those responsible for the overthrow of Peter III. Yet in office he was forced to rub shoulders with Glebov, the Vorontsov brothers (statesmen of Peter III), Bestuzhev, Riumin and Shakhovskoy (statesmen of Elizabeth), and to countenance the influence of Catherine's lover, Orlov. This balancing of interests guaranteed Catherine the longest reign of any Russian autocrat in the eighteenth century. Moreover, whilst ostensibly restoring the Senate in 1762, the almost immediate creation of an imperial council to serve as an intermediary between the monarchy and the Senate – and hence to act as main co-ordinator of national policy – and the breakdown of the Senate a year later into six departments, two in Moscow and four in St Petersburg, contrived to dilute and diffuse its authority. The difference apparent between court nobles and *dvorianstvo* was a constant in eighteenth-century history. By the reign of Catherine the Great, some of the former, such as Panin, had come to regard themselves as professional statesmen with an in-built right to conduct governmental affairs, the right to *consilium et auxilium* to which western European nobles laid claim. A move which cunningly deflected, rather than made an outright onslaught upon institutionalized noble power, was clearly an important achievement for an autocrat who was initially very tenuously entrenched. The Senate was prevented from blossoming into a German *Reichstag*.

Between 1762 and 1767 when the Legislative Commission met to consider the grievances of the *dvorianstvo*, the latter had time to contemplate their situation in peacetime. Clearly what disturbed them most was their fundamental insecurity *vis-à-vis* their land. They had no rights of hereditary tenure. Moreover, in an age of palace revolution, their serfs might be confiscated or redistributed. They were also clearly nervous about their own standing. Their programme, as it was to be presented aggressively and somewhat incoherently to Catherine in 1767, pivoted on three points: security of property, inalienable and exclusive tenure of serfs and immunity from arbitrary arrests and confiscations. Whereas the 1762 act left unclear the extent of noble privilege, the programme of 1767, not to be realized until 1785, formally spelt out what the *dvorianstvo* knew they needed before they could consider themselves a privileged elite.

Life in the provinces had made apparent the degree to which Moscow and St Petersburg had monopolized the resources of the nation, whether in terms of buildings, or facilities and social amenities such as schools and hospitals. It also made the *dvorianstvo* aware of the neglect of local government. Amongst the demands of 1767 can be found that for the total overhaul of local government so that it pass under the close direction of local noble families. If ceded, the demand might have converted the *dvorianstvo* into a gentry rather on the English model. This was very far from being Catherine's intention. In no way in 1767 was she prepared to cede a scrap of central control. All she permitted in the sixties was some formulation of noble control over the serfs by forbidding the serf any right of appeal against his master. She thus formally severed the last link between the proprietary serf and the sovereign. This was a significant step signalling a marked deterioration in the proprietary serf's legal standing if having little or no bearing at all on his actual socio-economic position. It was insufficient to satisfy the *dvorianstvo* but they had no power to make their dissatisfaction felt in the conditions of the late sixties. They were loyal to the ideal of an autocracy which was, after all, their livelihood. Their commitment to state service was equally total but the failure of their programme demonstrated their fundamental lack of leverage on the Russian monarchy.

Yet by 1785 the programme of 1767 was to be partially achieved. In the intervening years, a number of factors contributed to a changing relationship between *dvorianstvo* and autocrat. The first arose from the return in 1769 to war and the most significant expansion phase of Catherine's reign. The second followed from the chronic insecurity of monarchy in the aftermath of the Pugachev revolt. In a real sense 1769–75 saw a radical turning point in the relationship between the tsarina and her peoples and the Pugachev revolt in particular was evidence of social tensions emanating from military demands upon frontier territories. It also demonstrated latent hostility even within Muscovy itself which made apparent to the tsarina her need for support.

In many ways the Pugachev revolt was the single most revelatory incident of Catherine's reign, permitting at one and the same time an appreciation of peasant grievances and of the limitations of central control over frontier territories. The pretender phenomenon was no new one in Russian history and Kliuchevskii's dictum 'when the Russians are unhappy the way is open for a pretender' has peculiar relevance in the eighteenth century which knew, at a conservative estimate, at least 44 of them (compared with 23 in the previous century). Of these six were concentrated in the year 1764–5; six (including Pugachev) in the two years 1772–4 and a further five between 1782–6. None menaced central control more seriously than the revolt of Pugachev between 1773 and 1774.

Russian pretender movements do not appear to have been the particular product of dramatic instant deprivation – localized famine or sudden increases in the price of rye – but of attenuated deteriorating circumstances, part economic, part legalistic, part psychological. Most significantly they had a heartland which lay in a crescent belt stretching from the Urals across the black earth region and into Orenburg and were concentrated most heavily along the middle and lower Volga. Protest Russia was steppe Russia, the one which had known the Tartar hordes, and was once farmed only by warriors who took tardily to arable husbandry because of the unsettledness of their existence in face of marauders. Then it had been the refuge of runaway serfs seeking to scratch a livelihood in anonymity. Most recently, like everywhere else in Russia, the area had become largely peopled by bonded men and hired marginal labourers. The protester groups were Cossacks above all, but also Bashkirs, Kalmyk and Kazan Tartars who had been progressively alienated from what they regarded as Muscovite policy. They were frontier peoples – though Cossack territories penetrated deep into Russia – with a strong concept of identity and peculiarities which marked them off from the Muscovites. The Bashkirs dwelt with their Turco-Magyar past, still looking to their beys and to a trading world which stretched into Turkestan and Asia Minor. These were peoples whom a central government concerned with a national war policy – particularly one in adjacent Turkish lands – with increased taxation and troop recruitment must bring into line. But for Cossack, Bashkir and Tartar, the experience could only be one of reduction, a physical and psychological colonization by an intruding, alien, central power in the shape of bureaucrat, recruiting agent and a nobility hitched in interest to the crown.

Broadly speaking, there were two major types of serf: the one on *obrók* and the one on *barshchina*. *Obrók* serfs rendered quit rents to their lord in money and this was the dominant form of servitude in Muscovy and the forest regions where agricultural returns were low and experience had demonstrated to the lord that the peasant knew best how to raise money and was best left alone to get on with it. *Barshchina* was payment by labour services and in the course of the eighteenth century this emerged as the typical form exacted in the black earth belt, the south and the south-east. In these regions manpower was scarce but the land was fertile. If the lord could raise output on his domain he could find ready markets for the produce. Hence, and this was to be a particular feature of the sparsely populated areas of the Volga and the southern frontier lands, *barshchina* duties were intensified to incredible levels by greedy lords and the three-day normal service due to the lord was extended by working hours stretching from dawn to dusk. Moreover, in these regions, previous *obrók*-paying serfs were converted to serfs on *barshchina*. This did not necessarily imply an economic deterioration in an individual's standing but it did mean an intrusion into the traditional regulation of agricultural matters. Some of the worst riots were to occur where there had been such a conversion from *obrók* to *barshchina*. Russia as a whole experienced three-fold increases as well in the sixties and seventies in the level of *obrók* payments which may explain why Pugachev's rebellion threatened to extend into Muscovy.

There was another dissident social element. Above the serfs and below the *dvorianstvo* existed a social group known as the *odnodvórtsy* who in some areas constituted the bulk of the tax-paying population. They were particularly numerous in the black soil regions which were to be very riot-prone. The *odnodvórtsy* could own a restricted number of serfs but their rights over their lands were limited. They paid *obrók* to a lord, poll tax to the government and they did not escape military service. The victims of state demands, conscious of *dvorianstvo* opposition to their holding serfs, they were a dissatisfied grouping who looked to a happier past. Hence they were fuel for revolt.

The Bashkirs, the factory workers of the Urals and the Cossacks had further specific grievances. The Bashkirs had passed nominally under Russian control at the end of the sixteenth century but it was not until the reign of Peter the Great that their territory experienced fiscal demands or that the great metallurgical resources of the Urals became the prime basis, not only of the tsar's ambitious export plans but of the Russian armaments industry. The growth of this industry depended upon the creation out of the Bashkir peasants of factory workers. These were allowed to hold land against work in the factories or mines for a stipulated time each week – *barshchina* divorced from agricultural services. Camel traders, bee-keepers, livestock breeders and woodcutters with no interest in iron ore except as a means of making strong agricultural implements, the Bashkirs rebelled at least six times in the eighteenth century against central intrusion. Usually, however, they rebelled in isolation. Yet in 1773 they were to make common cause with the Cossacks. Cossack grievances stemmed from the continuance of Peter the Great's attempts to absorb the Cossacks into regular military service subject to Russian officer control. In 1765 as the Turkish War loomed, military service under a Russian officer class became mandatory.

There were further grievances: the government had claimed monopolies over salt extraction and perhaps as important, over fishing rights in the River Yaik, a crucial element in the Yaik Cossack economy. Recruiting agents and tax demands when the Turkish War broke out in 1768 obviously brought grievances to a head and a pretender issued forth from the Cossacks.

The pretender phenomenon in Russia has been convincingly explained by reference to a peasant psychology imbued with a dual conviction: the one of a natural justice – the land and all its produce is mine and no lord, landlord or bureaucrat has a stake in it – the other of the intrinsic bounty of the monarch. This bounty could only be deflected from his child, the peasant, by corrupt officials or courtiers or perhaps, if the monarch was seen to be palpably unjust, because the monarch was not the real monarch. Peter III, whom Pugachev, an illiterate ex-soldier, claimed to be, was an obvious candidate for resurrection because of the dubious circumstances in which he died after only a short reign, and because of the evident unpopularity of his wife, Catherine. The imagined virtues of the one could be contrasted with the known atrocities of the other. How far thinking people were convinced by Pugachev is impossible to discern, but they were prepared to accept him and the programme which he proclaimed. This embodied freedom from serfdom and, for the Cossacks, from recruiting levies, an end to the poll tax and guarantees in possession of land, salt lakes and fishing rights. On these issues Cossack and Bashkir found common ground. The Cossacks also pressed for a return to the 'old religion' and customs condemned by the government. Cossack military traditions, upon which Pugachev superimposed a 'college of war' almost on St Petersburg lines, marshalled the brave but disorganized Bashkirs in a way never experienced before. The revolt spread over territories comprehending about $4\frac{1}{2}$ million people and at times 30,000 men were reported in arms. The rebels burnt, pillaged and destroyed manorial registers, killed lords and their families with incredible brutality and actually crossed into Muscovy.

What held them back? The revolt sustained itself for a year. It was finally suppressed when the government made peace with Turkey and hence generals and troops were released for an immense military effort against the insurgents. The peace with Turkey obviously took the edge off some popular discontent. One evident failure of the rebels was to hold the towns and what was probably a decisive factor in bringing about peace was the lack of grain and livestock created by the rebellion. By August 1774 there was real famine in the Volga valley.

The details of the rising and of Pugachev's death are of less relevance than the consequences of a movement which had directly influenced the lives of a third of Russia's population and had seriously threatened central control and the fabric of Catherine's government. Probably the main results were to make an overwhelming imperative of local government reform. The provinces were dangerously undermanned. In Kazan, seat of revolt, eight virtually uninspected officials supposedly controlled a population of $2\frac{1}{2}$ million. The second result was that defeat spelt the death knell of Cossack and Bashkir pretensions to autonomy and thirdly it brought Catherine into a closer realization of the community of interests between herself and the nobility which carried her further in the direction of ceding to their corporate demands in 1785.

The reform of provincial administration as enacted in 1775 divided the Russian Empire into fifty *gubernii* of 800,000 inhabitants, further subdivided into districts of 60,000 inhabitants. In charge of the *guberniya* was the governor. In many ways the system resembled that of the French intendances as conceived by Colbert, that is to say, the governor was not a local man but hand-picked by the ruler for loyalty and ability and was in fact accountable to her alone. Because of the distance between the *gubernii* and the central government the governors enjoyed virtually limitless powers since there simply was not time to consult the Empress before making a step. In consequence, the Empress was careful to see that governorships fell to men she could trust. They were favourites and lovers, perhaps, but usually men of energy and initiative. Unlike the French intendant, the Russian governor had at his disposition all the military units in his *guberniya* which meant that any local disturbance could be met with immediate military repression without having to seek permission from St Petersburg. Financial administration and industrial development and social services – hospitals, schools and almshouses – were made the responsibility of a number of local boards.

There was also an apparently comprehensive reform of the judicial structure. A local board assumed responsibility for the administration of civil and criminal justice within a given area and below these, extended a network of separate courts dealing with, respectively, nobles, town dwellers and state peasants. Such a system pointed to the separate identity of the nobility and accorded it separate corporate status, but how far did the measures, taken as a package, go towards realizing the aspirations of the *dvorianstvo* to control local government? The answer is scarcely at all. A few posts, though they were not prestigious ones, were open to election on a class basis. The formal head of district administration, the *kapitan-ispravnik*, was an elective post and so was the marshal of the nobility, their spokesman to the governor. Similarly some high judicial posts were reserved to the *dvorianstvo*. The nobles had the right to meet in assembly with a view to formulating a common programme and electing their spokesman but the governor was neither open to pressure from the assembly nor was he obliged to accept their candidate if he considered him unsuitable. In short the *appearance* of concession was much greater than the actuality and there was nothing in local service to attract the *dvorianstvo* there rather than towards the professional, largely military service. The governors were the fifty men to whom real power was temporarily given and since they were the Empress's appointees, she ceded nothing.

Ten years later the Municipal Charter Act made more specific the mechanism for the government of towns, by creating six-man town councils (*duma*). Each of the men was the representative of one of six categories of townsmen, including the nobility and the merchants. These six then elected a mayor. But the governor's control was absolute. He and his bureaucracy controlled municipal elections and used the *duma* largely for the collection of taxes. Certainly Catherine achieved something no other Russian autocrat had achieved before her: that is the extension of more effective control into the provinces.

In 1785 the most significant of Catherine's measures concerning the *dvorianstvo*, the Noble Charter, finally resolved by careful definition the thorny question of noble privilege without attendant obligation. Why this should happen in 1785 is a difficult question to answer. Was it that a further crop of pretender movements troubled Catherine's psychological security so that she looked to bolstering her position with noble allies? Or was it that twenty-three years of political experience had convinced her that the *dvorianstvo*, if given privileged status, would not suddenly abandon state service and become a drone class? Was it that the real political question, that of who should govern the localities, had been effectively resolved in 1775 and that Catherine now had experience of the degree to which the local assemblies of nobles were basically disinterested in corporate activities and incapable of presenting a political threat to autocracy? Certainly the Charter of 1785 represented a compromise between the concept of nobility as a reward for service and that of nobility as transmitted by blood. By it, the law recognized equality between nobility of birth and that of service and confirmed and extended privileges granted over the previous sixty years. In particular these embodied security of person and property: a monopoly of serf ownership: exemption from taxation: trial by peers and immunity from corporal punishments. The guardians of privilege were the elected marshals of the nobility in the localities and these had the right to keep genealogical rosters though only the State Department of Heraldry had the right to decide who was, or was not, a noble.

From this point on the nobility could claim themselves a legally privileged elite though practice might occasionally depart from legality and governors in particular were known to act arbitrarily causing loss of liberty or property. Taken overall, the measures probably engendered little change in the way the *dvorianstvo* actually lived. They were still very much at the state's disposal and without the means or the desire to question the power of the state in any way. Lack of primogeniture meant that families could be beggared within three generations without a new inflow of resources from state salaries, rewards of serfs, or grants or loans. The rootlessness characteristic of the Petrine nobility continued and since state service carried the best educated and most able out of the localities, the assemblies of nobles acquired little significance in the political or social life of the state.

Yet something had changed. The achievements of Petrine Russia had been the achievements of a successful marriage between tsar and *dvorianstvo* but events, especially since 1775, had distanced the partners by interposing an officialdom emanating from the governor and engendering the conviction that tsarina and *dvorianstvo* were not one in interest. Heightening this conviction was the extension of the commoner elements in the bureaucracy in positions which did not confer noble status but demanded an efficient performance of routine office-work so that eventually the government could call upon professional functionaries long experienced in administrative toil. The central government itself progressively hemmed itself around with bureaux staffed by such functionaries. It paid them salaries and gave them neither rewards nor privileges. It hence liberated itself from dependence on the *dvorianstvo* in routine matters of government. To reach the ruler by petition the noble needed to work through offices staffed by commoners. A further wall was also gradually and perhaps unintentionally erected. By the Charter of 1785 the noble was permitted to travel abroad. His position as a westernizing cultural influence was not merely conceded but positively blessed by Catherine. This 'westernization' of the Russian nobility was to have some unexpected repercussions of which the most significant was the emergence of an intelligentsia whose education had been permeated with principles at odds with the political nature of an autocracy. Radischev, educated at Catherine's expense in Leipzig, is perhaps the outstanding example of a noble whose education turned him into a critic of both autocracy and serfdom. His *Journey from St. Petersburg to Moscow* expresses a paradox of late eighteenth-century Russian history: the encouragement, by the autocrat herself, of an education in principles fundamentally anti-autocratic.

'Westernization' continued throughout the eighteenth century to mean a number of economic, political and cultural processes. In economic terms it continued to signify the adoption of western technology and the gearing of the Russian economy to the important European export market in pig iron. In political terms it implied more efficient bureaucratization to achieve the fiscal means for military expansion. In military terms it never ceased to mean the adoption of tactics of weaponry on a western model. In cultural terms, however, a marked development took place in the second half of the century. Here it meant the airing of western ideas, the cultivation of refined taste and hence it implied a type of education and a degree of conspicuous consumption. The *dvorianstvo* since the 1730s had appreciated that education was the way to advancement in the service: hence their particular concern that the autocracy should provide subsidized noble academies. But this does not necessarily infer any predilection for a particular *kind* of education. The taste for an education inculcated by French tutors, such as Catherine gave to her grandson, whose intellectual content was based upon a western European literature, absorbed through the medium of French or German, was a phenomenon of the second half of the eighteenth century. For the tsarina, to have an educated elite responded to her own intellectual penchant. She was a gifted woman with an agile mind and a degree of intellectual vanity. If she enjoyed sharpening her mind against Diderot and Voltaire and examining the essence of *De l'Esprit des Lois* then we must presume she found it congenial to dwell with individuals of similar intellectual formation. The reorganization of the Cadet Corps and the foundation of the Smolny Institute in St Petersburg (for girls), and, more specifically, the emergence of sixty or so provincial academies, opened to elements in the nobility the prospect of a western-style education. Catherine also wished to extend schooling to the inhabitants of provincial capitals, if not to the rural masses, but the elementary and secondary schools which emerged were very feeble and limited in extent, and education remained basically the privilege of the nobility or, more specifically, of the 20 percent or so (at most) of the *dvorianstvo* who could afford academy fees or tutors.

A western-style education for a boy cost the equivalent every year of the rent from twenty *obrók*-paying serfs. To secure such an education opened for the young man the prospect of acceptance at court and in the influential circles that would achieve his social advancement and to purchase this prospect for their sons the *dvorianstvo* tried to increase their revenues. To a degree they did so with state connivance. The legislation tightening the lord's control over his serfs strengthened him in possession of the manpower which was his greatest asset, but the lord was powerless to raise rents beyond a certain level since one cannot get blood out of a stone and, great though the penalties were, peasant flight to frontier territories was still a reality. In the last analysis, western education and western consumption patterns in the form of fine cloth, cuisine (sugar, chocolate etc.), tobacco, and artefacts in precious metals, were financed by state loans. Indeed, loans to the nobility constituted by 1800 the largest drain on state revenues after military expenditure. It has been argued that to have the more influential members of the *dvorianstvo* thus tied financially to royal favour suited the autocrat's purpose and was a far from oblique way of ensuring loyalty.[1] In this way the Russian crown built up the traditional, well-known, patron-client relationship upon which western European monarchies had relied since the late middle ages. In Russian terms, it was a monetary substitute for rewards to servants which had previously been made in land and men when such disposable assets were in short supply, as they obviously were between the first two Partitions of Poland. The same intention of bolstering *dvorianstvo* revenues may have lain behind the government's more stringent legislation limiting serf acquisition by industrialists. This reversed the Petrine policy of stimulating industrial development by permitting the employment of fugitive serfs and allowing entrepreneurs the right to acquire men when industrial expansion demanded them. The *dvorianstvo* either feared that the price of labour might be increased or that radical shifts of manpower into industry from peasant flight or with state encouragement might jeopardize their revenues.

With such state help, and on aggregate, the *dvorianstvo* just about managed to maintain the numbers of serfs at their disposition. However there were wide discrepancies in patterns of ownership between the two extremes of petty nobles at one end of the scale and considerable holdings at the other, and at the bottom end of the scale, petty noble families were continually disappearing from the noble bracket. But whilst the numbers of serfs per household held relatively steady, imported luxury goods and the taste for foreign-style education grew apace. The Empress herself was not wont to count the cost as she indulged her architectural whims in the rococo grandeur of Tsarskoe Selo with its triumphal arches, Palladian columns and art collection of old masters culled from every corner of Europe. Her patronage encouraged native Russian artists and sculptors. Theatres sprang up all over Russia. By 1800 Moscow had fifteen. A book trade – though not without censorship – was born, partly concerned with foreign translations but progressively with an impressive array of Russian authors. Derzhavin, the poet, Karamzin whose memoirs contain some of the most pertinent commentaries on society and autocracy in Russia, Shcherbatov the historian and Novikov the satirist point to a flowering of literature unprecedented in Russian history. The purchasers of books,

1 A. Kahan, 'The Costs of Westernization in Russia', *Slavic Review*, 25, 1966.

the audiences in the theatres, the patrons of artists, the employers of architects, the wearers of elegant clothes and jewels in the salons where French was the medium of discourse and the successful conversational-ist could draw upon a galaxy of western authors and the critical apparatus of the European Enlightenment, all belonged to those mem-bers of the *dvorianstvo* (10–20 per cent) who could raise the means thus to involve themselves.

Much of this salon civilization was superficial. Voltairian anticleric-alism or deistical principles were singularly out of place in a Russian context whilst the political discourses and debates on the equality of man were fundamentally at variance with the Russian tradition. Cur-iously enough this situation was to breed two sets of critics, both, in a sense, the intellectually dispossessed of their generation. Those who accepted the western ideas of French tutors were drawn into belief in the rule of law and the rights of individuals and hence along a politi-cally radical path threatening to the monarchy, whilst another grouping recoiled before foreign influences. Novikov was one of the most pung-ent of these slavophiles who saw western influence as the medium whereby 'piglets' were transformed into 'perfect swine'. Though an admirer of western constitutionalism, Shcherbatov perceived the impli-cit contradiction of autocratic patronage of philosophies censorious of autocracy. Because Catherine could not support the conservative slavo-phile policy without admitting a need to reject a western European intellectual tradition, she was drawn into persecution of the slavophiles and used against them the mechanism of the police state with public burning of books, show trials and rigorous censorship. Novikov was imprisoned without trial in 1789 and emerged three years later an utterly destroyed man: Radischev became the first notable political exile in Siberia: and the Freemasons who had adopted a slavophile line but looked to humanitarian reform were driven underground. The victims however were not only to be on one side. The French Revolu-tion brought into the persecution net the politically radical and little by little, without admitting it, the state itself was pushed into a basically slavophile position.

The abortive Decembrist rising of 1825 and the secret societies of the nineteenth century were the logical corollary of changes taking place within Catherine's Russia. Far from being truly 'the golden age of the *dvorianstvo*' Catherine's reign saw their fundamental alienation from the peasantry and the bourgeoisie – whether industrialist or bureaucrat. Amongst the thinking elements, a profound malaise with the state they had helped to create became discernible. These were probably the most consequential developments of Russian society in this period, the price paid by the Russian state for a century of European expansion, great power status and a westernization process which involved philosophies so fundamentally at odds with the realities of Russian life.

Part III

The Western World

9

Vanished Supremacies: The Iberian Peninsula

Western Europe in the mid-eighteenth century had at least three members who had historically enjoyed a predominant role in Europe's political or economic life and whose overseas empires, or in the Dutch instance, maritime trade, still bore witness to that fact. Each had widely differing political structures yet all in the eighteenth century faced a common problem: the maintenance of empire and trade. Here comparison ends for each was to undergo radically differing political experiences, each in their way reflecting eighteenth-century trends. In Spain, essays were made in the direction of enlightened absolutism: in Portugal ministerial tyranny was thinly disguised in the trappings of 'enlightened' change and in the United Provinces the evolution of radical politics was to produce Europe's first revolutionary generation.

The history of eighteenth-century Spain is a curious hybrid, an amalgam of progress and reaction in which Enlightenment principles were applied by king and ministers to a society medieval in beliefs and outlook. Here an economically buoyant littoral of cities, flourishing trades and vital economic relations contrasted with an arid, scantily populated hinterland, the victim of recurrent droughts and pestilence. Spain was a country in which regional privileges and provincial demarcations seemed the very abnegation of the concept of a unified state. In an earlier epoch Spain's imported specie had seemed to set the pace for European economy. Her armies had determined the course of international politics and her religious convictions had nurtured mystics and Jesuits and made Spain the bastion of Counter-Reformation principles. Yet looking at Spain from the outside in 1730 what was perhaps most apparent was that she had undergone between 1680 and 1715 a period of immense crisis only partially resolved by the Treaty of Utrecht. In part the crisis had been a succession crisis and that had at least been resolved by the acceptance of Philip V, a Bourbon forced to renounce any pretensions to the French throne. But it was as well a crisis in which

Spain's future as a leading colonial power was severely questioned. Already at Utrecht inroads had been made by the British into Spanish trading monopolies and Spanish control of the Indies was far from secure. Crown finances from the early seventeenth century had been severely shaken by the alternate inflation/deflation policies of the Habsburg monarchs and South American gold and silver for more than a century had been viewed as a source of wealth not infinitely extendable, and hence far from being the answer to government financial problems. Clearly Spain must look to the preservation of her empire and her trading strength and hence above all to the maintenance of a navy.

The accession of a Bourbon merely confirmed what might in any event have been the case, that is a French connection, *la pacte de famille*, in which the two countries made common cause against the British whose trading and colonial ambitions and concepts of strategic interests menaced them more than anyone else. Colonial involvement dictated the pace of Spanish foreign policy and the French alliance was a reality which only the most daring (notably Esquilache) challenged. The importation of a Bourbon had other significant consequences. From 1715 onwards, Spanish monarchs began to view their territories as candidates for administrative reform very much along the lines adopted by Louis XIV in France some fifty years previously. Such reform was concerned above all with strengthening central control by reducing provincial boundaries and privileges: by making uniform the organs of provincial and municipal government by superimposing a new royal official, the *intendente* on a mass of hereditary and venal provincial offices to ensure the implementation of royal will: by abolishing or reducing the power of the erstwhile mighty *consejos*, the aristocratic councils which ran the provinces: and by creating what was to emerge as an unmistakable ministerial despotism.

A royal decision, made as early as 1705, to split the office of secretary of state into several secretaryships with special spheres of influence (state (foreign affairs), war, *hacienda* (treasury), *gracia y justicia* (justice), navy and the Indies) and to use the secretaryships to carry out the real work of government laid the foundations of ministerial power. Each secretary, chosen by the king, had the job of introducing policy in the Council of Castille and transmitting decisions to the provinces. Not surprisingly, the secretaryships for state (foreign affairs) and *hacienda* evolved as the most important posts offering most power to the incumbent. The secretary of the *hacienda* was the Spanish equivalent of the *contrôleur général*. He probably held the key position because concerned with finances, and he was helped in the formulation of economic policy by the *Junta de Comercio y Moneda*. More than one secretaryship could be held by any one individual concurrently – the decision was that of the king. Floridablanca for example held both the secretaryship of state and *gracia y justicia* which included ecclesiastical appointments. Government at the top obviously was the work of a small coterie and the monarch, having appointed his men, left them to get on with the job and bear the brunt of public ire. They were to be dismissed, as in the case of Esquilache, if they incurred too much hostility. Otherwise they could be left to attempt to force the pace of reform in Spain.

This distancing of monarchy from change makes it well nigh impossible to talk about enlightened despotism in Spain and much easier to think in terms of a reforming programme influenced in the second half of the eighteenth century by Enlightenment persuasions. The programme reflected the basic need of the Spanish government to extend the control of government, to achieve improvements in the fiscal system, to reduce the power of nobility and clergy and in the second half of the century to lift the economy by removing obstructions to the free movement of produce and reducing the amount of land open to transhumance (in particular ceasing to protect the sheep runs of the Mesta) or used for common pasture. The administrative changes are a continuing development throughout the century but the most wide-reaching reforms were to be the efforts of the ministers of Charles III after 1759.

Philip V (1714–46) embarked upon a policy of reducing separate governing enclaves within the major provinces and standardized provincial government at least in Castille, Aragon, Valencia, Mallorca and Catalonia. Of the provincial councils, Castille alone, the training ground of royal secretaries, remained a force for central government to have to consider. At the local level, government traditionally devolved upon *corregidores* of whom one existed in every town and controlled the surrounding rural area. These venal officials were hopelessly corrupt and Philip V sought to deflect their powers over financial affairs to *intendentes*. This step was taken cautiously, with only a handful of men, but was extended in 1749 and the *intendentes* were given yet more power in 1780 when the fiscal demands of the American War made closer control a necessity (though even then what was achieved in Aragon was not achieved in Castille). The *intendentes* were by the end of the *ancien régime* the most vital link in local government. Much weaker was government control over the cities and towns whose autonomy may have shrunk in the period but which remained notwithstanding, impressively strong.

In 1751 Ferdinand VI's minister, Ensenada, managed to oblige the towns to submit their accounts to the Council of Castille and after the insurrection in Madrid in 1766 an effort was made by Aranda to achieve a standardization of municipal government by decreeing the election of four representatives for every 1000 inhabitants. In many cases, however, this merely resulted in grafting more officials on to unchanged town councils. Several towns and cities were 'privately' owned by nobles, bishops, monasteries and the military orders. This meant control over taxation and justice was virtually denied to the monarchy. The census of 1797 showed that the nobility owned 15 cities, 2286 towns, 6380 villages and hamlets whilst the clergy had 7 episcopal cities, 395 towns and 3494 villages and hamlets. Even where towns were nominally in royal control officialdom in the shape of *corregidores*, tax officials and patriciates could divert revenue to line their own pockets. Royal officials sent into the localities could find themselves strangulated by meshes of local and individual privileges which extended to tax exemptions, personal possession of the fruits of certain royal taxes and the profits of justice.

Royal revenues were derived from a startling variety of sources: the ownership of saltbeds, mines, the tunny fisheries of Cadiz; income from the confiscated property of the military orders; the *servicio; moneda forera* (a tax on individuals in acknowledgement of being a Spanish subject and from which the nobility and clergy were exempted); an ecclesiastical subsidy (rather like the *don gratuit*); customs duties which at the beginning of the century in the sea ports were collected and hence distrained by the *municipios* (municipal councils); the *alcabala* or general sales tax (mercilessly creamed off by royal concessionaries); monopolies on the sale of salt, tobacco, quicksilver, playing cards etc; excise duties on a number of random commodities (*milliones*); some revenue from the Mesta for retention of its privileges; *tercios reales* (two-ninths of tithe) and certain special contributions from ecclesiastical revenues authorized by the popes in the sixteenth century. How much any of this could be made to yield at any particular time was a matter of speculation. To introduce reform into the situation was well nigh impossible. Philip V and Ferdinand VI's ministers tried improved bookkeeping and attempted to audit the account books of the *municipios* and to get the customs dues back from the sea ports but this did not make available substantial revenues. They were of course forced to borrow to survive. In normal years a loan from the *Cinco Gremios Mayores* (literally the Five Major Guilds, a powerful syndicate which borrowed from the public at 2 1/2 per cent and lent to the monarchy at 4 1/2 per cent might suffice but war could engender special expedients, such as recourse to loans from abroad.

Both Philip V and Ferdinand VI were cursed with wives whose dynastic ambitions ran counter to the interests of the Spanish treasury. Elizabeth Farnese's attempts in the thirties to forge Italian territories for her sons in Naples and Sicily and Spain's subsequent backing of Charles of Bavaria in the Austrian Succession War which brought the Dukedoms of Parma and Piacenza were irrelevant digressions from the need to protect the Spanish Empire. Ferdinand VI's minister, Ensenada, initiated in 1741 a programme of costly naval reform which in nine years produced 43 ships of the line and 9 frigates and which stretched budgetary resources to the full. Ensenada was a fervent protagonist of the French alliance and in the ensuing Seven Years' War Spain shared the humiliations of her ally entailing the loss of Minorca and Florida. The Peace of Paris marked a stage in the disintegration of the Empire.

In the course of the war, Spain acquired a new king, Charles III, and at the same time, a new set of ministers. Charles III had behind him twenty-five years' experience as ruler of Naples under the influence of Tanucci, an Italian notorious for his hard line towards clerical immunities and privileges and who *ab initio* was to become a protagonist of the policy of *regalismo* aimed at extending the power of the state at the expense of the church. Tanucci recommended to Charles III the importation, also from Naples, of a man regarded as a financial genius, the Marques de Squilacce, or Esquilache as he became known in Spain, and to this 'foreigner' was given the secretaryship of the *hacienda* and in 1763 that of war as well. Ensenada was dropped and Campomanes was made *fiscal* (financial expert) of the Council of Castille.

The reign of Charles III (1759–89) was to be the significant period of reform and attempted reform in eighteenth-century Spain. In part this reflected the predilections of an efficient 'outsider' king and, initially, of a group of foreign ministers who looked with alien eyes at the jumble of privileged individuals and corporate bodies which lay in the path of effective government and an uncluttered fiscal system and who could appreciate that reform was desirable. But the context within which they were operating, the sixties, in which the psychological and financial disasters of war were only too apparent also made reform a necessity. Recent Spanish historians stress that the era of reform was coincident with a period of economic growth but such an appreciation obscures two important considerations. First, Spanish economic growth was chronically uneven. To set against the burgeoning cities of the littoral, the ports whose wealth stemmed predominantly from the export of wines, spirits and fine wool and which were backed by a restricted hinterland of vineyards, lay an interior where, setting aside river valleys, production was low and markets virtually non-existent. Coastal Spain exchanged its goods with northern Europe and imported grain in return. In this way it was hitched to the economy of the Baltic and the entrepôt of Amsterdam and hence to the vicissitudes of the north European economy – an important consideration when we remember that in the sixties low Baltic harvests led to the adoption of, albeit temporary, protection policies and the Amsterdam money market was severely dislocated. The second consideration is that the government was, through the very nature of royal finances, ill placed to take full advantage of Spain's mercantile or landed wealth, yet it had no option but to attempt to increase government revenues if only to service the debts of war and to assure the future of the Spanish navy. No one assumed that the Peace of Paris was a lasting peace.

The first reforming package put forward by Esquilache focused upon a reform of the treasury with a view to introducing a single land tax without exemptions for the nobility, the clergy and the towns (which would entail a new land survey and hence could not be put into effect immediately). Secondly, there was to be a re-shaping of the Council of Castille to exclude the clergy and nobility and replace them by *manteistas* (a kind of lesser bureaucratic nobility deemed more amenable to fiscal change). Thirdly, Esquilache embarked upon a struggle with the *Cinco Gremios Mayores* to strip them of their monopoly of fixing the price of woollens, silks, jewellery and spices. The idea was that in the long run this would weaken them and loosen their stranglehold on monarchical finance. Fourthly, there was projected a reassessment of the church's contribution to government finances and decrees virtually preventing further land slipping into mortmain were intended to ensure that the church's wealth would remain static and would not further increase at the expense of the state.

Esquilache's reforms constitute a rather curious package understandable only with reference to the long-term view. In the here and now they offered nothing to the central treasury but they portended radical change to come. Immediately they secured for Esquilache a number of powerful enemies, the high aristocracy, the church, the *Cinco Gremios Mayores*, and to these must be added the protagonists of the French connection for Esquilache was overtly hostile to the family compact. Viewed objectively, Esquilache's proposals were the logical first steps in a physiocratic programme and might have passed smoothly into operation but for his approval of a grain policy which, whether it profoundly affected them or not, brought the working-class populace of Madrid into open protest in the most considerable Spanish rising of the eighteenth century, the *motín di Esquilache*.

The economic difficulties experienced by Spain in the 1760s were of course common to Europe and were, broadly speaking, the product of three factors. These were, first, a long-term demographic imbalance between population growth and economic development, second, a series of bad harvests – in particular those of 1763 and 1764 – and third, a profound dislocation in the delivery of Baltic grain supplies due to diminished Baltic harvests and the adoption in northern Europe of temporary protectionist policies. The ports of the Spanish littoral looked to the Baltic for provisioning. If they could not get grain there, then they must look elsewhere and become contenders for what there was to be had at home. In short, even in Catalonia whose economy was healthier than that of any other part of Spain one sees in the sixties certain manifestations of economic stress: an upsurge in banditry, the need for new repressive measures to counteract vagrancy and begging with violence. In the arid interior of Spain, the harvests of

1763 and 1764 were notoriously poor and if they improved during the next year, peasant debts had to be paid and hence the crisis could be prolonged.

Pierre Vilar has offered the following figures as representative of the movement in the price of wheat in the Madrid market (in *maravidies per fanega* – approximately a bushel).

1754	952	1761	843
1755	836	1762	1039
1756	529	1763	1360
1757	?	1764	1258
1758	680	1765	1657
1759	646	1766	(1054)*
1760	1009	1767	1791

* artificial figure due to a government subsidy.

Clearly from 1760 prices were retaining high levels. The interior of Spain knew little in the way of grain merchants but those who received rents in kind, such as tithe farmers and seigneurs, obviously had a surplus to be disposed of in the spring and summer months when prices were high, whilst in the post-harvest period when prices were at their lowest there was some buying up by almshouses, army suppliers and by private granaries, some charitable, some run by municipalities. The small private speculator was not unknown, but before 1765, his operations were illegal. Traditionally the grain trade was regulated by a system of price controls (*tasa de granos*) issued by the central government and enforced in the urban markets by municipal authorities. The level of the controlled prices reflected the supply of grain and the costs of transport. There was no internal or external trade in grain permitted before 1756–7 when it was allowed if prices in the interior fell below those of the coastal provinces, which they rarely did, and so the change was largely theoretical.

The degree of regulation was far greater in theory than in fact. It was believed that the *tasa de granos* kept prices down but they certainly did not stop them rising. Indeed, and the Spanish were far from unique in this respect, as long as traditional means were left to operate, whether or not they were effective, relative tranquillity prevailed – though whether it would have done so in 1766 is open to speculation. In July 1765 Esquilache's *Pragmática* was issued introducing freedom of the grain trade which permitted the purchase and sale of corn anywhere at any time providing merchants (who were defined as 'the holders of income from feudal or other dues or tithes or any others who obtain grain for trading purposes') were registered in their localities. Local authorities were simultaneously instructed to see that sufficient bread was locally available.

It is questionable whether these measures ever came into effect in face of the wariness of local authorities. Some urban magistrates actually bought up grain to guard against speculators. Certainly, with or without the implementation of the *Pragmática*, 1765–6 would have been a hard year but the fact that the government had sought to tamper with the grain trade meant that government measures could be blamed for the country's plight.

By the beginning of March 1766 a series of risings began, starting in Madrid but rippling through towns and large villages where an end was sought to the free trade measures. But the Madrid riots were different insofar as they went far beyond the simple bread riot and were clearly organized in the *tavernas* by agitators with political ends. A demonstration by 10,000 people in the streets on 23 March demanding lower bread prices succeeded in forcing Charles III to concede a lowering in prices and an end to free trade. But the riots did not stop. Lampoons and pamphlets circulated and on 24 March a crowd of 3000 (a very marked reduction), with a friar as their messenger, presented seven demands. The first was for the exile of Esquilache and his family: the second the demand that all ministers be Spanish: the third the abolition of the royal Walloon guard which was very unpopular: the fourth the suppression of the board of grain provisions: the fifth the lowering of food prices: the sixth the return of troops to their proper garrisons: the last the retention of the traditional aristocratic garb of long cape and broadbrimmed hat. To all these demands, Charles III ceded.

Much debate has raged over the engineers of these riots though there have been three favoured candidates, the Jesuits, the grandees, then the French together with the partisans of the family compact. Evidence suggests that though the Jesuits were opposed to the policies of *regalismo* of Charles III's government, as an order they were not involved in the riots though a handful of individual Jesuits may have been so. Clearly the grandees were resentful of replacement by *manteistas* and along with Ensenada's supporters, perhaps backed by French money, they are more convincing suspects. The mystery remains but what is clear is that Charles III's advisers, minus Esquilache and Tanucci, chose the church as a scapegoat and the *motín* provided the justification for two acts of major significance: the first the expulsion of the Jesuits (1767) and the second the purging of the Council of Castille of any 'Jesuit' – meaning anti-*regalismo* – elements.

The expulsion of the Jesuits, bringing Spain into line with Portugal and France, though done explicitly by reference to their unpatriotic influence over the people (they preached, said Campomanes the attorney general, the doctrine of regicide) allowed Charles III's government to assume their property and to destroy the main bastion of ultramontanism in Spain. Campomanes was also able to demonstrate the implication in the rising of Diego de Rojas, Bishop of Cartagena and president of the Council of Castille, and he was replaced in office by Count Aranda, the king's nominee. This, together with the ousting of a further 13 so-called 'Jesuits' (out of a total of 27 members) made the institution thoroughly the tool of Charles III's ministers. Perhaps the re-modelling of the Council was the most striking immediate consequence of the *motín*. With or without free trade, prices did not fall in the long run though in the seventies they were to level out and not until the 1780s did bread riot again become a recurrent aspect of the Spanish scene.

Modern Spanish historians regard the advent of Aranda to presidency of the Council of Castille (1766–73) as the most important result of the *motín*. Aranda enjoyed a particularly high reputation for several rea-sons. Firstly he was a native and his mode of thought based upon a development of indigenous Spanish practice. Unlike Esquilache who thought in terms of the efficiency of royal bureaucratic control, Aranda was more a partisan of what in France would have passed under the heading of limited monarchy or aristocratic constitutionalism. He was a grandee and hence opposed to what he regarded as bureaucratic tyr-anny. His ideas on politics, economics and administrative reform align him very much with the western European Enlightenment. He was a close friend of Voltaire and it is easy to appreciate why. Less easy is it to understand Charles III's readiness to lend an ear to Aranda who became progressively the leader of a grouping known as *el partido aragonés* (the Aragonese party) which included Jovellanos the economist, and which stood, in political terms, for monarchy tempered by aristocracy and ancient institutions against the *golillas* in the Council of Castille who were led by Floridablanca and Campomanes and who advocated stron-ger central and bureaucratic control. Charles III may indeed have viewed the one as an effective counter to the excesses of the other, since he was unwilling to see a repetition of the events of 1766. More-over, if Aranda's political concepts did not tally with those of the king, his economic ideas and particularly his projected agrarian law were in perfect harmony with Charles III and Campomanes.

Aranda's period of office saw the enactment of provisions, mostly formulated by Jovellanos (1766, 1768, finalized 1770), to divide all cultivable commons amongst legal claimants (a residence and land in the area in question made one qualify for up to eight acres, residence alone three acres) and the formation of *sociedades de Amigos del País*, agricultural societies which were intended to foster in the nobility and large landowners a consciousness of the need to stimulate agrarian development. Many of these societies were of course merely arenas of desultory debate which did far less to stimulate interest in agriculture than the rising grain prices which offered more positive incentives. But the involvement of the state which sought to use the Madrid *Amigos del País* as advisor and critic of its projected agrarian law gave some status to the societies. What emerged after eleven to fifteen years of debate and discussion was relatively little. The project included forcing the towns to divide and enclose their common land but neither the bureaucratic mechanism nor the capital effectively to carry out the plan were available. The same deficiencies added to peasant ineffectiveness in face of seigneurial hostility also nullified efforts to divide rural commons and waste.

Aranda and Campomanes were fervent opponents of Mesta privileges which gave a group of fifty or sixty individuals or institutions the right to use extensive sheep runs which precluded significant areas, particularly in Extremadura, from development. In that province by the 1770s were $\frac{1}{2}$ million people and 3 million sheep. The total return of the Mesta was estimated as an annual 75 million *reales* compared with a speculative national agricultural output of 5000 million *reales*. The crown itself drew important revenues from Mesta profits. The annual return on one Mesta sheep was $1\frac{1}{2}$ *reales* to the owner; $6\frac{1}{2}$ *reales* to the crown and $7\frac{1}{2}$ *reales* in pasture charges so that the crown in ceasing to protect Mesta interests was a financial loser. Not until 1786 in fact were any truly significant measures adopted against the Mesta when its right to use in perpetuity and at fixed rents any land it had previously used as pasture was abolished, and two years later landowners were given the right to enclose their lands and plant whenever they wanted.

Attempts to stop the sub-contracting of property (*foristos*) which began in 1763 so as to prevent the rapid rise in rents had not been implemented by the time of the Napoleonic invasions. In short, the economic reform plan was far from being a success in the agrarian sector – the area which mattered for the bulk of the Spanish population. Seigneurial and church levies, absentee landlordism, lack of water and manure, the slow acceptance of the potato and of rice and the evolution of a keener land market in an ambience of rising prices, all counted against the small peasant. Moreover, town and country were in progressive competition over supplies and the peasant in order to meet his rents expected high prices for such grain as he marketed. A riot occurred in Saragossa in 1776 to secure fixed grain prices which was put down by the surrounding peasantry whilst the authorities remained inactive.

Whilst the state sought freedom for grain producers it adopted the reverse of *laissez-faire* tactics in its attitude towards industrial enterprise, rigidly buttressing native industries from the late 1760s by prohibiting the import of foreign goods – particularly of cotton so as to protect the development of Catalan production and of iron so as to protect the Basque iron industry. There was, however, some effort to remove impediments to production at home firstly in 1785–6 by a reduction of the *alcabala* and secondly by continuing a frontal attack on the *Cinco Gremios Mayores*. There had been a great deal of opposition to women workers by these powerful guilds yet between 1778 and 1784 women were proclaimed free to work at industrial pursuits and laws of 1787 and 1789 permitted textile manufacturers to have an unlimited number of employees and relieved their products of guild inspection. It is difficult to assess the overall impact of such policy on industrial production. Protection against British goods was valuable to the Spanish cotton industry at a vital period of its growth. The zenith of this industry was 1783–c. 1795, that is to say between the end of the American War which had severed colonial markets and the delivery of supplies and the French Revolution. The opening up of industry to women and the reduction of guild inspection perhaps merely accelerated a drift of industry into the countryside. By the end of the eighteenth century woollen manufacturers were well into hard times which were not eased by multiplying the number of workers or bringing into industrial employment women who were prepared to work for less than their male counterparts.

The pattern of reforming legislation clearly followed the vicissitudes of Spanish foreign policy. In time of war for example even Charles III could not countenance a decline in income from the Mesta or a sacrifice of the *alcabala* to cut the costs of industrial goods or indeed an attack on the *Cinco Gremios Mayores*, though the lending capacity of that institution was by the American War of Independence a thing of the past.

Spain did not refuse to follow France into declaring war on Britain, her main colonial rival, in 1779, although Charles III had some misgivings about a colonial insurrection possibly setting a bad example to Spain's own colonies. Smarting under the earlier refusal of France in 1771 to co-operate with Spain in an ejection of Britain from the Falkland Islands, this time Spain sought a clear agreement with France as to her prizes for victory which were notably the restoration of Gibraltar. In fact, although in the course of the war Spain reconquered Florida and the Bahamas, seized British bases in Belize and recovered Minorca in 1782, Gibraltar was not a prize of the peace and Spain also handed the Bahamas back to Britain. Territorially, the peace looked advantageous enough but the price had been immense commercial dislocation striking a severe blow at bullion and cotton imports and preventing exports of wine and commodities to northern Europe. Britain may have been Spain's main commercial rival but she was also her main trading partner and through naval strength was able to sever Spain's commercial links. Unable to raise the level of taxation at home, or to step up loans from domestic or foreign sources, Charles III had recourse to issuing paper money, the *Vales Reales*, interest-bearing royal bonds which circulated as legal tender. In comparison with other European experiments of like nature the *Vales Reales* were quite successful. In the course of the war Francisco Cabarrús was authorized to found the first national bank of

Spain, the Banco de San Carlos (1782) with the purpose of redeeming the bonds. Peace in fact saved the day and the *Vales Reales* retained their value until the outbreak of the war with Revolutionary France when unprecedented financial disaster ensued.

During the last decade of Charles III's reign, his right-hand man was Floridablanca who, after 1776, became secretary of state (foreign affairs) and held the office of *gracia y justicia*. More committed to bureaucratic absolutism than Aranda, Floridablanca extended the use of the *intendente* but in other respects continued Aranda's work. A reform of the judicial structure aimed at greater uniformity of judicial procedure and was followed by a gradual ousting of torture and barbaric punishments as a feature of justice. One marked aspect was the decline of the Inquisition's strength. During the reign of Ferdinand VI there were 34 *auto-da-fé* to punish converted Jews who had relapsed, blasphemers, bigamists and sodomists, but such occasions became progressively rarer. A *cédula* of February 1770 defined the inquisitors' competence and confined it to heresy and apostasy. In fact, their demise was very much linked with that of the Jesuits with whom they had nothing else in common but their allegiance to a Roman faith. Inquisitorial denunciation of Aranda, Roda, Floridablanca and Campomanes for work done in the Council of Castille was not followed by proceedings against them. The inquisitors fulminated in vain over the projected single land tax but it was not their opposition so much as the logistics of abolishing the old taxes without an immediately assured income from the new which held back the central authority from implementation. Nor did the Inquisition succeed in stemming the flow of enlightened literature.

Spain, very cautiously, through the reign of Charles III was moving into the eighteenth century. The positive achievements may look scanty enough, yet there had been some breakdown of the tangle of provincial privileges and anomalies even if uniformity was still to be achieved. There was a little more contact, if not enough, between central government and the localities. Through the secretaries a greater cognizance of the country's problems was made possible. The power of the church could for the first time be said to be on the wane: the nobility by the cutting off of royal rewards and favours and the loss of power in the councils and the restriction of entail were pushed into greater commercial activity. Beccarian principles to a very slight degree had infiltrated Spanish primitive justice. Little of all this made much imprint on the way the bulk of the population lived nor were the reforms sufficient to realize the overriding preoccupation of the Bourbon monarchy, that is the preservation and exploitation of a large commercial empire. But they are sufficient to allow one to say that the French Revolution which converted Floridablanca and the new monarch Charles IV into arch conservatives, adamant partisans of censorship and strict social regulation, was indeed the proverbial fall of snow on blossoming trees.

Portugal, Spain's neighbour and traditional enemy in spite of repeated royal marriage alliances, stands out awkwardly in any generalizations made about Enlightenment influence upon eighteenth-century government, even though it had European linkages of geography, feudal traditions, seigneurial relationships, and social structure as well as an orthodox Catholic past. This is because although there was some attempt to introduce social and economic change through the action of the state, such actions scarcely reflected Enlightenment influence. Portuguese monarchs were indolent when it came to the work of government and prefered to abdicate powers of decision to autocratic ministers; firstly to Pombal (1750–77) and then to Pina Manique (1780–1803) whose concern was largely with the articulation of their own power. Pombal, though historically credited with a policy permeated by Enlightenment principles, was the scorn of intellectual Europe. Terrorism and senseless brutality, murder and torture were the hallmarks of his period of control.

Neither Portuguese society nor the apparatus of state were in any way receptive to change. More than any other country in Europe, Portugal, a land of under 3 million people and barren soil, was tied to its empire and trading stations which shored up government finance. Above all, the gold of Brazil, to which was added in 1728 the discovery of diamonds, gave the monarchy a significant independent income which since the early century had rendered unnecessary any calling of the Cortes to grant supplies. Such an income was patently inadequate to cope with the costs of the Spanish Succession War, but from the early eighteenth century Portugal had hitched her future to an alliance with Britain. This carried with it two major advantages and one serious disadvantage. The first advantage was that Portugal did not need to part with a major part of state income on defending her colonial interests against the Spanish, or in Asia, against the French. Secondly, the Methuen Treaty which formally opened up the Portuguese market to British textiles made available to the Portuguese a British customer for fortified wines. The taste for port, the produce of the Upper Douro Valley, amongst affluent sectors of British society provided Portugal with her most buoyant export trade. True the carriage of wine and olive oil – and later Brazilian gold, diamonds and the rich timbers, ebony and mahogany emanating from South America – was in British hands and British interests purchased a part of the vineyards of the Douro Valley setting up residences in that most harmonious of landscapes. Hence, it could be argued, as Pombal did, that native Portuguese did not themselves exploit their resources to the full. There was also something of a reduction in the amount of fortified wines produced by

the Portuguese in the course of the eighteenth century in favour of less
potent wines which sold well at home but less well abroad. Portuguese
society did not produce a population sufficient to man the trading
stations in Asia, notably Goa and Macau, or in Africa and there was
a perceptible growth in British involvement.

Portuguese economic historians often blame the British alliance, as
Pombal himself did, as constituting an impediment to Portugal's economic growth but one has to treat such an approach with circumspection. British textiles clothed the more affluent of the cities of the littoral
and those townships which dotted the river valleys of the Tagus, Douro,
Guadiana, Mondego and the Sado. Inland lay an impenetrable Portugal
characterized by a lack of roads and bridges which meant that such
commerce as existed took place by packmule and trading was largely
confined to wine, salt, honey, wax and dried fruit. The hamlets and
scattered farms provided their own basic clothing needs. Local industries (wool, silk, pottery, soap, iron, wood) especially in Trás-os-Montes, Beira Alta and Alentejo were insulated by poor communications
from outside competition and denied effective commercial contact with
the rest of Portugal.

In contrast with this virtually hermetically sealed world was Lisbon's
commercial nexus which was totally outward looking. Provisioned even
in grain from outside – particularly from the Azores and north Europe –
Lisbon's commercial activities were of truly international dimensions
and involved at least three-quarters of Portugal's foreign trade. Heavily
involved in the re-export of Brazilian commodities, sugar (not far short
of port exports), cotton (which jumped in the 1780s to approach sugar
in value), as well as timber and gold, Lisbon was a hive of commercial
activity.

Portuguese imports, however, considerably exceeded her exports and
re-exports in value.

Portuguese foreign trade in '000,000,000 *reis*

	Imports	Exports
1776, 1777 p.a.	6.55	4.90
1789	9.60	7.50 of which 3.25 domestic including 2.05 wine

Such a nagging realization was very disturbing to those aware of the
exhaustible resources of gold and diamonds which were rapidly falling
off from 1764.

Yet such vitality as Portugal had in the first half of the eighteenth
century focused entirely upon her commerce. Government at both the
central and the local level was inactive. Indeed, at the local level it was
virtually non-existent. John V (1706–50) was for the last twenty years

of his reign a sick man whose frail health may have contributed significantly to the rise of a clerical faction at court. During his reign had
emerged a number of secretaries of state – usually three in all – for state
(home affairs), war, and overseas and marine. Cardinal da Mota who
was both aged and inactive held the first office until he died in 1747 and
was replaced by his invalid nephew. A courtly but indecisive diplomat,
Diogo de Mendonça, held overseas and marine and foreign affairs were
in the hands of a friar, Gaspar de Encarnação. All were influenced by
another Portuguese cardinal, Nino da Cunha, whilst John V leant
progressively on a Neapolitan Jesuit, Padre Carbone who also died in
1750.

The strength of the clerical party in government perhaps only
reflected the strength of the church in society as a whole. Although
local studies progressively demonstrate the dearth of rural priests in the
remote Portuguese hinterland, the high percentage of free unions and
illegitimate births and the virtual absence in many parishes of catechetical instruction, the Portuguese were strong believers in their own
religious orthodoxy and racial purity. Moorish and Jewish penetration
had perhaps reinforced these elements in popular psychology. Certainly
the Inquisition, as an organ existing to guarantee religious orthodoxy,
was popular enough with the masses. Its periodical trials, burnings and
banishments of Marranos (Jews previously converted to Christianity,
forcibly or otherwise, and their descendants suspected of relapsing) and
Moriscos (converts from Islamic subjects of the Mozarabic Kingdoms
and their descendants) absorbed that instinct for hatred prevalent
amongst in-turning, under-educated, and economically deprived groups.
Saraiva has argued that in its search for Judaic practices the Inquisition
became itself a 'manufactory of Jews' and he cites individuals who
pointed out to the inquisitors that the Inquisition's techniques of
cross-examination under torture for confession to carefully described
Judaic ritual informed them for the first time of practices they had
previously never heard of. But the Inquisition got its business by public
denunciations and the crowds at an *auto-da-fé* were considerable until
the edict of 1774 which prohibited them in public and virtually suppressed the death sentence.

The Inquisition was as well a very solid part of the Portuguese
establishment. Theoretically the Portuguese nobility who were heavily
involved in trading and colonial activity, ought, given the subsequent
historiographical penchant for berating nobilities who scorned commerce, to have been one of the most open, modern and aware of the
intellectual and economic changes taking place in the eighteenth-
century world. In practice, something like the reverse was true. Rigidly
orthodox in religion, clinging to the concept of 'purity of blood' which
guaranteed entrée to significant offices and impervious to European
thought-processes, the Portuguese nobility was used by the Inquisition

as 'familiars', that is as filters for popular denunciations of the allegedly guilty, stationed in the localities. They took part in the ceremonial of the *auto-da-fé*. Those who had acquired colonial experience in office or had enriched themselves by colonial trade or by corruption appear to have returned to live in lordly state in provincial Portugal. As a small group whose inheritances were subject to royal confirmation so that all the dukes could claim kinship with the king and there were only nine marquises and thirty-three counts, they automatically expected offices, embassies and colonial governorships to come their way. This was, in short, a primitive society of conspicuously little movement, embodying every inequality and privilege, yet lacking a substantial body of indigenous critics.

Nevertheless, it was to be in Portugal that the attack on the Jesuits originated and where the ousting of a clerical party at court and the promotion of a policy of *regalismo* was most apparently complete. This was the achievement of the Marquis of Pombal who was appointed in 1750 to the ministry of foreign affairs and war, thus ousting the inert ecclesiastic Fr. Gasper de Encarnação. An element of mystery enshrouds the reasons for Pombal's promotion. His previous experience was that of diplomat in London and Vienna where he took a wife of ancient but impecunious lineage. Returning to Lisbon eight months before John's death, he found little room for manoeuvre in face of the omnipresent clerical party at court but he secured the support of Don Luis de Cunha, an influential noble critical of the existing stagnant government, and his Austrian wife came into close contact with the Austrian queen. This may have been crucial. When John died, his son José I (1750–77) had no apparent taste for government. His Spanish wife did not exert over him the influence of his mother Maria Ana, and the latter may well have urged upon José Pombal's promotion. Once in ministerial position, his quickness and ability to summarize business for the work-shy José perhaps assured his long-term influence over the king, and Pombal's ascendancy is co-existent with the life of that monarch. The sick da Mota and the elegant Diogo de Mendonça were no match for him but Pombal clearly felt that the clerical party still posed a menace. Moreover, from 1753 the queen mother, Pombal's protectress, became intensely attached to Gabriel Malagrida, an Italian Jesuit whose early reputation as prophet and holy man had been made in Brazil. It was probably a feeling of insecurity as well as the insatiable impulse for power which precipitated Pombal into an attack on the Society of Jesus. Pombal is known to have been a protagonist of *regalismo*. The Jesuits too may have aroused especial hostility by the intrigues which they sought to foster at the Portuguese court, in Spain and in South America over the Portuguese-Spanish negotiations on the issue of the exchange of Sacramento for part of Paraguay. Both Spain and Portugal favoured this exchange because Sacramento was of little value to the Portuguese, merely serving as a base whence British contraband could be discharged into Spanish South America whilst the portion of Paraguay in question was deemed of more intrinsic territorial worth. But Paraguay, although part of the Spanish Empire, was *de facto* governed by the Jesuits who erected a battery of fierce opposition to the measures. In some instances they marshalled the Indians into rebellion and exploited to the full their powers of intrigue at both the Spanish and Portuguese courts. In spite of this, they were unable to prevent the acceptance of the exchange which had been arranged by the two governments before Pombal took office. The Pombaline administration however was left with the implementation of the measure and Pombal was fully justified in assuming the Jesuits to be at the root of organized opposition. A handful were expelled from Paraguay and menacingly returned to Portugal.

Pombal perhaps exaggerated their efficiency in intrigue and was convinced they would concoct an alliance aimed at his downfall. A group critical of Pombal gathered around the king's brother, Dom Pedro, at Queluz and to this group the deported Jesuits made complaint. Dom Pedro was the favourite candidate for the hand of José's eldest daughter and hence a force to be reckoned with. Moreover the Queluz group included Mendonça who was obviously less than enthusiastic about his ministerial colleague. The Portuguese nobility had since Pombal's inception seen none of the plums of office going their way but directly into the hands of Pombal's family and those prepared to be his henchmen. Hence the Queluz critics included a number of ducal families. An alliance of powerful nobles and Jesuits, a conscience less than clear over manipulations of office and personally advantageous speculations in a number of commercial ventures, made Pombal sensitive as to the vulnerability of his position if he lost the king's favour. But he had to bide his time. The massive earthquake which shook Lisbon in 1755, followed by a tidal wave, together killed somewhere between 5000 and 15,000 people and gave rise to untold physical and psychological anguish. Pombal distinguished himself by his prompt and practical response to a national crisis with schemes for clearing rubble and rebuilding the city. These schemes were financed by an imposition, in face of mercantile hostility, of 4 per cent on all merchandise shipped through Lisbon. Nevertheless, the aftermath of catastrophe was marked by sermons and processions designed to associate disaster with the divine wrath incurred through national sin. The Jesuit Malagrida in particular published his *Judgment on the True Cause of the Earthquake* which so reeked of fire and brimstone that the papal nuncio acquiesced when the government urged his exile to Setúbal for spreading alarm amongst the people. The king, who was deeply devout, obliged Pombal to request in Rome that the Spanish Jesuit St Francis Borgia be made patron of Portugal and thereafter he was honoured on the anniversary of the earthquake.

Clearly the aftermath of earthquake was an unpropitious time to make an attack upon clerical strength or plotting nobles yet in less than two years Pombal had struck major blows at the Queluz group and at the Jesuits. The first was at Mendonça, implicated in a treasonable correspondence criticizing 'royal' policy, who was banished from court and replaced by Pombal's brother. Other critics who actually presented a petition of grievances to the king denouncing Pombal for his self-enriching speculation in mercantile companies included two Italian priests, Martinho Velho Oldenburg of a distinguished mercantile house, a group of noble suspects, and also by highly complex implication, the Duke of Lafões. The latter was sent by Pombal to Vienna and the rest were either imprisoned or sent to Angola. Thus the clique of Queluz was weakened and silenced. Then in May 1757, the administration of Paraguay was secularized and the Jesuit missions suppressed and the Indian population which they protected was freed. Pombal justified himself in his missives to Rome by denouncing Jesuit secular power and accusing them of enslaving the Indians for personal profit. The papacy raised no objections to the measures though Malagrida fumed from Setúbal and attracted to himself another grouping of noble critics, this time the Duke of Aveiro, the Marquis of Gouvea and members of the Marquis of Tavora's family. There is little to suggest these formed a group similar to the Queluz clique but Pombal could not leave them alone. In September 1758 an attempt was made on the life of the king, allegedly returning from a clandestine amorous meeting with the younger Marchioness of Tavora. A special court of enquiry was set up to find who was guilty and Pombal contrived to implicate the Duke of Aveiro, the Marquises of Tavora and Alorna, three counts, Malagrida and twelve leading Jesuits. Aveiro under torture implicated the Tavoras but they themselves revealed nothing. The commission of enquiry filled with Pombal's men urged the king to waive all clemency. The Tavoras and Aveiro were either beheaded or broken on the wheel along with their servants. The scaffold was then set alight. Then on 3 September 1759 José was persuaded, papal appeals for clemency set aside, to expel the Jesuit order from Portugal. As a particular manifestation of hatred, Pombal elected to have Malagrida condemned as a heretic by the Inquisition. The existing Inquisitor General refused to co-operate and was replaced by Pombal's younger brother. Malagrida was charged with regicide, blasphemy, and heresy and was publicly executed. All remaining Jesuits were confined.

Here was no gesture to the Enlightenment. The Jesuits were destroyed in Portugal because they appeared in some way as a threat to untrammelled Pombaline power and the vehicles of their destruction and that of the nobility were torture, public and humiliating execution and the Inquisition. Pombal's victory over any potential rivals was complete and it became no more than a question of filling all important posts with near relatives and placemen. One brother held the Ministry of Marine and Overseas, another the Inquisitor Generalship and was head of the corporation of Lisbon. A friar who retained Pombal's goodwill – Mansilha – presided over the *Junta do Comercio* and the royal board of censorship. In Pombaline Portugal enlightened criticism of despotic power was not allowed to infiltrate. Indeed, the works of Hobbes, Locke, Spinoza, Voltaire and Montesquieu were all prohibited books. The pretext of a proffered insult was used to expel the papal nuncio so that Portugal was still further cut off from outside influence. There was certainly no liberalism in Pombal's religious policy. Some nominal secularization of education followed upon the expulsion of the Jesuits in face of the clear vacuum left in the education of the nobility by their disappearance. The Inquisition was converted from a tool of the orthodox church to one of the state so that sentences had to be vetted by the government and, once Pombal's enemies were out of the way, that institution was stripped of the death penalty. True, persecution of Marranos was prohibited. The nobility were given clearly to understand that Pombal's favour was the only route to success. The abolition of the purity of blood qualification for office was quickly enacted.

Pombal was once credited with a coherent economic policy but it is difficult to discern a single scheme in the random measures adopted to cope with day to day exigencies. Without being anti-British, he believed, accurately enough, that Britain took too great a share of Portuguese trading profits and that the export of gold in particular must be curtailed. The job of the *Junta do Comercio* was to maximize Portuguese trading profits and a number of monopolistic trading companies, like the Upper Douro Company trading in port wine, were designed to supervise quality and to regulate the export trade. This particular company's activities indeed produced the most serious popular revolt Portugal knew in the course of the century, the so-called Boozers Revolt of Ash Wednesday 1757 in Oporto. Twenty thousand people who had gathered in the city for a public holiday, a religious festival, were encouraged in their rejection of the official monopoly of the Upper Douro Company by the clergy and the town's tavern keepers. The people were objecting to a measure which they saw as curtailing their right to market their goods according to traditional methods, and in particular refuted the right of the company to buy up at fixed prices whatsoever it wished. The tavern keepers supposedly saw their economic interests threatened by controls on the production of cheap wine. English mercantile interests may have put some money behind the drink which fuelled the rising. The clergy's part may be explained by sympathy towards the people or hostility towards any Pombaline measure. The official in the towns supposedly representing the government, the *juiz do povo*, was forced, allegedly from his sickbed, to lead the demonstration. No popular rising in the course of western European history in the eighteenth century was more severely punished. Troops were sent in, 17 people were hanged, a further 26 went to the galleys, 86 were banished and a further 56 were imprisoned. In addition the *juiz do povo* was severely punished and the office abolished in all small towns.

There is no evidence to suggest that Pombal's measures controlling the wine trade did any more than line the pockets of a number of individuals in the *Junta do Comercio*. The general trading slump of the 1760s had its repercussions in Portugal and it is impossible to know whether Pombaline protection measures mitigated, irritated or were irrelevant to Portugal's performance. An attempt to centralize the collection of customs revenues in 1766 at least ensured that more of what there was flowed into the central treasury. The attempts to foster protected industries of linen, glass, paper, porcelain and hat-making were to a large degree window dressing, though the protection of a cotton industry developing in Beira was in the long term more consequential. Portuguese society did not engender a sufficiently large affluent purchasing sector to lend constant support to a developing industry and nothing anyone did could reverse this.

Pombal lost office when José I died in 1777 and charges of peculation and tyranny – to which he was found guilty – were brought against him, though at seventy-eight he was left unpunished. The prison gates were opened and hundreds of victims of Pombaline terrorism found themselves at last free. The new queen Maria I, married to Dom Pedro, rehabilitated the Tavoras and individual Jesuits were permitted to return. The newly rebuilt Lisbon was a lasting memorial to Portugal's reign of tyranny and destined to be the continuing arena of political tyranny and repression. Pombal's successor, Pina Manique, was no less authoritarian though he looked to the lesser nobility for support. His period of office was largely remarkable for the creation of a Portuguese police apparatus to pursue literary liberals and enforce public order. At least three notable representatives of the Enlightenment were exiled Portuguese – Verney, Ribeiro Sanches and Oliveira – and their works may have reached noblemen and bureaucrats through the port of Lisbon. Yet there is no indication that such literary seeds fell on fertile ground, or that there was any widespread social response to central tyranny. Indeed, no society was to receive with a more deafening silence the message of the French Revolution.

10

The United Provinces

One overriding preoccupation has monopolized the historian's approach to the record of the United Provinces in the eighteenth century: what happened to the Dutch economic miracle of the previous century? Then the Dutch had monopolized the carrying trade of western Europe. In particular they had been masters of the key Baltic grain and timber trades. Dutch ports had been the entrepôts of the civilized world with vast distribution networks stretching into Germany and Amsterdam had been converted into the banking capital of Europe.

So striking does the contrast seem between a dynamic seventeenth century in which the Dutch fashioned new criteria for trading and business practice and the sluggish, allegedly decadent, performance of the eighteenth century that the record of overall decline has been indubitably exaggerated, obscuring several important nuances and neglecting the developing shift amongst Dutch merchants and business interests from active trading to financial speculation. Over the century as a whole one cannot point to any shrinkage in the actual volume of Dutch trade merely to a failure on the part of the Dutch to expand and lay hold of a preponderant proportion of world trade which was yearly increasing. Hence the decline in trading was merely relative. Was it that Dutch merchants did not seek or were they unable to capture new markets? Or was it that such new markets and new developments as did take place were merely substitutes for losses sustained in other sectors? The answer seems to be resoundingly the latter. Capturing the market for light textiles at Constantinople and Smyrna was no real or long-term substitute for the losses which occurred in the Atlantic carrying trade, but it argues firmly for some continuing dynamism in the Dutch mercantile sector. Inched out of the traditional carrying trade by the emergence of the British and French fleets which adopted, as far as in them lay, protectionist legislation over the carriage of colonial freight, stripped of traditional lucrative monopolies, like sugar refineries, by the rise of parallel establishments at Nantes and Bristol, forced to face active competition from new cloth trades – for example the English, Irish, Silesian and Elberfeld linen industries, the latter two competing for previous Dutch markets – the wonder is that the Dutch record was as good as it was.

Two factors above all others operated very strongly against continuing Dutch success in the eighteenth-century world. Firstly, the increasing reluctance of British and French merchants to purchase by sample from Dutch middlemen when they could, by using deliveries from their own merchants, be assured of the overall quality of a consignment – a consideration particularly applicable to linen deliveries whereby stores kept in warehouses awaiting a purchaser and a ship could readily become spotted with mildew. That is to say, it was possible in the conditions of the eighteenth century to ensure higher standards than it had been a century before, but the Dutch could in no way be guarantors of those standards. Secondly, and perhaps more significantly, Dutch trade in the seventeenth century had been remarkably integrated, vessels rarely travelling empty, which kept freight charges low. This applied particularly to the Baltic trade in timber and grain which for most countries was a heavy deficit trade since they took more out of the Baltic than into it and had to meet the difference in bullion. The Dutch however took in salt herring, salt from the pans of Setúbal in Portugal, together with wine, and, of course, in return dispensed Baltic timber and grain over the Mediterranean lands. The rise of competitive British, Irish and Danish fisheries and the loss of the Portuguese salt trade to the British profoundly disrupted this harmonious pattern. The British became rivals for timber. The Dutch share of the Baltic timber trade dropped from 65 per cent in the 1730s to 31.9 per cent in the 1780s. The industries which were generated by the timber trade, the sawmills of the Zaanstreek, the shipyards of Zaandam, the cordage and sail-making industries in turn experienced slump. Few European industries in our period underwent a more spectacular demise than the sawmills of the Zaanstreek between 1730 when their business reached its peak (256 mills) and the period 1740–65 when 47 went out of action. By 1795 only 144 remained at work. The decline of native supporting industries such as sail-making and the manufacture of naval supplies was also very extensive.

Yet performance varied very much from region to region and place to place. The first half of the eighteenth century in the United Provinces generally witnessed a decline of textile production in the old cities and a rise in lesser towns and in the countryside. This confirmed a general European trend. The linen production of the north was in fairly constant decline from 1725 in face of international competition and the woollen manufacture of Leiden seemed to fall in inverse proportion to the rise of the draperies of Brabant. (In 1671, Leiden produced 139,000 pieces of cloth; in 1725, 72,000, in 1775, 41,000 and in 1795, 29,000.)

These industries had all been geared to an international market. The Dutch population was small and demographically Dutch performance was fairly sluggish: a population of 1.85–1.95 million in 1700 had risen to 2.08 million by 1795–6. Some of the cities, Leiden, Delft, Haarlem, actually declined in population. Amsterdam and Rotterdam maintained a fairly even development and Schiedam, centre of the gin distilleries, the most burgeoning Dutch industry in the period, and The Hague, city of bureaucrats, alone sustained continued growth.

The agrarian population, setting aside enclaves in south Holland and the Nord Kwartier, clearly experienced limited growth in spite of devastating typhus and typhoid epidemics, the one predominantly the disease of the undernourished, and the other water borne. But if this demographic excess was pushed townwards it was not into the ancient Dutch cities. Brabant was a more promising pole of attraction. Dutch agriculture was highly specialized in cattle rearing both for dairy produce and meat and as such underwent some devastating setbacks in the eighteenth century. Cattle pestilence in 1744–5 and again in 1769 killed up to 75 per cent of the cattle in some provinces. Moreover, most of north Holland was under water during the winter, the lowest parts lying under water for as much as six months. There is some indication that from c. 1700 water levels were becoming higher and hence inundation more protracted, thus reducing the value of the land. More clearly there is evidence of the spread of *equesetum palustre*, a weed causing diarrhoea amongst livestock. There were areas in central Holland where the agricultural scene looked healthier and where landlords made significant experimentation with fodder crops. But the overall picture drives one irrefutably to the conclusion of declining standards of living for the working populace in both town and country, a conclusion reinforced by indications of static wage levels and rising prices and by the very evident pauperization of significant sectors (50–60 per cent in some areas) of the Dutch populace. It is always difficult to assess at a comparative level various national criteria for determining the point at which a family entered the ranks of paupers but it would seem that the United Provinces bade fair to rival parts of France in the numbers of beggars, vagrants and bandits it produced. Moreover, hungry town populaces were, as might be expected, highly volatile and subject to manipulation by political dissidents.

The Dutch merchant therefore operated from a home base which was truly depressed. He made his profits in spite of indigenous problems. His main concern was how to reinvest his profits. He shared this concern with traditional banking and financial interests into whose ranks many merchants were ultimately recruited and in any event the two were intricately connected in the business of borrowing and lending. Setting aside the distilleries, much Dutch industry repelled rather than attracted investment. Expansion into other branches of mercantile trade was limited by British and French advances. Interest rates at home were low. One area for investment however could absorb all the Dutch could proffer: loans to foreign governments. Though critics of foreigners holding the national purse strings abounded in England and grossly distorted the extent of Dutch involvement in the National Debt and one must take care not to present the Dutch as the major financiers of international conflict, a simple fact remains. Dutch mercantile activity engendered capital which sought to perpetuate and re-create itself in loans, whether small or large, and the British, the French, the Habsburgs, the Romanovs, the Spanish and the Americans were all eager borrowers when faced with imminent or actual conflict. This growth in lending was positive. (In purely economic terms offset against the relative decline in trade it makes it possible to talk of an overall increase in gross aggregate Dutch wealth.) It ensured in many instances that some Dutch businessmen had a healthy portfolio and that others suffered spectacular collapse. But it injected little into the Dutch economy as a whole and hence merely accentuated the division of Dutch society into the affluent few and the abundant poor – the two worlds. A moneyed banking and business grouping was of course an established feature of Dutch society and was traditionally recruited from the wealthiest elements in the mercantile community who progressively severed themselves from trade as invested capital engendered greater returns. Yet merchants and bankers did not necessarily have synonymous interests. A purely moneyed group of bankers and financiers profited from international conflict: trade and industry from the pursuit of peace. Home industries may well have been best served by the adoption of protectionist policies but the Republic clung doggedly to *laissez-faire* in order to preserve existing trading patterns and central revenues. It became progressively difficult to discern in whose interest the Republic was directed.

The removal of traditional enemies, hatred of Spain and fear of France which had proved some kind of cement for the seven provinces, left them more conscious of their differences than of any overriding common interests. The burden of taxation in the Republic was probably heavier than anywhere else in Europe and was largely indirect. The Estates General was torn with dissension as to whether the country should commit itself to strengthening its army and land defences (the recommendation of the southern provinces with straggling and, by definition, vulnerable frontiers) or to increasing naval strength to which the maritime provinces lent their support. In one sense England, as chief rival to the Republic's maritime and commercial strength, was a natural enemy and anglophobia ran deep in the maritime provinces. Yet Dutch moneyed interests were caught up in the London money market and traditionally the two Protestant powers had prevented French extension into the Netherlands. The House of Orange, the stadtholderate, had emotional ties with Britain. Nothing was clear cut. Whether or not, when the pros and cons have been weighed, gross aggregate Dutch wealth was declining or not in the eighteenth century is irrelevant to the sense of decline and the evident crisis of confidence experienced by thinking Dutchmen, and the consciousness of a lack of direction. Such a malaise owed nothing to the Enlightenment and everything to indigenous circumstances, circumstances which were to give rise to Europe's first revolutionary generation.

The political structure of the United Provinces was quite unique though inevitably it savoured, like all other eighteenth-century governments, of patronage and corruption. The strength of the United Provinces had traditionally been its towns and cities and, like those of Germany, northern Italy and Spain, these were virtually autonomous. The cities were dominated by patriciates, called regents. The regents had by the late seventeenth century virtually patrimonialized their offices so that, for example, by the beginning of our period some forty families dominated Amsterdam, drawing to themselves by marriage impressive financial alliances (and hence perpetuating even greater wealth) and dispensing offices by patronage. Naturally they were resented by lesser burghers. The latter in Holland, the wealthiest and most populous province, traditionally looked to the stadtholderate, an office which dated from the late middle ages and was now vested in the House of Orange. This individual's estates both in Holland and France dwarfed even the resources of the Amsterdam capitalists. The stadtholder was, in the first instance, a magistrate of five provinces and his post elective, insofar as the Estates of Holland exercised an option on his replacement at death. The towns sent delegates to provincial estates which in turn sent delegates to the Estates General in which the stadtholder had a very important role to play as head of the armed forces. A great deal of weight was also given in the Estates General to the grand pensionary – the nearest the country came to a minister of finance – who emanated from the province of Holland which paid the most taxes and hence might claim some right to call the tune over their deployment. Traditionally however politics polarized between regents and stadtholder, a tradition disrupted for the second time between 1702 and 1747 when, after William III's attempts to convert the stadtholderate into a kingship, no appointment was made. During this stadtholderless period the Estates General wore itself out with routine debate and clung rigidly to the policies of the past such as the English alliance, whilst in individual cities regents ignored or accepted at will the decisions of the central body, and the worst manifestations of venality were brought out into the open. Critics of policy during this period were able to point to the lack of a stadtholder as an immediate catch-all for Dutch problems and in particular to the desirability of such an official to crush for ever the power of the regents and in less specific terms to work for economic revival.

A diplomatic event, the French invasion of the Austrian Netherlands in 1747 in the course of the Austrian Succession War, and ensuing Dutch panic, precipitated the restoration of the office and its bestowal upon William IV of the Friesian line. His restoration was in fact the work of ultra-Orangists amongst whom the most prominent was Count William Bentinck but it also had broad popular support. The continuation of that support was conditional upon the association of the stadtholder with an attack upon the urban oligarchies and a revision of fiscal policy. The stadtholder was made aware of popular grievances in many ways. The meetings of 'Doelisten' (nicknamed after their meeting-place in Amsterdam) demanded an end to venality, or at least the sale of offices on the open market, a restoration of guild regulations (their demise being associated with economic decline) and an election of militia officers from the citizenry and not the use of partisans of the regents whose armed strength could thence subdue popular demands. Fierce rioting occurred in Amsterdam, Haarlem, Rotterdam and Leiden often against tax farmers and their officials. At Leiden popular leaders – though whether they were men drawn from the people is not clear – supported by unemployed textile workers, established a rival municipal government to that of the regents. Purge of the regencies became by 1748 an important part of the Doelisten platform and the movement mushroomed in the larger cities drawing in lesser burghers, amongst whom were some professional men, and tradesmen, actively petitioning the new stadtholder to combat oligarchical corruption.

The efforts of the Doelisten were misplaced. William IV was prepared to a limited degree to trim the power of the regents with a view to consolidating his own position and actually purged 17 out of 36 Amsterdam officers. But, they were replaced immediately by others of their kind, albeit ones who expressed allegiance to the House of Orange. Doelisten petitioners were imprisoned and demonstrations put down by troops at the command of the stadtholder. The reformers were truly crushed. Some change emanated from the city demonstrations of 1748 insofar as tax farming was abolished. But the Estates General clung to the idea of an excise in preference to a poll tax and probably for good reason. A poll tax would have demanded a fundamental reassessment of every individual's resources, a very lengthy process urged by reformers throughout Europe but shunned by governments who needed immediate funds. The stadtholderate itself – the entire House of Orange – was bound up in patronage and venality, links which it regarded as essential to its existence. Indeed, like William III before him, William IV was quick to stuff every municipal and provincial office in the provinces with 'his men' as guarantors of his authority. In this way, and the trend was not reversed after his death in

1751, he became an apparent part of a decadent corrupt establishment which in no time at all was associated with regent oligarchy. His successor was a minor initially directed by his mother and then by Louis of Brunswick, a foreign adventurer to whom by a secret act of advisorship William V signed away much of his power. The stadtholderate seemed to slide even further away from firm decision-making and made the process of alienation indeed complete. Some critics amongst the literate burghers condemned the entire system. Elements amongst the patriciates took the opportunity to present themselves as the true defenders of the Dutch republican tradition.

The Seven Years' War in which the Dutch maintained an astute neutrality formed a kind of watershed. During the war the Dutch, in spite of pressure from both France and England, were able to stand on the sidelines. Thereafter such a stance became impossible. The economic effects of the war are difficult to gauge. Bankers and financiers obviously profited from every aspirant borrower and Dutch trading in view of the disruptions in mercantile activity forced upon the belligerent states may have been improved. This did not prevent a marked slump in the aftermath of war when accumulated stocks of British and French goods flooded European markets and Amsterdam's warehouses were overflowing with goods it was almost impossible to dispose of. The sixties were also to see some dislocation in the Amsterdam money market attributable to the unhealthy state of government finances throughout Europe. Rulers struggled one after another to lift their finances by tax reform or spending cuts and European financial houses were disturbed by some unanticipated bankruptcies in financial quarters. Even the British looked unhealthy debtors. Politics focused on the apparently unresolvable question of Dutch defences: should money be put into the Dutch marine to protect Dutch commerce or into the army to safeguard her frontiers? These were not perhaps important questions when neutrality was the order of the day but during the seventies the course of international politics was flowing in a direction which could not but interest the Dutch and her involvement without adequate defences would not be sound. The American War of Independence opened up the prospect of destroying British dominance in the Atlantic and hence perhaps of a potential Dutch breakthrough. It thus appealed to the anglophobic Dutch mercantile interest and it excited every anti-Orangist for that house was associated with the traditional English alliance. It also brought into involvement in the American interest Dutch financial interests. John Adams's mission to the Netherlands was aimed expressly at finding financial support for the war and between 1782–8 some nine million *guilders* were raised by a consortium of financial houses. Dutch moneyed interests were perhaps drawn by the prospect of making a quick return on a stock they could readily dispose of to a gullible public excited by the prospect of British defeat.

Perhaps they simply did not know what to do with their money. But for an element in the Dutch populace, subsequently to be known as the Patriots, there was a political aspect to financial involvement. The Patriots saw in the American War and the Fourth Anglo-Dutch War (1780–84) a chance to introduce radical political and constitutional change into the United Provinces.

Conflict with England of course meant the abandonment of the neutrality which Dutch merchant interests were prone to regard as essential to their trade but Anglo-American conflict had in effect inhibited Dutch trade with the American continent by blockade and hence their traditional reluctance was removed. Theoretically the British regarded trading in weapons and 'warlike stores' as prohibited. Dutch merchants however were by 1775 carrying out an active arms trade with the colonies and stockpiling weaponry on the West Indian island of St Eustatius. When war broke out in 1776 the merchants demanded that the Estates General sanction the equipment of convoy vessels to allow them to run the blockade with armaments. The Estates General tried to stall on an issue which must push the Republic into conflict with Britain but events were outstripping such conservatism. Amsterdam merchants and the Americans were said to be discussing a possible trade treaty and the governor of St Eustatius was reputed to be recognizing the American flag and to be permitting American ships to take refuge in the harbours of St Eustatius. The French too were anxious that the Dutch be brought into open conflict and it became clear that an abandonment of the traditional British alliance would make possible a new rapprochement between the Republic and her former enemy. The formation, under the aegis of Catherine the Great, of the Armed Neutrality of the North, designed specifically to assert the independence of neutrals to trade at will with a belligerent power without any interference from that belligerent's enemy, was signed by the Dutch. Ten days later (December 1780) the more positive step of an actual declaration of war on the British was taken. It was an immensely popular step with the mercantile and banking sectors and with the Patriots, and a major blow to the stadtholder who incarnated the hereditary English alliance and who, as head of the armed forces, was placed in a situation he had desired to avert.

In spite of the popularity of the war, however, Dutch defeat was to be resounding. The Dutch colonies captured by the British were only restored at the peace through French help. The losses inflicted on shipping were substantial and the insurance houses were projected into successive bankruptcies. The commitment of the non-maritime provinces to the war was far less than that of Holland and as disaster loomed, the integrity of the United Provinces seemed far from assured.

Defeat by the British whilst their American friends emerged victorious merely fanned the flames of Dutch political criticism. 'America had held up a mirror to their own Republic in which they had glimpsed an idealized image of heroic patriotism.'[1] Public meetings, the growth of an acrimonious press, petition campaigns, agitation for a citizens' militia, marked the swelling tide of the Patriot movement. Who were these agitators? In an active sense they were a minority of the Dutch population though many more gave passive support. Some were aristocratic and wealthy like the Baron Joan Derk van der Capellen tot den Pol. Others were substantial and many more lesser burghers, merchants, bureaucrats, lawyers, professional men, guild members, and above all in numerical terms, artisans and craftsmen. Some pastors were involved and the pulpit as well as guild meetings were effective means for cementing attitudes and reaffirming zeal and for maintaining contacts in isolated small towns – for the countryside was in no way politically committed.

The pattern of political ferment was by no means analogous in each province and the traditional breakdown of differing attitudes between land and maritime provinces or between Holland and the rest does not in this instance apply. Holland was split into Patriot cities, including Amsterdam, and Orangist cities, notably Delft and Rotterdam, that is to say into cities in which the regents were prepared to go along with the Patriots and those outrightly rejecting them. Zeeland towns were on balance Orangist. Overijssel, Utrecht and Gelderland had some very active Patriot towns but the last two had provincial estates which remained loyal to the stadtholderate. In the land provinces the town (Patriot)/country (Orangist) split was at its most clear cut. These provinces were lacking in the powerful regent class found in the large cities of the maritime provinces, the burghers of the land provinces stood instead against a petty rural nobility entrenched in the provincial estates which equated its existence and its political dominance with the maintenance of Orangist power. In the maritime provinces, cities were split by regent factions who owed their existence to Orangist promotion and those who assumed the Patriots could be manipulated to serve regent anti-Orangism.

If, when counted against the overall Dutch population, the Patriots were a minority, when counted as a part of the politically aware population, they were much more significant. Moreover, they had a press with two widely-read journals and a programme demolitionist enough to gain broad urban support. This programme stood for the removal of the stadtholderate and most specifically of William von Brunswick from political power: abolition of corrupt oligarchic municipal control and of provincial estates weighted in the rural noble interest. A free press and a citizen militia completed the positive aspects

1 S. Schama, *Patriots and Liberators: Revolution in the Netherlands 1780–1813* (London, 1977).

of the Patriot package. There was a less clearly defined aspect. Though by European standards the Dutch Republic already seemed markedly decentralized, the Patriots were associated with a still greater recognition of provincial and local autonomy. One cannot perhaps endow their programme in this respect with too great precision since the thinking of the Patriots of Utrecht may well have differed from those of Gelderland. Nor did the Patriots dream of democracy but less specifically of an extension of political rights to those literate, articulate and at least of modest means, to men, in short, capable in their estimation of grasping political realities. In practical terms the Patriots achieved their step on the road to significance by their setting up of Free Corps or citizens' militias. These had had some historic existence in the defence of the Republic but now became the main arm of the Patriot movement and demonstrated to the stadtholder the strength of political dissidence. Confident of the discomfiture of William V in the midst of Dutch defeat at sea and the growth of the Patriot movement at home, the regents of Holland in 1782 launched an attack firstly on Brunswick who was forced to leave The Hague and secondly upon the stadtholder and his family who were also exiled from the centre of government.

Only then did the Patriot movement become more specific in its constitutional reasoning producing in June 1785 a draft constitution bearing a marked resemblance to the American Declaration of Independence. By then, however, the marked dichotomy of interests between regents and Patriots and between aristocratic estates and Patriots was becoming all too patent. Moreover, the coming of peace in 1784 did not mark a return to profitable quietude in the foreign sector. Joseph II had pre-empted a Scheldt crisis by sending an Austrian vessel into the waterways closed by the Treaty of Munster (1648) and, shaken by anything foreshadowing the opening of Antwerp, the Dutch looked to a French ally. But France was in no position to make threatening gestures, although a defensive alliance was engineered by the Free Corps Congress. Britain however was also closely involved and much readier to countenance a revival of a Dutch alliance, albeit through the Orangist medium, and the British ambassador Harris was in possession of funds to promote the Orangist cause. The revival of the Scheldt issue contrived to muddy still further the water of Dutch political life. The Patriot strongholds run by burgher councils tried to accelerate the pace of conversion of the countryside, and indeed had some success among the Catholic peasantry though this in many instances only served to push the rest further into a hard Orangist line. The Patriots were on the whole content to wait until the Estates General should, by persuasion, be filled with delegates of Patriot commitment but such an event was slow in materializing. In some provinces (Utrecht, Friesland) a tripartite political division of Patriots, nobles of the provincial estates and Orangists emerged with the last two moving into alliance. The Republic seemed to have reached political stalemate when the Princess of Orange in June 1787, smarting under exile, set off for The Hague. Roughly handled by a Free Corps detachment, she retired to Nijmegen. Her brother, the King of Prussia, invaded the Republic. The Patriots panicked and many fled to France and the Orangists were re-established at The Hague.

This was obviously a signal defeat but it equally clearly did not herald the end of the Patriots. The Orangists were not secure in their return and a Patriot press and meetings continued to exist. The trend of political events in France aroused great excitement and the Patriots drew strength from the analogies in the political development of the two countries, whilst stressing the original qualities of the Dutch situation and their particular identity. Progressively, they saw the political salvation of their country in a close allaince between themselves and French Revolutionary politicians. They had yet to experience the chastening effects of a French occupation in the name of political liberty.

France of the Old Regime

Amongst European countries, France enjoyed a certain pre-eminence, though one perhaps less than a French-based historiographical tradition has assumed. This pre-eminence reflected that country's demographic weight – there were more Frenchmen than any other grouping – its intellectual ascendancy over the west, its political traditions based upon the Versailles model which many other European monarchs strove to emulate and which presented to the world the image of a formidable despotism. France had easily the highest GDP in Europe and was one of the most economically developed countries even if it had regionally intense problems of poverty. Furthermore, French political life had an intrinsic frailty few could perceive in 1730 but which was all too apparent by 1789. The social and institutional framework of the old regime was a mixture of ancient, medieval and modern. In particular, there were two factors at work in the government of eighteenth-century France, each contriving to pull the country a different way. The first was a centralizing force composed of king and an impressive range of councils and ministers concentrated in Versailles and in close contact with the intendants in the localities. The second was the older decentralizing force of provincial estates, *parlements, bailliages* and *sénéchaussées* which asserted older rights and sought to restrain monarchical encroachments upon local powers and privileges. *L'ancien régime*, wrote Marcel Marion, *ne détruisait rien, il préférait laisser végéter*. This sentence summarizes the spirit of *ancien régime* administration. It reposed upon a bed-rock of medieval law courts and gatherings and of venal officials, undisturbed and indeed undisturbable in their tenure. On top of these had been placed in the seventeenth century royal councils and intendants who did most of the actual work of government. Some of the medieval survivals were indeed so effete as to be ineffectual (e.g. the tax courts or *élections*) but others (*parlements* and some provincial estates) were living and vital. Moreover, on occasion, the apparently moribund could find sufficient spirit to rise in defence of its interests. *Ancien régime* administration was haunted by ghosts of whom few were content to remain eternally quiet. By 1730, it must have seemed that the deadest of all was the Estates General.

At the head of the administrative and judicial structure was the king, supreme law-maker. Nominally he made decisions after consultation with the councils, though he need not be swayed by them. Six in number by 1740, these councils were: the *conseil d'état (d'en haut, secret)* presided over by the king and filled with ministers chosen by him to deal with the great affairs of state, particularly foreign affairs: the *conseil des dépêches*, concerned with the day-to-day running of the country: the *conseil des finances* which dealt with taxation and whose business was sometimes allied with the *conseil de commerce*: a *conseil de conscience* which dealt mainly with presentation to benefices, and a *conseil privé* or *des partis* which dealt largely with conflicts of jurisdiction. Filled with ministers nominated by the king, with the *secrétaires d'état, chancelier* and *contrôleur général* and with eighty or more *maîtres des requêtes* to the *conseil privé*, the councils were, in Alfred Cobban's phrase, a mere façade, for the real work of government was done by a handful of officials alone. Of these, the *contrôleur général* probably wielded the greatest influence because most problems were in essence financial and he was responsible for royal finances, agriculture, industry, bridges and highways. Next were the four *secrétaires d'état* (for foreign affairs, war, navy, and the royal household). These were capable of independent initiative and took decisions with which the monarch was usually happy to comply. Most prestigious was the office of *chancelier* who was held to be the embodiment of justice. All ministers and *secrétaires* were royal appointees as were the intendants, the executive agents of royal will in the localities. All thirty-four of these had responsibility at the local level over their *généralité* for the same business as the *contrôleur général* had at the national level. They were not policy makers but they could determine how much of royal policy was felt in the localities and, using material supplied by their largely unpaid agents, the *subdélégués*, they were important agents of information for the central government and could often, albeit indirectly, force its hand.

The royal will was generally expressed by means of edicts. Before an edict could pass into law it needed ratification by the separate provincial *parlements* which considered the compatibility of the edict with existing law since the function of each *parlement* was to stand as the guardian of a particular provincial law. Each *parlement* had a right of remonstrance or protest against any edict which could halt its passage into law. But this remonstrance could be overridden by a summons from the monarchy to a *lit de justice* wherein the king personally ordered the *parlements* to register his edict. Since in the royal presence no contradiction was possible the *parlements* could be forced to concur or accept exile. Obviously such trials of strength were to be avoided if the country was to be administered smoothly. Equally obviously the *parlements* represented a barrier to the untrammelled extension of monarchical power. By 1740 Montesquieu was probably already at work upon *De l'Esprit des Lois* which emphasized the special obligation of the *parlements* to act as a check upon despotism and as guardians of the law. Already in espousing the Jansenist cause and in opposing monarchy over the registration of the *Unigenitus* (see pp. 217–19) a foretaste of the bitter struggle between *parlement* and monarchy which characterizes French history in this period had been given. Suffice it to say at this juncture that this aristocratic *elite* (for the *parlementaires* were noble and allegedly closing ranks) disposed of an unsatisfactory form of negative power. It could frustrate and even stop the ministers of the crown doing what they wanted to do and in so doing could effectively topple ministers, but it could not determine the policies of the crown.

It is customary to represent the *parlements* as an important decentralizing force in French history and doubtless they were so despite their contrary allegation that it was their existence guaranteeing everyone's historical rights which made a unified state possible at all. No such case was put forward by the provincial estates. Confined by the eighteenth century to the provinces of Languedoc, Brittany, Burgundy, Walloon Flanders, Provence and enclaves of the Pyrenees, and having strength only in the first three instances, the provincial estates had a single simple purpose, to protect provincial privilege. Most meaningfully this meant consultation as to the amount of tax payable by the province and supervision of the tax levy by provincial methods. In the provinces with such estates (*pays d'états*), the influence of the intendant was weak (because he was essentially a finance official) and indeed was confined to a single individual per province. How could one man effectively administer a province the size of Brittany or Languedoc?

The answer is, not at all, and that moreover, his hands were bound more and more in the last fifty years of the *ancien régime* by an increasing assertiveness on the part of the estates which was particularly marked in Brittany. There existed the general conviction that the brunt of taxation was borne by the *pays d'élections* (areas without provincial estates) since the negotiating power of the estates ensured more favoured treatment. This was doubtless true as was the evident immunity of some of the *pays d'états* (Brittany, Flanders) from the brunt of the salt tax (*gabelle*).

The concept of the province ran deep through much of France. Breton, Flamand, France Comtois, Lorrain, Alsacien, Auvergnat, etc. had a highly developed concept of provincial identity and where provincial boundaries were historically fluid, as in the case of much of Languedoc, this was replaced by a kind of regionalism – the Gévaudois or the man from the Pays de Velay thought in terms of his immediate locale rather than the provincial entity. Such sentiments were in part merely emotional but they reflected a mistrust of the man from outside, a suspicion of anything national and central. On the eve of the Revolution, the government sought to win support for itself by wooing this sentiment and deflecting the fiscal powers of the intendant in the *pays d'élections* to provincial assemblies, modelled upon the estates of Languedoc. Such a move did not save *ancien régime* government but it reflects the intrusiveness of provincial decentralization upon a nominally centralized state.

One cannot treat constitutional and financial issues in isolation because in *ancien régime* France these were intrinsically interrelated matters.

Eighteenth-century financial and constitutional history is permeated by a dual persuasion which has been the terms of reference of much text-book writing. The first is that French financial difficulties were uniquely the result of the exemptions of the privileged, nobility and clergy, from the system of taxation, an immunity preserved by the policy of the *parlements*. This was the line urged upon the Assembly of Notables by Calonne in 1787 and if he did not convince them of its rationality, he appears to have convinced succeeding generations. The implication of such a persuasion emerges from the first and is that the French financial system was sound but for selfish fiscal immunities. The second persuasion concentrates upon the relationship, an endlessly bellicose one, between king and ministers with the *parlements*. This is presented as a battle between government reformers interested in fairness and efficiency and the privileged with vested self-interests[1] and hence, by extension, between good and bad. Such a view is perhaps written with an eye to the Revolution. For those in the nineteenth century who condemned the Revolution and its excesses, it was possible to discern amongst the king's ministers a programme of reform, stifled by the opposition of the *parlements*, which if carried out might have made the Revolution unnecessary. Even to Alfred Cobban, the Revolution came as 'a fall of snow on blossoming trees' and 'the *ancien régime* would have stood a better chance of survival if there had been room in it for a minister like Turgot'.[2] Turgot, and this would have come as a surprise to his contemporaries, has been singled out for the particular approval of posterity perhaps for two reasons. If one posits ministerial virtue against *parlementaire* malevolence then his fall after the defeat of his Six Edicts can be presented as ultimate proof of *parlementaire* moral turpitude. Secondly, as protagonist of a physiocratic policy of

1 'the obscurantist defenders of vested interests'. Cobban, *In Search of Humanity*, p. 164.
2 *A History of Modern France*, p. 104.

laissez-faire, he was suspected and derided by the *parlements*, but was more than acceptable to nineteenth-century free-traders. Hence historiographic attitudes towards Turgot, sacrificial lamb of *parlement's* blood lust, might be said to symbolize the persuasion that all virtue lay in the king's side and all myopic self-interest upon that of the *parlements*.

Modern research has understandably challenged such simplistic assumptions and has insisted that monarchical despotism, ministerial mishandling and anti-constitutional behaviour, inconsistency of direction and frankly contradictory attitudes towards financial reform should be borne in mind before apportioning praise and blame. In particular, one should approach the constitutional issues with an eye as much to monarchical aggression as to *parlementaire* hostility and alleged interest in undermining monarchical authority. One should also consider other fundamental weaknesses of the fiscal structure besides privileged immunities, not least the actual mechanisms whereby tax was imposed and collected which rested in the hands of vend official down

'Arbitrary government, where the only law is the Prince's will, does not exist in well-ordered states; it has no place amongst us; it is manifestly opposed to legitimate government' (Bossuet). These words were written not by an eighteenth-century *philosophe* intent upon broadening the basis of government, but by a seventeenth-century theologian, confessor to Louis XIV, a monarch who defined his authority by reference to the divine right of kings. In such a view of *ancien régime* monarchy royal power was conceived as an authority which fell short of despotism because tempered by the restraining influence of the law. The main guardians of that law were the *parlements*, protectors perhaps of individual and corporate privileges but only insofar as these privileges were a fundamental part of French law and custom. Any infringement of law and custom on the part of the monarchy was tantamount to a shift in monarchical power in the direction of undesirable despotic or arbitrary government.

In the 1640s the *parlements* had naturally resisted Mazarin's attempts to raise money by anti-constitutional means, that is, by using financiers who advanced money to the monarchy against the proceeds of extraordinary, unsanctioned levies upon the general populace. But the Parlement of Paris at least had taken the fatal step of carrying its opposition to the point of violent civil war. It paid for that decision with the revulsion of a war-weary populace which in effect permitted monarchy in the second half of the seventeenth century to strip the *parlements* of the right of remonstrance against royal edicts and hence released Louis XIV from ever having to have recourse to a *lit de justice*.

Yet, that said, Louis XIV did not seek to push his control further. He abandoned recourse to irregular taxation. When his minister sought tentatively to impose a duty upon a privileged province, Brittany, he incurred open revolt and largely backed down. He did not destroy the *parlements* or indeed ever contemplate so doing for he believed in what Bossuet defined as legitimate government and legitimate government in France perforce entailed recognition of the law and its guardians.

The penchant for strong monarchy born of the disorders of the Frondes did not survive the seventeenth century. Military demands, financial disorders which were the product of heavy war expenditure, and economic distress due to crop failure and plague turned the tide of popular sentiment. The death of Louis XIV was the occasion of the regent's restoration of full powers to the *parlements* in order to secure the nullification of Louis XIV's testament limiting the regent's powers.

The restored *parlement* was very far from being obstreperous. If it had learned any lesson from the previous fifty years it was that its survival was linked with the maintenance of public order and a rigid definition of its traditional role. It was that role which the regent, Orleans, and later Louis XV's first minister, Fleury, tried most blatantly either to ignore or deny. For the first, the restoration of the right of remonstrance was the purchase price for liberation from the intrusions of a regency council by *parlement*'s abrogation of the king's will. That achieved, on two vital issues, the registration of the Bull *Unigenitus* and financial matters, both the regent and Fleury occasionally showed total contempt for *parlementaire* authority except in time of crisis. In so doing they provoked a sour, defensive attitude in which compromise on either side became increasingly impossible.

In the case of the Bull *Unigenitus*, Fleury in 1730–31 carried the conflict far beyond religious issues on to the uncomfortable constitutional ground of whether the king should act within the law or independently of it. The issue might appear to posterity as theoretical enough. *Parlement*'s objection to the Bull *Unigenitus*, promulgated in 1715, which condemned the work of the Jansenist Quesnel, was that it contravened the so-called Gallican Liberties of the French Church – not least the tendentious article 91 which asserted that a judgement in spiritual matters of the universal church was incapable of modification. Between 1715 and 1730 the issue appeared almost to have worn itself out, having rent both the ecclesiastical hierarchy and the secular power. But Fleury's revival of the issue in 1730 by a declaration demanding that 'the Bull *Unigenitus*...being a law of the church...should be regarded too as a law of our kingdom...' again brought the matter to the fore. A *lit de justice* in April 1730, demanding submission, measures forbidding the magistrates to discuss legislation enforcing unqualified submission to the Bull and an attempt to force recognition through the *Grand' Chambre*, the most docile of all the chambers of the Parlement of Paris, all failed to win over the *parlements*. Most extreme of all was a decree of the royal council of March 1731 which guaranteed the church's right to enforce its spiritual censures without reference to any secular power. Such a move clearly aroused all those questions of the relative authority of temporal and spiritual powers whose roots lie deep in medieval Christendom. A decree of *parlement* in September 1731 stressed the total independence of the secular power which alone had powers of coercion: the subordination of clerics to temporal law: the impotence of ecclesiastical authority to fix the boundaries between it and the secular power. As a rejoinder, Fluery curtailed the magistrates' right to freedom of speech on the question of the authority of the two powers, though he assured them that this was only for a provisional period.

Cold comfort indeed, but worse was to come. Public opinion for undefinable reasons rallied to the Jansenist cause and around the tomb of an ascetic young deacon named Pâris, a bitter opponent of the Bull *Unigenitus*, miracles were reputed to occur and crowds flocked to pay tribute. As a result, in January 1732, the government ordered the closure of the church-yard of Saint-Médard and, though the *parlementaires* were not hostile to the closure, for good measure forbade *parlement* to debate any matter at all relating to the Bull.

Such an arbitrary curtailment of *parlement*'s privilege provoked an immediate response. The magistrates declared themselves ready for a judicial strike. Fleury arrested and exiled the main opponents whereupon the bulk of the magistrates of the Parlement of Paris resigned *en bloc*. Matters could not remain there. The right to free remonstrance on any issue was restored but a royal declaration insisted that the *Grand' Chambre* alone should decide whether or not a piece of legislation was compatible with the fundamental laws of the kingdom and forbade legal strikes. *Parlementaire* hostility was countered by a *lit de justice* forcing registration of this declaration and when the magistrates remained obdurate, 139 of them were exiled. The result was judicial chaos in which the monarchy was the loser, ultimately purchasing compromise by suspending the very declaration forced through by a *lit de justice*. But this represented the only victory to the *parlements* for, as long as Fleury held office (until 1736), he forbade the courts to interfere in any matter relative to the recognition of the Bull *Unigenitus*.

The struggle over the *Unigenitus* has significance both in the history of the French monarchy and in the history of the *parlements*. Louis XV backed Cardinal Fleury in his demands perhaps because, as Cobban suggests, he was under the influence of the *dévot* party at court, or perhaps because he had committed himself to one man, a first minister, believing, like many French monarchs before him, that this placed him more directly in control of politics. It was a misalliance and one which gave rise to innumerable problems. For Fleury stripped the French monarchy of the firm support of the Gallican tradition, thus reducing the authority of the crown in spiritual matters. Even more importantly, he attacked the entire basis of what Frenchmen regarded as legitimate sovereignty, a sovereignty based on the rule of law and which, as Bossuet reminds us, fell short of arbitrary government. Enlightenment philosophy was swiftly eroding the concept of a monarchy based upon the divine right of kings and substituting for it, admittedly more gradually, an ideal of monarchy tempered only by law. The registration of the Bull *Unigenitus* was 'carried through in a thoroughly arbitrary manner with little respect for the normal processes of law. It demonstrated not the power but the impotence of the law in the face of royal authoritarianism.'[3]

At the same time, the 1730s were an important point of departure for the *parlementaires*. On the whole, throughout the struggle over the Bull *Unigenitus*, their behaviour was responsible, restrained and they were insistent that they intended no slight to monarchical authority – indeed the Gallican tradition which was their concern was an aspect of that authority – and that their main concern was the sovereignty of the law. Both the regent and Fleury had treated the Parlement of Paris with nothing short of contempt, using arbitrary and illegal action at will. From the 1730s the *parlements* emerged cynical, disillusioned and defensive. *Unigenitus* was the first nail in the coffins both of the French king and the sovereign courts.

In comparison with the turmoil engendered by the Bull *Unigenitus*, financial issues during Fleury's tenure of office caused relatively little trouble, though even here the minister chose to force registration of problem measures directly by a *lit de justice* without reference to the courts. It is worth considering attitudes towards taxation before one contemplates the frailty of the French fiscal system because some understanding of these is crucial to an understanding of the difficult relationship between king and *parlement*.

The first conviction was that the king should live off his own in peacetime and by 'his own' was understood the product of the royal domain, the traditional direct tax, the *taille*, and customary indirect taxes. In time of war extraordinary direct taxation might be levied with the consent of *parlement*. Already inroads had been made into the principle of noble exemption from direct taxation by the *capitation* of 1695 but a principle not violated until the regency was the introduction of new direct taxes without the justification of war. Alongside this first conviction lay an ingrained suspicion of any deviation from traditional methods of financing the French state, and of finance ministers, particularly foreigners, suspected of lining their own pockets by devious means. The use and abuses of the *traitants* by Richelieu and Mazarin which was at the basis of the Frondes was not ancient history. The opposition of the *parlements* to John Law's schemes during the regency should be seen in a context of mistrust for a foreigner of dubious repute

3 J. Shennan, *The Parlement of Paris* (1968), p. 307.

with an untried, flamboyant policy questioned not only by the *parlements*, but by other ministers – including the chancellor and Parisian commercial interests. The *parlementaires* were conservative by very definition. They were not men of vision and they can readily be understood for their disquiet over the feasibility of Law's schemes, the more particularly when the regent had defaulted in respect of interest payment (*rentes*) on loans to the state and had shaken the government's creditors. Thereafter and throughout Fleury's tenure of office, opposition focused either upon the government's efforts to levy new direct taxes in peacetime (1725, the *cinquantième*) or in 1733 and 1741, upon the monarchy's refusal to set a time limit on the imposition of a *dixième* tax levied on all sectors of the populace and initially only granted to cover the expenditures of the Polish Succession War. In short, there was no question at this juncture of a totally intransigent attitude towards a universal tax. Indeed, one might argue, as Shennan does, that the principle of taxation of privileged as well as unprivileged was implicitly and explicitly ceded by the magistrature between 1695 and 1741. What was not ceded was any recognition of the need to restructure the entire tax system (Calonne's radical proposal of 1787) or the principle that existing taxation was perfectly adequate to cover peacetime needs. The existing structure was the one which had behind it the force of law as well as suiting those with privileged immunities.

Certainly that last assertion was incontestable. But how realistic was the attitude relative to the adequacy of existing taxes to cover reasonable day-to-day peacetime expenditure? Put another way, how sound were government finances?

The fiscal framework of *ancien régime* France reflected something of the conflict between national direction and provincial and individual privilege. The most onerous of royal taxes was the *taille* levied in the north upon all landholders who were neither noble nor ecclesiastic and in the south upon those who held non-exempted land (for here *taille* was *réelle* i.e. the land not the individual bore the status). Riddled with immunities purchased by towns and privileged individuals, contested with the provincial estates, administered by intendant and *élection* courts and collected by a member of the peasant community, this tax alone had never been adequate to cover government expenditure. Since the sixteenth century the monarchy had tried to interpose its own direct agents or to levy new indirect taxes. The result had been provincial rebellion, the tax revolts which peppered the mid-seventeenth century, and from which a wiser monarchy had withdrawn, reconciled to the idea of leaving the mechanism for the collection of *taille* in the localities, where much of it stuck, and to looking elsewhere for ready money. A further essay in direct taxation, the *capitation* or poll tax, introduced in 1695 but since made permanent and which extended to the nobility, had become in many instances a mere addition to the *taille* though its allocation was more directly in the hands of the intendant.

Direct taxation was insufficient to meet the costs of running the country. For day-to-day expenditure, the monarchy leant on the profits of indirect taxes. These were legion: the *gabelle* (salt tax), *aides* (taxes on food and drink), monopolies, particularly on tobacco, taxes on leather, internal and external customs and the *affaires extraordinaires* which largely came down to the sale of offices and patents of nobility. Colbert had bequeathed an important legacy to eighteenth-century French monarchs in the shape of the *Ferme Générale*, a syndicate of financiers who leased the right to levy indirect taxes (setting aside the *affaires extraordinaires* and certain customs dues) against a lump sum, payable in advance and usually held for a nine-year term before renegotiation. The financiers were themselves borrowers and the *Ferme* was a steady source of investment paying $2\frac{1}{2}$ per cent interest. This system had two solid advantages for the monarchy. First, it provided precious funds *in advance* and preserved the government from erratic returns and the unwieldy job of collection. Second, it shifted the unpopular imposition of indirect taxes from the monarchy to private individuals who then bore the brunt of public odium. The eighteenth century knew no revolts against royal taxes at the popular level and this, if we consider the history of the Frondes, revolts of the Croquants, and the Nus Pieds, or the Révolte du Papier Timbré of the previous century, was a kind of achievement. True, *commis des aides* were regularly strangled or stabbed and the employees of the *Ferme Générale* were frequently discovered dead and mutilated by smuggling bands, but that was someone else's problem.

The element of private enterprise in government taxation which so characterized the *Ferme Générale* was not limited to that august body which contained some of the wealthiest men in France. It extended, in one form or another, to every government department concerned with financial administration. Whilst the posts of ministers – and in particular that of *contrôleur général* and membership of the royal councils – were political appointments dependent upon royal favour and influence in court circles, there existed for the actual running of government finances a vast network of accountants and financial agencies staffed with venal office holders in contractual relationship with the crown. There was no real centralized royal treasury and though a treasury existed much of the business was enacted through a number of accountants (*comptables*) who were part of, or managed, individual *caisses* (payment offices) which carried out the crown's business according to contracts and instructions. These accountants, who were all men of wealth, had an eye ever open to advancement. They either inherited or bought their offices. They were prepared to sell if a better opportunity occurred. They also accumulated venal positions. In the letters of provision which bestowed an office nothing required an accountant to confine himself to the royal service and stay out of private business and finance nor suggested that he might not use his office for his own advantage. He received fees, a proportion of the funds he handled, gratuities, pensions and emoluments, but not a salary. Though he was required to submit accounts, and to give loyal service, nothing restricted his independence. He could not be called an official in the modern sense of the term.

The accountant's *caisse* received and/or paid out a large part of the crown revenues without their ever reaching the royal treasury and many of these funds were not even recorded in treasury ledgers. If the *Ferme Générale* was the most organized and powerful of the groups of accountants, there were other powerful though less coherent groups such as the receivers general (*receveurs généraux*) each with his own *caisse*, but committed to pay into a common *caisse* of the royal treasury the net returns of royal direct taxation and each responsible, in whole or in part, for a particular *généralité*. Each receiver general, a venal official, had a contract with innumerable *receveurs particuliers* (also venal officials) who in turn had contracts with parish officials for the collection of individual taxes. Since taxes were slow in coming in, the system was highly dependent *within itself* upon short-term borrowing, though this did not mean that real money changed hands. Rather, the receiver general issued promissory notes to whomsoever he was required to do so by the *Conseil des Finances*. These notes derived their value only from the personal credit of the receiver general himself and they were negotiable instruments tantamount to a bill of exchange. Some of the officials such as the treasurers general, responsible for making payments for particular purposes (e.g. marine and colonies), issued credit notes which were regarded as very solid currency by *ancien régime* society.

What did such a system cost to run? No one really knew. This network of accountants was a continually growing phenomenon. Whenever and wherever the government borrowed, a new group of accountants had to be created to cope with the payment of interest. Guardian of this system was the *Chambre des Comptes*. To this body, needless to say a law court, an accountant was supposed to submit his accounts and any measures necessary to protect the crown's financial interests were its concern. Even the *contrôle général* had to submit its accounts to the *Chambre des Comptes* six months after the expiry of the fiscal year. Moreover, the venal magistrates of the *Chambre des Comptes* had the right to remonstrate against royal acts bearing upon financial matters in much the same way as the *parlements*.

The chief hallmark of the entire system was its inflexibility. If French government expenditure had not outstripped taxable resources, the government could not effect radical changes either in the levy or the mechanism for collection without bringing upon itself endless problems. Everyone – kings, ministers, *parlements*, people – believed the whole system to be snarled up with corrupt fortune seekers and were convinced that financial crimes distrained an important part of revenue. French history is peppered with its Jacques Coeurs and Fouquets who were monarchical scapegoats for financial disorders and their elimination of psychological rather than genuine financial effect. Beyond this persuasion, however, there was no common ground. The *parlements* consistently refused to accede to any royal demand for new taxation except as an extraordinary measure. Successive *contrôleurs généraux*, whom it should be remembered were men chosen by the monarchy and forced to survive in a court ever open to intrigue and hence were not necessarily men of percipience and talent, often sought varied and contradictory means for bringing the situation under control. Up to 1756 these might be described as frankly illegal methods of forcing the registration of new and/or extraordinary taxation. In this period the *parlements* were irrevocably alienated. After 1763 approaches then began to diverge wildly. Terray, Turgot and Necker sought to bring the system of venal accounts under closer central control by the abolition of particular *caisses* and by an attack upon the principle of venality, by the deflection of business from accountants and *caisses* to the royal treasury and by greater scrutiny by the treasury of overall funds – in short, by more accurate book-keeping. Joly de Fleury (1781–2) believed that such an approach undermined the credit of the accountants upon whom the monarchy was entirely dependent and sought to halt the move towards the destruction of venality and greater centralization. Finally Calonne came forward with the idea of a uniform land tax to replace all other taxes and aimed the brunt of his reforming efforts against privileged immunities and the system of royal pensions. What no *contrôleur général* could do was liberate the government from recourse to loans and the elaborate mechanism of venal accountants and *caisses* whereby the French debt was serviced made any fundamental reform indeed impossible for it was largely beyond the control of the central government.

The answer to our initial question as to the adequacy of government income from taxation to meet normal expenditure in time of peace must remain largely unanswerable. Until Necker's *Compte Rendu* in 1781 no one had ever tried to get an overview of total income in relation to total expenditure, and when Necker did so he allegedly made a number of fundamental miscalculations which proved disastrous for the claims of monarchy. The essay of the *Comité des Finances* in 1791 was largely based on guesswork and assumptions (we know monarchical expenditure to have been large, therefore we shall concoct a suitably gross sum). It would seem that payment of interest on contracted loans accounted for about a half of government expenditure in the late

1780s and substantially less before.[4] This proportion was exactly the same as in the British instance, though the French government paid a rate of interest about twice as high (6 per cent), a rate of interest very attractive to an international money market of Dutch and Swiss financiers, as late as 1785. In short, there was perhaps little remarkable about either the size of the French debt or the amount required to service it. What was remarkable was the degree to which government finance reposed on private credit and individual financiers and hence was exposed to private business performance, the state of the French economy, even the international money market, and was capable of being torn apart by crises of confidence in which loans simply dried up. Each of these features played a significant role in the history of French government finance, most particularly between 1770 and 1789.

Without the thorny questions of finance, the ill-will generated during Fleury's tenure of office by *Unigenitus* might have had little long-term significance. As it was, it was the prelude to a long-drawn out struggle of which the salient features of the period 1740–55 were two. The first was a marked growth in militancy and political pretensions of the *parlements* expressed in the production in 1748 of Montesquieu's *De l'Esprit des Lois* wherein the magistracy appeared as guardians of fundamental and statutory law and monarchy was seen as under, not outside, the law. The *Grandes Remontrances* of 1753 built upon this basic work. These were produced by the *parlements* in response to a further religious dispute over *Unigenitus* in which the monarchy endeavoured to remove disputes arising out of refusals by anti-Jansenist clergy to administer the sacraments to any opponent of *Unigenitus* out of the *parlements* to the *Grand Conseil* where monarchy and ministers had control. The remonstrances were published and included the assertion that 'when there is a conflict between the king's absolute power and the good of his service, the court respects the latter rather than the former, not to disobey but in order to discharge its obligations'. This statement is a neat encapsulation of a growing vision of their role as judges of royal policy.

The second development was equally significant. It comprised a growth in contact and coherence of action between the Parlement of Paris and its provincial equivalents so that opposition which had formerly only been Paris based now extended to Bordeaux, Rennes, Rouen, Toulouse etc. Against this background of growing militancy, Machault d'Arnouville in 1749 sought to introduce a new tax to cope with the debts arising from the Polish Succession War. The *contrôleur général* envisaged this tax, the *vingtième*, as one to be levied on all sectors of society and all forms of income (property, manufacturing industry and office). When *parlement* stalled in face of a new tax in

4 F. Braesch, *Finances et monnaies*, II, p. 202.

peacetime Machault had recourse to a *lit de justice*. In fact, the principle upon which the new tax was to be levied was eroded *not* by the *parlements* in this instance but by the clergy who saw in this essay in compulsory state taxation the opening of a floodgate to untrammelled royal demands. They pulled out every weapon in their arsenal, including the threat to abandon their churches. They were supported by the *dévot* party at court, embracing in this instance, the queen, the dauphin, the princesses of the blood and even the secretary for war, d'Argenson, who ran his own personal feud with Machault. In 1751, Machault was forced to concede the principle of clerical immunity.

The struggle over the *vingtième* represented a victory for someone but hardly for either the nobility or the *parlements* for the second order was taxed in 1749, albeit on a temporary basis, and was taxed in peacetime. Yet in 1756 the *parlements* were to win a battle in war which was very much of Machault's making. Shifted from finance to the chancellorship, he was the architect of a number of royal acts designed to reduce the capacity of the *parlements* for counteracting royal proposals. These acts were ratified only by the authoritarian means of a *lit de justice*. They included the prohibition of judicial strikes and repeated remonstrances, suppressed two of five *chambres des enquêtes* and shifted the power of political debate into the more amenable *Grand' Chambre*. Had Machault been able to get away with it, *parlement* would have been a very reduced institution. As it was, all five *chambres des enquêtes* resigned followed by half the *Grand' Chambre* and in unprecedented fashion, the provincial *parlements* rushed to support the Parlement of Paris. Hence the government for the first time had to cope with a formidable united magistracy. For the entire duration of the costly Seven Years' War, the King was to be pushed in turn into a defensive situation in which royal prestige suffered a grave blow at the hand of the *parlements*. Machault was transferred to the navy office; the royal acts – with the exception of those suppressing two *chambres des enquêtes* but this rendered tolerable by the transference of their personnel to the other three *chambres* – were suspended. In return the *parlements* accepted *pro tem* extraordinary taxation, in this instance a temporary *vingtième* levy (1756, 1759). They did so, of course, without for an instant sacrificing the principle of consistency. Indeed, consistency became a predominant theme of *parlementaire* propaganda during what we might call the war interlude. Because of the monarchy's need for money, justifiable in actual terms of military expenditure, the monarchy adopted a relatively submissive line. This is not to imply a harmonious relationship. Stung by experience and exhilarated by a new-found unity, *parlementaire* pretensions during this period underwent some rapid developments. The publication of arguments which stressed the limitations on monarchy or the indefensibility of any fiscal change which offended custom – even the discussion of the historical

importance of an institution, the Estates General, apparently long dead
– belongs *par excellence* amongst the wartime propaganda of the *parlements*. Perhaps they were equipping themselves for a renewed monarchical onslaught regarded as inevitable with the return of peace. Be this as
it may, intransigently convinced of the intrinsic rectitude of their position, they were at least a match for central government up to 1770. In a
very real sense the end of the war in 1763 marked the beginning of yet
another act in this drama in which all parties were ultimately to perish.
The first victim to fall in this act was the *contrôleur général*, Bertin.

The fall of Bertin was, to a degree predictable. It stemmed from the
impasse which occurred when Bertin, as *contrôleur général*, was
responsible for the introduction of an edict authorizing the prolongation of the ordinary taxation of the Seven Years' War. This edict had to
be registered by a *lit de justice*. Immediately a welter of *parlementaire*
criticism in the shape of remonstrances insisting upon their right to
sanction taxation assailed the monarchy. The monarch at this juncture
was not prepared for confrontation. If Louis XV ever experienced a
crisis of confidence, it was in 1763 after a disastrous war in whose
diplomacy he had been closely involved. There was no European monarchy involved in that war which did not, as a direct result, find itself in
deep financial trouble – even the British were forced to think in terms of
taxing the colonies – but perhaps loss of face was experienced most
keenly by the French and Austrian monarchies. Some renewal of conflict was regarded as inevitable but temporarily all the belligerent
powers needed some breathing space. Louis XV then chose, rather
than become involved in a head-on collision with the *parlements*, to
sacrifice Bertin and most of his unpopular edicts and to recognize the
validity of *parlementaire* right to sanction taxation. A further expression of monarchical weakness at this time was Louis XV's acceptance in
November 1764 of the suppression, under *parlementaire* pressure, of
the Society of Jesus.

The 1760s need very careful consideration. The classical interpretation
of the immediate post-war years is of a period given over to army and
navy reform with the Duc de Choiseul in control of foreign affairs, in
anticipation of imminent Franco-British conflict. Choiseul is presented
as a man geared to this single end and to achieve it he was prepared to
temporize with the *parlements*, allowing them to suppress the Jesuits
and perforce giving up any prospect of financial reform. A nonentity as
contrôleur général in the shape of de l'Averdy, himself an ex-*parlementaire*, was not going to depart from such a policy. The most significant
achievements of these years were a considerably reformed navy, an
improved artillery and measures guaranteeing greater centralization
for recruitment and the provision of equipment in the Ministry of
War. On the deficit side, there was a recrudescence in *parlementaire*

power apparent not only in general struggles of common interest over the Jesuits and taxation but in particular ones such as the resignation of the entire Parlement de Bretagne in 1765. This arose out of several disputes over taxation and the question of the construction of new military roads, which were to be a linkage with Quiberon and the Breton ports, in anticipation of a new Atlantic struggle. The issue was about who should pay for, build and manage these roads and Brittany, poverty-stricken as she undoubtedly was amongst French provinces, resisted the shifting of this and other financial burdens in whole or in part on to her shoulders and ran a constant battle with the provincial governor, d'Aiguillon. The resignation of the Parlement de Bretagne was counteracted on the King's side by the creation of a new judicial court at Rennes. At this point other *parlements* rushed to Rennes's support and remonstrances demonstrating *parlementaire* solidarity were presented. This did not prevent the arrest of La Chalotais, *Procureur-Général* of the Parlement de Bretagne who had been involved in court intrigues to gain ministerial power. The affair reached a climax with a *lit de justice* on 3 March 1766 – a celebrated occasion known as the *séance de la flagellation* – in which Louis XV rejected the constitutional claims put forward by the *parlements* since 1740, the idea of a union of *parlements* or the claim that they possessed sovereign power.

The attempts of the Parlement of Paris to try d'Aiguillon were squashed by the monarchy in 1770 and the chancellor Maupeou two months later presented the celebrated November edict which prolonged the first *vingtième* and forbade the *parlements* to evoke the concept of *parlementaire* unity and stipulated that all edicts, whether registered normally or by a *lit de justice*, must be immediately executed. The whole edict was forcibly registered in a *lit de justice*.

In short, any cession of ground by the monarchy to the *parlementaires* was only for a short duration. According to the traditional interpretation, Choiseul's fall was the result of alienation between himself and Louis XV who wisely refused to be pushed into war with England in support of Spanish claims over the Falkland Islands. This growing alienation had already had some expression in Louis XV's bringing of Maupeou into the ministry as chancellor and the Abbé Terray as *contrôleur général*. Certainly both these ministers were committed to a harder line towards the *parlements*. Both were ambitious and neither had any love of the Choiseuls. The Falkland Island crisis, seen by Choiseul as an opening for conflict, was the occasion of a session in the royal council in December 1770 in which a bitter slanging match occurred. Terray opposed the idea of conflict by exposing the disastrous state of royal finances and blamed this on the intransigence of the *parlements* and Choiseul retaliated by attributing difficulties to Terray's financial maladministration. Louis XV stood by Terray and Maupeou and dismissed Choiseul. Hence began the period of Maupeou's ascendancy (1771–4) 'last of the great ministers of the Bourbon dynasty'[5] in which, in the traditional interpretation, a real stand was made against the *parlements* and financial reform was undertaken and the French monarchy was set on a firm path which, had it not deviated from it in 1774, might have saved it from revolution.

This simple political narrative has been questioned and lent sophistication by a recent interpretation of Maupeou which sees him less as a clear-sighted reformer, intent *ab initio* on ridding monarchy of a self-interested obstacle to change, than as an ambitious intriguer whose search for power brought him into seeking the means to engineer the fall of Choiseul and whose policy towards the *parlements* was unnecessarily aggressive and probably counterproductive. Choiseul's sway at court depended upon the imminence of war which in turn implied the need for a reasonably harmonious relationship with the *parlements* whose sanction was required for war taxation. To secure Choiseul's fall Maupeou deliberately set out to antagonize the *parlements* by an intransigent line over the d'Aiguillon affair and by expressing forcible antipathy to *parlementaire* pretensions in the November edict. He thus ensured that there was no chance whatsoever of realizing Choiseul's war programme and Choiseul was forced out of office. Maupeou did not necessarily envisage a further attack on *parlementaire* power. With Choiseul out of the way, a real attempt was made to take the heat out of relations between central government and *parlement*, though Maupeou could not withdraw the November edict.

It was Maupeou's refusal to withdraw this contentious piece of legislation and the equal refusal of the *parlements* to see their power thus diminished which forced the next step, the exile, dissolution and remodelling of the Parlement of Paris and, in its train, the abolition of three provincial *parlements* (Rouen, Douai and Metz) and the remodelling of the rest. The quintessential features of this remodelling were firstly a dimunition of the power of the Parlement of Paris in particular *from below* by the setting up of a number of *conseils supérieurs* within the area of its jurisdiction designed to have sovereign judgement over all civil and criminal cases, exclusive of matters relating to the peerage. These *conseils* had no political role whatsoever. They registered laws but had no rights of remonstrance. The power of the Parlement of Paris was limited to Paris and its immediate hinterland. Power was also fundamentally shifted from the Parlements of Toulouse and Rouen to similar *conseils*. Elsewhere remodelling was confined to eliminating redundant office-holders. Perhaps the most fundamental and consequential change of all was the abolition of venality and hereditary right in regard to higher office. That principle established, the actual personnel chosen were obviously existing magistrates with the safe

5   Cobban, *A History of Modern France*, p. 97.

knowledge for the government that these were neither irremovable *nor* endowed with political power. They were much reduced in number but compensation was to be paid to any ousted magistrate who chose to make a claim.

Certainly Maupeou's reforms removed the potential for strikes, mass resignations and concerted action between the *parlements*. What they did not totally eliminate were remonstrances against Terray's financial reforms though many of these were of a token muted nature. What one has to ask is how much difference the effective elimination of *parlementaire* pressure between 1771–4 made to the issue of French finances? What evidence is there that the remodelling of the *parlements* was with a view of giving the government greater freedom of action in financial matters?

These questions are far from easy to answer. So far our narrative of this struggle between king, politicians and *parlements* has used finances merely as a *casus belli* – lent edge by the particular post-war financial situation. But there were other considerations as well. It now seems as if the sixties were a crucial turning point in French economic growth and that from that juncture there seems to have been, in many regions, an evident imbalance between population and supply. Something of this is reflected in de l'Averdy's edicts on begging and vagrancy in 1767 which set up new houses of correction for the vagrant and the attempted reforms of the French police force to cope with the growing problems arising from the agrarian situation. A further expression of it was Terray's attempts in 1770 to tamper with the grain trade in the belief that what was most to be feared was shortage in the cities and hence he sanctioned government purchases of enormous stocks of grain. From this grew the widespread persuasion that Terray was the architect of a plot, *le pacte de famine*, whereby he or the government were out to make money by buying grain when it was plentiful to sell at extortionate prices when scarcity bit and, by extension, that the minister was himself the architect of dearth. Certainly no one could manipulate the grain trade without arousing popular suspicion. Equally certainly, however good his intentions, Terray's action enhanced, rather than detracted from crisis.

It now seems to financial historians that economic crisis could be, if not productive of, at least a significant contributory factor in, government financial crisis. The accumulated debts of the Seven Years' War and the preparations for the next conflict were obviously still burdensome to all governments. But the French government was peculiarly dependent upon private credit and private credit in the France of the late sixties was a sickly plant. Herbert Luthy has spoken of 1769–70 as the year of 'la crise générale de commerce': 2500 business failures allegedly took place. Up and down the French social scale, the innumerable office-holders who issued letters of credit on their particular *caisses* or in their own names found themselves faced with difficulties. In part, this may have just been the difficulties experienced in getting in taxation from a peasantry forced in the abnormal times to become purchasers. In part, the crisis may have reflected withdrawal of foreign money on the part of international lenders. This 'crisis of confidence' remains to be fully documented and explored but one can have no doubt of its existence or of the bankruptcy of several important financial officials on a scale which did not occur again until 1787 and which forced a number of stringent emergency measures upon Terray. The crisis certainly gave a new edge to the government's relationships with *parlement* in 1770 which had nothing to do with the purely political rivalries between Choiseul and Maupeou. Maupeou's remodelling of the *parlements* ought to have made possible some financial reform; what would Terray do with his opportunities?

The emergency measures by which Terray saved royal credit and prevented bankruptcy were first and most draconian, a suspension of payment on any short-term credit notes issued by government *caisses* in anticipation of the revenues of 1770 so that tax revenues could be used as security for new issues of notes to cope with government spending (this measure preceded the November edict). Secondly, the edict of November 1771 made perpetual the first *vingtième* and a second *vingtième* was now prolonged until 1781. One might say that these measures probably would not have passed the *parlements* without Maupeou's reforms nor, perhaps, would plans for reassessing liability to the *vingtième* on a more equitable basis. But most fundamental of all was to be an assault on financial officials themselves in the same way that Maupeou had attacked venality in the *parlements*. Terray has been credited with taking the first steps towards a centralized royal treasury with a view to giving the royal government greater control over its finances. These steps however were perforce of a very tentative nature. It was relatively easy in course of Maupeou's suppressions to be quit of a number of lesser financial officials, less easy to attack the world of finance without rocking the boat of credit.

Still, one can note for example the reduction of the Treasurers General for Marine and Colonies from four to two, and the Treasurers General of the King's Household from two to one. Moreover, the means for controlling the financiers seem to have been steadily improved from Terray's tenure of office. It marked a turning point in the relationship between government and financiers in which the latter came under closer scrutiny and were much more vulnerable. The Farmers General, for example, were forced into harsher leases which yielded more to the crown and 1770 marked something of an ebb-tide in the fortunes of financiers, a phenomenon as remarkable amongst the provincial financiers of Languedoc as amongst the moneyed houses of

Paris. But, and this is important, one should not paint Terray as a man with a vision of fundamental financial reform, or imagine that in the absence of a *parlement* able to put up staunch opposition, such reform was possible. Apart from the *vingtième*, a very insignificant tax viewed in the context of French taxation as a whole, at no point did Terray seek to reform or in any way tamper with the traditional structure of direct or indirect taxation. Those who have most vaunted Terray's achievements hesitate to say that the steps in the direction of the creation of a royal treasury were towards a more economical or efficient way of raising taxes – all that can be claimed is that such reforms were in the direction of increasing central control over an unwiedly out-of-date system. This system could not be overhauled from top to bottom without a thorough survey of income throughout the country even before one considers the existence of provincial privilege. One could not overnight demolish a source of crown revenue without immediately creating another. Such steps could not and did not enter into Terray's thinking. He was interested solely in gaining a breathing space for the monarchy in which new private credit could be raised *within the existing system* and to hold the monarchy's debts at arm's length. If necessary, on the strength of the extra revenue from the *vingtième*, he could contract new debts. Indeed, his tenure of office is remarkable for having extended financial chaos into municipal finances by re-introducing venality of office in 1770. He was loathed by a hungry populace as architect of a *pacte de famine*, at loggerheads with the intendants over all manner of matters from the virtual breakdown in some cases of municipal government as a result of his edict, to the failure adequately to finance *dépôts de mendicité* and a newly-reformed police force.

It must also be questioned whether Terray did not shake royal credit still further. The government's handling of the financial crisis of 1770 engendered a nervousness amongst investors and financiers which could only contribute to the long-term financial difficulties of the crown. If loans did not dry up, the propensity for credit to be frozen in times of constitutional crisis, and for creditors to associate their fate with that of the *parlements*, were obviously recurrent phenomena after 1770. In short, the concept of 1770–74 as a period in which the royal government showed how reform-minded it was without the restraining hand of *parlement* is a distorted one. Maupeou and Terray merely purchased for the monarchy four relatively easy years in which royal business could be more speedily transacted. This does not mean that Maupeou's edict produced quicker or more efficient justice. The salaries of the members of the *conseils supérieurs* seem to have pushed up the overall cost of justice and the reform of the jungle of French provincial law was not broached. Perhaps most significant of all, was the alienation of public opinion from Louis XV who died in 1774 a hated man, a tyrant, *le plaisir des dames*, and the employer of a minister capable of running a *pacte de famine*. The obverse side of that alienation was warm public sympathy for the *parlements*.

There seems little doubt that the new king, Louis XV's grandson, was aware of the alienation and that consciousness of it was to be one of the factors which pushed him, against his real feelings, into a restoration of the *parlements*. In part, the decision stemmed from political predilections. The politics of absolute monarchy are the politics of factions. Maupeou and Terray were a faction. They were defined initially, along with d'Aiguillon, by their opposition to Choiseul and his faction who had been prepared to temporize with *parlements* to secure military ambitions. Nothing recommended them to the well-intentioned young royal couple. The King himself looked to his aunt, Madame Adelaïde, for advice and was recommended Maurepas, exiled in 1749 through loss of royal favour – or rather the favour of the King's mistress. If Maurepas had a political philosophy it reposed on the tenet *sans parlement point de monarchie*. D'Aiguillon at the war office had pleased no one and was immediately replaced by the Comte de Vergennes. A relative outsider with friends in court circles, given ministerial office was Turgot, an ex-*maître des reqûetes* as well as former intendant who was in favour of a qualified recall of the *parlements*. Convinced by Maurepas of the ill-will generated throughout the country by the policy of Maupeou, in August 1774 the King dismissed both Maupeou and Terray. Demonstrations in the capital, including an invasion of Maupeou's *parlement*, were evidence to the King and his ministers of popular commitment to the old *parlements* and along with the proclivities of the bulk of the new ministers decided the new monarch to restore them. Before he did so, he took an important step in replacing Maupeou as chancellor by Miromesnil, a *parlementaire* who had suffered at Maupeou's hands.

Louis XVI's recall of the *parlements* was not a leap in the dark simply made under pressure without some thought for the consequences. Government Louis XV style had come closer to despotism between 1771 and 1774 than French monarchy had perhaps ever done. Throughout his reign Louis XV had shown himself very jealous of power, an attribute made manifest not only in his attitude to the *parlements* but also in his tolerance of bitterly hostile factional in-fighting amongst his ministers which he deemed the means whereby no one man ever became too powerful nor forgot that he owed his position to the monarch. Louis XVI's ministerial choice was of men who were, at least in 1774, more or less at one on vital issues – and none more vital than the relationship between central government and *parlement*. Maurepas, in his seventies, was of a conciliatory disposition: Miromesnil was a shrewd operator who understood the inner workings of the *parlements* and indeed was suspected of having his agents, spies and manipulators within the *parlements* themselves. Maurepas's choice of Turgot as *contrôleur général*, was of a man obsessed with the economy and not of a man adept at court intrigue. Indeed he had no talent whatsoever for politics, whilst Vergennes found his real momentum in foreign affairs. This ministry was to run smoothly until 1776 when Turgot and Miromesnil clashed over the Six Edicts, a clash which meant that one of them had to go in a style of government which demanded ministerial harmony and consistency.

The restored Parlement of Paris was not intended to be quite like its predecessor. On the one hand a certain amount of judicial business was removed from below by raising the jurisdictional status of the old *présidial* courts so that a great deal of practical business was kept out of the *parlements* and secondly, from within, the power of the *Grand' Chambres* (traditionally the sector of the *parlements* most consistently amenable to royal interests) was increased at the expense of lesser *chambres*. There was a new edict of disciplinary procedure reminiscent of Maupeou's edict, in which strikes, mass resignations and judicial obstructions to registration were curbed. Similar safeguards were to be imposed upon the provincial *parlements*. The question everyone was asking at the French court and in foreign embassies was how this would work in the long term and what were the odds on contriving a viable relationship between royal government and *parlement*. The traditional view is that after an initial year in which the *parlements* trod a careful path, they soon relearnt their obstreperous tactics and embarked upon that heedless policy of obstruction which ultimately killed themselves and monarchy. More recently, however, it has been argued that the *parlements* played a very quiet hand between 1774 and 1787 and were remarkably amenable over the registration of new loans and the extensions of the *vingtième*. They never, in fact, recouped the unity between Parisian and provincial *parlements* which had been a feature of the pre 1770 situation. Moreover, the provincial *parlements* were characterized after 1774 by internal quarrels between those who had accepted office in Maupeou's *conseils supérieurs* and pared-down *parlements*, and those who had remained untainted and office-less, which made the *parlementaires* somewhat ineffectual defenders of traditional liberties against royal despotism.

The dismissal of Turgot is now seen to have been brought about less by the refusal of the *parlements* to register his Six Edicts than by general ministerial opposition to a policy which ruptured the ministerial harmony which the monarchy esteemed so highly. Moreover, the crisis of the late 1780s in which *parlementaire* opposition brought about the calling of the Estates General is now interpreted as a response to the spectre of revived despotism in the style of 1770 and ministerial vacillation of the type which had characterized Louis XV's government. Such a view puts the events of 1774–89 into a different perspective, as something far more complex than a renewed battle between king and *parlement* opened up by Louis XVI's folly in allowing this destruction-bent institution to be restored.

There are innumerable myths surrounding the ministry of Turgot (1774–6). His background as intendant at Limoges was remarkably sound and he had demonstrated a conspicuous awareness of the problems of poverty and low agricultural productivity in a region dominated by small farms where there was little capital input into improvement. But he was ill fitted for court politics. Moreover, as a minister of finance he cannot be considered as of anything but minor significance amongst eighteenth-century *contrôleurs généraux*. His policy was largely that of continuing Terray's efforts in the direction of centralizing the royal treasury by attempts, perforce of a token nature, to reduce the numbers of accountants and *caisses* (e.g. the consolidation within each *élection* or *sénéchaussée* of multiple offices into the single office of *receveur des impositions*) by increased invigilation of accounts, and by a tough line towards the *Ferme Générale* and financiers. His record, as far as the contraction of new loans is concerned, is cleaner than Terray's but his term of office was shorter and he was not operating in the same difficult financial atmosphere as his predecessor who had had to cope with the problems arising from the crisis of 1770. He differed from Terray and indeed from any other *contrôleur général* of the eighteenth century in being preoccupied less with finances than with the economy and hence in seeking to use his period of office in a way that no one other than Colbert had ever done, that is as an opportunity to influence French economic development. One can of course question whether in eighteenth-century terms one can talk of a French economy at all and may even be forgiven scepticism over the degree to which governments can at any time influence economic growth. Nevertheless, in eighteenth-and nineteenth-century terms, Turgot's belief in an economy which could be boosted by government intervention had a singularly modern ring. As a physiocrat, he understood by government intervention the removal of obstacles to free market conditions and industrial expansion. Indeed, three of his controversial Six Edicts were concerned with the freedom of the grain trade and the abolition of the guilds. In short, Turgot sought to convert Enlightenment economic ideas into action.

But how germane were Turgot's economic measures to France's real economic problems and were they likely to provide any palliative? By the mid-seventies population growth in France had outstripped economic growth in the direction that mattered, that is, the production of more grain to feed more mouths. This of course was not necessarily totally apparent to a government which was only just beginning to look to statistical data as a basis for policy-making (a revolution of a kind which is to be attributed to Terray). Turgot, had considerable experience of the vulnerability of the smallholder to the least fluctuation in the harvest of his staple crop – which in that region could be the chestnut or the potato or coarse grain – but, endowed with a cosmic vision of France, he believed that the surplus of one region could be used to bolster the inadequacies of another, that as long as an export trade outside the country was illegal, total production was adequate to French needs. In a free market, grain would be channelled where it was needed.

It was a policy which was obviously producer-orientated. A man who can shift his grain wherever he wills, can get the best price for it and might be thus stimulated into greater production. This is a perfectly reputable intellectual stance. In the context of the 1770s however it was doomed to failure for three good reasons. Firstly, however enthusiastically producers may have welcomed free trade, consumers, who were after all the bulk of the French population, were adamantly hostile. For them, free trade in grain meant higher prices. Secondly, Turgot's proposals were to be tried out in a year of mixed harvests, decidedly poor in the south and far from abundant in the north. The sight of grain in transit clearly destined for a market other than the purely local one could only provoke trouble. Thirdly, and something Turgot could perhaps not know, one simply could not, in any way whatsoever, tamper with the *carte de ravitaillement* (provisioning map) of eighteenth-century France without encountering opposition from a population which dwelt in fear of hunger. By this one means that each locality was accustomed to draw its food from a particular zone and grain producers were *obliged* to use particular markets. Most complex of all was the *carte de ravitaillement* of Paris and it is significant that Turgot in 1774 exempted Paris and its grain-provisioning zone from his measures. Any tampering at all with the age-old traditions of provisioning was apt to arouse popular panic.

The immediate response of local officials to Turgot's initial free-trade measures of 1774 abolishing the requirement for producers to sell in stipulated markets, was to attempt to stall, so appalled were they at the prospect of putting them into effect. Rising prices caused rioting in spring at Dijon, Tours, Metz, Reims and Montauban but most significant of all was to be the Flour War which broke out at Beaumont sur l'Oise in April 1775. This was a spontaneous popular movement, like many other grain riots, but much more extensive. It aimed at reducing grain from the elevated level of 25 *livres* the *septier* to 12 *livres* – the level at which it had stood in the early sixties. The high prices may have just been a reflection of the condition of the harvest but they were associated with free-trade policy. The aim of the movement was to oblige merchants to sell their grain at a just price and if they failed to do so to seize it and sell it for such a price. This was known as *taxation populaire*. The movement spread to Pontoise where the populace attacked grain convoys destined for Paris, thence to Saint Germain en Laye, and to Versailles. Everywhere local officials backed down and ordered merchants and bakers to sell at the people's price only to find themselves arrested on Turgot's instructions or to have their decisions revoked. Measures exempting Paris from the free-trade legislation did not stop prices rising in the capital nor rioting in early May. The Flour War passed also into the Brie where it became not only an attack on merchants but on large farmers themselves and then abruptly about 10 May it petered out – perhaps because the death penalty was introduced for rioting in the capital.

This repressive measure was sanctioned by the Parlement of Paris on 4 May but the Parlement added that the King should take measures to reduce the price of bread to a rate proportionate to the means of the people and the ruling, with this comment, was posted in the Paris streets. Moreover *parlementaires* protested against the setting up of a *commission prévôtale* to try the insurgents as a deflection of power from the *Grand' Chambre*. A *lit de justice* ultimately forced through this measure but not before remonstrances had thoroughly demonstrated the Parlement's insistence on the principle of the people's right to bread at 2 *sous* the pound.

The attitude of the Parlement of Paris was not inconsistent. It had registered an edict promising the exemption of Paris and was now confronted with an evident breakdown in public order which the police could not contain. Informed at the *lit de justice* that Turgot's measures had been undermined by a plot 'to lay desolate the countryside, to impede navigation, to hinder the transport of grain on the highways, and to starve the large towns, above all Paris', they put themselves behind the monarchy in the interests of public order. Both Turgot and Louis XVI professed belief in a conspiracy to undermine free trade and suspects ranged from the Prince de Conti, the Abbé Terray, the French clergy, leading *parlementaires*, to the English – but such theories have never been found to have substance.

The summer of 1775 saw some attempt to bring down bread prices in the towns by the abolition of municipal taxes (*octrois*) on grains and flour and the central government remained committed to a free-trade policy. That said, one must be careful to explain who one has in mind when one talks of central government for the whole experience of the Flour War was to drive a wedge between Turgot and his most influential ministerial colleagues. Turgot was an intellectual civil servant and no politician. His political support at court, where such support mattered, shrank in the summer of 1775. Maurepas, for example, was clearly alienated and apprehensive of the actions of the *contrôleur général* and Miromesnil, whose attitude towards the imminent Six Edicts would be overtly hostile, was already critical. A bevy of lesser secretaries of state like the d'Ormessons and the Trudaines were behind Turgot but they were far from being men of significant political repute. Throughout 1775 and into 1776 Louis XVI wholeheartedly backed his *contrôleur général* and in the ministry Malesherbes was perhaps alone firm in support. His estrangement in the course of the battle over the Six Edicts was to be crucial. A man of political talent might have seen the futility of proceeding without more considerable ministerial backing. It was this lack of support at court which was responsible for Turgot's dismissal. The opposition of the *parlementaires* was far from sufficient to topple the minister: it merely contributed to the general hostility towards him.

Three of the Six Edicts extended to Paris measures relating to the freedom of the grain trade. A fourth abolished a host of minor offices which existed to impose minor levies on the meat trade which added to consumer costs and raised little for the treasury. The fifth, and probably the most damaging in terms of Turgot's reputation at the popular level after the measurese freeing the grain trade, abolished the guilds which controlled admission to certain branches of industry and to artisanal training and which were anathema to current economic thinking as restricting industrial development. The sixth commuted the *corvée*, an inefficient road tax exacted in peasant labour, into a money tax to be levied on all proprietors of land. These last two measures have been presented as a fundamental attack on privilege of which the *parlements*, regaining their old assertiveness, were the constant champions. Yet the *parlements* did not stand out in opposition to registration of these measures by a *lit de justice*. Moreover to represent these measures as an attack on privilege and nothing more is to gloss over their implications for a broad social spectrum. The abolition of the guilds was a logical step in a physiocratic programme. The best means to promote industrial growth, it was believed, was to remove any obstacles to its free development.

In a global economic sense economic performance was not determined by the existence or non-existence of guilds. The masters of the urban guilds were not necessarily wealthy men. Indeed, the bulk of them were men without capital who could go under at the least vicissitude in their personal circumstances as well as in the wider economic situation. Turgot's edict was not the first nail in their coffin. In 1762 an edict had permitted the extension of uncontrolled industry to the countryside, a measure which had in many circumstances had the most devastating effect upon urban industry. Rural production was cheaper, the work force being partially buttressed by smallholdings and prepared to accept lower wages. Coupled with the bad harvests of the late sixties the ill-will engendered by this edict had been immense and particular industries – notably Languedocian production for the Levant as centred at Clermont de Lodève and Carcassonne – had been severely hit by an exposure to free market circumstances they could not stand. The crisis in this case was one of overproduction of shoddy cloth which stuck with the producer and left him resourceless. Everywhere the edict of 1762 set town against country. Turgot's edict threatened to set towns-men against each other. In physiocratic thought people were meant to go to the wall if their enterprises could not compete in a free market. In the long term this might lead to healthy production but it was certainly not a policy which considered immediate human factors and opposition to Turgot's policy was not just that of 'privilege'; it was an opposing and not inhumane viewpoint, a different interpretation of what industry should be about.

The opposition which mounted over the commutation of the *corvée* could also be represented as something other than the mere response of privilege to much needed reform. Certainly a straight money tax was a more efficient way of financing road-building and certainly some intend-ants had already begun to move in that direction. But the smallholder, unemployed in any case in the dead season could have little doubt as to where his predilections lay Why should he, as a member of the unpriv-ileged, tax-paying population be asked to pay more when those who carriages used the roads were exempt? In opposing this measure, the *parlements* could only enhance their popular support. Any increase in taxation was to be resisted.

When the edicts had been registered at a *lit de justice* the cracks in ministerial solidarity were only too apparent. Malesherbes wanted to resign immediately and the strength of antipathy against Turgot was borne in on Louis XVI. In vain Turgot tried to discredit his colleagues to Louis XVI who finally broke silence and within two months dismissed a minister whose actions had created far more problems than they had solved. The ministry of Turgot had destroyed the ideal of united direc-tion which Louis XVI had sought to create in 1774. Perhaps that destruction would have taken place without Turgot but the process of disintegration might have been slower.

The choice of Turgot's successor, de Clugny, whom death removed prematurely from the scene a year later, was of little consequence in the history of French government finances in comparison with the ever-increasing certainty that France would enter the American War of Independence which broke out in 1776. Though the decision, made in 1778, when American success seemed a distinct probability, seems to posterity to have been a disastrous one, it was a logical one in the light of the continuity of Franco-British hostility and the distinct setback to French colonial fortunes received in 1763. Since that time, France had been engaged in an arms race. Now the opportunity seemed at hand for revenge and possible gain, if not in terms of territory at least in terms of trade. Moreover, the country was clearly as ready for war as she ever would be. The actual cost of war was not seen as a direct threat to government. Whilst engaged in war, recourse could be made to extraordinary taxation which *parlement* would concede because of precedent and somehow the funds would be found to service debt. Nothing suggested that the difficult situation which had existed in the aftermath of the Seven Years' War might be repeated since the new conflict, like all wars at the outset, was envisaged as a successful enterprise from which ill-defined benefit would flow. Vergennes and Sartine (*Secrétaire d'Etat de la Marine*) were insistent upon seizing the opportunity. Maurepas showed that he thoroughly grasped the implications of the situation when he pressed upon a hesitant Louis XVI the elevation from *directeur du trésor royal* to *contrôleur général* of a Genevan, Jacques Necker, a wealthy banker and self-made man who knew the international money market to an unparalleled degree and who had contacts in every capital, and whose bank (though he no longer directed it) had been a considerable lender to government during Terray's tenure of office. This man, if anyone, would know where the hard cash to finance war might be found.

We must take a long look at Necker who until relatively recently has been the whipping boy of *ancien régime* historians, the man to whom, as arch-borrower of allegedly untold profigacy, might even be attributed the fall of *ancien régime* government. His most recent biographers and historians of financial institutions have made a plea for recognition of Necker in one instance as perhaps the greatest finance minister of the century. Certainly the most meaningful point of departure is that Necker's very presence as a Genevan Protestant in a French Catholic court was only justified by the need to borrow and his success in this sphere was undoubted. Between 1778 and 1781 he raised for the monarchy about 150 million *livres* per year and that largely in *emprunts viagers* (loans made against a pension payable on the life span of a given individual). Other methods such as lotteries and direct loans from major financial companies and anticipation of revenues from annual 'extraordinary' taxes (for example, on officeholders) by offering a cut rate to those who would pay eight years in advance, all helped to swell the flow of government funds and the very presence of Necker served to create an atmosphere of confidence amongst creditors. This is not to say that the *contrôleur général* was an unquestioning purveyor of finance. The relationship between himself and Sartine, over naval expenditure and the navy office's arbitrary methods of raising money without consulting the *contrôleur général*, caused constant conflict which resulted in Sartine's dismissal in October 1780.

Moreover, if borrowing was a crucial aspect of Necker's policy, there were other aspects too. Confidence was the prerequisite of credit, and confidence depended upon what Necker termed 'conduite économe et sage'. This meant the pursuit of a kind of financial reform which did not open up untold social and political conflict but which promised greater central control of French finances. Necker did not, like Turgot, indulge in fanciful overviews of the French economy. He was not, for example, a protagonist of free trade but approached the grain question from the point of view of the consumer, only advocating free-market conditions in the event of a glut which threatened farmers with unduly low profits. In many ways Necker was the most pragmatic *contrôleur général ancien régime* France knew. He is remarkable, for example, for having introduced an element of rationality into the financial management of *hôpitaux* and charitable foundations by allowing them to sell their property to pay off the debts which inevitably arose with swelling numbers of indigent. But for our purpose, most significant was his work in extending central control over the tangle of venal officials, treasurers, receivers, etc. against whom Terray had made a tentative assault. Working on the premise that the more *caisses* involved, the greater the possibility for financial mismanagement, he aimed at overall reduction and abolished many venal positions for example in the offices of the marine treasurer and war treasurer. He attempted direct ministerial control over remaining *caisses* and strict supervision of book-keeping together with direct control on short-term advances and the use of paper notes by accountants and others who had custody of royal funds. Indeed, a regulation of 1778 insisted that *caisses* could only issue credit notes when authorized by the department of finance and in 1780 a further step attempted to ensure they were guaranteed by the Crown and not merely by an issuing accountant. Necker also made an assault on the tax empire of the *Ferme Générale* by shifting to the *Régie Générale* (a group of salaried civil servants) the collection of royal domain rights and excise duties, by reducing the numbers of *Fermiers Généraux* from 60 to 40 and by a much stricter lease which cut their profits. Significant economies were made and were seen to be made. What Necker jettisoned was the recourse to a new tax or to futile efforts to make more simply by increasing old taxes.

Certainly Necker made enemies and some very powerful ones. In particular Vergennes detested him partly because of his overt hostility to the extent of French involvement in the American War but more because of Necker's conviction that war expenditure should be the responsibility of the *contrôle général*. Accountants and venal officials in general claimed themselves the victims of ministerial tyranny and the world of office-holders felt itself threatened. Opposition at court was to secure Necker's downfall and it may have been consciousness of the ubiquity of his critics which impelled him to publish the *Compte Rendu au Roi par M. Necker, Directeur Général des Finances, au mois de janvier 1781*, a work which has procured an almost general obloquy from *ancien régime* historians since it allegedly engendered a spurious optimism in the state of French finances and was a major obstacle to Necker's successors when they sought to make radical financial reforms.

More recently it has been interpreted as the first public airing of royal finance; an attempt to put an erstwhile secret exercise before the public gaze. Moreover, the critics of the *Compte Rendu* have been accused of leaning too heavily on the evidence of Calonne, who had a vested interest in showing Necker to be in error. On one point historians agree. The *Compte Rendu* was announced on the same day as Necker announced the creation of 6 million *livres* of *rentes viagères* and hence was intended as an assurance to would-be creditors that the interest on their loans was guaranteed.

The public nature of the *Compte Rendu*, rather than its inaccuracy, incensed ministers. Necker was accused of being something less than a Frenchman. Vergennes gave to Louis XVI an opinion of the *Compte Rendu* which encapsulated this point of view: '...the example of England where accounts are made public is that of a calculating, selfish, troublesome nation. To apply such principles to France is a national insult: we are people of feeling [*sentimental*], trusting and devoted to the person of the King...' and he went on to spell out that the *Compte Rendu* was a slight to monarchy. Maurepas adopted a similar stance and threatened the King that all the ministers would resign if Necker's demands to bring the expenditure of the ministries of war and the marine directly under the supervision of the *contrôle général* were conceded. The King yielded and Necker lost office.

The consequences of that loss of office were multiple. For example, the ministries of war and the marine were released from the threat of financial supervision. Again, the new *contrôleur général*, Joly de Fleury, directly reversed Necker's policy of transforming the system of *caisses* and venal accountants. He re-created some of the offices Necker had suppressed and strengthened the system of independent *caisses* in the belief that the short-term credit of government depended upon the personal credit of the accountants. Most tantalizingly for posterity, all that really remained of Necker's policy were the continuing interest payments on debt and the *Compte Rendu* which could be, and was, challenged as fraudulent.

Was Necker profligate or was he a realistic banker? The question is impossible to answer fully but we can go some way towards making Necker and his policy more understandable if we survey the financial context within which he operated and recognize that his main critic, Calonne, in 1786 was not seeking to reverse the policy of borrowing but to offer a different kind of guarantee to creditors. We must recognize that the scale of borrowing did not decelerate with Necker's fall: indeed both Joly de Fleury and Calonne borrowed more heavily than he did.

	Annuity Loans	Other Types	Total
Necker, 1777–81	233,813,722	79,000,000	312,813,722
Joly de Fleury, 1781–2	177,299,160	170,000,000	347,299,160
Lefevre d'Ormesson, 1783		48,000,000	48,000,000
Calonne, 1783–7	194,810,120	226,978,540	421,788,660
Loménie de Brienne, 1787–8	187,000,000		187,000,000
Totals, 1777–88	792,923,002	523,978,540	1,316,901,542

Our point of departure must be that France's need to borrow for the war was met by a readiness on the part of foreign and French bankers to lend on a scale probably unprecedented in European history. On a foreign level, the main creditors were Dutch, Genevan and Genoese and their initial propensity to lend reflected less confidence in the health of French finances than a positive dearth of other sources of investment. In particular the decade 1775–85 saw a turning from England as a country whose debt was excessive and whose political system seemed prone to stress in the face of colonial conflict as a market for government borrowing. In the United Provinces and Switzerland there existed superabundant capital but the relative stagnation of Dutch commerce after 1730 and the underdevelopment as yet of industrial potential caused would-be investors to look outside the domestic market to place their surplus funds. It was this money which was courted by French *contrôleurs généraux* as loans to carry the war. They did so by offering high-yield annuities that could not be rivalled on any other market.

The avidity with which these annuities were snapped up until the mid-1780s engendered an amazing speculative boom. Like many other booms of its kind it had an intrinsic fragility which the percipient banker might in the long run have anticipated but, whilst it lasted, loans to the French state certainly looked like an investors' bonanza in which money could be borrowed from the cautious at 4 or 5 per cent, invested by a banker in French state loans at 8 or 10 per cent, and the profits derived might be used either to liquidate the loan or to increase the investment. In short, capital growth could be accelerated and be the more remarkable if the speculator had embarked with little or no capital of his own.

To Necker and the speculators of 1780–81 the exercise was relatively safe if backed by the evidence that French ordinary revenues from taxation produced sufficient slack to pay the interest on the loans. The *Compte Rendu* was designed to demonstrate that such slack existed by showing that ordinary revenues offset against ordinary (i.e. the day-to-day running of the country) expenditure showed a healthy surplus of some 10 million *livres*. Necker's book-keeping distinguished carefully between ordinary and extraordinary expenditure (the latter predominantly on war) and ordinary and extraordinary income (the latter predominantly in the form of loans). Calonne's case against Necker was that he had falsified the situation in 1781 in a number of ways. Firstly he had not deducted from the gross amount collected by the *caisses* responsible for treasury receipts (i.e. ordinary income) the extraordinary expenditure of those *caisses*, which in fact meant the ordinary revenues were 9 million *livres* less than Necker stated. (Terray, let it be said, had followed Necker's practice.) Secondly, his estimate of the *vingtième* for 1781 was in fact not realized until the early months of 1782 and hence *ordinary* income from this source was 120,000 *livres* less than stated. Thirdly, Necker counted as *ordinary* income, income which was in fact *extraordinary*. Here Calonne needs examining very carefully. For example, he asserted that the *don gratuit* was extraordinary revenue whilst Necker held it to be ordinary revenue. Insofar as the clergy held themselves free from any real obligation to donate their 'free gift' Calonne was right and 3–4 million *livres* should have been shifted to extraordinary income. But, on the other hand, the clergy invariably made their contribution and hence modern book-keeping would accept Necker's approach. Similarly Calonne disputed the shifting of some military and naval expenditures into extraordinary expenditure on the grounds that military and naval expenditure to an amount far greater than Necker allowed was borne in time of peace. (Yet Joly de Fleury proceeded along the same lines as Necker.) Calonne placed the discrepancy here at almost 4 million *livres*. By shifting Necker's extraordinary expenditures into ordinary expenditures into ordinary expenditures Calonne contrived overall a deficit of ordinary expenditure over income of 56 million *livres* in 1781 and hence, in 1786, sought to demonstrate that a surplus had never existed.

We are here confronted with something more than a difference in methods of book-keeping. Without painting Necker as a lilywhite incapable of falsifying the books, his was without doubt the approach of the seasoned banker, though one who made a number of miscalculations. Calonne's approach was that of a man hell-bent upon demonstrating a certain point in order to achieve very specific ends. Calonne's record in office had been that of a heavy borrower and a heavy spender, scrupulous in payment of interest, almost profligate in the field of public spending. He purchased Saint-Cloud and Rambouillet for the Crown: paid the debts of the King's brothers: encouraged great *urbanisme* enterprises at Bordeaux, Marseilles and Lyons and undertook the construction of Cherbourg harbour: finished the Canal du Centre and the Canal de Bourgogne. In short he did everything to encourage confidence before 1786.

Yet by 1785 steam was going out of the speculative bonanza. In part this may well have reflected internal pressure. In particular, the Parlement of Paris had remonstrated violently against the annuity loans created in December 1784 and December 1785 and the public image of bankers was akin to that of *partisans* in the seventeenth century. These had been fortune hunters who gained a stranglehold on government. At the international level the years 1785–6 were remarkable for a reluctance on the part of financiers to become further involved in French finances perhaps because of cold feet or because Dutch financiers in particular were given the opportunity to vary their portfolios by investing in the American debt and in Russian outlets. Even investment in Britain assumed a more attractive appearance to the world of international finance. This is not to say they withdrew such investments as they held – and indeed Amsterdam remained the most important centre for French loans – but that the credit flow formerly moving at flood level began to ebb. A would-be borrower could only seek to attract capital by offering further inflated interest rates (12–16%). Even then he was not guaranteed success. Already heavily involved financiers like Clavière changed their speculative techniques and demanded better guarantees.

This, then, was the context of Calonne's denunciation of Necker's *Compte Rendu* and his demand of Louis XVI in August 1786 that he acknowledge an annual deficit of at least 100 million *livres* (166 for 1786) and embark upon a state reform of the tax structure. This reform would, if accepted, expand the ordinary revenues of the crown by bringing into the tax net the privileged orders. In order to achieve this end as quickly as possible an assembly of notables, not the *parlements*, was to be summoned which could be directly swayed by Calonne's bleak picture and would not have to express reservations about its constitutional competence to accede to such a request. The British envoy had little doubt as to what Calonne was about: his summoning of the Notables 'under whatever pretext it may be disguised has certainly been adopted with a view to reanimate, if possible, the calamitous credit of the Government and *to pave the way to fresh loans*' (my italics). If this was the view of the British envoy how much more so that of the Notables. But we must look a little further. Calonne's logic as to the means of solving French financial problems has convinced posterity to an extraordinary degree. Every schoolboy since the nineteenth century knows that the crisis could only be resolved by taxing the privileged and accepting Calonne's proposals and that only the nobility's untrammelled selfishness in defence of their fiscal privileges prevented this happy consummation. But was this really so? For many sound reasons Calonne's logic was less apparent to contemporaries with experience of government. The new *subvention territoriale* was to be a tax *in kind* levied upon the harvest, attractive perhaps to the doctrinaire physiocrat but scarcely so to the actual producer who was far more resentful of levies in kind upon his crops than to fixed money taxes levied by the government. To levy such a tax would necessitate a complete new cadastral survey and teams of new officials. Hence it was far from offering an immediate solution. Secondly, the putative (and it could be no more) revenue from such a levy was estimated at 80 million *livres* – almost a half of the deficit Calonne estimated for 1786. Such a sum might service a debt but it would not obliterate it nor remove recourse to further borrowing. In short, it did not offer, to the seasoned examiner, a different answer to the problem.

Calonne threw in other so-called reforms of a highly contentious nature. The first was a return to free trade in grain to favour producers' revenues and hence to make the new *subvention* healthier. Another was a return to a money *corvée*. The Notables had lived through the Flour War and the Six Edicts and here was another physiocrat threatening to expose the country to the untold upheaval such policies might produce. It is not to be wondered at that the Notables threw out Calonne's proposals. What is to be wondered at is that Calonne succeeded in convincing posterity that he possessed the instant solution, an achievement perhaps attributable to a continuing penchant in the nineteenth century for *laissez-faire* and the inner conviction that privilege alone was the bedrock of financial disorder. Here we pass to a related consideration. The intellectual climate of the day to which the world of international finances and the European literate public belonged believed firmly in the perniciousness of privilege and the virtues of a free-market economy. Hence Calonne's proposals amounted to a propaganda campaign aimed at appealing to those very convictions in a desperate attempt to restore the government's borrowing power. The rejection of his projects however left behind it the public airing of a gross deficit and the knowledge that Calonne had failed in his attempts to cut it.

We are all familiar enough with the existence of an economic crisis and with an economic crisis intensified by talking about such a crisis. This was the legacy bequeathed by Calonne (dismissed February 1787) to his successor Loménie de Brienne, together with the knowledge that the Assembly of Notables was no solution to his problems. It is incredible that Brienne succeeded in raising 187 million *livres* in loans against annuities though he did so on very unfavourable terms to the monarchy and through an Amsterdam which was reluctant to admit the fragility of its past investments. The sum was, in any case, quite incapable of meeting government demands. For added to Brienne's problems, the problems of international finance, were other particular problems reminiscent of 1770. The disastrous harvests of 1786 slowed down the collection of tax revenues and caused considerable defaulting on payments and hence precipitated amongst accountants a number of bankruptcies which reverberated throughout the French fiscal system. The credit of accountants depended totally upon the expectation of tax revenues: who would use their credit notes if the likelihood of redemption was reduced? Hence Brienne found himself confronted with likely troubles in the absorption of ordinary revenues into the government treasury. When he carried his projects for tax reform before the *parlements* it was as a desperate man stripped of any line of action other than pleading with this body to widen the tax net.

The French monarchy, and not for the first time, had become ensnared in its debts. Unless reform offered guarantees to creditors, repudiation of the debt offered the only way out. But Louis XVI and his ministers did not see this as a viable alternative perhaps because private credit so permeated the entire fabric of government finance. Hence the futile final confrontation with the *parlements* which was to bring down both monarchy and aristocracy. The crisis of the *ancien régime* was in first instance a crisis of credit. It was also a crisis in which the very essence of monarchical power and the foundations of government were up for debate. A whole Pandora's box of discontents was abruptly opened and the discussions of previously armchair philosophers gained topical relevance.

The Old Order Changeth

After the mid-1760s Europe as a whole, but the west in particular, had moved into an age of crisis whose repercussions are apparent in almost every aspect of government and social and economic life. It was in the west that the demographic upsurge had by the sixties produced an uncomfortable imbalance between population and economic performance. Even in years of normal harvests the number of those unable to make their resources stretch without recourse to begging was rapidly growing – a phenomenon remarkable even in Britain where the best balance between population and supply had been struck.

The road to destitution usually lay through accumulated debt. The farmer borrowed to see his way through one agricultural year against the proceeds of the next harvest. Each year of personal difficulty saw fresh borrowing until his credit-worthiness was used up and he was either driven townwards in search of labour or took to the road. France in 1767 saw the most stringent attempts ever made to stem the rising tide of vagrancy by penal legislation, increasing the police force (though even then it only represented 4800 individuals for a population of almost 26 million) and setting up *dépôts de mendicité* (houses of correction) for vagrants without recent work records. All this met with relatively little effect and no more successful were work projects to employ the rural poor during the dead season.

The poor themselves were not protestors but the same could not be said for those fighting to remain on the right side of the line marking sufficiency from destitution. The vehemence of city riots in London, Madrid and several French towns in the north and east, Nancy, Metz, Amiens, Lille, in the late sixties is a significant manifestation of strain after decades relatively free from such disturbances. Setting aside London riots many of these were simple grain riots in which the towns enacted traditional patterns of protest against rising prices. Sometimes, as we have seen in Madrid, they were exacerbated by government essays in *laissez-faire* and sometimes political dissidents used such discontent to further their ends. By a European reckoning London in the sixties and again after the Gordon Riots of the eighties had the worst reputation in this respect. All western capital or large provincial cities, lived on their nerves. Another aspect of the crisis of the sixties was the slump in traditional woollen industries manifest throughout Europe. This slump projected thousands in England, France, the Dutch Republic and Germany into severe difficulties.

Governments could not remain immune to the crisis. The Seven Years' War had strained the financial resources of almost every participant to the full. In every state in Europe in the aftermath of war some vital decisions had to be taken to cut government costs and to restore funds to a healthier state. From this period we have seen that Russian monarchs, for example, sought to cut costs by reducing the numbers of nobles in state service whilst increasing attacks were made in the Habsburg lands on clerical property etc. and the thorny question of tax reform hovered ubiquitously. Those monarchies which looked to land tax as a basis for government revenue were in particular difficulties because to lift taxation meant both a debate with those institutions whose right it was to contest the level of these taxes with the monarchy and because how much one could wrest from a rural populace depended upon how much that populace contributed to church, seigneur and landlord. The financial crisis of the late sixties in France had demonstrated the utter vulnerability of that country's fiscal system. Since the land tax stretched low down the scale to men who became during protracted bad harvests unable to make ends meet, and since revenues were collected by a hierarchy of accountants advancing sums against recoupment from below, widespread defaulting at the bottom could provoke a major fiscal crisis.

Yet neither this crisis, nor the battle with the *parlements* which triggered off their exile, provoked revolution. European governments in the main survived the difficult sixties and the early seventies by avoiding armed conflict and by attempting to strengthen the control of the central government over state revenues or by recourse to new fiscal expedients. In the early seventies the Dutch money market settled down after a period of dislocation and was to continue relatively steady until the embroilment in the American War.

Yet the crisis of the late sixties and early seventies had some psychological importance and it increased the sensitivity of government creditors, a sensitivity which extended down the social scale to every man of moderate means. The French government and the government agencies, the *Ferme Générale*, the different provincial estates, even the general assembly of the French clergy, borrowed from a broad social spectrum at moderate interest rates and were caught up in the process of state finances. The fortunes of the *rentiers* were hence involved in the continuing solvency of the French monarchy.

The crisis of the late sixties in France was almost a dress rehearsal for that of the eighties. A crisis of government credit existed within the framework of a social and economic crisis, the product of diminished harvests and industrial slump and of the longer-term unfavourable balance between population and supply. The important difference was that in 1774 the dismissal of the *parlements* sparked off no further change. If there was a section of society with political aspirations it did not formulate its grievances. It was to be quite otherwise in the eighties.

In 1788 the Notables called for no tax reform without the summoning of the Estates General and the monarchy saw no alternative but to accept. Necker who had replaced Brienne proposed a doubling of the Third Estate which was presumed to indicate voting by head and not by order at the Estates General. Suddenly, a simple constitutional redeployment was made available which within the framework of the existing constitution could realize the aspirations of the politically discontended. This group had been nurtured on a vociferous, critical pamphlet literature. Its political muscles had only been flexed in salon, or provincial academy. Before 1788 there was certainly little consensus about a way forward or a vision of the Estates General as a means to power sharing. Perhaps the critics of government had believed that the *parlement*'s stand against despotism was on their behalf. If that is so, then *parlement*'s shunning of any change in the historic structure of the Estates General was a major disillusionment, rupturing any concept of aristocracy united with the Third Estate against despotism and replacing it by one of overt conflict between aristocracy and bourgeoisie. Theoretically it might seem this replacement should have made possible, by the time the Estates General met, an alliance between monarchy and bourgeoisie since the clear opponent of the one to this point had been the aristocracy. But this was not really a possibility. The monarchy gave in to a call for the Estates General because it could see no way out of an impasse. It was buying time. It did not see itself as ceding ground even to aristocratic constitutionalism let alone to power-sharing with any broader section of society. When the speech from the throne opened the Estates General and Barentin, Keeper of the Seals, made explicit that in spite of the doubling of the Third Estate vote by order was intended, then the Third Estate became aware of its isolation. It perceived itself as stranded somewhere between a monarchy with pretensions to despotism and an aristocracy with claims of sole right to temper monarchical decisions and it realized that both were prepared to use the Third Estate to their own ends but not to recognize its claims to a periodic voice in the government of the land.

The confidence born of several decades of discussion and belief in the quintessential rectitude rectitude of their struggle strengthened the collective will of the Third Estate to stand firm. Believing the monarchy was about to dissolve the Estates General by force and was attempting to inhibit the discussions of the Third Estate by the closure of its place of assembly, the members withdrew to a local tennis court and, shaking in their shoes, refused in the Tennis Court Oath of June 1789 to disband until the monarchy had ceded two basic constitutional points: the one vote by head and not by order: the other the periodic recall of the Estates General. Insistence upon these demands constitute what historians have defined as the bourgeois revolution of 1789 which left aristocratic pretensions to power-sharing a long way behind. Like their Dutch and other western European counterparts, the members of the Third Estate had behind them a vast political literature. They shared a profound disillusionment with the ineptitude of government and they believed they could do better.

We are singularly well informed as to who represented the Third Estate in 1789. The unit of election for the Estates General was the *bailliage*, a territorial unit used in the middle ages for the administration of civil justice, and the *bailliage* court itself was charged with conducting the final elections to which villages and towns sent their elected delegates. At municipal elections, professional men, officeholders and municipal councillors were in effect accorded a double vote for professional bodies were allowed to elect two representatives for every hundred members, guild members only one per hundred and lawyers often had a quadruple chance of representation, as members of the corps of lawyers, as office-holders in particular courts, as village syndics (very commonly chosen by villagers) or as town councillors. Not surprisingly the elections resulted in an overwhelming victory for lawyers and officials who filled something approaching 85 per cent of the overall delegation. Literate, articulate, with some experience of administration in the localities, two months spent at Versailles brought them together as a group with identifiable interests. During these weeks the nuclei of political clubs formed and certain persuasive figures like the Abbé Sieyès, author of *Qu'est-ce que le Tiers Etat*, and Mirabeau, rebel son of the physiocratic Comte, who had a mastery for synthesis and considerable oratorical talents emerged as spokesmen so that an inchoate grouping rapidly acquired something approaching coherence. Even so, many were afraid to leave the meeting hall where they had taken a corporate oath lest they should be arrested. A vacuum of political power had made possible their appearance in the limelight: that they remained on stage was assured by the behaviour of two other major actors in this drama of epic dimensions. The first was the monarchy: the second the revolt of the people of Paris. A third factor was the reluctance of any major foreign power to intervene in French political life.

When the monarchy had summoned the Estates General it had done so with little or no idea of what would happen or what would be the next step. The resignation of Brienne and the retaking of Necker into the ministry had been in part a sop to public opinion and in part an assurance to the *rentiers* that the government would honour its debts and not pronounce itself bankrupt. But neither Necker's presence nor the stand taken by the Third Estate was something the monarchy was prepared to countenance in the long term. During the spring and early summer, a time of great personal suffering for Louis XVI and Marie Antoinette for their eldest son died, Louis XVI took two decisions. The first was to disperse the Estates General by force by calling 30,000 troops into Versailles. The second was to dismiss Necker and presumably pronounce the bankruptcy of the French state which would mean a complete repudiation of the government debt and hence the failing of some important financial houses. What the King intended to do next is far from clear and there is every indication that he himself was now putting his trust in time – a quick re-seizure of initiative from the Estates and a cooling period. If so, the miscalculation was considerable.

On 12 July, news filtered into Paris of Necker's dismissal. The events of the next day, Sunday, are something of a mystery, but as a non-working day, the exposure of the populace to political agitation coming either from the rebel politicians at Versailles or soap box orators or the henchmen of the *rentiers* are obvious possibilities. Public opinion, shaped by high prices, demagogy, a scurrilous pamphlet literature which undermined the position of the royal family by vilifying the Queen and rendering the King as the victim of her machinations within a corrupt court, moved in support of the perpetuation of the Estates General. The Palais Royal was the arena of much haranguing and what is clear is that even in working-class *faubourgs* the populace identified its future well-being with the existence of the Estates and saw the dismissal of Necker as the prelude to their closure by force. On 14 July occurred the great revolt of Paris which consisted of a bifurcated attack, first on the Bastille, symbol of despotism, but also reputedly the arsenal of Paris, and second on the Invalides where more arms were kept. Insofar as the symbol of despotism was maintained by a mere handful of royal troops and found only to contain a madman and a couple of debtors – it was, after all, a rather high-class prison – and its resources in arms and munitions were scantier than anticipated, the attack on the Bastille was a less heroic episode than it was subsequently made out to be in the legend of Revolution. But the newly accumulated troops in the capital, who were to have been the agents whereby the recalcitrant Third Estate was dismissed, neither tried nor deemed themselves able to confront the insurgent Paris masses. The means to contain the capital were simply not there and the revolt of Paris demonstrated that royal authority did not run in the capital. This revolt consolidated and made possible the continued existence of the Estates General.

Why Paris rose in this way has been recounted a thousand times. The difficult conditions described for the sixties were repeated with a new force in the second half of the eighties. France experienced after 1784 a run of bad harvests reaching a climax in 1788 with one of the worst on record for the eighteenth century. In Brittany harvest failure was accompanied by virulent typhus and typhoid epidemics. In Gascony, Champagne, Alsace, France Comté and Languedoc it was coincident with a crisis of over-production in the wine industry, visible for many years, which depressed prices. In the industrial regions of Normandy and the north-east and in Lyons grain shortage and industrial slump caused mass destitution. Into the cities, and into the capital in particular, poured the hungry of the countryside in the belief that there the attention of authorities would be focused on their plight. Paris had in particular a work project at Montmartre which during the winter served as a magnet for the unemployed hungry of the Ile de France and many had to be turned away. These rural immigrants were in competition with the indigenous poor for charitable resources and were a dissident and crime-prone force in the streets. Even if he was in work, the indigenous Paris day labourer was only in command of rates which, given bread at high costs, would as to 80 per cent be consumed on the purchase of this one commodity alone. The rising of Paris, as far as it can be ascertained, was a rising of the native working populace and not of the dispossessed of the countryside but it was a movement wherein high prices and suffering were connected with *ancien régime* government. Whatever direction was given to the rising of Paris by orators and journalists, such a persuasion was omnipresent. The Bastille and the Invalides stormed, the crowd's next significant accomplishment was the lynching of Bertier de Sauvigny, the intendant responsible for the provisioning of the capital.

It is worth looking at the Revolution on 15 July and asking what had been achieved. What did the Revolution mean so far? What the insurgent Third Estate had achieved was a clear extension of political power to themselves, to men of education and moderate means, an achievement confirmed by the Constituent Assembly's subsequent enactment of the active/passive citizenship qualification with only the former, taxpayers of a sum equal to three days' labour and above, actually enfranchised. *Ancien régime* monarchy had been brought to an end. Yet the representatives of the Third Estates were monarchists and the bulk prepared to concede extensive powers to the monarchy, though it was to be a constitutional monarchy. Along with the collapse of *ancien régime* monarchy was implied the abolition of *ancien régime* institutions of government, councils, ministers, intendants, provincial estates, *parlements* and law courts with their hordes of venal officials. A new and streamlined system must replace the tangle of overlapping authorities and this would allow the power-sharing principles of the

Revolution to extend into the localities. The Constituent Assembly was placed in a position to do what no *ancien régime* monarch had ever been able to do, to abolish an entire institutional structure and create a new one from first principles.

There was of course the stumbling block of venality, the fact that in these obsolete courts the personnel owned their positions. One aspect of all the revolutions of the late eighteenth century was their commitment to the sanctity of property, a commitment to be embodied in the Declaration of the Rights of Man and of the Citizen. But the men of '89 reconciled their belief in the sanctity of property with the abolition of venal office by the simple promise of compensation.

The Declaration of the Rights of Man and of the Citizen owed something to its American precedent but it stands as one of the most significant summaries of European Enlightenment principles. The rights with which it was concerned, equality before the law, freedom of opinion, of the press and of the individual from arbitrary arrest, the abolition of privilege based on birth or the purchase of titles, *la carrière ouverte aux talents*, spoke to the convictions of the critics of *ancien régime* government and society. The new France was to be a place of upwardly mobile educated men of means. If the language of rights looked universal it soon became clear when the first constitution was drawn up that full citizenship was only for men with a property quali-fication. Women were deemed irrelevant to the scheme and the position of colonial slaves had yet to be worked out. Viewed as a whole, and in spite of the length of the Declaration, the concept of rights was an important point of departure from which over the next two centuries further developments would occur. The men of '89 had yet to embark upon fiscal reform but they would do so under the physiocratic persua-sion of the desirability of a single land tax without exemptions and as men of the eighteenth century attempting to run a state in financial difficulties, the property of the Catholic Church would be the first sacrifice. This was a logical Enlightenment stance.

But would the newly empowered men of the Constituent Assembly confront the problems of rural France? They were hardly given the choice. Within a fortnight of the revolt of Paris occurred the fourth rising in the Revolutionary quartet, that of rural France, which in purely social terms was probably the most consequential of them all. Rural France had recorded its grievances in the spring of '89 about tax levels, about the multiplicity of venal officials, about the tithe which went to the wrong clerics, and above all about the seigneur and his agents who took a cut of the crop and gave nothing in return. The *cahiers* had requested the abolition of *cens* and *champart* (usually by redemption) and had listed the inconveniences attached to *banalités* and the delays, costs and inadequacies of seigneurial justice. Curiously enough, the dues were the least of the triple tolls (of church, government and seigneur) made upon the peasant's income. Usually they did not exceed 2 per cent of the total (though they could rise to 10 per cent). Yet in 1789 they were to bear the brunt of peasant hostility. This phenomenon is the more remarkable when a century previously peasant protest had been almost entirely focused upon government levies. Such a shift was once explained by the increasing onerousness of the dues in the eighteenth century as a deliberate piece of seigneurial policy to make the seigneurie more lucrative. More recently, historians have rejected such an interpretation in favour of a thesis positing a contraction in peasant hostility to government taxation once the government abandoned the extraordinary taxes it had sought to impose in the seventeenth century. With this contraction came a focusing of antipathy instead upon a man who was increasingly irrelevant to the rural community. In particular is noteworthy over the century a decline in the judicial services to the community offered by the seigneur, forcing the peasants into the costly and inconvenient royal courts for business, particularly minor land litigation, which needed prompt and urgent attention. The seigneurial prison lay everywhere in ruins. The peasant risings against the seigneur in 1789 were not the proverbial storm in the hitherto cloudless sky. The growth in sociability patterns based on the *cabaret* (inn or bar) speculatively contributed to a growth in peasant propensity to overt anti-seigneurial hostility in the last decades of the *ancien régime*. There is also evidence to suggest that many small seigneurs, lacking a team of agents and officials, had difficulties in getting in their dues, particularly where the peasant was actual owner of his own land and hence where the threat of eviction or a progressively unfavourable lease had no significance. Moreover, by 1788, after a run of unfavourable harvests and with a slump in supporting rural industries, communities were ensnared in debt to an inordinate degree. In the debt web the seigneur was often involved, sometimes allowing the dues to remain unpaid, sometimes advancing grain to see the peasant through difficult months against the forthcoming harvest. In this way debts could build up and anti-seigneurial resentment could intensify.

There were other problems too arising from the particularly difficult circumstances of 1788–9. Hunger put people on the roads: vagrants prepared to catch as catch can: town dwellers – dismissed servant girls, apprentices, textile workers convinced their rural relatives would share what they had – made treks for villages: rural dwellers persuaded they might make out better in the towns made in the opposite direction. All were dangerous insofar as they might seek to wrest by force what they could not get by other means. In the summer of 1789 there were unprecedented numbers on the roads. The summer months were the worst for the hungry because of the running out of the old supplies. The French call such a period *la soudure* (literally the joining or welding) because whilst the next harvest was imminent, prices and supplies reflected the conditions of the previous year. At such a time many hands were unemployed awaiting the harvest and the fear grew that the hungry and idle might cut down the grain before it ripened in the field. This fear was one of the two apprehensions which made up the Great Fear. The other was that the seigneur and local authorities in order to keep the peasant in tax bondage were withholding the news that the Constituent Assembly had in fact abolished the dues. Somehow, and how this happened can only be explained by reference to peasant psychology, to poor communications and ignorance of what was going on in Versailles and Paris, fear of the seigneur and of 'brigands' (desperate men who would desecrate the crops) became linked and the brigand was seen as the putative henchman of the seigneur. Isolated vagrants were exaggerated into forerunners of armies of brigands about to terrorize the peasantry.

The result, in the last weeks of July, was a series of rural risings with a number of epicentres, notably Burgundy, which then rippled along river valleys and significant arteries, leaving out enclaves like the Seine Valley, the Beauce, Brittany and most of Languedoc, and which were almost uniform in their characteristics. The peasantry attacked the *châteaux*. They burned the registers of the seigneurie. They mishandled seigneurial agents. In the north and east the only weapons used were pitchforks and farm tools: in the south a few shots were fired. But what was truly significant was the lack of real violence it required to destroy seigneurialism. Seigneurial authority, of which the dwindling and often pathetic spectacle of a prison-less, court-less, police-less seigneurial justice was just one manifestation, was, setting aside a few huge employers of men and resources like the recently studied family of Saulx-Tavanes, a house of cards. It stood because it had been considered part of the establishment, state, church and seigneur, but once royal authority had collapsed in 1789 its days were numbered. A police force of under 5000 for 26 million people was no deterrent force. The army had no means to hold the masses in check. Intendants had abandoned office and the urban elites looked on afraid and helpless as the rural revolt shook most of France. The peasantry, or more specifically the small and modest landowners and holders (those who paid dues on the one hand and had something to fear from the depredations of the down and out on the other), had driven a wedge right through the Constituent Assembly's intrinsic respect for the sanctity of property. Someone had owned those dues and though the Assembly concurred on 4 August in their abolition, it sought to draw an impossible line between dues which had brought in a revenue and for which compensation should be paid, and those which consisted of servile labour services which should go without redemption.

The elaborations of the Assembly had no meaning for the rural masses. Those amongst them who owned their land but had had to pay seigneurial levies of something between 2 and 10 per cent of their gross proceeds now held on to this portion of their revenues. Those who had a landlord in the long run found they had to countenance a rise in rent over and above the amount previously paid in dues. Yet the French peasant had been drawn into line with his English and Netherlands counterpart. From henceforth the only sacrosanct property was the ownership of land. *Ancien régime* privilege had been struck a very consequential, indeed as far as the bulk of the populace was concerned, its hardest blow. For the modest owner/occupier it was the last beneficial thing he was to get out of the Revolution.

Conclusion

An American Revolution which destroyed an empire, a Dutch revolt, however abortive, the cities of the Austrian Netherlands split into rival factions linked only by bitter, overt hostility to Vienna, Magyar nobles insurgent, Poland rousing itself to attempt a rising to forestall total elimination, the evolution of radical politics in Britain, a revolt in Geneva to broaden the basis of city-state government and the beginnings in France of one of the world's most consequential political upheavals, brought the *ancien régime* to a noisy and violent close. Equally obviously these were only the major episodes in a disruptive push against established government. By 1792 a monarch lay murdered in Sweden by a noble plot. Twenty years previously an 'enlightened' reforming minister, Struensee, was decapitated in denmark. Ireland for most of the 1760s and 1780s at least in Munster and Ulster was rent by antitithe riots and vicious agrarian disturbances. The White-boys, Peep-o-day boys and Ribbon men, founding fathers of Irish rural opposition, came into being and in the eighties the Volunteer movement to gain Ireland a separate legislature emerged. Religious revolt was brewing in northern Italy which would erupt in the 1790s in the Viva Maria risings. What caused all this discord? Can any common thread be found running through this disturbed, uneasy Europe which might be used as an explanation or was it mere coincidence that all this hostility was virtually contemporaneous? Why did the *ancien régime* not die a natural seemly death splendidly encased in baroque decadence, a girl on a swing in a *fête galante* grown sour, feeble and disagreeable in old age? Who wanted change and why and, if change was needful, why could it not be achieved without revolt and revolution?

Text-books need titles and titles are proffered as instant though often inadequate signposts to the spint or flavour of a period. The closing decades of the *ancien régime* have been dubbed the 'Age of Enlightenment' or the 'Age of Enlightened Despotism'. Forty years ago they were heralded by R. R. Palmer as the 'Age of the Democratic Revolution' trimmed down by French consensus to the 'Age of the Atlantic Revolution'. Then more than three decades ago, Alfred Cobban proffered the 'Age of the Aristocratic Reaction'. All these qualifications were intended to pick out a common link and in all of them one recognizes something of the truth. Yet none can totally satisfy for none can simultaneously express the omnipresence of decaying institutions, social inequalities, privileges sometimes designated liberties, political corruption and financial disorder on the one hand and on the other the complexities of the movement for radical change or that for restoring a previous *status quo*. Moreover what applies to one or a group of states is without universal application. We have seen that the Enlightenment was in many ways a formidable intellectual movement and one which gives the eighteenth century much of its greatness in its dauntless demolition work and occasional constructive strength as embodied in the American or French Declaration of Rights. But in other ways it was an eclectic, diffuse and highly restricted phenomenon and one marked by lack of consensus which became ever more apparent after 1789. Similarly, enlightened despotism had hardly given Europe a common experience for it was an egregious experience of greatest moment in the fragmented conditions of the Empire and never had any relevance to 'Atlantic Europe'.

The 'Age of the Aristocratic Reaction' proffers an alternative because it points to the evident confrontation between monarchy and aristocracy which in at least five instances, those of the Austrian Netherlands, the traditional Habsburg lands, Hungary, Sweden and France, left the monarchies without a clear body of support. Yet this thesis has been stretched to posit a ubiquitous growth in noble social power and political pretensions throughout the eighteenth century which simply does not stand up to close analysis. The thesis rests upon four considerations. The first is the apparent increase in noble claims against government. The second is the attempt by some nobilities (Russian in particular) to slough off state service but hold on to economic privilege. Thirdly there is an argued, though now shown to be undemonstrable, increase in noble monopolization of the best jobs in army, church and state. Lastly in support of the thesis is advanced a speculative increase in the weight of seigneurialism attributable either to the reimposition of lapsed seigneurial dues and a reconversion of payments in kind or to the evident increase of serf obligations in Russia and the apparent failure of the emancipation movement in Prussia and the Habsburg lands. In short the thesis of the aristocratic reaction embraces a clearly definable resurgence of noble power at the expense of monarchy and of the rest of society – in particular at the expense of a bourgeoisie jealous of a noble stranglehold on the best jobs and an increasingly oppressed peasant sector.

Yet when each national record is pursued there is nothing to suggest that the number of noble bishops, intendants, bureaucrats or army officers was any greater in 1789 than what it had been a century before. Even the much cited Ségur ordinance of 1781 which restricted entry into the highest military grades in France to those of noble origin did not alter the noble/commoner ratios in the army. True an analysis of the Swedish officer class of 1760 showed that two-thirds were noble whilst in 1719 only a third had been so but this reflected the abnormality of the officer death rate and promotional prospects in the somewhat difficult conditions of the Great Northern War. Where there are apparent increases in noble council power in Prussia we find that this was a deliberate attempt on the part of the monarchy to curtail not noble, but bureaucratic control.

In gross aggregate terms noble wealth was almost certainly increasing since the nobility was in command of land, rents and surplus commodities and insofar as the opportunities were available, was able to put money into commerce and government borrowing. But this does not necessarily mean that the nobility's grip on the rest of the populace was tighter than ever before. The extensionof serfdom in Russian lands was attributable to the policy of a monarchy interested in extending fiscal control over frontier peoples. Austrian nobles saw no economic advantage in retaining serfdom since there was a buoyant labour market and put up no opposition to its abolition. On the other hand, there is no evidence to suggest that the Prussian or the Austrian peasant courted an emancipation which did not embody guarantees of a land settlement.

Then there is the fashionable thesis of the seigneurial reaction lent weight in France by two types of evidence: on the one hand manuals which appeared with increasing frequency after 1760 to show seigneurs how to maximize their profits and on the other hand the *cahiers* of grievances of 1789 which enumerate peasant woes concerning seigneurial oppression. Resentment, presently to be explored further, is however one thing, actual widespread evidence of an aristocratic reaction in social or economic terms, quite another.

This brings us to politics. The tendency of continental states in the seventeenth and eighteenth centuries was for a maximization of royal power at the expense of those institutions which acted in any way as a check on central authority, provincial estates, diets or in the French instance the *parlements*. The record of France in the late seventeenth century suggests that on the whole such institutions were more tractable than they subsequently became. On the other hand, never had they been more tested or flagrantly abused by ministers and monarch than they were in the course of the financial squabbles of the eighteenth century in which the French monarchy sought to bludgeon the *parlements* into acceptance of measures beyond their constitutional competence.

The French state was far from being the only one in which privileged institutions were the only check upon monarchical despotism and hence the only real source of organized opposition daring to question royal decisions. In this sense much eighteenth-century political protest was perforce aristocratic in origin even if, in the cases of France and the Austrian Netherlands, its basis widened in the conditions of the eighties, simply because aristocratic institutions were the most available forum of debate.

Joseph II made an outright attack on the political autonomy of the Netherlands and Hungary and however self-interested the Belgian patriciates may have been in their overt hostility, their opposition had a popular basis and was initially at least directed towards recoupment, not extension, of their authority. The same largely holds true of the curious spectacle of Swedish politics. From the 1720s the Swedish state bounced back and forth between an aristocratic constitutionalism as highly developed as that of Great Britain and in the seventies and eighties despotic monarchical control. Power was reseized by the nobility in 1792 after a noble plot had ensured the elimination of Gustavus III. The oscillations of Swedish politics were determined largely by foreign policy. In 1730 the Diet or *Riksdag* was divided into four estates and a written constitution drawn up during Charles XII's absence in Russia had reduced the king's power to relatively little. A council of sixteen was responsible to the *Riksdag* which met every three years – a truly regularized parliamentary practice. The aristocratic grouping in the *Riksdag* supported the Hat party, protagonists of a French alliance, and was severely discredited after a disastrous involvement in the Seven Years' War. The Caps, who had a basis of support in the other three estates – clergy, burghers and free peasants – seized the opportunity in the 1760s to introduce a number of liberal reforms which included freedom of the press and a reduction in military expenditure. The Caps looked to a Russian alliance as the best way of guaranteeing Sweden's continuance in Pomerania and Finland. A population of a little over two million was ill-fitted to support a dynamic foreign policy and Sweden's main concern was the preservation of what she had got. In 1771 the King, Gustavus III, engineered a veritable *coup d'état* and formulated a new constitution reducing the power of the *Riksdag* and increasing that of the king. Gustavus looked to the free peasants for support for his policies as Charles XI had done when he had persuaded them to surrender their constitutional privileges in order to curtail those of the aristocracy. Piecemeal attempts were made to stimulate economic growth establishing free cities and ports at Marshand and in Finland which bore little or no relevance to Swedish economic performance and Gustavus III indulged in some of the window-dressing of classic enlightened despotism.

But his ambitions in the foreign sector included in 1786 war with Russia which threatened to increase taxation and the Act of Union in 1789 was intended to nullify the power of the *Riksdag*. Faced with a loss of constitutional powers and a foreign policy transcending national resources, the nobility eliminated the ambitious king. This could be pointed to as a prime example of an aristocratic reaction but it would be difficult to claim the Swedish aristocracy had done much more than protect the traditional Swedish constitution and prevent a repetition of the disasters of the Northern War. Nor did the death of one king leave the nobility dictators of Swedish politics.

Only in Poland where noble claims paralysed government and ultimately destroyed the state, and in Britain where lords and gentry virtually shared power between them, could it be claimed that the aristocracy was throughout the period in control of the struggle with monarchy or able to assume the initiative to force the pace of political events. Elsewhere the nobility merely exploited its constitutional powers of rejection to the full until in the 1780s in France, the Austrian Netherlands and Hungary they felt themselves pushed into an impossible position by monarchical encroachment upon their traditional powers and as guardians of essential 'liberties' adopted a more assertive role. In the case of the Austrian Netherlands it was a question of protesting against national extinction. The French *parlements* never parted for one instant from the path of constitutionalism, merely insisting that the monarchy, if it needed fundamentally to tamper with the tax structure of France, should consult the Estates General. In so doing they opened the flood gates to a movement which left them a long way behind and which was a radical departure from previously experienced political life.

In the struggle between monarchy and aristocracy it is fair to say there were no victors. Neither could exist without the other. Insofar as European aristocracies ranged themselves in the west against despotism then, in political terms, the late eighteenth century was the 'Age of the Aristocratic Reaction' but such a concept does not take us far enough. Contemporaneous with, or arising out of, or in the special case of Great Britain, provoking a kind of aristocratic reaction, existed another movement aimed at broadening the basis of political and social power. This movement, recognizable in the North American Colonies in the 1770s, in the Dutch Republic in the early 1780s, in Geneva, in the Austrian Netherlands, in Britain and France in the late eighties, is the one baptized by Palmer as that of the 'Democratic Revolution'. He identified this movement as one defined by its unanimous opposition to aristocracy, the rule of self-perpetuated, self-constituted bodies. It aimed to extend participation in political life and make governments, whose record was far from satisfactory, accountable to some broader political spectrum. Historically, it looked back to a medieval past in which political organs had been more fully representative whereas since the sixteenth century they had been sacrificial lambs to encroaching monarchical authority. But the movement also justified itself by reference to more modern theories of natural law and the contractual basis for power. With the very special exception of the Westminster Committee in England no part of this movement demanded universal suffrage. It recognized the apathy of 75 per cent and upwards of society towards an extension of political rights though it talked in terms of the sovereignty of the people. It conceived of 'people' however in a very limited sense. As the French ambassador commenting to his government on the characteristics of the Dutch patriot movement noted: 'By people is not meant the most wretched part of the nation, men deprived of means of living in a condition of comfort. Only the class of bourgeois possessing a certain capital and contributing in a certain proportion to the expenses of the Republic is included in this term.'

Events in Geneva permit one to see such principles at work with close statistical precision. The Genevan revolt was directed against the monopoly of power by a narrow aristocracy, a closed oligarchy who directed the city state from the Legislative Council of Two Hundred and the yet more elite Small Council, or Senate, which had the right to veto the decisions of the Council of Two Hundred. This Council nominally represented 3000 *citoyens et bourgeois* who held General Council or town meetings for electoral purposes. The adult male population of Geneva, however, also included 4000 *natifs* (professional men and those of moderate means) and 4500 *habitants* (these were manual workers and servants). Opposition crystallized amongst the *natifs* who from 1766 appealed for a broadening of political power to allow a proportion of the *natifs* political representation which effectively would have converted them into *bourgeois*. At the town meeting in 1781 the *bourgeois* conceded that 460 *natifs* should be thus given voting power but the Small Council applied its veto and in face of such intransigent hostility a coup was engineered to overthrow the oligarchic constitution. At this juncture, the guaranteeing powers of the Genevan Constitution, France and Zurich helped by Sardinia responded with a military blockade and after a virtual siege the main leaders of the revolt fled, some like Clavière to Paris to enjoy some limelight during the Revolution as a hack-writer for Mirabeau and as a collaborator with Brissot.

To endow the movements in Geneva or in the Dutch Republic or those of the Belgian Patriots or the French Third Estate with the qualification, democratic, is obviously to use the word in a sense very different from that current in our times. Indeed, these movements look much more like the liberal constitutional movements of Restoration Europe in their cautious approach to an extension of political power to the wealthy and literate. For this reason, the French long preferred the concept of an Atlantic Revolution as lacking the commitment of the democratic qualification. Insofar as the movement for the broadening of political power was confined to the United States, where it also had some claim to being democratic in the fullest sense, to England, perhaps Ireland, certainly to France and the Low Countries – though it had no relevance to Spain and Portugal whilst Geneva was hardly ocean-washed – the description is fair enough yet a mere geographical expression cannot convey the desire for political change which Palmer tried to capture. This is a pity because it was the pressure for political change which distinguished certain societies in the closing decades of the *ancien régime* and in France events were carried far beyond an aristocratic revolt – which alone might merely have resulted in stalemate – to challenge and then destroy the political foundations of the *ancien régime*. Whereas in Geneva, the United Provinces and the Austrian Netherlands, lawyers, bureaucrats, merchant bankers and shopkeepers proved incapable of unseating the holder of political power, in France circumstances and developments allowed the professional classes, lawyers, office-holders and bureaucrats, gain control of political events.

Why was radical political agitation confined to that part of western Europe characterized by a diverse political tradition, municipal autonomy, limited monarchy or *despotisme légal*? This question is perhaps simple to answer. There were countries with a history of authority hedged about with checks and balances where the cry was for an *extension* and rational formulation of power sharing not the question of power sharing *per se*. It was a matter of natural growth in which the most articulate and substantial citizens sought to share in government structure. Behind them lay a century or more of publicized debate on the distribution of power which rejected out of hand any kind of authoritarianism. The agitation for an extension of the franchise in Britain, although in London and large provincial cities it embraced the principle of extension to the working classes, only envisaged a revision of the British constitution to dispel the abuses in the corrupt and decadent voting system where rotten boroughs and patronage, hustings based on free beer etc., were the incredible means whereby the aristocracy perpetuated its political power. In Geneva, it was merely a question of broadening the electorate by some 10–15 per cent. In the Netherlands where power had historically shifted between Orangists and estates on the one hand and urban oligarchies on the other or occasionally between maritime and inland provinces, the Patriots sought an elimination of the Orangists and an ill-defined reorganization of provincial and municipal power to break the power of landed nobility and urban oligarchies and to give political say to a larger wedge of men of at least modest affluence. This demanded the forging of a new, if not radically new, constitutional basis which was never carried out because of foreign intervention. In the Austrian Netherlands opposition began as an aristocratic reaction against Joseph II's reforms. Factions then emerged, some aiming merely at the restoration of the *status quo* and others demanding a broader distribution of power within provinces whose autonomy was to be restored. Even in France, a breakdown of events in 1788–9 shows the more radical proponents of political change focusing attention upon an antique institution, the Estates General, as the means whereby French political life was to be given a broader basis.

Clearly then the movements of the eighties have a common thread. The success of France in achieving what the Dutch, Belgians and Genevans sought in their own way to realize, stemmed perhaps more than anything else from a confirmation of the politicians' stand by the intervention of Paris and the reluctance of foreign powers to attempt an intrusion upon French territory. Once in power the intervention of the peasantry gave a breadth to change which far transcended any reform programme envisaged elsewhere.

Between May and August 1789 the most populous country in Europe underwent a metamorphosis. There was a shift in political power to a broader constituency and the wholesale destruction of an institutional framework embracing medieval courts and provincial estates. Provincial immunities which stretched back to a time when France was not a united country were destroyed. The end of the *parlements* whose proud boast had been that they limited despotism by ensuring that it in no way contravened the fundamental laws of provincial France was abruptly achieved. Personal and corporate privileges based on birth were stifled, the ownership of office or of seigneurial rights in land disappeared. Obviously France would never be quite the same again and, because she exported the changes at bayonet point, nor would much of western Europe.

What had been destroyed was monarchical authority limited by privilege which it was not strong enough to countermand. What now existed was a smoother state absolutism which involved the intrusion of government more and more and with greater efficiency into the lives of communities and human beings and permitted no exemptions. As a result of events in France in 1789 the Constituent Assembly sought to lay down for future generations a constitutional monarchy in which the Assembly initiated and debated policy and the monarch confirmed its decisions. The state became potentially much more intrusive in the lives of citizens and communities. Government gained greater control not less.

Monarchs like Joseph II drawing upon the German cameralists had dreamed of cutting through the web of privilege to extend the influence of the state into the lives of the many and had failed conspicuously because the basis of absolutist monarchical power was insufficiently strong and to survive had to rest upon aristocratic consensus. The movements of the late eighteenth century contrived to give the state extended control by broadening the basis of its authority and destroying curtailments upon its power.

The set of prints which demonstrated the French *ancien régime* peasant burdened by noble and cleric illustrated his emancipation by reversing the roles and sitting the peasant upon the noble's shoulders and in turn, the noble sought support from the church. Around the new peasant grew bigger cabbages and the rabbits and pigeons which had picked at his crops, previously the quarry of the noble alone, lay slaughtered by the peasant's hand and were clearly on the way to his stewpot. The image was conceived in fantasy. The elimination of privilege gave the state an access to noble wealth and the means to re-assume church land and hence a kind of equality was achieved. But in no way was the peasant's tax burden lessened nor his obligations to the state diminished and the shift in political power did not mean the discovery of a magic switch to give food and employment to the needy. There were no larger cabbages; rather the reverse. The institutions of the *ancien régime*, taken cumulatively, had been considerable employers and consumers and the towns especially suffered from their demise. Indeed one has yet to discover a village or town which profited from the destruction of the *ancien régime* and what change invariably meant was the substitution of a new set of hate figures, intrusive government officials, for the old ones of seigneur and employee of the *Ferme Générale*.

Decadent privileged Europe was not of course ubiquitously destroyed in 1789. Even in France, heartland of Revolution, many of the changes of 1789 were temporary or underwent many vicissitudes. The wealthiest families in France in 1815 were still from the ancient *ancien régime* nobility but they were taxed. Moreover, the anachronistic institutional framework of government had disappeared irrevocably. Spain and Portugal where a privileged establishment was equated with national liberty clung to old ways and in Britain the establishment underwent an 'aristocratic reaction' hardening itself against the cry for political reform lest Britain and Ireland should go the way of France. Indeed, it was in England that in order to justify his condemnation of events in France, Edmund Burke wrote panegyrics to corruption as an 'infallible sign of political liberty'. Russia and the heart-lands of the Habsburg dominions contrived to preserve an immunity and an antique society and privileged institutions thus slipped into the nineteenth century. But the psychological underpinning shoring them up had undubitably been eroded. That process of erosion was the particular legacy of the eighteenth century.

Select Bibliography

Introductory Reading

Anderson, M. S., *Europe in the Eighteenth Century, 1713–1783* (1987).
Black, J., *Eighteenth Century Europe, 1700–1789* (1990).
Cobban, A., ed., *The Eighteenth Century* (1969).
Doyle, W., *The Old European Order 1660–1800* (1992).
Dukes, P., *A History of Europe, 1648–1948* (1985).
Gershoy, L., *From Despotism to Revolution 1763–1789* (1944).
Merriman, J. A., *History of Modern Europe*, vol. 1 (1996).
Tapié, V. L., *L'Europe de Marie Thérèse* (1973).
Venturi, F., *The End of the Old Regime in Europe 1768–1776* (1989).
Woloch, I., *Eighteenth Century Europe: Tradition and Progress, 1715–1789* (1982).

Chapter 1   Social and Economic Development

General

Abel, W., *Crises agraires en Europe XIIIe–XIXe siècles* (1973).
Berg, M., *Markets and Manufactures in Early Industrial Europe* (1991).
Berg, M. and Bruland, K. *Technological Revolutions in Europe: Historical Perspectives* (1998).
Bonney, R., ed., *Economic Systems and State Finance* (1995).
Braudel, F., *Civilisation and Capitalism, 15th–18th centuries*, 3 vols (1981–4).
Cipolla, C. M., ed., *Fontana Economic History of Europe*, vols 3 and 4 (1976).
Clark, P., *Small Towns in Early Modern Europe* (1995).
Davis, R., *The Rise of the Atlantic Economies* (1973).
DuPlessis, R., *Transitions to Capitalism in Early Modern Europe* (1997).
Hohenberg, P. M., and Lees, L. H., *The Making of Urban Europe* (1985).
Landes, D. S., *The Unbound Prometheus: Technological Change in Europe since 1750* (1969).

Post, J. D., *Food Shortage, Climatic Variability and Epidemic Disease in Pre-Industrial Europe. The Mortality Peak in the Early 1740s* (1985).

Rabb, T. K., and Rotberg, R. I. (eds), *Population and Economics* (1986).

Slicher van Bath, B. H., *The Agrarian History of Western Europe* A. D 500–1850 (1962).

Taylor, B., *Society and Economy in Early Modern Europe, 1450–1789. A Bibliography of Postwar Research* (1989).

Vilar, P., *A History of Gold and Money, 1450–1920* (1991).

de Vries, J., *The Economy of Europe in an Age of Crisis, 1600–1750* (1976).

de Vries, J., *European Urbanization* (1984).

Woolf, S., *The Poor in Western Europe in the Eighteenth and Nineteenth Centuries* (1986).

(a) Austrian Empire

Wright, W. E., *Serf, Seigneur and Sovereign; agrarian reform in eighteenth-century Bohemia* (1966).

(b) Dutch Republic

Van Houtte, J. A., et al., *Algemene Geschiedenis der Nederlanden*, vol. vii (1954).

de Vries, J., *The First Modern Economy: Success, Failure and Perserverance of the Dutch Economy, 1500–1815* (1997).

(c) France

Braudel, F., and Labrousse, E., *Histoire économique et sociale de la France 1660–1789* (1970).

Forster, R., 'Obstacles to agricultural growth in eighteenth century France', *American Historical Review*, (1970).

Hufton, O. H., *The Poor of Eighteenth Century France, 1750–1789* (1974).

Hufton, O. H., 'Social Conflict and the Grain Supply in Eighteenth-Century France', *Journal of Interdisciplinary History* XIV, 2 (1983).

Kaplan, S., *Provisioning Paris* (1984).

Labrousse, E., *Esquisse du mouvement des prix at des revenus en France au XVIIIe siècle*, 2 vols (1973).

Labrousse, E., *La crise de l'économie française à la fin de l'ancien régime et au début de la Révolution* (1944).

Morineau, M., *Les faux semblants d'un démarrage économique; agriculture et démographie en France XVIIIe siècle* (1971).

Norberg, K., *Rich and Poor in Grenoble 1600–1814* (1985).

(d) Germany

Gagliardo, J., *Germany under the Old Regime 1600–1790* (1991).

McIntosh, T., *Urban Decline in Early Modern Germany: Schwäbisch Hall and its region, 1650–1750* (1997).

Moeller, R. G., *Peasants and Lords in Modern Germany: recent studies in agricultural history* (1986).

Ogilvie, S. C., *Germany: a new social and economic history*, 3 vols (1996).

Sabean, D. W., *Property, Production and Family in neckerhausen 1700–1870* (1990).
Sagarra, E., *Social History of Germany 1648–1914* (1977).

(e) Italy
Woolf, S. J., *A History of Italy 1700–1860: the Social Consequences of Political Change* (1991).

(f) Poland
Cieslak, E., *Changes in Two Baltic Countries: Poland and Sweden in the eighteenth century* (1990).
Topolski, J., 'La régression économique en Pologne du XIVe au XVIIIe siècles', *Acta Poloniae Historica VII (1962).*

(g) Portugal
Marcadé, J., *Une Comarque Portugaise-ourique entre 1750 et 1800* (1971).
Silbert, A., *Le Portugal méditteranéen à la fin de l'ancien régime*, 2 vols (1966).

(h) Russia
Blum, J., *Lord and Peasant in Russia from the Ninth to the Nineteenth Century* (1961).
Clendenning, P., 'The Economic Awakening of Russia in the Eighteenth Century', *Journal of European Economic History* (1985).
Confino, M., *Domaines et seigneuries en Russie* (1966).
Jones, R., *The Emancipation of the Russian Nobility, 1762–1785* (1973).

(i) Spain
Casey, J., *Early Modern Spain. A Social History* (1999).

(k) Sweden
Barton, H. A., *Scandinavia in the Revolutionary Era, 1760–1815* (1986).
Hecksher, E. F., *Economic History of Sweden* (1954).

Demography

Flinn, M. W., *The European Demographic System, 1500–1820* (1981).
Guillaume, P., and Poussou, J. P., *Démographie historique* (1970).

Family History.

Anderson, M., *Approaches to the History of the Western Family 1500–1914* (1980).
Burghière, A., Klapisch-Zuber, C., Segalen, M., and Zonabend, F., *A History of the Family* vol. 11, The Impact of Modernity (1996), Part 1.

History of Women

Hufton, O., *The Prospect before Her. A History of Women in Western Europe 1500–1800* (1995).
Duby, G., and Perrot, M., eds, *A History of Women* (Cambridge, MA, 1992) vol. 3, Davis, N. Z., and Farge, A., eds, *Renaissance and Enlightenment Paradoxes.*

History of Childhood

Aries, P., *Centuries of Childhood* (1960).
Cunningham, H., *Children in Western Society since 1500* (1995).
Levi, G., and Schmitt, J. C. eds, *A History of Young People in the West* (Cambridge, MA, 1997).

Cultural History.

Roche, D., *The People of Paris. An Essay in Popular Culture in the Eighteenth Century* (1987).
Roche, D., *The Culture of Clothing: Dress and Fashion in the Ancien Regime* (1994).
Pardailhe Galabrun, A., *The Birth of Intimacy: Private and Domestic Life in Early Modern Paris* (1991).
Aries P., and Duby, G., eds, *A History of Private Life* (1987–1991).
Delumeau, J., *Sin and Fear: The Emergence of a Western Guilt Culture, 13th–18th centuries* (1987).
Chartier, R., *The Cultural Uses of Print* (1987).

Chapter 2   The World of Privilege

Nobility

General
Bush, M. L., *Noble Privilege* (1983).
Bush, M. L., *Rich Noble, Poor Noble* (1988).
Clark, S., *State and Status: The Rise of the State and Aristocratic Power in Western Europe* (1995).
Dewald, J., *The European Nobility 1400–1800* (1996).
Goodwin, A., ed., *The European Nobility in the Eighteenth Century* (1953).
Meyer, J., *Noblesse et pouvoirs dans l'Europe d'Ancien Régime* (1973).
Scott, H. M., *The European Nobilities in the Seventeenth and Eighteenth Centuries* (1995).

(a) Austria
Jelnsic, K., 'La noblesse autrichienne', *Annales*, viii (1956).

(b) Dutch Republic

Rowen, H. H., *The Princes of Orange: The stadholders in the Dutch Republic* (1988).

(c) France

Chaussinard-Nogaret, G., *The French Nobility in the Eighteenth Century* (1985).
Doyle, W., *Officers, Nobles and Revolutionaries: Essays on Eighteenth Century France* (1995).
Forster, R., *The Nobility of Toulouse in the Eighteenth Century.* (1960).
Forster, R., 'The Provincial Noble: a re-appraisal', *American Historical Review* 68 (1962–3).
Forster, R., *The House of Saulx-Tavanes, Versailles and Burgundy, 1700–1830* (1971).
Smith, J. M., *The Culture of Merit: Nobility, Royal Service, and the Making of Absolute Monarchy in France* (1996).

(d) Russia

Confino, M., 'A propos de la noblesse russe au XVIIIe siècle', *Annales* (1967).
Meehan-Waters, B., *Autocracy and Aristocracy: The Russian Service Elite of 1730* (1982).

(e) Spain

Callahan, W. J., 'Crown, Nobility and Industry in Eighteenth Century Spain', *International Review of Social History* xi (1966).
Callahan, W. J., *Honour, Commerce and Industry in Eighteenth Century Spain* (1972).

Clergy

Aubert, R., and Beckmann, J., *The Church between Revolution and Restoration* (1981).
Beales, D., and Best, G., *History, Society and the Churches* (1985).
Callahan, W., *Church, Politics and Society in Spain, 1750–1874* (1984).
Chadwick, O., *The Popes and European Revolution* (1981).
Cragg, G. R., *The Church in the Age of Reason 1648–1789* (1984).
Gross, H., *Rome in the Age of Enlightenment* (1990).
Hoffman, P. T., *Church and Community in the Diocese of Lyon 1500–1789* (1984).
Kley, D. van., *The Jansenists and the Expulsion of the Jesuits from France, 1757–1765* (1975).
McManners, J., *Church and Society in Eighteenth Century France* (1998).
Nicholls, D., *God and Government in an Age of Reason (1995).*
Ravitch, N., 'The Social Origins of French and English Bishops in the Eighteenth Century', *Historical Journal* VIII (1965).

Stroup, J., *The Struggle for Identity in the Clerical Estate: Northwest German Protestant Opposition to Absolutist Policy in the Eighteenth Century (1984)*.
Tackett, T., *Priest and Parish in Eighteenth Century France* (1977).
see also **Religious Belief and Criticism (ch. 3)**.

Privileged Institutions

Bluche, F., *Les Magistrats du Parlement du Paris au XVIIIe siècle* (1961).
Carsten, F. L., *Princes and Parliaments in Germany from the Fifteenth to the Eighteenth Century* (1959).
Durand, G., *Etats et institutions XVIe–XVIIIe siècles* (1969).

Chapter 3   The World of Ideas

General

Cobban, A., *In Search of Humanity* (1960).
Gay, P., *The Enlightenment: An Interpretation* (1996).
Hampson, N., *The Enlightenment* (1990).
Hazard, P., *European Thought in the Eighteenth Century* (1954).
Im Hof, U., *The Enlightenment* (1994).

(a) Politics, Philosophy and Government

Caparnetto, D., and Ricuperati, G., *Italy in the Age of Reason, 1685–1789* (1987).
Chisick, H., *The Limits of Reform in the Enlightenment: attitudes towards the education of the lower classes in eighteenth-century France* (1981).
Cranston, M., *Philosophers and Pampleteers: political theorists of the Enlightenment* (1986).
Fox-Genovese, E., *The Origins of Physiocracy: economic revolution and social order in eighteenth-century France* (1976).
Gagliardo, J. G., *Enlightened Despotism* (1967).
Hartung, F., *Enlightened Despotism* (1957).
Mason, H. T., *Voltaire: A Biography* (1981).
Maxwell, K., *Pombal: paradox of the Enlightenment* (1995).
Payne, H. G., *The Philosophes and the People* (1976).
Scott, H. M., *Enlightened Absolutism* (1990).
Szabo, F., *Kaunitz and Enlightened Absolutism, 1753–1780* (1994).
Venturi, F., *Utopia and Reform in the Enlightenment* (1971).
Wisner, D., *The Cult of the Legislator in France, 1750–1830: a study in the political Theology of the French Enlightenment* (1997).

(b) The Republic of Letters, Political Culture, Public Opinion

Becker, M., *The Emergence of Civil Society in the Eighteenth-Century: a privileged movement in the history of England, Scotland and France* (1994).
Baker, K. M., ed., *Inventing the French Revolution: Essays on French Political Culture in the Eighteenth Century* (Cambridge, 1990).

Cochrane, E., *Tradition and Enlightenment in the Tuscan Academies 1690–1800* (1961).

Darnton, R., *The Forbidden Bestsellers of Pre-Revolutionary France* (1997).

Darnton, R., 'The High Enlightenment and the Low Life of Literature in Pre-revolutionary France', in D. Johnson, ed. *French Society and Revolution* (Cambridge, 1976).

Dölmen, R. van., *The Society of the Enlightenment: the rise of the middle classes and enlightenment culture in Germany* (1992).

Farge, A., *Subversive Words: Public Opinion in the Eighteenth-Century France* (1994).

Goldgar, A., *Impolite Learning: Conduct and Community in the Republic of Letters, 1680–1750* (1995).

Goodman, D., *The Republic of Letters: a cultural history of the French Enlightenment* (1998).

Hahn, R., *The Anatomy of a Scientific Institution, the Paris Academy of Sciences 1666–1803* (1971).

Menhennet, A., *Order and Freedom: Literature and Society in Germany from 1720–1805* (1973).

Roche, D., 'Academies et politique au siècle des lumières: les enjeux pratiques de l'immortalité' in K., Baker, ed., *The French Revolution and the Creation of Political Culture*, vol. 1, *The Political Culture of the Old Regime* (1987).

Religious Belief and Criticism

Callahan, W., *Church, Politics and Society in Spain, 1750–1874* (1984).

McManners, J. C., *Death and the Enlightenment* (1981).

Nicolls, D., *God and Government in an Age of Reason* (1995).

Palmer, R. R., *Catholics and Unbelievers in Eighteenth-Century France* (1939).

Rosa, M., *Riformatori e ribelli nel' 700 religioso italiano* (1969).

Vovelle, M., *Piété Baroque et Déchristianation: les attitudes devant la mort en Provence au XVIIIe siècle* (1973).

Whaley, J., *Religious Toleration and Social Change in Hamburg 1529–1819* (1985).

Chapter 4   Armies, Interests and Conflict

General

Anderson, M. S., *War and Society in Europe of the Old Regime, 1618–1789* (1998).

Childs, J. C. R., *Armies and Warfare in Europe, 1648–1789* (1982).

Duffy, C., *The Military Experience in the Age of Reason* (1987).

Luard, E., *The Balance of Power: The System of International Relations, 1648–1715* (1992).

McKay, D., and Scott, H. M., *The Rise of the Great Powers, 1648–1815* (1983).

Parker, G., *The Military Revolution and the Rise of the West, 1500–1800* (1988).

Parry, J. H., *Trade and Dominion: The European Overseas Empire in the Eighteenth Century* (1971).

Williams, G., *The Expansion of Europe in the Eighteenth century* (1966).

(a) Austria
Anderson, M. S., *The War of the Austrian Succession 1740–1748* (1995).

(b) Dutch Republic
Carter, A. C., *Neutrality or Commitment: the Evolution of Dutch Foreign Policy (1667–1795)* (1975).

(c) France
Olive, L. J., *Misalliance: French Policy in Russia during the Seven Years' War* (1964).
Tarrade, J., *Le commerce coloniale de la France à la fin de l'ancien régime* (1972).

(d) Germany
Wilson, P. J., *German Armies, War and German Politics 1648–1806* (1998).

(e) Poland
Kaplan, H. H., *The First Partition of Poland* (1962).
Leslie, R. F., *The Polish Question (Historical Association Pamphlet, 1964).*
Lukowski, J., *The Partitions of Poland, 1772, 1793, 1795* (1999).

(f) Prussia
Duffy, C., *The Army of Frederick the Great* (1975).
Duffy, C., *Frederick the Great, a Military Life* (1985).
Showalter, D. E., *The Wars of Frederick the Great* (1996).
Spencer, F., 'The Anglo-Prussian breach of 1762', *History* 41 (1956).

(g) Russia
Madariaga, I. de., *Britain, Russia and the Armed Neutrality of 1780* (1962).
McNeill, W. H., *Europe's Steppe Frontier, 1500–1800* (1964).

Chapters 5 and 6   The Holy Roman Empire

General

Aretin, K. O. F. von, *Heiliges Römanisches Reich*, 2 vols (1967).
Beales, D. E., *Joseph II, Holy Roman Emperor, 1741–1790* (1987).
Gagliardo, J. G., *Reich and Nation: The Holy Roman Empire as Idea and Reality, 1763–1806* (1980).
Wheatcroft, A., *The Habsburgs: embodying Empire* (1995).

(b) Austria and Hungary
Balázs, E. H., *Hungary and the Habsburgs, 1765–1800: an experiment in enlightened absolutism* (1997).

Barker, T. M., *Army, Aristocracy, Monarchy. Essays on War, Society and Government in Austria, 1618–1780* (1982).
Blanning, T. C. W., *Joseph II* (1994).
Frey, L., *Societies in Upheaval: Insurrections in France, Hungary and Spain in the Early Eighteenth Century* (1987).
Kosáry, D., *Culture and Society in Eighteenth Century Hungary* (1987).
Ingrao, C. W., *The Habsburg Monarchy, 1618–1815* (1994).
Murr Link, E., *The Emancipation of the Austrian Peasant, 1740–1798* (1949).
Szabo, F., *Kaunitz and Enlightened Absolutism* (1994).

(c) Germany
Benecke, G., *Society and Politics in Germany 1500–1750* (1974).
Blanning, T. C. W., *Reform and Revolution in Mainz 1743–1803* (1974).
Friedrichs, C. R., *Urban Politics in Early Modern Germany* (2000).
Gagliardo, J. G., *Germany under the Old Regime* (1991).
Holborn, H. A., *History of Modern Germany*, vol II 1648–1840 (1982).
Hughes, M., *Early Modern Germany, 1477–1806* (1992).
Ingrao, C. W., *The Hessian Mercenary State: Ideas, Institutions and Reform under Frederick II* (Cambridge, 1987).
Luebke, D. M., *His Majesty's Rebels: Communities, Factions and Rural Revolt in the Black Forest 1725–1745* (1997).
Parry, G., 'Enlightened Government and its Critics in Eighteenth century Germany', *Historical Journal*, vol. VI (1963).
Vann, J. A., *The Making of a State: Württemburg 1593–1793* (1984).

Chapter 7   Prussia

Asprey, R. B., *Frederick the Great: the magnificent enigma* (1988).
Carsten, F. L., *A History of the Prussian Junkers* (1989).
Craig, G. A., *The Politics of the Prussian Army 1640–1945* (1955).
Gawthrop, R., *Pietism and the Making of Eighteenth-Century Prussia* (1993).
Hubatsch, W., *Frederick The Great* (1976).
Johnson, H. C., *Frederick the Great and his Officials* (1976).
Rosenberg, H., *Bureaucracy, Aristocracy and Autocracy: the Prussian Experience, 1660–1815* (1958).

Chapter 8   Russia

Alexander, J. T., *Catherine the Great: Life and Legend* (1989).
Alexander, J. T., *Autocratic Politics in a National Crisis. The Imperial Russian Government and Pugachev's revolt* (1969).
Avrich, P., *Russian Rebels 1600–1800* (1972).
Dixon, S., *The Modernisation of Russia 1676–1825* (1999).
Dukes, P., *The Making of Russian Absolutism 1618–1801* (1990).
Dukes, P., *Catherine the Great and the Russian Nobility* (1967).
Erickson, C., *Great Catherine* (1994).
Gleason, W. J., *Moral Idealists, Bureaucracy and Catherine the Great* (1981).

Kahan, A., 'Continuity in Economic Activity and Policy during the Post-Petrine period in Russia', *Journal of Economic History* (1965).

Kahan, A., 'The Costs of Westernization in Russia. The Gentry and the Economy in the Eighteenth Century', *Slavic Review* (1956 and 1959).

Le Donne, J. P., *Absolutism and Ruling Class: The Formation of the Russian Political Order, 1700–1825* (1991).

Le Donne, J. P., *Ruling Russia: Politics and Administration in the Age of Absolutism* (1984).

Longworth, P., 'The Last Great Cossack-Peasant Rising', *Journal of European Studies*, no. 3 (1973).

Madariaga, I. de., *Russia in the Age of Catherine the Great* (1981).

Madariaga, I. de., *Politics and Culture in Eighteenth Century Russia. Collected Essays* (1998).

Madariaga, I. de., 'Catherine II and the Serfs', *Slavonic Review* (1974).

Raeff, M., *The Origins of the Russian Intelligentsia* (1966).

Raeff, M., *Plans for Political Reform in Imperial Russia, 1730–1905* (1966).

Raeff, M., 'The Domestic Policies of Peter III', *American Historical Review* (1970).

Raeff, M., *The Well Ordered Police State: Social and Institutional Change through the Law in the Germanies and Russia, 1600–1800* (1983).

Troyat, H., *Catherine the Great* (1994).

Poland

Davies, N., *God's Playground. A History of Poland (1981) vol. 1.*

Chapter 9   Vanished Supremacies: The Iberian Peninsula

Spain

Callahan, W., *Church, Politics and Society in Spain 1750–1874* (1984).

Cruz, J., *Gentlemen, Bourgeois and Revolutionaries: Political Change and Cultural Persistance among the Spanish Dominant Groups, 1750–1850* (1996).

Frey, L., *Societies in Upheaval: Insurrections in France, Hungary and Spain in the Early Eighteenth Century* (1987).

Herr, R., *Rural change and Finances in Spain at the End of the Old Regime* (1991).

Herr, R., *The Eighteenth Century Revolution in Spain* (1958).

Lynch, J., *Bourbon Spain 1700–1808* (1989).

Rodriguez, L., 'The Spanish Riots of 1766', *Past and Present* 59 (1973).

Rodriguez, L., 'The Riots of 1766 in Madrid', *European Studies Review* (1973).

Portugal

Boxer, C. R., *The Portugese Seaborne Empire 1415–1825* (1969).

Livermore, H., *A New History of Portugal* (1966).

Oliveira Marques *History of Portugal* (1972).

Silbert, A., *Le Portugal méditéranéen à la fin de l'ancien régime* (1966).

Chapter 10   The United Provinces

Buist, M. G., 'The Sinews of War: The Role of Dutch Finance in European Politics c. 1750–1815', in Duke, A. C., and Tamise, C. A., *Britain and the Netherlands* vi (1977).

Brake, W. P. te., *Regents and Rebels: the Revolutionary World of an Eighteenth-Century Dutch City* (1989).

Carter, A., 'Dutch Foreign Investment, 1738–1800', *Economica* XV (1953).

Israel, J., *The Dutch Republic; Its Rise, Greatness and Fall, 1477–1806* (1998).

Leeb, I. L., *The Ideological Origins of the Batavian Revolution* (1973).

Rowen, H. H., *The Princes of Orange: The Stadholders in the Dutch Republic* (1988).

Schama, S., *Patriots and Liberators: Revolution in the Netherlands 1780–1813* (1977).

Wilson, C., 'The Decline of the Netherlands', *Economic History and the Historian* (1969).

Chapter 11   France of the Old Regime

Adams, C., *Visions and Revisions of Eighteenth-Century France* (1997).

Antoine, M., *Louis XV* (1989).

Campbell, P. R., *Power and Politics in Old Regime France, 1720–1745* (1996).

Cobban, A., *A History of Modern France*, vol. 1 (1957).

Doyle, W., *Venality: The sale of offices in eighteenth-century France* (1996).

Hardman, J., *Louis XVI* (1993).

Kaplan, S. L., *Bread, Politics and Political Economy in the Reign of Louis XV* (1976).

Matthews, G. T., *Royal General Farms in Eighteenth Century France* (1958).

Riley, J. C., *The Seven Years' War and the Old Regime in France: The Economic and Financial Toll* (1986).

Rudé, G., *London and Paris in the Eighteenth Century* (1970).

Shennan, J. H., *The Parlement of Paris* (1968).

Velde, J., 'The Financial Market and Government Debt Policy in France', *Journal of Economic History* 52 (1992).

Chapter 12   The Old Order Changeth

Amann, P., *The Eighteenth Century Revolution: French or Western?* (1963).

Baker, K. M., *Inventing the French Revolution: Essays on French Political Culture in the Eighteenth Century* (1990).

Blanning, T. C. W., *The French Revolution – Civil war or Culture Clash* (1998).

Bossenga, G., *The Politics of Privilege: The Old Regime and Revolution in Lille* (1991).

Cobban, A., *The Social Interpretation of the French Revolution* (1963).

Doyle, W., *The Origins of the French Revolution* (1980).

Johnson, D., ed., *French Society and the Revolution* (1976).

Kley, D. van, *The French Idea of Freedom. The Old Regime and the Declaration of Rights of 1789* (1994).

Lefebvre, G., *The Coming of the French Revolution* (1947).

Palmer, R. R., *The Age of the Democratic Revolution* (1961).

Taylor, G. V., 'Non-capitalist Wealth and the Origins of the French Revolution', *American Historical Review* (1967).

Vovelle, M., *The Fall of the French Monarchy 1787–1792* (1984)

Index

Page numbers in **bold** type indicate main or detailed references